P...
RUGBY UNION
ANNUAL 1996-97

1st edition

**Edited by Bill Day and
Brendan Gallagher**

HEADLINE

First published in 1996
by HEADLINE BOOK PUBLISHING

Cover photograph: Lawrence Dallaglio
(Wasps and England) by Colorsport

10 9 8 7 6 5 4 3 2 1

ISBN 0 7472 5612 8

Typeset by
Letterpart Limited, Reigate, Surrey

Printed and bound in Great Britain by
BPC Paperbacks Ltd
A member of The British Printing Company Ltd

HEADLINE BOOK PUBLISHING
A division of Hodder Headline PLC
338 Euston Road
London NW1 3BH

Contents

Editorial Preface

The new *Playfair Rugby Union Annual 1996-97* is published to coincide with the remarkable and revolutionary change that is taking place in the game of rugby union football. The handbook makes its debut in high-street bookshops at a time of unprecedented change, when all the trappings of amateurism that the game guarded so zealously for so long have finally been kicked high and unceremoniously into touch, forever.

We hope *Playfair* will become essential reading for all rugby enthusiasts preparing to embrace this brave new professional age when chequebook transfer deals and share issues have become more important than a bygone age when amateurism reigned and the brotherhood of rugby believed: 'My word is my honour.' Its contents have been deliberately tailored towards this new world, with the emphasis firmly on internationals, the leagues and exciting new tournaments like the Heineken European Cup.

Playfair arrives at the end of a summer of bitter argument over the onset of the new age of professionalism. It is our wish that this acrimonious chapter represents rugby's darkest hours before the dawn of a new era of co-operation instead of confrontation.

First came the wounding power struggle between the English Professional Rugby Union Clubs (EPRUC) and the RFU, which required the intervention of outgoing RFU president Bill Bishop before an uneasy compromise was found. Cliff Brittle led the RFU negotiating team and as he flexes his muscles as chairman of the RFU executive further conflict cannot be ruled out. The Courage League 1996-97 season begins without agreement on relegation from League One and promotion from League Two and there is a real danger of a repeat of the farce at the end of 1995-96 when, by any criteria, Saracens and West Hartlepool should have been relegated. League rugby is worthless under such circumstances and the goalposts should be set now and never moved.

Meanwhile, in Wales the senior clubs have been negotiating to conclude a TV deal with Sky against the expressed wishes of the WRU, which continues the search for a sponsor to replace Heineken, quitting the Welsh domestic scene after six years of stalwart support.

In Ireland the international squad staged a sit-down protest at training in July when it emerged that their contracts did not include insurance cover against loss of earnings due to personal injury while representing Ireland. And in Scotland the ongoing debate between clubs and districts simmered and threatens to erupt again.

Then came the most acrimonious dispute of the close season, England's extraordinary expulsion from the Five Nations Championship after they arrogantly concluded and independently negotiated an £87.5 million deal with BSkyB which included live coverage of all their home Five Nations games. England's stance, in turn, provoked an unattractive holier-than-thou response from Wales, Scotland, Ireland and France, who de facto announced that England were no longer part of the Five Nations tournament and, instead, they would organise a Four Nations championship.

Incredibly, France, who have always concluded their own lucrative television deals, worth over three times more than the other nations', were perversely deemed fit to sit in judgement of England. Belatedly meaningful negotiations broke out and as the *Playfair Rugby Union Annual* goes to print all parties are seemingly inching towards a compromise, for that is the only sensible way forward. The desire to preserve big games on terrestrial TV is understandable, but equally Sky must be allowed to play a major role if professional rugby union is to become established.

A common thread embroiders all these cliff-hanging disputes, namely too much power has been invested in too few individuals, with the same old faces sitting across the table and plotting behind the scenes. Beware the cult of the all-powerful rugby administrator.

Happily, there have been antidotes to all this misery. After 101 years of bitter rivalry, the barriers between union and league have come crashing down and it is with real excitement and anticipation that we relish the appearance of Martin Offiah, Henry Paul and many others in the union game. If such an historical rift can be healed, surely union can resolve a few little domestic difficulties without too much bloodshed.

Meanwhile, the clubs are recovering from the busiest close season in their histories to meet deadlines imposed by the game's new structure. It was well into August 1996 before some clubs revealed the identities of their full squads, many of them showing considerable change from the personnel they bade farewell to at the end of the previous season.

It was a summer, too, of massive upheaval in boardrooms, as some clubs called press conferences to introduce millionaire backers, while others unveiled the identities of consortia prepared to plunge countless thousands into the coffers. The overwhelming majority of clubs maintained their 'Right to Decide' stance, remaining amateur with a 'they won't change us' attitude.

The fixture list for the 1996-97 season is given a new dimension by the belated inclusion of Courage League giants Bath, Leicester, Harlequins and Wasps in the Heineken European Cup competition. As with the development of European club soccer competition from the 1950s, so this new platform for rugby clubs to parade their talents for a wider audience is certain to become a money-spinner and a welcome change from domestic competition for the players, with midweek dashes to Heathrow, Gatwick and East Midlands airports becoming an essential part of players' itineraries.

An unprecedented number of players changed clubs in the close season to add another major point of interest for the new season. The Richmond team will be unrecognisable from the side that played last season, with Ben Clarke, Scott Quinnell and Brian Moore among their major signings. Bedford, the little club with big ideas, unleash ex-Wigan star Martin Offiah at defences and most of the other major clubs will parade at least one big signing for their wide-eyed supporters.

The new professional age demands first-rate infrastructure and many clubs are looking at their grounds with increasing dismay, wondering whether they can find new accommodation large enough to generate the gates their rich benefactors will demand for a return on their investments.

All of this exciting change is reported in this first edition of the *Playfair Rugby Union Annual*. It is our express wish that this lightweight handbook packed with heavyweight information will become vital equipment for all rugby enthusiasts on match days this season.

Acknowledgements

We are indebted to Stuart Farmer for his selfless devotion to the production of statistical information. Many thanks also to RFU, IRFU, SRU, and WRU officials, UNISYS, Ian Marshall at Headline, Roger Shackleton Associates, Michael Humphreys and Partners, Christina Harrison at CIS, the RFU's Media and PR agency, Reg Hayter's sports agency, George Mackay, Mark Jones, Rupert Bates, Katie Coker, John Harding, Mark Nelson and all the hard-working club secretaries, press officers and directors of coaching at clubs who have willingly dug deep for information.

BILL DAY
BRENDAN GALLAGHER
August 1996

Guide to Courage League Club Section

The following is a guide to the clubs and players in the top two divisions of the Courage League. The player biographies start with an individual's date of birth, height, weight and career. Players who have stated they are professional are listed as PRP (professional rugby player) but many are still choosing to pursue a career outside rugby. Where details are known they are listed. Then follows information concerning their playing career. For example, Lawrence Dallaglio (6, SA95, 1t-5pts) indicates that Dallaglio, at the start of the 1996-97 season, had won six full England caps, having made his debut against South Africa in 1995. During those international appearances he has scored one 5-point try. Details are also given, where possible, of an individual's appearances at A/B level. Hence Dallaglio has played four A internationals, making his debut against France in 1994, but has yet to score.

Abbreviations for various countries are standard:

ARG	(Argentina)	ROM	(Romania)
AUS	(Australia)	SA	(South Africa)
CAN	(Canada)	SC	(Scotland)
ENG	(England)	SP	(Spain)
FIJ	(Fiji)	TON	(Tonga)
FR	(France)	USA	(USA)
IRE	(Ireland)	USSR	(former Soviet Union)
IT	(Italy)	WAL	(Wales)
JAP	(Japan)	WS	(Western Samoa)
NAM	(Namibia)	ZIM	(Zimbabwe)
NZ	(New Zealand)		

Records of A/B appearances also include tour games against such opposition as B Col (British Columbia), S Aus (South Australia), Vic (Victoria), Nat (Natal). International records for this season's book include Wales's summer tour of Australia and Scotland's visit to New Zealand.

Other representative honours at national level are then listed in descending order before a record of divisional appearances. Barbarians (95-96) indicates that Dallaglio made his Barbarians debut in that season and full details of points scoring for the Barbarians will follow in next season's *Playfair* CLR: 11t-55pts, indicates that Dallaglio has scored 11 five-point tries in the Courage League for Wasps. Where a player has scored points for more than one Courage League club, his points total is given by club. If no CLR is given, this means the player has not scored any points. Again, comprehensive details of a player's appearances in the Courage National Leagues are being prepared and will appear in next season's *Playfair* annual. After a player's CLR there follows details about him, his playing style, his interests, etc. Where details of birth, height, weight etc are not given, this is because we were unable to track down such information.

Courage League One

BATH

Formation of Club: 1865
Ground: The Recreation Ground, London Road, Bath. Tel: 01225 425192
Capacity: 9,000
Colours: Blue, white and black
Honours: Pilkington Cup: Winners: 1984, 85, 86, 87, 89, 90, 92, 94, 95, 96.
  Courage League: Champions: 1988-89, 90-91, 91-92, 92-93, 93-94, 95-96
Last season: CL1: Champions. Pilkington Cup: Winners
Most capped player: Jeremy Guscott (England) 45
Manager: John Hall
Coach: Brian Ashton
Captain: Phil de Glanville

ADAMS, Gareth (Hooker)

Born Wakefield, 12.9.70. 5'11", 13st 13lb. Career: Student. Rep hons: England A (2, S Aus95), Students, U21, 18 Group. South West (1). Barbarians (92-93) CLR: 2t-10pts. Yorkshire-born, educated at Batley GS and an England Schools cap at flanker before he arrived at Bath, Gareth now regards himself as a hooker and kept Graham Dawe out of the 1995 Pilkington Cup final team.

ADEBAYO, Adedayo (Wing/centre)

Born Ibadan, Nigeria, 30.11.70. 5'9", 14st 7lb. Rep hons: England A (13, Sp91, 6t-28pts), Students, U21, U18, England 7s. South West (7, 2t-10pts), London (1). CLR: 22t-104pts. Has overcome a serious knee injury (1991) to gradually fulfil the potential he first displayed at Kelly College and Swansea University. Toured Canada with an England XV in 1993 and South Africa with England in 1994. Was a valuable member of the England World Cup Sevens winning team in 1993 and represented England in Hong Kong in March 1996.

BUTLAND, Richard de Villiers (Fly-half)

Born Cape Town, South Africa, 5.11.71 5'11", 13st. Career: Student. Rep hons: England Students, U21. CLR: 1t, 9c, 5pg-38pts. Grandfather played for Natal, but Richard is of Anglo/South African stock, and his family returned to England ten years ago. Educated at Wellington College (Berks), initially joined Harlequins but moved to Bath in 1994. Studying Mechanical Engineering at Bath University.

CALLARD, Jonathan Edwards Brooks (Full-back)

Born Leicester, 1.1.66. 5'11", 12st 10lb. Career: PRP/Western Freights Haulage Logistics. Rep hons: England (5, NZ93, 3c, 21pg-69pts), A/B (3, Sp89, 1t, 2c, 5pg-23pts). South West (7, 1t, 9c, 14pg-65pts). Wales U21. Barbarians (94-95). CLR: 19t, 84c, 121pg-620pts. Educated at Bassaleg College, Newport, and St Paul's College, Cheltenham, Jon made his senior debut for Newport against Bath before moving to the Rec and opting for England. Scored a try in Bath's 1990 Pilkington Cup triumph over Gloucester but then struggled to claim a First XV place as Jon Webb rediscovered his best form. Returned in style in 1993-94 season, making a victorious England debut against New Zealand and securing a dramatic victory over Scotland before he took the blame for a shocking team performance against Ireland. Scored 237 League points last season and poached Bath's solitary try against Wigan at Maine Road in May.

CATT, Michael John (Utility back)
Born Port Elizabeth, South Africa, 17.9.71 5'10", 13st 8lb. Career: PRP. Rep hons: England (18, Wal94, 2t, 1dg-13pts), A (1, NZ93), England U21. South West (2). Eastern Province U21. CLR: 10t, 4c, 4pg, 3dg-79pts. Anglo/South African who would be playing for Gloucester had somebody picked up the phone at Kingsholm when he was visiting relatives in Lydney in 1992 – he then dialled Bath and the rest is history. Talented utility back, Mike was educated at Grey School, Port Elizabeth, and played for Eastern Province U21 before moving to England and almost immediately won selection for the England U21 squad to Australia (1993). Made his full England debut against Wales as a replacement in 1994. Has generally been preferred as a full-back by England since impressing as a replacement for Paul Hull against Canada in December 1994. Former Eastern Province junior triathlete champion.

COOK, Jeremy (Wing)
Born 5.5.77. 6', 12st 5lb. Career: Student. Rep hons: England Colts, 18 Group. Promising former Millfield schoolboy who proved a deadly goal kicker during England Schools' Grand Slam of 1995. Son of former Richmond and Barbarians Peter Cook who won two England caps (1965).

DAWE, Graham Richard Reed (Hooker)
Born Plymouth, 4.9.59. 5'11", 13st 8lb. Career: Farmer. Rep hons: England (5, Ire87), England A (14, Aus90). South West (11). Cornwall. Barbarians (90-91). CLR: 5t-23pts. The most respected hooker on the club circuit, it remains a mystery why Graham has won just five England caps. A farmer at Milton Abbot on the Devon/Cornwall border, he played scrum-half and full-back for Launceston before switching to hooker and joining Bath aged 26, making the 300 mile round trip twice a week ever since. Graham made his England debut against Ireland in 1987 but his international career was blighted by the unsavoury game against Wales that season when England chose to discipline him and Richard Hill, Gareth Chilcott and Wade Dooley. Was capped again in the 1987 World Cup against USA but had to wait until 1995 for his next appearance, against Western Samoa. Has benched a record 34 occasions for England. Keen bell ringer and successful livestock breeder in the south west.

DE GLANVILLE, Phillip Ranulph (Centre)
Born Loughborough, 1.10.68. 5'11", 13st 6lb. Career: Marketing consultant. Rep hons: England (16, SA92, 1t-5pts), A (13, It89, 3t-12pts), Students, U21. South West (6). Barbarians (93-94). CLR: 19t-91pts. Phil celebrated his first winter in charge at the Rec by leading Bath to a hard-fought League and Cup double. Educated at Bryanston and Durham University before winning a Blue from St Catherine's College, Oxford. Represented England, and scored two tries, in their inaugural U21 international against Romania (1989) and soon graduated to the B squad. Made his full debut as a replacement against South Africa in 1992. Has won 16 caps, sat on the bench 21 times and become an invaluable member of England's squad. First captained Bath in the 1995 Pilkington Cup final when he deputised for the injured John Hall.

EWENS, Joe (Centre)
Born 16.12.77. 6', 13st. Career: Student. Rep hons: England 18 Group. Won nine England 18 Group caps over the last two seasons, captaining the side in 1995-96. Also helped Colston's Collegiate win two consecutive *Daily Mail* U18 Cup titles. Appeared as a replacement against Wigan at Twickenham.

FRENCH, Gary James (Hooker)
Born St Helens, 2.12.67. 5'11", 15st. Career: Chartered accountant. Rep hons: Emerging England. North (4). CLR: Orrell (2t-10pts). Educated at Cowley HS where father, TV commentator and dual international Ray, taught rugby union. Gary was a first team regular at Liverpool-St Helens and Orrell before joining Bath in 1994.

GEOGHEGAN, Simon Patrick (Wing)
Born Knebworth, 1.9.68. 6', 13st. Career: Solicitor. Rep hons: Ireland (37, Fr91, 11t-51pts), A, U25, Students. Barbarians (92-93). CLR: London Irish (15t-67pts), Bath (8t-40pts). London Irishman whose family hail from Galway. Educated St Edmund's College, Ware and Holborn Law School and now works as a solicitor with Rosling King in Fleet Street. Played Colts rugby for Wasps before joining London Irish and beginning his international career against France at Lansdowne Road, scoring a try in each of the next three games against Wales, England and Scotland. Joined Bath at the start of the 1994-95 season.

GUSCOTT, Jeremy Clayton (Centre)
Born Bath, 7.7.65. 6'1", 13st 10lb. Career: Business development officer with British Gas. Rep hons: England (45, Rom89, 18t, 2dg-83pts), British Lions (5, Aus89, 1t-4pts), A/B (3, Aus88). South West (8, 2t-8pts). Barbarians (89-90). CLR: 36t, 8c, 1dg-178pts. Gifted runner who has delighted fans throughout the world. Educated at Ralph Allen Comp – a soccer school – Jerry learned his rugby with Bath's Mini and Junior sides. Scored three tries on his England debut against Romania in Bucharest and was then called up by the 89 Lions to replace the injured Will Carling. A key member of England's Grand Slam sides in 1991, 1992 and 1995 and RWC91 and 95 squads, he missed the 1994 season with a serious pelvic/groin injury. Scored his 18th England try, against Wales, last season which puts him joint second with Cyril Lowe and Rory Underwood. Blossoming TV and modelling career which included the Body Heat Show and, more improbably, a children's series on opera. Keen golfer.

HAAG, Martin (Lock)
Born Chelmsford, 28.7.65. 6'5", 16st 7lb. Career: Insurance official. Rep hons: England A/B (6, Sp92, 1t-4pts). South West (3). Barbarians (94). CLR: 6t-28pts. An underrated lock and sevens specialist, Martin was educated at Penwith College and was everpresent for England Schools in 1986 before joining Bath. Toured Zimbabwe with Barbarians. Member of the Bath team that won the 1994 Middlesex and Snelling Sevens.

HILTON, David Ivor Walter (Prop)
Born Bristol, 3.4.70. 5'10", 16st 4lb. Career: Butcher. Rep hons: Scotland (16, Can95, 1t-4pts), A. England Colts. Barbarians (94). CLR: 2t-10pts. The Scotland prop with a broad Bristol accent, David qualifies for Scotland by virtue of his Edinburgh-born grandfather, Walter. Educated at Ashton Park, Bristol, the same school as Gareth Chilcott, David joined Bath from Bristol in 1992 and soon established himself as Chilcott's successor. Made his Scotland debut in 1995 when coming on as a replacement for former Bristol colleague Alan Sharp.

LUMSDEN, Audley (Full-back/wing)
Born London, 6.6.67. 6', 13st 7lb. Career: Teacher. Rep hons: England A/B (1, Fr89, 1t-4pts), Students, Colts, South West (5, 2t-10pts). CLR: 18t-86pts. A graduate both of Bath and Oxford Universities and now a physics teacher at Millfield School, Audley has continued at the top level despite suffering a serious broken neck in 1989. After finally

gaining a Blue in 1992 he missed the 1991 match with a broken ankle he reappeared in League rugby three and half years later against Bristol. Sevens specialist.

McCARTHY, Neil (Hooker)
Born Slough, 29.11.73. 5'9", 14st 6lb. Career· Construction work. Rep hons: England U21, Colts. Represented England Colts for a record three years at prop, captaining the side in his last season, but has switched to hooker.

MALLETT, John (Prop)
Born Lincoln, 28.5.70. 6'1", 16st. Career: Teacher. Rep hons: England (1, WS95), A (3, Ire94), Emerging, Students, Colts, Schools. South West (2). CLR: 1t-4pts. A product of Millfield School and West London Institute, John finally won a full cap as a replacement against Western Samoa in RWC95 after touring South Africa the previous year with England. Powerful and increasingly respected scrummager.

NICOL, Andrew Douglas (Scrum-half)
Born Dundee, 12.3.71. 5'11", 13st 4lb. Career: Management trainee. Rep hons: Scotland (9, Eng92, 1t-4pts), A, U19, Schools. Barbarians (91-92). CLR: 4t, 1dg-23pts. Powerful Scots scrum-half who was educated at Dundee HS and played for Dundee HSFP before joining Bath. A career-threatening cruciate knee ligament injury delayed his Bath debut but he has gradually recovered the form he displayed for Scotland in 1992-93 which earned a brief appearance (seven minutes) on the 1993 British Lions tour of New Zealand as a replacement for Robert Jones.

OJOMOH, Stephen Oziegbe (Backrow)
Born Benin City, Nigeria, 25.5.70. 6'2", 15st 10lb. Career: Repo-broker. Rep hons: England (11, Ire94), England A/B (13, N Otago92, 3t-12pts), U21, Colts, Schools. South West (4, 1t-5pts). Barbarians (94). CLR: 2t-10pts. Schoolboy decathlete of note who attended West Buckland School and the West of England University. Steve joined Bath from Rosslyn Park and toured New Zealand and Canada with England before winning his first cap against Ireland. Outstanding for England in South Africa (1994) and a member of England's RWC95 squad.

PAUL, Henry (Utility back)
Born New Zealand, 10.2.74. 5'10", 14st 8lb. Career: PRP. Rep hons: New Zealand RL. One of the world's most talented rugby league players. Henry joins Bath on a £2,000-per-match winter contract from Wigan which ends in January after impressing everybody at the Recreation Ground in May's cross-code games. Identified by his distinctive white shoes and capable of playing anywhere behind the scrum, Henry also hooked for New Zealand in their World Cup semi-final against Australia. Elder brother of the equally talented Robbie Paul (Bradford RL).

PEARCE, Edward (Backrow)
Born Bristol, 2.9.75. 6'6", 17st. Career: Student. Rep hons: England U21, U18. South West (1). Proud owner of size 16 boots, Ed was educated at Clifton College and has developed into an exceptional age group international. Performed well in the cross-code game against Wigan at Twickenham.

PETERS, Eric William (Backrow)
Born Glasgow, 28.1.69. 6'5", 16st 6lb. Career: Chartered surveyor. Rep hons: Scotland (15, Can95, 5t-25pts), A. England Students, U21. Barbarians (92-93). Played his early rugby for Brentwood School and Loughborough University, where he studied Economics, and captained Cambridge University. Played for Saracens before joining Bath in 1993 and opting for Scotland, the land of his birth, having represented England in the World Students Cup (1992). Made his Scotland debut against Canada in 1995 and has not looked back since. Impressed during Scotland's summer tour of New Zealand, scoring a try in each Test.

REDMAN, Nigel Charles (Lock)
Born Cardiff, 16.8.64. 6'4", 17st 2lb. Career: Technical rep. Rep hons: England (18, Aus84, 1t-4pts), A/B (17, It86, 1t-4pts), Colts. South West (20, 1t-4pts). Barbarians (85-86). CLR: 7t-31pts. Educated at Priory Comprehensive School and South West Bristol Technical College, Ollie made his England debut at 19 against Australia in 1984 and has moved in and out of the squad ever since – after being voted the RFU Player of the Year in 1994 he was promptly dropped! Unfortunately, much of his career has coincided with emergence of Paul Ackford, Wade Dooley, Martin Bayfield and Martin Johnson to name just four world-class English locks. Has made a record nine winning appearances with Bath in the Pilkington Cup final and helped the club to six Courage League titles.

REED, Andrew Ian (Lock)
Born St Austell, 4.5.69. 6'7", 17st 10lb. Career: Western Freights. Rep hons: Scotland (10, Ire93). British Lions (1, NZ93). England Colts. Cornwall. Back to competitive action after a serious back injury. Educated at Bodmin Comprehensive, Bristol Polytechnic and Cheshire College of Agriculture, Andy arrived at the Recreation Ground via Bodmin, Camborne, Plymouth Albion and England Colts, but soon used his Scottish ancestry to win international honours for them. Toured New Zealand with 1993 British Lions, playing in the first Test. A member of Cornwall's County Championship winning side in 1991 and a former Cornwall Schools goalkeeper.

ROBINSON, Andrew Richard (Flanker/Assistant coach)
Born Taunton, 3.4.64. 5'9", 13st 12lb. Career: PRP. Rep hons: England (8, Aus88, 1t-4pts), A/B (6, Fr87, 1t-4pts), British Lions tourist (89). South West (20, 2t-9pts). Barbarians (88-89). CLR: 9t-39pts. A former club captain who led Bath to the double in 1992, Andy joined Bath in 1986. Two years later, he won England recognition and was voted European Player of the Year but untimely injury reduced his effectiveness during the 1989 Lions tour of Australia and thereafter vertically challenged flankers became virtually extinct at international level. England's loss was Bath's gain and Andy has been an influential figure throughout Bath's 'glory' years. Was recalled by England against South Africa last autumn but was again jettisoned. Has just stepped down as Head of Sport at Colston's Collegiate in Bristol, who he guided to consecutive *Daily Mail* U18 Cup titles. Hopes to continue his coaching career at Bath. Confirmed Elvis Presley freak.

SANDERS, Ian (Scrum-half)
Born Penzance, 22.1.71. 5'9", 12st. Career: Police officer. Rep hons: England U21 South West (1). Cornwall. CLR: 4t-20pts. Proud Cornishman who impressed Wigan as an emergency hooker in their cross-code encounter at Maine Road in May. Educated at St Ives School and Pentwith College, he made his Bath debut in 1990 as a replacement against London Scottish.

SLEIGHTHOLME, Jonathan Mark (Wing)
Born Malton, 5.8.72. 5'10", 13st 5lb. Career: Teacher. Rep hons: England (4, Fr96, 1t-5pts), England A (9, Ire95, 3t-15pts), Emerging, U21, Colts, England 7s. North (5, 1t-5pts), South West (2). Barbarians (92-93). CLR: Wakefield (27t-127pts), Bath (9t-45pts). Pacey Yorkshireman who made an instant impact on the international scene last season with his powerful running and tigerish defence. Educated at Whitgift School, Grimsby, and Chester College, John played for Grimsby and Hull Ionians before moving to Wakefield where he scored 42 tries in 60 appearances. Gradually became established at Bath, made England A debut against Ireland in January 1995 and full debut at Parc des Princes in February 96. Younger brother Andrew has also played for England U21 and Colts – on the wing of course.

UBOGU, Victor Eriakpo (Prop)
Born Lagos, Nigeria, 8.9.64. 5'9", 17st. Career: Entrepreneur. Rep hons: England (21, Can92, 1t-5pts), A/B (8, Aus90, 4t-16pts), Students, 18 Group. South West (4). CLR: 11t-51pts. Victor has lived in England since he was 13 and was educated at West Buckland School, Devon, Birmingham University and Oxford. Numbers Richmond and Moseley among his previous clubs and made his senior England debut against Canada at Wembley in 1992. Director of London-based security firm Cobrawatch and a co-owner of Shoeless Joe's, a sports bar and restaurant on the King's Road.

WEBSTER, Richard Edward (Flanker)
Born Morriston, 9.7.67. 6'2", 17st. Career: PRP. Rep hons: Wales (13, Aus87, 1t-5pts). British Lions tourist 1993 (NZ). Signed on a match contract, Richard went 'north' to play for Salford RL after returning from the 1993 British Lions tour of New Zealand where he stood out as a whole-hearted grafter in the Midweek XV. Richard first attracted attention as an outstanding Wales Youth international in 1985-86, winning six caps, and was enjoying a summer playing club rugby in Australia the following year when he was dramatically called into the Wales team for their RWC87 play-off game against Australia in Rotorua. On his return, Richard was plagued by the first in a long series of knee injuries but earned another 'cap' against the Barbarians (1990) and produced solid performances in RWC91 against Argentina and Australia. Ever-present in the 1992 and 1993 Five Nations before turning professional.

YATES, Kevin (Prop)
Born Medicine Hat, Canada, 6.11.71. 5'11", 17st. Career: Project manager. Rep hons: England A (4, Vic95, 1t-5pts), U21. Barbarians (94). CLR: 3t-15pts. Affable, fleet-footed prop who was educated at John Bentley School, Calne, before learning his rugby at Chippenham and joining Bath. Toured Australia and Fiji with England A (1995).

REVIEW

Wobbled slightly in April with unexpected defeat at Gloucester and a dramatic 38-38 home draw against Sale, but over the long haul Bath were again undoubtedly the best team in the land and deserved to complete another double. Under the guidance of coach Brian Ashton, captain Phil de Glanville and manager John Hall they produced a more expansive game than in 1994-95 with backs and forward interacting superbly on occasions. Cup victory over Leicester, albeit in controversial circumstances, represented an incredible 10th consecutive Pilkington victory at Twickenham. Enjoyed their unique cross-code series against Wigan and earned much respect from RL supporters for accepting the challenge. Their financial future has been secured by the £3 million investment of local businessman Andrew Brownsword; while the emergence of young-sters such as Ed Pearce and Joe Ewens suggests that Bath will remain the team to beat. Recent signing of Henry Paul from Wigan RL could prove a master-stroke.

BATH in the Courage League 1995-96

Sep 9	West Hartlepool	A	Won	20	15	Sleightholme(T) Callard(5P)
16	Gloucester	H	Won	37	11	Lumsden(T) Nicol(T) Sleightholme(T) Callard(2C, 5P) Catt(D)
23	Leicester	A	Won	14	9	Adebayo(T) Callard(3P)
30	Orrell	H	Won	55	20	Adebayo(2T) Callard(2T, 6C, P) Catt(T) De Glanville(T) Guscott(T) Ubogu(T)
Oct 7	Wasps	A	Won	15	6	Adebayo(2T) Callard(C, P)
14	Bristol	H	Won	52	19	Guscott(3T) Catt(T) Clarke(T) Geoghegan(T) Ojomoh(T) Callard(4C, 3P)
21	Harlequins	A	Won	19	13	Lumsden(T) Callard(C, 4P)
28	Saracens	H	Won	52	16	Geoghegan(2T) Sanders(2T) De Glanville(T) Guscott(T) Lumsden(T) Penalty(T) Callard(6C)
Nov 4	Sale	A	Won	30	18	Lumsden(2T) Callard(T, 3C, 3P)
11	West Hartlepool	H	Won	34	22	Clarke(T) Guscott(T) Lumsden(T) Penalty(T) Callard(4C, 2P)
Jan 6	Leicester	H	Lost	14	15	Adebayo(T) Callard(3P)
Feb 17	Wasps	H	Won	36	12	Dawe(T) De Glanville(T) Nicol(T) Sleightholme(T) Yates(T) Callard(4C, P)
Mar 30	Bristol	A	Won	43	5	Geoghegan(2T) Guscott(2T) De Glanville(T) Hilton(T) Lumsden(T) Callard(4C)
Apr 6	Harlequins	H	Won	41	15	De Glanville(T) Guscott(T) Sleightholme(T) Callard(C, 6P) Catt(D) Nicol(D)
10	Gloucester	A	Lost	10	16	De Glanville(T) Butland(C, P)
13	Saracens	A	Won	21	15	Adebayo(T) Dawe(T) Callard(C, 3P)
20	Orrell	A	Won	44	11	Haag(2T) Sleightholme(2T) De Glanville(T) Nicol(T) Callard(4C, 2P)
27	Sale	H	Drew	38	38	Catt(T) Lumsden(T) Nicol(T) Sleightholme(T) Walters(T) Callard(2C, 3P)

BRISTOL

Formation of Club: 1888
Ground: The Memorial Ground, Filton Avenue, Horfield, Bristol BS7 0AQ.
  Tel: 0117 951 4448
Capacity: 12,000
Colours: Navy blue and white
Honours: Pilkington Cup: Winners: 1983. Losing finalists: 1973, 84, 88
Last season: CL1: 6th. Pilkington Cup: Q/F (lost 19-12 to Bath)
Most capped player: Robert Jones (Wales) 54.
Coaches: Alan Davies, Mike Davis
Rugby Development Manager: Mark Tainton
Captain: Martin Corry

ADAMS, Phil (Lock)
Born 2.2.63. 6'6", 17st. Career: Plasterer. Rep hons: Gloucestershire. Reliable grafter in the second row, Phil captained Bristol United in 1995-96. Became a first team regular after Simon Shaw injured his ankle.

ARMSTRONG, Robert (Flanker)
Born Liverpool, 17.8.67. 6'4", 17st. Rep hons: South West (1). Combined Services. CLR: Plymouth (2t-8pts). Corporal Bob Armstrong is a Royal Marine drill instructor based at the Commando training centre at Lympstone. A former Marines Super Heavyweight Boxing champion, Bob made his Combined Services debut in 1988 and played a prominent role in the Services' fine showing against the 1993 All Blacks at Devonport.

BARROW, Craig (Backrow)
Born 26.2.69. 6'6", 17st. Career: Teacher. Rep hons: England Students. Midlands (2). South West (1). CLR: 3t-14pts. Versatile backrow forward who joined from Exeter. Sevens specialist.

BREEZE, Ben (Wing)
Born Exeter, 8.4.74. 5'10", 13st. Career: Student. Rep hons: South West U21, Colts. CL: 1t-5pts. Educated at Queen Elizabeth, Credition, and Loughborough University, Ben graduated through Bristol Colts and U21 and made his first team debut against Clifton (December 95). League debut against Harlequins (January 96).

BURKE, Paul Anthony (Fly-half)
Born London, 1.5.73. 5'8", 12st. Career: Teacher. Rep hons: Ireland (7, Eng95, 11c, 14pg, 1dg-67pts), A, U21. Ireland 7s. England U21, Colts, Schools. Barbarians (94). CLR: London Irish (3c, 12pg, 7dg-63pts). Anglo/Irishman who was educated at Epsom College and came up through the English age group system, captaining England Colts, before opting for Ireland – his father is from Galway and mother from Kildare. Moved from London Irish to Cork Constitution in 1994 and made his senior Ireland debut against England in 1995, in tandem with club colleague Michael Bradley. Was dropped after his next game, against Scotland, but returned as a replacement against Wales. RWC95 was confined to a game against Japan and although he performed well against Fiji and USA last autumn, Eric Elwood and David Humphreys were preferred for the Five Nations.

14

CORKERY, David Sean (Backrow)
Born Cork, Ireland, 6.11.72. 6'4", 16st 2lb. Career: PRP. Rep hons: Ireland (14, Aus94, 3t-15pts), A, U21, Schools. Barbarians. Abrasive, no-nonsense flanker who arrived at the Memorial Ground from Cork Constitution, having previously played for Terenure. David is a product of the Christian Brothers College in Cork and was an outstanding Irish Schools blindside flanker in 1991. Emerged through the U21 set-up and made a big impression on his full debut against Australia in 1994. Retained his place against USA but was dropped after the England game in the Five Nations and only reappeared in the RWC95, when he was Ireland's best forward.

CORRY, Martin (Backrow)
Born Birmingham, 12.10.73. 6'5", 17st. Rep hons: England A (6, Vic95), Emerging, U21, 18 Group. CLR: Newcastle (7t-35pts), Bristol (4t-20pts). Former Newcastle forward emerged as Bristol's most consistent player in 1995-96 with his excellent form commanding a regular place in the England A line-up having toured Australia and Fiji with England's second string in 1995. Educated at Tunbridge Wells GS and Newcastle Polytechnic, Martin played lock for the England Schools' Grand Slam side in 1992.

DENNEY, Mark (Centre)
Born Epping Forest, 25.7.75. 5'8", 14st 7lb. Career: Student. Rep hons: England Students, U21, Colts, U18. South West (5). CLR: 3t-15pts. Former Bedford Modern schoolboy and now a student at Bristol University, Mark spent two seasons in the England Schools' 18 Group team, captaining the side in his final year.

DIXON, Iain (Flanker)
Born Inverness, 2.3.66. 6'1", 14st 13lb. Career: Teacher. Rep hons: Scotland B, Anglo-Scots, Combined Services. CLR: London Scottish (6t-24pts). Former Royal Marine who joined Bristol in 1995-96 from London Scottish.

HINKINS, David (Prop)
Born Exeter, 20.10.66. 6'1", 17st. Career: College lecturer. Rep hons: Emerging England, Students and 18 Group. South West (6). A PE and science teacher at the John Cabot City Tech, Dave is a solid prop who also contributes usefully in the loose. Educated at Plymouth College and St Paul's College, Cheltenham, Dave played for England in the 1988 Students' World Cup and enjoyed a short spell with Moseley before joining Bristol and making his first team debut in a 58-4 win over Met Police (1989).

HULL, Paul Anthony (Full-back)
Born Lambeth, London, 17.5.68. 5'9", 12st 10lb. Career: PRP. Rep hons: England (4, SA94), A/B (19, Fiji89, 6t, 6c, 3pg-50pts), Emerging, U21, Colts. South West (10, 2t, 2c, 3pg, 1dg-26pts). Combined Services. Barbarians (94). CLR: 18t, 4c, 12pg-127pts. Versatile back who has finally settled on full-back as his preferred position. Outstanding for England in South Africa (1994) when he won two caps but was unluckily dropped on his return after getting injured against Canada. Captained England A on their tour of Australia and Fiji (1995) and also led Bristol in 1995-96. Educated at Gordon Boys' School in Woking, Paul had soccer trials for Southampton FC before concentrating on rugby.

JONES, Robert Nicholas (Scrum-half)
Born Trebanos, 10.11.65. 5'8", 11st 8lb. Career: PRP. Rep hons: Wales (54, Eng86, 3t-14pts). British Lions (3, Aus89). After resisting the overtures of Harlequins earlier in the season, Robert finally decided to move from Swansea when Bristol went searching for a quality scrum-half following the departure of Kyran Bracken. Slick distributor who reached the height of his powers in Australia in 1989. Impressed for many seasons in moderate Welsh teams but increasingly fell out of favour during Alan Davies' spell as coach. Obviously there were no grudges because Davies moved quickly to secure Jones' services when Bracken went to Saracens. A talented cricketer who represented Wales at three age group levels.

KEYTER, Jason (Wing/centre)
Born Port Elizabeth, South Africa, 20.12.73. 5'11", 14st 2lb. Career: Sales executive. Rep hons: England A (2, Vic95), Emerging, Colts. London (1). CLR: Harlequins (5t-25pts). Talented but inconsistent utility back, Jason arrived in England in 1986 and played his junior rugby with Weston-Super-Mare. Joined Harlequins as a Colt and made rapid progress before quitting the club and joining Bristol midway through 1994-95 season. Toured Australia and Fiji with England A in 1995.

KNIBBS, Ralph (Utility back)
Born Bristol, 3.8.64. 6'1", 13st. Career: Personnel officer at Bristol RFC. Rep hons: South West (13, 1t-4pts). CLR: 9t, 2dg-45pts. Wonderfully gifted, if eccentric, runner who has served Bristol loyally since scoring a try on his first team debut against Pontypridd in March 1982. Has made 436 appearances placing him fourth on the all-time Bristol list behind Alan Morley (519), Dave Watt (512) and Peter Polledri (466).

LATHROPE, Andy (Hooker)
Born Bristol, 6.2.66. 5'10", 13st. Career: Telecom engineer. Rep hons: Somerset. Loyal second team hooker who never lets Bristol down when deputising for Mark Regan. Has made over 100 Bristol United appearances.

MAGGS, Kevin (Centre)
Born 3.6.74. 5'11", 14st. Career: Builder. Rep hons: England Colts, South WestU21 CLR: 1t-5pts. Former captain of Bristol Colts and U21 who is rapidly making an impression at senior level.

MARTIN, Simon (Centre)
Born Thornbury, Bristol, 24.1.75. 5'10", 13st 7lb. Career: Student. Rep hons: South West U21, Colts, 18 Group. Proved an outstanding captain of Bristol's successful colts section in 1994-95 and has impressed on his first team appearance to date.

PEARSON, Joel (Flanker)
Born Bradford-on-Avon, 8.3.70. 6', 15st 10lb. Career: Broker. Rep hons: England U21, Colts. South West (1). A flanker of some potential but has yet to reproduce his outstanding form when in Bristol's junior teams.

REGAN, Mark Peter (Hooker)
Born Bristol, 28.1.72. 5'11", 16st 2lb. Career: Work coordinator for Avon Cranes. Rep hons: England (6, SA95), A (7, Ire95, 2t-10pts), Emerging, U21, Colts, 18 Group.

South West (1). CLR. 3t-15pts. Educated at that well-known Bristol nursery St Brendan's College and a former member at Keynsham, Mark is a fine advert for the England age group system and finally displaced Brian Moore last season against South Africa and was subsequently ever present in the Five Nations. Toured Australia with England U21 in 1993 and made a big impression on England A's tough trip to Australia and Fiji in 1995.

ROLLITT, Eben David (Backrow)
Born Bristol, 23.11.72. 6'3", 16st 5lb. Career: Architect. Rep hons: England Students, U21, 18 Group. South West (3). CLR. 3t-15pts. Educated at St Paul's School, London, and Cambridge University where he won a Blue (1994), Eben has also played club rugby for Randwick in Sydney and Richmond. Son of former Bristol favourite Dave Rollitt who won 11 caps for England between 1967-75.

SHARP, Alan Victor (Prop)
Born Bristol, 17.10.69. 5'9", 17st. Career: Construction. Rep hons: Scotland (6, Eng94), A, U21, U19. England A/B (1, Sp89), Colts, 18 Group. South West (3). Anglo/Scot who has veered between the two nations, representing Scotland U21 and the Anglo/Scots before playing for England B against Spain and becoming a member of the full England training squad. Eventually opted for Scotland and won six caps, the last being against South Africa in 1994 before a back injury interrupted his international career. Educated at St Brendan's, Alan played for the school's Old Boys and Clifton before joining Bristol.

SHAW, Simon (Lock)
Born Kenya, 1.9.73. 6'9", 19st. Career: Student. Rep hons: England A (3, Ire95), Students, U21, Colts, 18 Group. London (2). Barbarians (94-95). CLR: 2t-10pts. Immensely promising lock who became the biggest ever schools international when he made his debut against Ireland at Thomond Park in 1991. Simon was 6'8" and 18st 4lb that day and for such a big man is a superb athlete. Brought up initially in Spain, he attended Godalming Sixth Form College and was playing a Colts final trial when the selectors realised he was still a schoolboy. Won a Colts cap the next season and rapidly moved through the age groups before being called up as a replacement for England's tour to South Africa (1994) and producing two eye-catching performances. Recent career has been badly disrupted with serious injuries against touring sides when he damaged a knee against Northern Transvaal and an ankle against New South Wales.

TAINTON, Mark (Fly-half)
Born 10.3.69. 5'7", 12st. Career: Sales engineer. Rep hons: England Colts. South West (1, 1c, 2pg-8pts). CLR: 59c, 160pg, 7dg-619pts. Loyal club servant and prolific goal kicker. Bristol again turned to Mark when fighting relegation at the end of 1995-96 when he was once more their leading points scorer in the League with 120. Became Bristol's rugby development manager in July.

TIUETI, David (Wing)
Born Tonga, 6.6.73. 6', 14st 2lb. Rep hons: North Harbour CLR. 2t-10pts. Made five senior appearances for North Harbour before moving to England. Bristol debut at Bridgend in March 1996, followed by League debut against Bath.

WATERS, Fraser (Centre)
Born Cape Town, South Africa, 31.3.76. 6', 13st 9lb. Career: Student. Rep hons: England U21, Colts, Schools. CLR: 1t-5pts (Bath). Former Harrow schoolboy who shared in England Schools' Grand Slam in 1994. Learned many lessons appearing against Wigan at Maine Road. Signed from Bath in August 1996.

REVIEW

Bristol took their eye off the ball immediately after Christmas and carelessly slipped into the 'relegation' zone although they responded to that indignity with some spirited performances. Bristol remain a club of huge potential but have consistently underperformed. A lack of penetration behind the scrum would still seem the main problem and the arrival of Wales fly-half Arwel Thomas brought little satisfaction and ultimately ended in tears when he joined Swansea in May. Paul Burke's arrival from Cork Constitution and his partnership with former Wales and British Lions scrum-half Robert Jones will help but Bristol still need to find finishing power out wide. The pack was solid, as usual, but will benefit by the signing of Ireland flanker David Corkery and Martin Corry's decision to resist Newcastle's overtures. The return to fitness of Simon Shaw is also greatly welcomed.

BRISTOL in the Courage League 1995-96

Sep	9	Wasps	A	Lost	5 33	Regan(T)
	16	West Hartlepool	H	Won	12 3	Tainton(4P)
	23	Harlequins	H	Lost	25 31	Bracken(T) Corry(T) Hull(T) Tainton(2C, 2P)
	30	Saracens	A	Won	24 11	Maggs(T) Shaw(T) Tainton(C, 4P)
Oct	7	Sale	H	Won	30 6	Corry(T) Wring(T) Tainton(C, 5P) Hull(P)
	14	Bath	A	Lost	19 52	Archer(T) Tainton(C, 4P)
	21	Gloucester	H	Won	22 16	Hull(T, C, 4P) Thomas(D)
	28	Leicester	A	Lost	6 43	Hull(2P)
Nov	4	Orrell	H	Won	33 14	Corry(T) Shaw(T) Thomas(T, 3C, D, 3P)
	11	Wasps	H	Lost	9 17	Thomas(3P)
Jan	6	Harlequins	A	Lost	3 28	Thomas(D)
Feb	17	Sale	A	Lost	6 15	Tainton(D, P)
Mar	30	Bath	H	Lost	5 43	Thomas(T)
Apr	6	Gloucester	A	Lost	14 18	Sharp(T) Thomas(3P)
	13	Leicester	H	Lost	29 43	Bracken(T) Rollitt(T) Tainton(2C, 5P)
	20	Saracens	H	Won	21 7	Bracken(T) Regan(T) Tainton(C, 3P)
	27	Orrell	A	Won	29 26	Tiueti(2T) Bracken(T) Thomas(T, 3C, P)
May	5	West Hartlepool	A	Won	37 15	Rollitt(2T) Breeze(T) Corry(T) Tainton(4C, D, 2P)

GLOUCESTER

Formation of Club: 1873
Ground: Kingsholm, Kingsholm Road, Gloucester, GL1 3AX.
  Tel: 01452 520901
Capacity: 12,000
Colours: Cherry and white
Honours: Pilkington Cup: Winners: 1972, 78, 82 (shared title).
  Losing finalists: 1990. Courage League: Runners-up: 1988-89, 89-90
Last season: CL1: 8th. Pilkington Cup: S/F (lost 19-10 to Bath)
Most capped player: Mike Teague (England)/Tom Voyce (England) 27 caps
Director of Coaching: Richard Hill
Coaches: Mike Rafter, Dave Pointon, Peter Kingston, Viv Wooley
Captain: David Sims

ANDERSON, Eral (Wing)
Born 29.10.73. 5'7", 13st. Rep hons: England U21 CLR: Moseley (5t-25pts). Fiery wing who joined Gloucester from Moseley at the end of 1995-96.

BECK, Lawrie John (Scrum-half)
Born Cheltenham, 2.1.71. 5'10", 13st 5lb. Career Drayman. Rep hons: England U21 Gloucestershire. CLR: Reliable scrum-half who joined Gloucester from Cheltenham. Represented South West Juniors at water polo.

BENTON, Scott (Scrum-half)
Born Bradford, 8.9.74. 5'11", 13st 2lb. Career: PRP. Rep hons: England U21, Colts. CLR: Morley (6t-30pts). Joined Gloucester from Morley, the former England Colts captain was an instant hit with the Gloucester crowd, not least for his brilliant try-making run against Bath.

BULLOCK, Warwick (Prop)
Born Stowbridge, 9.2.70. 5'11", 17st. Career: Construction. Rep hons: Warwickshire. Hard-scrummaging prop who joined from Coventry and made his first team debut in September 94 in Gloucester's 63-7 win over Stroud.

CASKIE, Don William (Centre)
Born Almondsbury, 12.12.67. 5'8", 13st 4lb. Career Sales manager for agricultural products. Rep hons: Scotland B, Students, U21. Scottish Exiles. CLR: 4t-17pts. Gloucester stalwart in midfield who had soccer trials with Swindon, Bristol City and Plymouth in his youth. Represented Scotland in the 1988 World Students Cup.

CATLING, Chris (Full-back)
Born 17.6.76. 6'1", 14st. Career Student. Rep hons: England Students, U21, 18 Group. Cultured full-back who signed from Exeter in June. Educated at Whitgift School in Croydon, Chris was ever-present in the England Schools Grand Slam team of 1994, captained by Gloucester's Phil Greening, before moving to Exeter University. Member of England's World Students Cup squad in South Africa this summer.

CORNWELL, Mark (Lock)
Born Gloucester, 22.2.73. 6'7", 17st. Career: PRP. Rep hons: England Colts. CLR: 1t-5pts. Promising lock who joined from Old Richians. Another who spent the summer playing for the Hamiltons club in South Africa.

CUMMINS, Damian (Centre)
Born Tenby, 8.12.64. 5'11", 14st. Career: Teacher. Rep hons: Anglo-Scots, Anglo-Welsh. CLR: 7t, 3dg-38pts. Tenby-born teacher whose rugby travels have resulted in spells for Newport, Exeter University, Borough Road College and Tenby. Played for Middlesex CCC Second XI (1982-86).

DEACON, Andrew (Prop)
Born Gloucester, 31.7.65. 6'2", 17st. Career: Drayman. Rep hons: Gloucestershire. CLR: 3t-15pts. Experienced former Gloucester captain who joined the club from Longlevens.

DEVEREUX, Simon (Lock)
Born Gloucester, 20.10.68. 6'3", 16st 10lb. Career: Product engineer. CLR: 1t-5pts. Former Spartans lock who received a nine-month prison sentence after being found guilty of assault in a second team match against Rosslyn Park in 1995, when he broke an opponent's jaw with a punch. Hard-grafting second row who had just broken into Gloucester's first team when sentenced. The club stood by him throughout his ordeal and offered a two-year contract on his release from Leyhin Prison in July.

FENWICK, Gareth (Full-back)
Born Gloucester, 9.9.73. 5'10", 13st 7lb. CLR: 2c, 10pg-34pts. Underrated full-back, Gareth was with Old Richians before moving to Kingsholm where he became the youngest-ever Gloucester first team player, appearing against New Brighton in 1991, aged 17.

FIDLER, Robert (Lock)
Born Gloucester, 21.9.74. 6'5", 16st 8lb. Career: PRP. Rep hons: England U21, Colts, 18 Group. Son of former Gloucester and England lock John Fidler, Robert was educated at Cheltenham College and is developing into an uncompromising forward in the best Gloucester tradition.

FORTEY, Chris (Hooker)
Born Gloucester, 25.8.75. 6', 16st 7lb. Career: Joiner Rep hons: South West U21 Promising young hooker who has represented SWU21 alongside identical twin brother Lee, a useful prop. Bench reserve for England U21 in 1995-96.

GLANVILLE, Peter (Flanker)
Born Gloucester, 10.6.71. 6'3", 16st 2lb. Career: Sales manager Rep hons: South West (5, 1t-5pts). Gloucestershire. Formerly with Longlevens, Peter has become a first team regular at Kingsholm and performed well for the South West in the CIS Divisional Championship 1995. Sales manager for his father's tyre firm.

GIBSON, Colin (Backrow)
Born Belfast, 15.6.72. 6'4", 16st 4lb. Career: Trainee solicitor. Rep hons: Ulster schools. Son of British Lions and Ireland centre Mike, Colin made his full league debut against Leicester in April 96 after joining Gloucester from Swansea University.

GREENING, Philip Bradley Thomas (Hooker)
Born Gloucester, 3.10.75. 5'11", 17st. Career: PRP Rep hons: England A (3, WS95, 1t-5pts), U21, Colts, 18 Group. South West (1). Dynamic, aggressive hooker who captained England Schools and Colts and earned England A selection during his first season of senior rugby. Educated at Kingsholm Junior, Chosen Hill and Gloucester College, Phil originally played centre for the junior sides at Spartans before switching to hooker.

HAWKER, John (Hooker)
Born Gloucester, 17.5.63. 5'11", 13st 9lb. Career: Computer programmer. Rep hons: South West (5). CLR: 2t-8pts. Tough, durable hooker who has earned the respect of opponents, John arrived at Kingsholm from the Matson club. Lists gymnastics and juggling among his hobbies.

HOLFORD, Paul (Wing)
Born Gloucester, 2.12.69. 5'11", 13st. Career: PRP/Bricklayer. Rep hons: England A (2, Vic95, 1t-5pts), Emerging. South West (9, 2t-10pts). CLR: 17t-85pts. Quick and strong, Paul has done well for Gloucester since signing from Chosen Hill FP and was their top try scorer in the League in 95-96 with five. Has become a regular in the South West Division – he scored their winning try against London at Twickenham to take the 1994 title – and played for Emerging England against New Zealand, Canada and Spain.

KIMBER, Martyn (Fly-half)
Born Auckland, New Zealand, 20.9.68. 6', 13st 10lb. Career: Engineer. Rep hons: New Zealand U19 cricket. CLR: 1t, 2c, 4pg, 12dg-57pts. Better known as an accomplished club cricketer with Stroud CC before he joined Gloucester from Stroud RFC and made a smooth transition into top rugby. Dropped goal specialist who landed six in the League in 1995-96.

LLOYD, Mike (Wing)
Born 21.7.70. 6'2", 15st. Rep hons: South West (1) CLR: Bath (1t-5pts), Bristol (5t-22pts). Powerful wing who enjoyed spells at the Memorial Ground Bristol and the Rec, Bath, before arriving at Gloucester.

MAPLETOFT, Mark Sterland (Full-back)
Born Mansfield, 25.12.71. 5'7", 13st 8lb. Career: Sports development officer/PRP Rep hons: England U21, 18 Group, England 7s. Midlands (1). CLR: Rugby (10t, 14c, 45pg, 3dg-217pts), Gloucester (2t, 9c, 26pg-106pts). Hugely talented back, Mark's career was nearly halted by a series of serious knee injuries. Educated at Bawnmore Middle and Lawrence Sheriff School in Rugby and Loughborough University, he starred for England 18 Group before he first damaged his knee. Recovered in time to make an outstanding contribution on England's U21 tour of Australia (1993) but after joining Gloucester, and making a good early impression, he again injured knee ligaments, against West Hartlepool. Briefly signed for Bath in the summer of 1995 but had second thoughts and returned to Kingsholm. Started playing senior rugby again towards the end of 1995-96 season. Represented Coventry City Reserves as a schoolboy.

MASLEN, Daniel Magellan (Scrum-half)
Born Torbay, 23.3.72. 5'10", 13st 2lb. Rep hons: South West U21 Educated at Rendcomb College, Dan has played for Gloucestershire at all levels and won a Blue for Cambridge (1995) although he had to depart in the first half with bad concussion. Joined Gloucester from Cheltenham.

MATTHEWS, Neil John (Fly-half/centre)
Born Gloucester, 11.4.70. 5'10", 13st 7lb. Career: Leisure goods hire. Rep hons: England A/B (2, N Otago92), U21. South West (3). CLR: 1pg, 1dg-6pts. Talented utility back whose career has spluttered after a serious cruciate ligament injury to his knee. Formerly with Longlevens and Cheltenham, Neil toured New Zealand with England B in 1992 and enjoyed a short spell at Bristol before returning to Gloucester.

MILES, Peter (Lock)
Born Gloucester, 4.6.67 6'7", 18st. Career: Engineering manager. Rep hons: Gloucestershire. CLR: 4t-17pts. Laid-back lock who is a considerable performer when moved; witness the vital Bath game in April 1996. Formerly with both Bristol and Bath. Keen golfer.

MORRIS, Simon (Centre/wing)
Born Gloucester, 3.5.69. 6', 13st, Career: Policeman. Rep hons: England Colts. South West (7, 3t-15pts). CLR: 12t-55pts. Another Gloucester back who has been sorely tested by long-term knee injuries, having previously suffered with a cracked sternum. Simon is a well balanced, aggressive runner. Formerly with Lydney.

MULRAINE, Charles (Scrum-half)
Born Leamington, 24.12.73. 5'8", 12st 10lb. Career: Newspaper advertising rep. Rep hons: England 18 Group. Joined Gloucester in November 95 from Moseley. Former first-class cricketer with Warwickshire.

OSBORNE, Lee (Utility back)
Born Cinderford, 7.3.70. 6', 12st 7lb. Job: Metal buyer. Rep hons: Gloucestershire, South West U21. CLR: 6c, 15pg-57pts. Gloucester's Mr Versatility, Lee provides cover in all positions behind the scrum. Educated at the Royal Forest of Dean GS, Lee made his Gloucester debut in 1991 against Clifton. Formerly with Berry Hill.

PETERS, Mike (Wing)
Born Trinidad, 21.10.68. 6', 14st. Joined Wasps in 1994-95 on arriving in England from Trinidad but moved to Bristol to attend the University of West of England and was spotted playing in a sevens tournament by former Gloucester stalwart Tim Smith.

POWLES, Adrian (Prop)
Born Cowsford, 14.3.67. 5'11", 17st 2lb. Career: Heating engineer Rep hons: Gloucestershire. Another of Gloucester's front row squad, Adey arrived at Kingsholm via the Berry Hill club.

ROBERTS, Martin (Centre)
Born Gloucester, 21.1.68. 6'3", 15st 2lb. Career: Builder. Rep hons: Gloucestershire, South West U21. CLR: 2t, 6c, 13pg-61pts. Powerful hard-tackling centre and useful back-up goalkicker who joined Gloucester from Cheltenham.

SAVERIMUTTO, Alastair (Centre)
Born 4.3.70. 5'9", 12st 8lb. CLR: Bristol (8t-4pts), Coventry (2t, 1dg-13pts). Much-travelled, talented centre who has previously played for Bath, Bristol and Coventry. Brother of Christian and Robin.

SIMS, David (Lock)
Born Gloucester, 22.11.69. 6'7", 17st 10lb. Career: Youth Development officer. Rep hons: England A/B (18, Sp92, 1t-5pts), U21. South West (12, 1t-4pts). Barbarians (95-96). CLR: 8t-38pts. Powerful all-purpose forward who provided excellent leadership during Gloucester's fight against 'relegation' last season. The grandson of former Cheltenham and England forward Thomas Price, Dave was educated at Churchdown School, played his early rugby for Longlevens and enjoyed a spell with the Sunnybank club in Brisbane before representing England U21 and touring New Zealand with England B (1992). Bench reserve when Gloucester lost 1990 Pilkington Cup final to Bath, Dave was recalled by England A in 1995-96 and remains a respected opponent throughout League One.

SMITH, Ian Richard (Flanker)
Born Gloucester, 16.3.65. 6'1", 14st 5lb. Career: Civil engineering technician. Rep hons: Scotland (18, Eng92), A, Anglo/Scots. England B. South West (2). Barbarians (95-96). CLR: 8t-38pts. Ian was in outstanding form for Scotland last season and remains an influential figure at Gloucester where he is a former club captain. Educated at the Thomas Rich School in Gloucester and the son of former Gloucester lock Dick Smith, Ian was an England Schools final trialist and played for England B against Spain (1989) before opting for Scotland, being qualified through his paternal grandfather. Made his Scotland debut against England in 1992 and has appeared regularly until the Cambridge University axis of Iain Morrison, Eric Peters and Rob Wainwright left him on the bench throughout the 1995 Five Nations and restricted him to just one game, against Ivory Coast, in RWC95. He certainly returned with a vengeance in 1996.

STANLEY, Andrew Anthony (Flanker)
Born Gloucester, 15.9.65. 6', 14st 7lb. Career: Lecturer in construction at Gloucester College. Rep hons: Gloucestershire. Educated at Kingsholm primary and Oxstalls, Andrew is starting his 12th season with Gloucester having previously played for Gordon League and Sunny Bank in Brisbane. Captained Gloucestershire to victory in the CIS County Championship 1995-96. Players' rep this season.

WINDO, Tony (Prop)
Born Gloucester, 30.4.69. 6', 16st. Career: Warehouseman. Rep hons: England U21 South West (2). CLR: 5t-25pts. Another of Gloucester's array of powerful props, Tony joined the club from Longlevens.

REVIEW

Looked dead and buried before Christmas, but the arrival of former Bath and England scrum-half Richard Hill as director of coaching signalled a revival at Kingsholm, with traditional attributes of forward power and commitment coming to the fore. Any possibility of relegation was avoided with a home victory over Saracens on the final day, although the RFU were later to agree that no team should make the drop. Hill demanded much higher levels of fitness and attention to basics and was eventually rewarded on the pitch. Victory over Bath under the floodlights at Kingsholm was an occasion to relish and indicative of the team's potential, as was a useful run in the Pilkington Cup. David Sims, Phil Greening and Peter Glanville led by example up front, while the emergence of Scott Benton at scrum-half was a major plus. The signing of England U21 full-back Chris Catling could allow Mark Mapletoft to play at outside half although the abilities of Kiwi Martyn Kimber should not be underestimated.

GLOUCESTER in the Courage League 1995-96

Sep	9	Sale	H	Lost	17	22	Sims(T) Osborne(3P) Smith(D)
	16	Bath	A	Lost	11	37	Holford(T) Osborne(P) Kimber(D)
	23	West Hartlepool	A	Won	27	19	Holford(2T) Deacon(T) Kimber(2C, P) Sims(T)
	30	Leicester	H	Lost	14	27	Holford(T) Kimber(3P)
Oct	7	Orrell	A	Lost	3	21	Smith(P)
	14	Wasps	H	Lost	15	26	Smith(4P) Kimber(D)
	21	Bristol	A	Lost	16	22	Kimber(T) Smith(C, 3P)
	28	Harlequins	H	Lost	13	24	Fenley(T) Smith(C, 2P)
Nov	4	Saracens	A	Lost	16	19	Windo(T) Smith(C, 2P) Kimber(D)
	11	Sale	A	Lost	13	21	Miles(T) Sims(T) Smith(P)
Jan	6	West Hartlepool	H	Won	17	16	Beim(T) Smith(3P) Osborne(P)
Feb	17	Orrell	H	Won	27	0	Roberts(T) Windo(T) Fenwick(C, 4P) Kimber(D)
Mar	30	Wasps	A	Lost	10	21	Penalty(T) Fenwick(C, P)
Apr	6	Bristol	H	Won	18	14	Fenwick(3P) Mapletoft(2P) Kimber(D)
	10	Bath	H	Won	16	10	Holford(T) Smith(C, 3P)
	13	Harlequins	A	Lost	19	33	Raymond(T) Smith(T, 3P)
	24	Leicester	A	Lost	6	28	Mapletoft(2P)
	27	Saracens	H	Won	17	10	Windo(T) Mapletoft(3P) Kimber(D)

HARLEQUINS

Formation of Club: 1866
Ground: The Stoop Memorial, Craneford Way, Twickenham. Tel: 0181 892 0822
Capacity: 8,500
Colours: Light blue, magenta, chocolate, french grey, black and light green
Honours: Pilkington Cup: Winners: 1988, 91. Losing finalists: 1992, 93
Last season: CL1: 3rd. Pilkington Cup: Q/F (lost 24-9 to Leicester)
Most capped player: Will Carling (England) 66
Director of Rugby: Dick Best
Coaches: Simon Halliday, Kent Bray
Captain: Jason Leonard

ALLISON, Gareth Vincent (Flanker)
Born New Malden, London, 31.1.70. 6'5", 16st 2lb. Rep hons: England Colts. London (1, 1t-5pts). CLR: Rosslyn Park (6t-30pts), Harlequins (3t-15pts). Educated at St Paul's and an England Colts cap at full-back, Gareth continued his studies at Reading University and Oxford University where he graduated with an MSc in Management Studies and won a Blue at flanker (1994). Gareth, who also played for Toulouse and Rosslyn Park last season, developed apace at wing forward with Harlequins last season and is poised to challenge for international honours.

BENEZECH, Laurent (Prop)
Born Palmiers, France, 19.12.66. 6', 16st 5lb. Career: PRP. Rep hons: France (15, Eng94), A, Students, Armed Forces. Fell out of favour after the autumn series against New Zealand (1995), but remains an international class prop. Originally joined Toulouse as a young lock, he joined Racing in 1989 and helped them win the French Championship final (1990). International debut against England in 1994, Laurent is the president of the French players' union.

BROMLEY, Spencer Paul (Wing)
Born Manchester, 12.12.69. 6'1", 14st 10lb. Rep hons: England Students, U21. North (3, 2t-8pts). CLR: Liverpool St Helens (2t-8pts), Rugby (2t-10pts), Harlequins (11t-55pts). Educated at Cardinal Langley HS, John Moores University and Oxford where he gained a Blue (1994), Spencer benefited from Quins' free-running approach last season and scored 11 League tries.

CABANNES, Laurent (Flanker)
Born Pau, France, 6.2.64. 6'3", 14st 6lb. Career: PRP. Rep hons: France (45, NZ90, 2t-8pts). Western Province. Barbarians (1991). World-class flanker arrives at the Stoop on a two-year contract 'for the last great rugby adventure of my career' after signing from Racing Club. Originally played his rugby for Pau but joined Racing in 1986 and helped them to the 1987 French Championship final. Overcame a serious car accident and returned to help Racing to the 1990 championship before making his international debut against New Zealand that November. Has been an automatic choice ever since but was 'disciplined' last autumn for arriving back late from South Africa where he played for Western Province. Appeared throughout the 1996 Five Nations but made himself unavailable for France's summer tour of Argentina and could have played his last international.

CARLING, William David Charles (Centre)
Born Bradford on Avon, 12.12.65. 5'11", 14st 2lb. Career: Managing director/PRP. Rep hons: England (66, Fr88, 12t-53pts), British Lions (1, NZ93), A/B (1, Fr87). North (9, 1t, 2pg-10pts), London (5, 3t-13pts). Barbarians (86-87). CLR: 17t, 1pg-78pts. Will Carling OBE is England's most-capped centre and stepped down as captain after the Ireland game in March with a record of W44 D1 L14 during his 59 games in charge. His captaincy encompassed three Grand Slams (91, 92 and 95), a World Cup final (1991) and a World Cup semi-final (1995). Educated at Sedbergh, where England's only other back-to-back Grand Slam captain Wavell Wakefield learned his rugby, Will attended Durham University on an army scholarship, graduating in psychology. Made his international debut against France (1988) and succeeded Richard Harding as captain against Australia that autumn. Missed the 1989 Lions tour of Australia with shin splints and the Lions provided further disappointment in 1993 when Gavin Hastings was preferred as captain and he lost his Test place to Scott Gibbs. Intends to enjoy his last couple of seasons and has even threatened to dabble at fly-half.

CHALLINOR, Paul Andrew (Fly-half)
Born Wolverhampton, 5.12.69. 6', 13st 2lb. Career: Self-employed business consultant. Rep hons: England A/B (10, Fr93, 3t, 5c, 12pg, 2dg-67pts), 18 Group. London (3), Midlands (3, 2t-10pts). CLR: 13t, 27c, 62pg, 10dg-333pts. Returned to favour at fly-half midway through last season and contributed to Harlequins' strong finish. Educated at RGS Guildford, Paul made his Quins debut against Cardiff in December 1990 and has always been a prolific goalkicker. Keen club cricketer.

CORCORAN, Michael (Wing)
Born 29.11.69. 6'3", 14st 6lb. Rep hons: Ireland Development XV, Irish Exiles. England 18 Group. Chelsea FC. CLR: 22t, 64c, 165pg, 1dg-730pts. Reliable former London Irish wing and goalkicker who scored 301 League points in 1995-96, including 8 tries. Educated at John Fisher School, Purley, Michael toured Australia with England Schools in 1988 and was a professional footballer at Chelsea before concentrating on rugby.

DIX, Richard Shaun (Fly-half)
Born Brighton, 27.5.73. 5'10", 12st 4lb. Rep hons: South West. Former Millfield schoolboy and Cambridge Blue who also played for Llandovery before joining Harlequins.

HAMILTON-SMITH, Jim (Hooker)
Born Nassau, Bahamas, 6.10.71. 5'10", 13st 7lb. Career: Schoolmaster. Mobile hooker who has provided reliable cover for Brian Moore and Simon Mitchell since making his Quins debut against Blackrock in September 1993.

HENDERSON, Crawford (Wing)
Born London, 11.2.69. 6'1", 14st. Career: Reinsurance broker. CLR: 1t-5pts. Strong-running wing who provides useful back-up for Daren O'Leary and Spencer Bromley.

JACKSON, Adam (Lock)
Born Blackpool, 28.1.73. 6'6", 17st. Career: Student. Rep hons: England Colts. Strapping Lancastrian lock who appeared in three Colts County Cup finals for Lancashire at Twickenham.

JENKINS, Rory Harry John (Flanker)
Born Leicester, 29.6.70. 6'2", 15st 12lb. Career: Solicitor. Rep hons: England A (1, It94, 1t-5pts), Emerging, Students, U21, 18 Group. London (4). CLR: London Irish (3t-13pts). The son of former Leicester and Cambridge University lock John Jenkins, Rory was also educated at Oundle and Cambridge University where he won Blues in rugby, cricket and athletics. Formerly with Brixham he joined London Irish and played against the 1993 All Blacks for London before joining Harlequins.

KITCHIN, Robert (Scrum-half)
Born Chertsey, 25.7.71. 5'9", 12st 5lb. Career: Bond broker. Rep hons: England A (2, Aus95), Emerging, Students. South West (4, 1t-5pts). CLR: Bristol (14t-9pts), Harlequins (8t-40pts). Took over the captaincy when Jason Leonard was injured last season but finished the season as a reserve to Nick Walshe. Educated at Sherborne and Exeter University, Rob scored 7 League tries in 1995-96. Quick enough to play on the wing while at Bristol, Rob captained the South West in 1994-95 and will be determined to regain his first team place.

LEONARD, Jason (Prop)
Born Barking, 14.8.68. 5'10", 17st 2lb. Career: Business development manager/PRP. Rep hons: England (49, Arg90), British Lions (2, NZ93), A/B (2, Fiji89), U21, Colts. London (11). Barbarians. CLR: Saracens (1t-4pts), Harlequins (2t-9pts). Despite a career-threatening neck injury which required a bone graft from his hip, Jason has missed just one England international since his debut in 1990, sitting out the RWC group game against Western Samoa in Durban in 1995. He is now England's most capped prop. Educated at Warren Comprehensive School, Chadwell Heath, Jason joined Barking RFC before moving to Saracens. Won his first England caps against Argentina in 1990 from Saracens but then moved to Harlequins where he proved an outstanding and popular captain last season. Moved to tight head last season to accommodate Graham Rowntree in the England team, a position he filled with honour on the 1993 Lions tour.

LLEWELLYN, Gareth Owen (Lock)
Born Bradford-on-Avon, 27.2.69. 6'6", 17st 10lb. Career: PRP. Rep hons: Wales (48, NZ89, 5t-24pts), B, Youth, U19. Barbarians (89-90). Gareth Llewellyn has joined Harlequins from Neath having led the Welsh All Blacks to the Heineken League championship in 1995-96 and a SWALEC Cup final appearance against Pontypridd. The most capped Welsh lock in history, he has also captained his country against Zimbabwe and Namibia on tour and against France (twice), Italy and South Africa. Gareth was educated at Bryntirion Comprehensive and won Youth and U19 honours from Llanharan before moving to the Gnoll. Made his international debut against New Zealand in 1989. Switched briefly, without conspicuous success, to blindside flanker during RWC95 but was restored to lock for the quarter-final against Ireland and remained here through the 1995-96 international season.

LLEWELLYN, Glyn (Lock)
Born Bradford-on-Avon, 9.8.65. 6'6", 17st 8lb. Career: PRP. Rep hons: Wales (9, Nam90), U21, U18. Formerly with Llanharan, Bridgend, London Welsh and Llanelli, Glyn joins Harlequins from Neath after failing to agree terms with Wasps. Enjoyed a successful career with Neath that culminated in the Heineken League championship in May. Keen windsurfer and former Welsh Schools basketball international.

LUGER, Dan (Wing)
Joins from Orrell, Dan was formerly with Richmond. Played for London U21 against NZ U21 in 1994 and appeared for England Students and U21 in 1995-96. A member of England's squad in the World Students Cup this summer.

MENSAH, Peter (Centre)
Born Ghana, 10.11.66. 6', 13st 8lb. Career: Rep hons: England A (5, S Aus95, 1t-5pts). London (3, 2t-10pts). CLR: 8t-40pts. Came to the senior game late when he joined Quins from Old Millhillians in 1994, Peter has slotted in well at the Stoop and has also earned England A honours. Scored three tries for an England Select XV against a Springbok Veteran XV in a fund-raising game for Max Brito in Ghana in May 96.

MULLINS, Andrew Richard (Prop)
Born Blackheath, 12.12.64. 5'11". 16st. Career: Broker. Rep hons: England (1, Fiji89), A/B (19, Aus88), Students, 18 Group. London (6). Barbarians. CLR: 2t-9pts. Educated at Dulwich College and Durham University. Andy played for England in the 1988 World Students Cup and won his solitary cap against Fiji at Twickenham the following year. Made his Harlequins debut against Llanelli in September 1987 and has been a marvellous club servant ever since.

O'LEARY, Daren (Wing)
Born Harold Wood, 27.6.73. 6', 13st 10lb. Career: Bond dealer. Rep hons: England A (1, I196), Emerging, U21, Colts, Schools. London (12, 2t-10pts). CLR: Saracens (3t-15pts), Harlequins (26t-130pts). Try-poacher par excellence, Daren returned to his best form in 1995-96 with 14 League tries, topping the scoring chart. Educated at Campion School and West London Institute, Daren developed his try-scoring habits at Saracens before moving to Harlequins in 1993, making his debut that September against Lansdowne. Was called into the England training squad for the 1993 Five Nations but is still waiting patiently to make his senior debut.

OZDEMIR, Alton (Prop)
Born Cyprus, 3.9.74. 5'9". 16st. Rep hons: England 18 Group. Powerful prop, Alton moved from Cyprus at the age of six, was educated at Hurstpierpoint College and joined Harlequins after a short spell with Bristol.

PEARS, David (Full-back/Fly-half)
Born Workington, 6.12.67. 5'10", 12st 7lb. Career: Equities broker. Rep hons: England (4, Arg90), A/B (14, Aus88, 1t, 7c, 24pg, 2dg-96pts). North (6, 1t, 4c, 11pg, 1dg-54pts). Barbarians (91-92). CLR: Sale (3t, 3c, 26pg, dg-102pts), Harlequins (7t, 55c, 83pg, 14dg-431pts. The much-injured but ever-game David Pears underwent another operation on his damaged ankle last season following an accidental clash with Mike Catt when Harlequins played Bath, further aggravating the injury when he played for London against Western Samoa. Previous mishaps have seen Pears damage almost every part of his body, including neck, broken hand, broken nose, ribs, groin, hamstring, concussion and knee. He played in just one League match in the 1992-93 season and none at all in 1993-94. Made his full England debut on tour against Argentina (1990). Educated at Workington GS, David is a former captain of the Cumbrian schools soccer side and played for both Aspatria and Sale before joining Harlequins.

PICKUP, Ian (Backrow)
Born York, 27.6.69. 6'4", 16st. Career: Schoolmaster. Rep hons: England Univs. CLR: Coventry (1t-4pts), Rosslyn Park (4t-20pts). Dependable performer who played for Coventry and Rosslyn Park before joining Quins in September 1995.

RUSSELL, Mark (Back five forward)
Born Nairobi, Kenya, 16.12.65. 6'4", 17st 6lb. Rep hons: England A/B (4, N Otago92, 1t-4pts). London (4, 1t-4pts). Western Province. CLR: 2t-9pts. Arrived back in England after playing for Cape Town University and Western Province. Quins debut against Gosforth in February 91 and an England B tourist in New Zealand (1992).

SNOW, Alex Charles (Lock)
Born Chelsea, 29.4.69. 6'7", 17st. Career: Equities broker. Rep hons: England A (2, B Columbia), Emerging, Students. Scottish Univs, Edinburgh. London (9, 1t-5pts). CLR: 2t-10pts. Educated at Harrow School and St Andrew's University, Alex came to prominence as a lineout jumper with England in the 1992 World Students Cup.

STAPLES, James (Full-back)
Born Bermondsey, 20.10.65. 6'2", 13st 10lb. Career: Bond trader with Societé Général. Rep hons: Ireland (22, Wal91, 5t, 2c-25pts), B, U25. Barbarians (92-93). CLR: London Irish (14t, 1dg-59pts), Harlequins (9t, 5c, 2pg, 2dg-67pts). Jim, who is no stranger to injury, again suffered last season when a nasty knock and concussion saw him lose his place in the national side to Richmond's Simon Mason. Was educated at St Mary's, Sidcup, and played for Sidcup before joining London Irish. Played for the Irish Wolfhounds in the 1989 Hong Kong 7s and won three U25 caps against Italy, USA and Spain before making a try-scoring international debut against Wales in 1991. Starred for Ireland in RWC91 and did well to survive a crude late and high tackle from Scotland's Finlay Calder in their group games. Prolapsed disc and serious knee-ligament injury problems blighted his career after the tour to Australia in 1992 but, after joining Harlequins, returned to the international arena against France in 1995. A useful footballer who once partnered Arsenal's Ian Wright up front for Greenwich Borough.

THRESHER, Peter (Lock)
Born Farnborough, 9.6.70. 6'7", 16st 9lb. Career: Options trader. Rep hons: England Students, U21. London. CLR: 1t-5pts. Educated at Sevenoaks School, University of Wales and Oxford, where he won a Blue in 1991, Peter is a formidable lineout operator who made his club debut against Cardiff in December 1990.

WALSHE, Nick (Scrum-half)
Born Chiswick, 1.4.73. 5'11", 13st 4lb. Career: Student. Rep hons: London U21. CLR: Rosslyn Park (2t-10pts), Harlequins (1c-2pts). Formerly at Rosslyn Park, Nick impressed at full-back for London U21 v NZ U21 in 1994 but is scrum-half by preference and ousted Rob Kitchin as first choice at the end of 1995-96.

WATSON, Michael (Backrow)
Born Sunderland, 2.8.65. 6'6", 18st. Career: Broker. Rep hons: North (3, 1t-5pts), London (3, 2t-10pts). Combined Services, Army. CLR: West Hartlepool (8t-40pts), Harlequins (5t-25pts). Abrasive but highly effective ex-Army backrow star who joined Quins from West Hartlepool, having also represented Alton RFC. Despite deputising at lock on occasions last season, Mick scored five tries and remains one of the strongest running forwards in the game. Club debut against Nottingham in February 1995.

WOOD, Keith Gerard Mallinson (Hooker)
Born Limerick, Ireland, 27.1.72. 6', 15st 10lb. Career: PRP. Rep hons: Ireland (6, Aus94), A, U21, Schools. Missed all of last season with Garryowen after re-injuring a shoulder in the opening minutes of Ireland's group game against Japan in RWC95. The

son of former Ireland and British Lions hooker Gordon Wood, Keith was educated at St Munchin's College, Limerick. He was an exceptional age group international, and made his full debut on the Australian tour (1994).

WRIGHT, Chris (Utility back)
Born Heswell, 8.2.68. 5'6", 11st 10lb. Career: Financial adviser. Rep hons: North U21 CLR: Orrell (6t-24pts), Wasps (1t-4pts), Harlequins (2t-10pts). Educated at Birkenhead School and Caldey Grange GS, Chris played for New Brighton, Orrell and Wasps before becoming Quins utility man behind the scrum. Club debut against Lansdowne in September 1994.

REVIEW

Entertaining as ever, Harlequins added a genuine touch of steel under the captaincy of Jason Leonard and directorship of Dick Best and now command the respect of even Bath and Leicester. A talented back division, with Will Greenwood emerging as a class centre alongside Will Carling and Daren O'Leary rediscovering his try-scoring touch, was capable of running riot and frequently did – notably against West Hartlepool and Sale. Greenwood's move to Leicester in the summer was a surprise and he will be missed. In the forwards, the front row was always competitive, Mick Watson coped manfully at lock with Alex Snow, and a backrow of Rory Jenkins, Chris Sheasby and Gareth Allison was among the best units in the Courage League. With massive financial backing from sponsors NEC, and investors Riverside Leisure, and ambitious rebuilding plans at the Stoop, Harlequins are poised to hit the professional era running and the recruitment of Laurent Benezech, Laurent Cabannes, Keith Wood, Glyn Llewellyn, Gareth Llewellyn and Michael Corcoran has only strengthened their hand.

HARLEQUINS in the Courage League 1995-96

Sep	9	Orrell	A	Won	23	9	Kitchin(T) Mitchell(T) O'Leary(T) Pears(C, D, P)
	16	Wasps	H	Won	29	20	Bromley(T) Sheasby(T) Pears(2C, 3D, 2P)
	23	Bristol	A	Won	31	25	O'Leary(2T) Bromley(T) Greenwood(T) Pears(C, 3P)
	30	West Hartlepool	H	Won	34	18	Bromley(T) Brown(T) Carling(T) Kitchin(T) Sheasby(T) Pears(3C, P)
Oct	7	Saracens	H	Won	23	15	Allison(T) O'Leary(T) Pears(2C, D, 2P)
	14	Sale	A	Lost	11	29	Staples(T) Pears(2P)
	21	Bath	H	Lost	13	19	O'Leary(T) Pears(C, D, P)
	28	Gloucester	A	Won	24	13	Bromley(T) Challinor(T) Staples(T, 2C) Wright(T)
Nov	4	Leicester	H	Lost	25	29	Mensah(T) O'Leary(T) Sheasby(T) Challinor(2C, 2P)
	11	Orrell	H	Lost	21	25	Kitchin(T) Mensah(T) Pears(C, 3P)
Jan	6	Bristol	H	Won	28	3	Kitchin(3T) Bromley(T) Watson(T) Carling(P)

Feb 17	Saracens	A	Won	13	6	Mensah(T) Challinor(C, 2P)
Mar 9	Wasps	A	Won	34	3	O'Leary(2T) Bromley(T) Challinor(T, D, 3P) Walshe(C)
23	West Hartlepool	A	Won	91	21	Allison(2T) Bromley(2T) Greenwood(2T) O'Leary(2T) Staples(2T) Watson(2T) Challinor(T, 9C, P) Mullins(T)
30	Sale	H	Won	55	0	Bromley(3T) Staples(2T, D) Watson(2T) O'Leary(T) Challinor(3C, D, P)
Apr 6	Bath	A	Lost	15	41	Challinor(T, C, P) Kitchin(T)
13	Gloucester	H	Won	33	19	O'Leary(2T) Challinor(T, C, D, P) Greenwood(T) Staples(T)
27	Leicester	A	Won	21	19	Mensah(T) O'Leary(T) Challinor(C, 2D, P)

LEICESTER

Formation of Club: 1880
Ground: Welford Road, Aylestone Road, Leicester, LE2 7EF.
  Tel: 0116 2540276 or 0116 2541607
Capacity: 14,000
Colours: Scarlet, green and white
Honours: Pilkington Cup: Winners: 1979, 89, 91, 93.
  Losing finalists: 1978, 83, 89, 94, 96.
  Courage League: Champions: 1987-88, 94-95. Runners-up: 1993-94, 95-96
Last season: CL1: Runners-up. Pilkington Cup: Losing finalists.
Most capped player: Rory Underwood (England) 85
Director of Rugby: Bob Dwyer
Coaches: Ian Smith, Paul Dodge
Captain: Dean Richards

AUSTIN, Greg (Centre)
Born Cootamundra, Australia, 14.6.65. 5'10", 13st. Career: PRP. Rep hons: New South Wales Schools (RU). Prolific try-scoring centre who joins Leicester from Huddersfield RL having previously played for North Sydney, Rochdale Hornets, Salford and Halifax. Has logged over 300 tries in his RL career, including 52 in 1994-95 when he set a Regal Trophy record by scoring nine in one game for Huddersfield against Blackpool. Born in the same village as cricket legend Don Bradman, Greg's father Roy is a regular winner of the World Veterans' sprint championship and at 60 is still running 11.1 seconds for the 100m.

BACK, Neil Anthony (Flanker)
Born Coventry, 16.1.69. 5'9", 13st 12lb. Career: Senior pensions supervisor. Rep hons: England (5, Sc94, 1t-5pts), A/B (23, Aus90, 9t-44pts), U21, Colts, 18 Group, 7s. Midlands (9, 2t-8pts). Barbarians (90-91). CLR: Nottingham (2t-8pts), Leicester (13t-64pts). Ineligible until 4 November after receiving a six-month ban for pushing referee Steve Lander to the ground after Tigers' 16-15 defeat in the Pilkington Cup final in May. Educated at Woodlands School, Coventry, Neil played for Earlsdon and Barkers' Butts before moving to Nottingham and then to Welford Road. Toured New Zealand and Canada with England A. He made his full international debut against Scotland (1994). Fitness fanatic and useful cricketer.

COCKERILL, Richard (Hooker)
Born Rugby, 16.12.70. 5'10", 14st 7lb. Career: PRP. Rep hons: England A (3, It95), Emerging, U21. Midlands (10). Barbarians (90-91). CLR: 3t-15pts. Voluble hooker who has become a favourite at Leicester. Formerly an antiques restorer, he is now a full-time professional. Educated at Harris Church of England School, Richard played for Newbold-on-Avon and Coventry before joining Leicester. Missed out on the England A tour of Australia and Fiji (1995), but used the summer to improve his fitness and is now breathing down Mark Regan's neck at national level.

DELANEY, Paul Kenneth (Centre)
Born Wellsbourne, Liverpool, 17.10.74. 6', 13st 7lb. Career: Student. Rep hons: Midland U21. Learned his rugby under Mike Slemen at Merchant Taylors' School, Crosby. Paul is now a student at Leicester University.

DRAKE-LEE, William Michael (Flanker)
Born Kettering, 9.8.70. 6', 15st. Career: Estate agent. Rep hons: British Polytechnics, Midlands U21. Educated at the Irwin Academy and De Montford University in Leicester, Bill joined Leicester from Kettering and is the son of former England prop Nick Drake-Lee. Reliable backrow back-up who has made 13 Courage League appearances to date.

FIELD, Robert John (Lock)
Born Coventry, 2.6.71. 6'6", 17st 10lb. Rep hons: English Universities. Robert was educated at King Henry VIII School, Coventry, and Leicester University and joined Leicester from Coventry in 1994. Has made two Courage League appearances to date.

FLETCHER, Neil (Lock)
Born 4.6.76. 6'7", 17st. Career: Leisure centre supervisor. Rep hons: England U21 squad member. Midlands U21 Promising lock who joined Leicester from Moseley in June.

GARFORTH, Darren James (Prop)
Born Coventry, 9.4.66. 5'10", 16st 10lb. Career: PRP. Rep hons: England A (16, Sp93, 3t-15pts), Emerging. Midlands (10). Barbarians (90). CLR: Nuneaton (2t-8pts), Leicester (3t-14pts). Rugged tight-head prop with a surprising turn of speed, Darren enjoyed his best-ever season in 1995-96 and became a regular in the England A team. Educated at Binley Park School, Coventry, he played for Nuneaton before moving to Leicester in 1991-92.

GREENWOOD, William John Heaton (Centre)
Born Blackburn, 20.10.72. 6'3", 14st. Career: Merchant banker. Rep hons: England A (8, S Aus95, 4t-20pts), Students, U21. North. CLR: Waterloo (1t-5pts), Harlequins (6t, 1c, 5pg-47pts). Signed from Harlequins in June. Comes from the same Sedbergh/Durham University stable as former Quins colleague Will Carling. Will was an influential figure for Quins last winter. Formerly with Preston Grasshoppers and Waterloo, he toured Australia with England U21 (1993). Scored a hat-trick for England A against Western Samoa in December 1995.

HACKNEY, Steve (Wing)
Born Stockton-on-Tees, 13.6.68. 5'11", 13st 7lb. Career: Sales executive. Rep hons: England A (12, Aus88, 12t-56pts), Colts, 18 Group, England 7s. Midlands (19, 3t-13pts). Barbarians (88-89). CLR: Nottingham (2t-8pts), Leicester (21t-101pts). Educated at Ian Ramsey Church of England School and Loughborough University, Steve toured Canada with England A in 1993 and Australia and Fiji in 1995. Scored six League tries in 1995-96 including a length-of-the-field team effort against Bristol that was voted try of the season. Also scored a startling individual effort against the World XV at Twickenham.

HEALEY, Austin (Scrum-half/wing)
Born Wallasey, 26.10.73. 5'9", 13st 2lb. Career: PRP. Rep hons: England A (1, NSW96), Students, U21, England 7s. North (7, 2t-10pts). Barbarians (95-96). CLR: Waterloo (3t, 1dg-18pts), Orrell (4t, 2c, 1pg-27pts). Transferred from Orrell after switching from wing to scrum-half in 1995-96, Austin possesses exceptional pace off the mark. Educated at St Anselm's College, along with Richmond's Simon Mason, he first joined Birkenhead Park and came to national prominence when helping Waterloo to a third

round Pilkington Cup victory over Bath. A try scorer in December 1994 when England U21 beat New Zealand U21, Austin made his A team debut against New South Wales at Leicester in January 1995. Would have been called Jensen had he been born a girl!

JELLEY, Derek Arthur (Prop)
Born Nuneaton, 4.3.72. 6', 16st 10lb. Career: Construction engineer. Rep hons: Midlands U21. Educated at Earl Shilton College, Derek joined Leicester from Market Bosworth. Has made eight League appearances for Tigers.

JOHNSON, Martin Osborne (Lock)
Born Solihull, 9.3.70. 6'7", 17st 12lb. Career: Midland Bank. Rep hons: England (24, Fr93), British Lions (2, NZ93), A (8, Fr92, 1t-5pts), U21, Colts, 18 Group, New Zealand Colts (U21). Midlands (12, 2t-10pts). Barbarians (91-92). CLR: 2t-10pts. The world's outstanding front-of-the-line jumper and a formidable all-round forward, Martin has been an immense force for England since making his debut against France in 1993 after a last-minute call-up for Wade Dooley. Was touring Canada with an England XV in May 93 when he was again called on to replace Dooley, this time for the Lions in New Zealand, immediately winning Test selection. Educated at Welland Park and Robert Smythe Upper School, Market Harborough, Martin had already represented England Schools when he travelled to New Zealand to play for King Country and subsequently toured Australia with New Zealand Colts (U21).

JOINER, Craig Alexander (Wing)
Born Glasgow, 21.4.74. 5'10", 13st 12lb. Career: PRP. Rep hons: Scotland (17, Arg94, 4t-20pts), A, U21, Schools. Elusive Scottish wing who joins Leicester from Melrose, Craig was educated at Dunfermline HS and Merchiston Castle School where he was a national schools sprint champion and won 10 schools rugby caps. Made his international debut while on tour in Argentina (94), Craig was ever-present throughout Scotland's RWC95 campaign. Scored a try against New Zealand at Dunedin in June.

JONES, Matt Brian (Fly-half)
Born Tonbridge, 3.1.76. 6', 13st 8lb. Career: Student. Former Millfield schoolboy who was a member of England's Grand Slam side in 1994. U21 international. Student at Aston University, member of England Students World Cup squad 1996.

KARDOONI, Aadel (Scrum-half)
Born Tehran, Iran, 17.5.68. 5'8", 12st. Career: City broker. Rep hons: England A/B (6, N Otago92, 1t-4pts), Students, Schools. Midlands (8). CLR: 16t-74pts. Educated at Sherborne, Aadel was ever-present in the 1986 England Schools team and played one League game for Wasps before joining Leicester where he has become a Tigers stalwart. Toured New Zealand with England B (1992), playing in both 'Tests'

LILEY, John Garin (Full-back)
Born Wakefield, 21.8.67. 6', 13st 10lb. Career: Accountant and marketing executive. Rep hons: England A/B (4, Nam90, 6c, 7pg-33pts). Midlands (7, 8c, 20pg-76pts). Yorkshire. CLR: Wakefield (2t, 4c, 2pg-22pts), Leicester (22t, 105c, 188pg, 1dg-875pts). Prolific points scorer, John was educated at Eastmoor HS and played for Sandal and Wakefield before joining Leicester. Broke his own club record of 441 points in a season in 1995-96, raising the total to 446. Toured Argentina, perhaps prematurely, with England (1990) but is a much better player now. Underrated runner, John

captained Leicester to victory in the Middlesex sevens title in 1995 and at the Madrid Invitation tournament in 1996.

LILEY, Robert (Fly-half)
Born Wakefield, 3.4.70. 6'1", 12st 8lb. Career: Insurance inspector. Rep hons: England U21, Students. North (2, 1t, 10c, 3pg-34pts). CLR: Wakefield (3t, 23c, 51pg, 2dg-219pts), Sale (3t, 28c, 44pg, 2dg-209pts). Numbers Sandal, Wakefield, Sale and Cahors in France among his previous clubs; Rob is the younger brother of John and shares many of his footballing skills. Served a patient apprenticeship under Paul Turner at Sale but emerged in 1995-96 to amass 167 League points before signing for Leicester. Yorkshire debut against Cumbria in 1992. Enjoys classical guitar.

MALONE, Niall Gareth (Fly-half)
Born Leeds, 30.4.71. 6', 13st 5lb. Career: Sales executive. Rep hons: Ireland (3, Sc93, 3pg-9pts), A, Students, U21, Schools. English Universities. Irish Exiles. CLR: 1pg, 1dg-6pts. Educated at Methodist College, Belfast, and Loughborough University, Niall also won a Blue for Oxford (1992) and earned his first full cap two months later, against Scotland. Made his Leicester debut on tour in South Africa (1993) and disputed the fly-half spot with Jez Harris for two seasons. Scored a try in the 1995-96 Pilkington Cup final.

MILLER, Eric Roger Patrick (Backrow)
Born Dublin, Ireland, 23.9.75. 6'3", 15st 7lb. Career: Student. Rep hons: Ireland A, U21, Students, Schools. Promising Irish backrow forward who was educated at Wesley College, Eric spent two seasons in the Irish Schools XV. Although his opportunities have been limited at Leicester he made his Ireland A debut against Scotland in February 1996.

OVEREND, James (Centre/wing)
Born Leeds 1.12.74. 5'11", 13st 9lb. Career: Student. Rep hons: England U21, 18 Group. CLR: Otley (2t-10pts). Talented young centre who made two appearances for Leicester last season. Season finished disappointingly when he injured an ankle in the Pilkington Cup quarter-final against Harlequins.

POOLE, Matthew David (Lock)
Born Leicester, 6.2.69. 6'7", 18st. Career: Sales rep. Rep hons: England Emerging, U21, Colts, 18 Group. Midlands (13, 3t-15pts). CLR: 3t-15pts. Unsung but invaluable member of Leicester's pack, Matt has toured Argentina (1990) and South Africa (1994) with the senior England squads without being capped. Educated at Roundhill and originally a member of Syston College he made his Tigers debut in 1989 against Oxford University.

POTTER, Stuart (Centre)
Born Lichfield, 11.11.67. 5'11", 14st. Career: Insurance development officer. Rep hons: England A/B (17, It93, 5t-25pts), Midlands (13, 3t-15pts). Barbarians (93-94). CLR: Nottingham (5t-20pts), Leicester (8t-40pts). Powerful centre who toured Canada with England A (1993) and South Africa with England (1994). Educated at Friary Grange School, Stuart first came to prominence with Nottingham and helped the Midlands win the Divisional Championship (1991) before joining Leicester.

RICHARDS, Dean (No 8)
Born Nuneaton, 11.7.63. 6'4", 17st 8lb. Career: PRP. Rep hons: England (48, Ire86, 6t-24pts), British Lions (5, Aus89), A (1, Sp93, 1t-5pts), U23, 18 Group. Midlands (18, 4t-17pts). Barbarians (82-83). CLR: 12t-51pts. Leicester's talisman and captain, Dean Richards has been a magnificent servant for club and country. Educated at St Martins RC School and John Cleveland College, Dean won schoolboy international honours at lock but soon reverted to the backrow. Despite a career badly disrupted by serious shoulder injuries and falling out of favour with the selectors, he is now the world's most capped No 8 having overtaken Mervyn Davies. First capped in 1986 against Ireland, when he scored two tries, he possesses an uncanny ability to read the game and a huge physical presence in the tight. Key member of the 1989 Lions pack that subdued Australia, Deano also enjoyed a successful tour of New Zealand with the Lions four years later. Enjoys rough shooting.

ROWNTREE, Graham Christopher (Prop)
Born Stockton-on-Tees, 18.1.71. 6', 17st 2lb. Career: Insurance broker. Rep hons: England (8, Sc95), A (4, B Col93), U21, Colts, 18 Group. Midlands (4). Barbarians (93-94). CLR: 1t-5pts. Graham was ever-present in England's Triple Crown winning side last season at loose head, having made his debut the previous season as a replacement against Scotland. Also appeared in the World Cup against Italy and Western Samoa and toured South Africa with England in 1994 without being capped. Educated at Hastings HS and John Cleveland College in Hinkley, Graham emerged from the Nuneaton club and was an outstanding age group international. He toured Canada with an England XV in 1993 playing in both 'Tests' and underlined his potential for the Midlands against New Zealand that autumn.

UNDERWOOD, Rory (Wing)
Born Middlesbrough, 19.6.63. 5'9", 13st 8lb. Career: RAF pilot. Rep hons: England (85, Ire84, 49t-210pts), British Lions (6, Aus89, 1t-5pts), A/B (1, Ire82), U23, Colts. North (26, 14t-57pts). Combined Services. Barbarians (83-84). CLR: 36t-157pts. England's most-capped player and record try scorer with 49. Educated at Barnard Castle School along with Rob Andrew, Rory first came to prominence with England Colts in 1983 and won his first senior cap the following year, scoring against France in Paris. Involved in England's Grand Slam triumphs in 1991, 1992 and 1995 and all three World Cup campaigns, he equalled Dan Lambert's England record of 1907 by scoring five tries against Fiji at Twickenham in 1989. Winner of six Lions caps, Rory scored a memorable try against New Zealand in the second Test in 1993.

WELLS, John Martin (Flanker)
Born Driffield, 12.5.63. 6'2", 15st 7lb. Career: Police officer. Rep hons: England A/B (4, Fr88, 1t-4pts), Students, U23, 18 Group. Midlands (21, 1t-4pts). Barbarians. CLR: 8t-34pts. Uncompromising backrow forward and loyal club man, John is a former captain of Leicester and led the side to victory in the 1993 Pilkington Cup over Harlequins. Educated at Magnus GS and capped at lock by England Schools, John developed his rugby skills at Loughborough University before moving to Leicester. His appearance in the Pilkington Cup final in May 96 was John's 338th first team game, including 101 in the League, for Leicester, more than any individual currently playing at the club.

WEST, Dorian Edward (Hooker)
Born Wrexham, 5.10.67. 5'11", 15st 8lb. Career: Police officer. Rep hons: British Police, Midlands. CLR: Nottingham (6t-30pts). Understudy to Richard Cockerill, Dorian was educated at Ibstock and Ashby GS and is a former captain of Nottingham.

WINGHAM, Oscar John (Flanker)

Born Fareham, 8.3.72. 6'2", 15st 7lb. Career: Student. More than useful openside whose opportunities have been limited to date. Brother James is a useful prop.

REVIEW

A hugely disappointing final fortnight left Leicester dreaming of what might have been. But the Tigers remain one of Europe's great club sides who are helping to shape the new professional era. After losing their Courage League title on the final afternoon – John Liley's injury-time penalty against Harlequins was, retrospectively, for the championship – Leicester then suffered the agony of conceding a penalty try in the 79th minute at Twickenham which allowed Bath to retain the Pilkington Cup. Controversy had also raged a month earlier when Tony Russ was dismissed as coaching director, to be replaced eventually by Australia's World Cup winning coach Bob Dwyer. The arrival of Austin Healey, Craig Joiner and prolific Huddersfield RL centre Greg Austin would hint at a renewed attempt to expand their playing style, but Leicester would be foolish to ignore their massive strengths up front.

LEICESTER in the Courage League 1995-96

Sep 9	Saracens	H	Won	31	3	Hackney(T) Robinson(T) Underwood(T) Liley(2C, 4P)
16	Sale	A	Won	16	12	Potter(T) Liley(C, 2P) Malone(P)
23	Bath	H	Lost	9	14	Liley(3P)
30	Gloucester	A	Won	27	14	Back(T) Kilford(T) Liley(C, 5P)
Oct 7	West Hartlepool	A	Won	19	12	Cockerill(T) Garforth(T) Liley(3P)
14	Orrell	H	Won	22	3	Hackney(T) Liley(C, 5P)
21	Wasps	A	Won	21	11	Liley(T, C, D, 2P) Tarbuck(T)
28	Bristol	H	Won	43	6	Cockerill(T) Hackney(T) Underwood(T) Liley(2C, 8P)
Nov 4	Harlequins	A	Won	29	25	Penalty(T) Underwood(T) Liley(2C, 5P)
11	Saracens	A	Lost	21	25	Hackney(T) Robinson(T) Liley(C, 3P)
Jan 6	Bath	A	Won	15	14	Liley(5P)
Feb 17	West Hartlepool	H	Won	48	15	Kardooni(3T) Hackney(2T) Back(T) Liley(6C, P) Harris(D)
Mar 30	Orrell	A	Won	38	10	Underwood(2T) Liley(T, 3C, 4P) Wells(T)
Apr 6	Wasps	H	Won	15	12	Liley(4P) Malone(D)
13	Bristol	A	Won	43	29	Underwood(2T) Liley(T, 4C, 4P) Potter(T) Harris(D)
17	Sale	H	Won	32	10	Harris(2C, P) Kardooni(3T) Richards(T) Back(T)
24	Gloucester	H	Won	28	6	Liley(T, 2C, 3P) Underwood(T) Garforth(T)
27	Harlequins	H	Lost	19	21	Back(T) Liley(T, 3P)

LONDON IRISH

Formation of Club: 1898
Ground: The Avenue, Sunbury-on-Thames, Middlesex, TW16 5EQ.
  Tel: 01932 783034
Capacity: 7,500
Colours: Emerald green
Honours: Pilkington Cup: Runners-up: 1980.
  Courage League 2: Runners-up 1990-91, 95-96
Last season: CL2: Runners-up. Pilkington Cup: S/F (lost 46-21 to Leicester)
Most capped player: Brendan Mullin (Ireland) 55 caps
Coach: Clive Woodward
Captain: Gary Halpin

BIRD, Ciaran (Flanker)
Born Chingford, 29.11.71. 6'2", 16st. Career: Surveyor. Rep hons: England U21.
London U21. CLR: 5t-25pts. Destructive openside, Ciaran was educated at Davenant
Foundation School and is a former Wasp.

BISHOP, Justin (Wing)
Born Crawley, 8.11.74. 6', 13st. Career: Student. Rep hons: Ireland U21. England U21.
CLR: 4t-20pts. Elusive runner who arrived at London Irish from East Grinstead RFC,
Justin helped Ireland U21 to victory over England at Northampton in 1995-96 before
declaring for England and playing centre for England U21 against Italy. A student at
West of England University, Bristol.

BRIERS, Nick (Scrum-half)
Born Liverpool, 19.11.71. 5'9", 12st 6lb. Rep hons: England Students. CLR: 2t-10pts.
Educated at Wirral GS, Nick joined Irish from Liverpool-St Helens.

BURNS, Sean (Centre)
Born Nuneaton, 10.8.71. 5'10", 13st 11lb. Career: Teacher. Rep hons: England Students, U21, 18 Group. Ireland Students. CLR: Nuneaton (2t-8pts), London Irish
(1t-5pts). Chunky centre with speed off the mark, Sean was educated at King Edward
VI, Nuneaton, and represented Ireland in the Students World Cup (1992).

COBBE, Owen (Fly-half)
Born Dublin, Ireland, 26.9.72. 5'8", 12st 4lb. Career: Teacher. Rep hons: Ireland U21,
Schools. CLR: 1t, 2c, 6pg, 3dg-36pts. Reliable and underrated fly-half throughout
much of 1995-96 before the arrival of David Humphreys. Educated at Presentation
College, Bray, and St Mary's, Strawberry Hill, Owen was previously with Greystones.

COSTELLO, Victor Carton Patrick (Backrow)
Born Dublin, Ireland, 23.10.70. 6'6", 18st 3lb. Career: Company director. Rep hons:
Ireland (4, US95), A, U21, Schools. Made a huge impression in 1995-96 Five Nations
with his powerful surges off the backrow and his commitment. Vic was educated at
Blackrock College and was a Schools and U21 cap before concentrating on athletics. A
tremendous shot putter, has had a world-class personal best of 19.93m and competed
in the Barcelona Olympics before returning to the rugby fold. Toured Australia with

38

Ireland 1994 and finally made his senior debut against USA in Atlanta in January 1996. Despite an impressive performance, was dropped for the Five Nations opener against Scotland but was the outstanding Irish forward in the remaining three games. Father Patrick was capped against France (1960).

COVENEY, Patrick Francis (Lock)
Born Cork, Ireland, 23.10.70. 6'6", 17st. Won two Blues at Oxford (94 and 95) while studying for a MPhil in Management Studies at Templeton and a DPhil at New College. Originally from Congowes Wood College, Kildare, and University College, Cork, where he graduated in Commerce.

DAVIDSON, Jeremy William (Back five forward)
Born Belfast, 28.4.74. 6'6", 17st 3lb. Career: Student. Rep hons: Ireland (5, Fiji95), A, U21, Schools. Abrasive young forward from Ulster who was educated at Methodist College, Belfast, and University of Ulster in Coleraine. Toured New Zealand with Ireland Schools in 1993 and was in the southern hemisphere 12 months later with the full squad in Australia. Made his Ireland debut against Fiji (1995) and was ever-present in the 96 Five Nations.

DOUGAN, Andrew (Flanker)
Born Armagh, 14.10.74. 6'3", 16st. Career: Student. Rep hons: Irish Students. CLR: 4t-20pts. Gritty flanker who captained Brunel University in 1995-96.

EWINGTON, Tim (Scrum-half)
Born Sydney, Australia, 10.2.68. 6', 12st 7lb. Career: Broker. Rep hons: Sydney, New South Wales. CLR: 1t-5pts. Rugged Australian who performed well last season before breaking an ankle in the Pilkington Cup semi-final against Leicester.

FLOOD, Paul Jonathan (Centre)
Born Birmingham, 25.11.70. 6', 13st 10lb. Career: Chartered surveyor. Rep hons: England Students, U21, Schools. CLR: 2t, 1dg-13pts. Educated at Stonyhurst, Swansea University and Cambridge, where he won Blues in 1992 and 1993. Paul was an England Schools cap in 1988 and represented England Students at 1992 World Cup. Played for Bridgend while studying in Wales.

FULCHER, Gabriel Mark (Lock)
Born Surrey, 27.11.69. 6'5", 17st. Rep hons: Ireland (16, Aus94, 1t-5pts), B, U21. Powerful former Cork Constitution lock who joined the Exiles at the end of last season. Gabriel came of age internationally last season and has become a well-respected front-of-the-line jumper. Educated at Rockwell College, he toured Australia with the Irish Schools in 1987 and took Business Studies at University College, Dublin. Won his first senior cap on tour in Australia (94) after coming through strongly on the Ireland Development trip to southern Africa the previous summer.

HALPIN, Garrett Francis (Prop)
Born Dublin, Ireland, 23.12.66. 6', 17st 6lb. Career: Teacher. Rep hons: Ireland (11, Eng90, 1t-5pts), U23, Schools. Leinster. Barbarians (94). Ireland Athletics. CLR: 8t-40pts. Inspirational skipper who sacrificed a lucrative year of international rugby to devote himself to the Exiles' cause. Educated at Rockwell College, Tipperary, Gary won Schools caps in 1983 and 1984 before attending University of Manhattan on an

athletics scholarship. He represented Ireland in the hammer at the 1987 World Championships in Rome and has a personal best of 73.84m. First capped against England in 1990, Gary won six caps in the next five years before becoming first choice at RWC95, which he will remember chiefly for a tapped penalty try against New Zealand . . . and the celebrations.

HENDERSON, Robert (Centre)

Born Dover, 27.10.72. 6'1", 15st 4lb. Career: PRP. Rep hons: Ireland XV, A, Exiles, U21. CLR: 17t-85pts. Powerful centre who benefited greatly from the coaching of Clive Woodward and was rewarded at the end of 1995-96 season by playing for the Ireland XV against the Barbarians, scoring a try. Had attracted much attention earlier in the Pilkington Cup semi-final with a fine try against Leicester before injury slowed him up. Originally a footballer, Rob was asked to make up the numbers when Kingston found themselves short and hasn't looked back since. Educated at Tiffin and St Mary's, Teddington, he qualifies for Ireland via his mother, who comes from Wexford, though Scotland will be distressed to hear his father hails from north of the border. The target of numerous big-money offers throughout the summer.

HOWE, Tyrone Gyle (Wing)

Born Newtownards, 2.4.71. 6', 13st 4lb. Rep hons: Ireland A, Students. Ulster. Last year's Oxford University captain, Tyrone graduated with an MA in European Literature having previously taken an MA in German and International Relations at St Andrew's University. A well-balanced runner and fierce tackler, Tyrone is a product of Banbridge Academy whose rugby career only blossomed on reaching university.

HUMPHREYS, David George (Fly-half)

Born Belfast, 10.9.71. 5'10", 12st 3lb. Career: Trainee solicitor. Rep hons: Ireland (3, Fr96, 1c, 1pg, 1dg-8pts), A, U21, Students, Schools. CLR: 2t, 1dg-13pts. Educated at Ballymena Academy, David captained Ireland Schools to a Triple Crown in 1990 and subsequently studied for a law degree at Queen's University, Belfast. Progressed to the B team and produced an outstanding performance against Wales A at Newport, but his career then stalled as Ireland experimented with various fly-halves. A year at Oxford regenerated his enthusiasm culminating in a virtuoso 19-point display in the 1995 Varsity match. A similar display for Ulster against New South Wales in February clinched his Ireland selection and David managed to shine in adversity against France before more confident performances against Wales and England.

IONS, Philip Charles Marriott (Flanker)

Born Chalfont St Giles, 6.2.70. 6'3", 16st. Rep hons: England Schools. South West U21. Irish Exiles. CLR: 1t-5pts. Hard-working flanker who was educated at Wellington College (Berks) and Loughborough University before gaining a Blue at Cambridge.

JOY, Michael Tennant (Full-back)

Born Vancouver, Canada, 23.8.71. 6'2", 13st 7lb. An adventurous runner, Michael was educated at Marling School, Stroud, and joined the Exiles from the Stroud club. Won three Blues at Oxford (92, 93 and 94).

KELLAM, Robert (Hooker)

Born Newbury, 4.2.71. 5'10", 15st 2lb. Rep hons: England Students, U21, British Polytechnics. CLR: 1t-5pts. A combative hooker, Rob is a graduate of Portsmouth University and was formerly with Wasps Colts and Newbury.

MEADOWS, Alistair (Lock)
Born Kendal, 20.4.71. 6'5", 17st. Career: Chartered surveyor. Rep hons: England Students, U21. Educated at Sedbergh, Newcastle University and Cambridge, where he won Blues in 1993 and 1994. Alistair is a former member of the Newcastle club.

MOONEY, Liam Thomas (Prop)
Born Dublin, Ireland, 18.5.73. 6', 17st 10lb. Rep hons: Ireland Students, U21. Irish Exiles. England Students, Schools. Welsh Universities. Devon. Educated St Boniface College, Plymouth, and Cardiff University, Liam joined London Irish from Plymouth in 1991. Earned Blues at Cambridge in 1993 and 1994.

O'SHEA, Conor Michael Patrick (Full-back)
Born Limerick, Ireland, 21.10.70. 6'2", 15st. Rep hons: Ireland (13, Rom93, 1c, 3pg, 1dg–14pts), A. Leinster. CLR: 10t–50pts. Adventurous, pacey full-back who joined the Exiles from Lansdowne in 1995 and scored 10 valuable League tries. Conor was educated at Terenure College and University College, Dublin, and was an outstanding U21 international before representing Ireland in the World Students Cup in 1992. Made his international debut against Romania in 1993 and played in ten consecutive internationals before losing out to his friend and rival, Jim Staples, against France in March 1995. Staples' injury against New Zealand in Ireland's opening game of RWC95 saw O'Shea called in against Japan, Wales and France, but Staples and the emerging Simon Mason were preferred in 1995-96 season.

REDMOND, Anthony (Prop)
Born Wigan, 14.1.71. 5'10", 15st 10lb. Career: Teacher. Rep hons: England Students, Welsh Universities. Reliable front row back-up.

WALSH, Barry Joseph (No 8)
Born Limerick, Ireland, 27.5.68. 6'6", 15st 8lb. Career: Physiotherapist. Rep hons: Ireland A, Exiles. Ireland athletics. CLR: 6t–30pts. Another exceptional athlete, Barry won a decathlon bronze medal at the European Junior Championships in 1986. Took up a sports scholarship at Penn State University and was the East Coast Colleges champion three years in succession before returning to Britain where he took the AAA title in 1994. Educated at Crescent College, Limerick, Barry was a schools rugby international before pursuing his athletics career. Since returning to rugby he has already performed well for Ireland A and is chasing a full cap.

WOODS, Niall Kevin Patrick John (Wing)
Born Dublin, Ireland, 21.6.71. 6', 12st 13lb. Rep hons: Ireland (7, Aus94, 1t–5pts), A, Students, U21. Schools. Ireland 7s. Barbarians (93-94). Elusive wing who finally cemented his place in the Ireland side last season. Educated at Blackrock College, he moved to the Blackrock club and was soon a regular with Ireland U21. Toured southern Africa with Ireland (1993) scoring three tries in their 53-15 win over South Africa Provinces. First capped on tour in Australia (1994), he suffered with injury in 1995.

REVIEW

The London Irish clubhouse was buzzing again last season, thanks not only to a successful team but also to the exciting brand of rugby they produced in securing promotion. Off the field, however, it's been a troubled summer with coach Clive

Woodward, having turned down overtures from Leicester, storming out of the annual meeting accusing certain members of racial bigotry for insisting that only those of Irish birth or descent should serve on the club's committees. Happily peace eventually broke out because a split could prove disastrous. Woodward, along with captain Gary Halpin, has become the key figure in the Exiles' surge into League One. The duo masterminded the club's campaign and can be proud of their achievements. Justin Bishop and Rob Henderson developed into top-flight backs and, in the forwards, none did better than former Olympic decathlete Barry Walsh. With Irish recruiting enthusiastically over the summer   promising St Mary's lock Malcolm O'Kelly was their latest acquisition   there's cause for optimism at Sunbury despite the internal politics. It was ever thus.

LONDON IRISH in the Courage League 1995-96

Sep	9	Northampton	H	Lost	32	65	O'Shea(2T) Corcoran(T, 3C, P) Nolan(T) Cathcart(D)
	16	London Scottish	A	Lost	15	19	Cobbe(T) Penalty(T) Corcoran(C, P)
	23	Waterloo	A	Won	50	16	Corcoran(2T, 4C, 4P) Dougan(2T) Henderson(T) O'Shea(T)
	30	Moseley	H	Won	49	8	O'Shea(3T) Bishop(T) Corcoran(T, 3C, P) Halpin(T) Kellam(T) Neary(T)
Oct	7	Nottingham	A	Won	22	9	Walsh(T) Corcoran(C, 5P)
	14	Wakefield	H	Won	31	7	Corcoran(T, 2C, 4P) Flood(T) O'Shea(T)
	21	Bedford	A	Won	46	29	Walsh(2T) Bishop(T) Corcoran(T, 3C, 5P) Penalty(T)
	28	Blackheath	H	Won	32	9	Corcoran(T, C, 5P) Flood(T) Walsh(T)
Nov	4	Newcastle	A	Won	23	19	Burns(T) Corcoran(5P) Flood(D)
	11	Northampton	A	Lost	24	52	Corcoran(T, 3C) Halpin(T) Henderson(T) Haly(D)
Jan	6	Waterloo	H	Won	39	16	Henderson(3T) Ewington(T) Hall(T) Corcoran(4C, 2P)
	13	London Scottish	H	Won	21	20	Corcoran(7P)
Feb	17	Nottingham	H	Won	39	27	O'Shea(2T) Dougan(T) Henderson(T) Corcoran(2C, 5P)
Mar	9	Moseley	A	Won	29	26	Peters(T) Walsh(T) Corcoran(2C, 5P)
	30	Wakefield	H	Won	31	19	Bird(T) Briers(T) Humphreys(T) Corcoran(2C, 4P)
Apr	6	Bedford	H	Won	25	13	Bishop(T) Briers(T) Halpin(T) Humphreys(T) Corcoran(C, P)
	13	Blackheath	A	Won	46	23	Halpin(2T) Bird(T) Dougan(T) Henderson(T) O'Shea(T) Corcoran(2C, 4P)
	27	Newcastle	H	Won	29	28	Henderson(2T) Corcoran(2C, 4P) Humphreys(D)

NORTHAMPTON

Formation of Club: 1888
Ground: Franklins Gardens, Weedon Road, Northampton, NN5 5BG.
  Tel: 01604 755149
Capacity: 8,500
Colours: Black, gold, green
Honours: Pilkington Cup: Runners-up 1991.
  Courage League Two: Champions (1995-96)
Last season: CL2: Champions. Pilkington Cup: 4th round (lost 12-3 at Bath)
Most capped player: Gary Pearce (England) 36
Director of Rugby: Ian McGeechan
Captain: Tim Rodber

ALLEN, Matt Charles (Centre)
Born Farnborough, 28.2.74. 6'2", 15st 2lb. Career: Trainee manager. Rep hons: England Students, U21, Colts. Midlands (1). CLR: 22t-110pts. Educated at St Dunstans and Loughborough University, Matt is a powerful centre who powered over for 20 League tries in 1995-96, often reaping the benefit of Gregor Townsend's chicanery. Should relish the physical nature of League One rugby.

BAYFIELD, Martin (Lock)
Born Bedford, 21.12.66. 6'10", 19st. Career: PRP, formerly a policeman. Rep hons: England (31), Fiji91), British Lions (3, NZ93), A/B (8, Aus90 3t-12pts). Schools. Midlands (16). Barbarians (91-92). CLR: Bedford (1t-4pts), Northampton (5t-24pts). Unceremoniously dropped after the Wales international in February 1996, Bayfield remains one of the world's top lineout operators and will be determined to oust Gareth Archer this season and travel to South Africa with British Lions. Educated at Bedford School, where he now coaches on a part-time basis, Martin was the tallest ever schoolboy international (6'10") and initially played for the Metropolitan Police and Bedford. Joined Northampton in 1990 and won first cap against Fiji the following year. Not included in England's RWC91 squad but played in the 1992 Five Nations and then toured New Zealand with England B. Outstanding for the British Lions when he returned to NZ the following year.

BEAL, Nick David (Utility back)
Born York, 2.12.70. 6'2", 13st 8lb. Career: Sales consultant. Rep hons: England A (8, Ire93, 1t-5pts), England 7s. South West (12, 4t, 1dg-23pts). Barbarians (94). CLR: 11t, 11c, 10pg, 1dg-110pts. Sevens expert who represented England in the RWC Sevens in 1993 and Hong Kong (96). Nick was educated at RGS High Wycombe and 'discovered' playing for High Wycombe. Almost too versatile for his own good, he is nonetheless an invaluable member of Northampton's squad.

BEDDOW, Timothy Arthur Ronald (Hooker)
Born Dudley, 20.12.68. 6', 15st 11lb. Career: Investment consultant. Rep hons: England Students. Midlands (2). CLR: 1t-5pts. Former Bath hooker who has proved a reliable back-up to Allen Clarke. Represented England Students in the 1992 World Cup.

BELL, Jonathan Charles (Centre)
Born Belfast, 7.2.74. 5'11", 15st. Career: Student. Rep hons: Ireland (14, Aus94, 1t-5pts), A, Students, U21, Schools. Ulster. Barbarians (94). CLR: 5t-25pts.

Exceptional schoolboy talent at Coleraine Academical Institution, John blazed a rapid trail through Ireland's representative teams and won his first cap on tour in Australia in 1994. Has the pace and versatility to have played on the wing for Ireland, while many Ulster supporters argue he is a better full-back. His 1995 season was hampered by a hamstring injury, but he enjoyed a useful RWC95 in South Africa before joining Northampton from Ballymena. A PE student at Loughborough University, John struggled for full fitness after Christmas last season following a virulent flu bug but is sure to be an important member of their exciting back division this winter.

CLARKE, Allen Thomas Hartley (Hooker)

Born Dungannon, Ireland, 29.7.67. 5'9", 14st. Career: Special needs teacher. Rep hons: Ireland (3, Fiji95), U21, Schools. CLR: 1t-5pts. Educated at the Royal School, Dungannon, and Nene College, Northampton, Allen joined the Saints in 1991 and is now a special needs teacher at the nearby Raeburn School. His early career at Franklins Gardens was hindered by a nasty ankle injury and for a year he dropped down to local junior side Northampton Men's Own, but returned to senior rugby thereafter and played for Ulster against Northern Transvaal in February 1995. Broke into the A squad, won a first cap against Fiji last year as a second half replacement for Terry Kingston and earned selection against Wales and England in the Five Nations.

DAWSON, Matthew James Sutherland (Scrum-half)

Born Birkenhead, 31.10.72. 5'11", 12st 10lb. Career: Teacher. Rep hons: England (5, WS93), A (10, Fr93, 7t-35pts), U21, 18 Group. Midlands (7, 1t-5pts). Barbarians (94). CLR: 16t, 1c, 2pg, 1dg-90pts. Finally overcame nagging hamstring injuries last winter to complete a full Five Nations season for England alongside club colleague Paul Grayson. Matt was an outstanding schoolboy player at RGS High Wycombe and won caps at 18 Group, when he partnered Paul Burke, who later opted for Ireland. Played junior rugby for the Marlow club and represented England U21 at centre before reverting to scrum-half and successfully challenging Kyran Bracken for the senior berth. Useful wicketkeeper and played soccer for Chelsea Boys.

DODS, Michael (Full-back/wing)

Born Galashiels, 30.12.68. 5'10", 11st 9lb. Career: Medical sales rep. Rep hons: Scotland (8, Ire94, 3t, 1c, 21pg-80pts), A, U21, U18, Scotland 7s. South of Scotland. Barbarians (93-94). CLR: 7t, 12c-59pts. Surprisingly left out of Scotland's tour party to New Zealand, Michael, a full-back by preference, spent much of the 1995-96 season filling in for Scotland and Northampton on the wing. The younger brother of former Scotland full-back Peter Dods, Michael was educated at Galashiels Academy and made his senior debut for the local club against Vale of Lune in 1987. He represented Scotland A against New Zealand and Italy in 1993 and France the following year when he also made his senior debut, as a replacement, against Ireland. Subsequently won two caps on tour against Argentina and was ever-present in 1995-96 international season, enjoying a memorable afternoon against France when he scored all 19 points including two tries. Represented Scotland in the Hong Kong 7s in 1995 and 1996.

FOALE, Simon (Lock)

Born Northampton. 6'4", 16st 9lb. CLR: 1t-5pts. Proud product of the local Bugbrook RFC, Simon is a versatile young back five forward who made four Courage League appearances last season. Joined Saints in 1990 and has scored 20 tries in 90 games for the club.

FOUNTAINE, Mark Simon (Backrow)
Born Kenilworth, 7.6.67. 6'5", 16st 10lb. Career: Teacher. Rep hons: Warwickshire. Educated at Park Hill School and now a teacher at Bablake, Mark featured prominently in Warwickshire's County Championship campaign last season. Arrives at Franklins Gardens from Bristol.

GRAYSON, Paul James (Fly-half)
Born Chorley, 30.5.71. 6', 12st 7lb. Career: Insurance broker. Rep hons: England (5, WS95, 3c, 22pg, 3dg-81pts), A (8, B Col93, 13c, 19pg, 3dg-92pts), Emerging, U21. North (7, 6c, 22pg, 44pg-90pts), Midlands (3, 3c, 3pg-15pts). CLR: Waterloo (1t, 8c, 29pg, 6dg-126pts), Northampton (6t, 97c, 99pg, 6dg-593pts). A convert from soccer, Paul enjoyed an excellent debut season for England scoring 58 points in the Five Nations. Educated at Parklands High in Chorley and Dr Tuson College, Preston, Paul arrived at Northampton via Preston Grasshoppers and Waterloo, who he starred for in their famous Pilkington Cup victory over Bath in 1992. Useful club cricketer.

HEPHER, Alistair (Fly-half)
Born 3.10.74. Career: Student. Rep hons: Midlands U21. CLR: 1dg-3pts. Exciting young fly-half who captained East Midlands in their CIS U21 County Championship final at Twickenham in April. Alistair hails from the village of Yardley Gobian, is a student at Newcastle University and his brother Simon is a promising backrow forward.

HUNTER, Ian (Full-back/wing)
Born Harrow, 15.2.68. 6'2", 14st 10lb. Career: Self-employed product designer. Rep hons: England (7, Can92, 3t-15pts), A/B (16, Aus90, 10t, 1c-44pts), Students. North (11, 1t-4pts). Barbarians (90-91). CLR: 13t, 3pg, 1dg-69pts. Richly talented but injury-prone back who has the ability to excel in the top flight. Educated at Lake School, Windermere, Ian scored two tries on his international debut against Canada at Wembley and another on his Five Nations debut against France before injuring an eye against Wales. Selected for the 1993 British Lions tour of New Zealand, Ian was forced to return home after damaging a shoulder and has subsequently been plagued by knee complaints. Reappeared for England against Wales in 1994 and in RWC95. Finished last season in apparently good health and lives in hope.

HYNES, Martin Peter (Prop)
Born Wigan, 23.8.68. 5'9", 16st. Career: Electrician. Rep hons: England A (10, N Otago92). North (7). Lancashire. CLR: Orrell (1t-4pts). Tough scrummager, Martin was educated at Wigan Tech and moved to Northampton from Orrell. Played in the inaugural U21 international when England beat Romania 54-13 in Bucharest and helped Lancashire to a 32-9 win over Middlesex in the 1990 County Championship final. Was a bench reserve for England throughout the 1992 Five Nations.

MERLIN, Dave (Backrow)
Born 22.5.72. 6'4", 16st 5lb. Career: Physiotherapist. Rep hons: England U21. CLR: 4t-20pts. Former Worcester utility forward with impressive mobility and improving ball skills.

MOIR, Craig (Wing)
Born 25.10.73. Career: Student. Rep hons: Wales U21, Schools. Wales 7s. CLR: 10t-50pts. Welsh speedster from Milford Haven who played for Llanelli in 1991-92

before attending Nene College and joining Saints. Made his Courage League debut against Wasps in 1993-94 and was in outstanding form last season, on one occasion scoring four tries against Waterloo. Has represented the Welsh seven in Taipei and Uruguay and spent much of last summer playing and coaching at Sciotto Valley in Columbus, Ohio.

PHILLIPS, Jon-Lee (Utility back five)
Born Peterborough, 16.8.72. 6'6", 17st. Career: Engineer. Rep hons: England U21, Colts. Midlands (6). CLR: 3t-15pts. Raw-boned utility forward who came of age on the England U21 tour of Australia in 1993 when he forced his way into the Test side.

POUNTNEY, Tony Charles (Flanker)
Born Southampton, 13.11.73. 6'2", 15st. Career: Student. Rep hons: England Students, U21. Midlands (1, 1t-5pts). CLR: 10-50pts. Tireless scavenging flanker in the old-fashioned style, 'Budge' enjoyed a terrific 1995-96 season for Saints. A former member of Winchester (1989-91) before studying in Bedford and joining Northampton. Member of England's squad in the 1996 World Students Cup.

RODBER, Timothy Andrew Keith (Backrow)
Born Richmond, Yorkshire, 2.7.69. 6'6", 16st 7lb. Career: Army Lieutenant in Green Howards. Rep hons: England (25, Sc92, 2t-10pts), A/B (6, Fr90, 2t-8pts), U21. England 7s. Midlands (8, 3t-13pts). North (5). Barbarians (92-93). CLR: 13t-62pts. Tim led Saints straight back into League One last season with a perfect record of 18 victories and, although dropped for England's games against France and Ireland, he remains very much in the selectors' minds. Educated at Churchers Hampshire and Oxford Polytechnic, he played for Petersfield and Oxford Old Boys before joining Northampton. Developed rapidly under the tutelage of All Black Wayne Shelford and made his England debut against Scotland in 1992 and was a member of England 1993 RWC Sevens winning team. Performed wonderfully well in South Africa during England's 1994 tour, but career suffered a blip when dismissed for punching against Eastern Province at Port Elizabeth. Played throughout England's RWC95 campaign and did well in Hong Kong (1996) with the England Seven.

SEELY, Grant Lionel (Backrow)
Born Aylesbury, 7.1.74. 6'4", 16st 2lb. Career: Student. Rep hons: England U21. Midlands (1). CLR: 18t-90pts. Like Pountney, has learned from playing alongside Rodber in the backrow. Grant has developed out of all recognition since joining Northampton from Aylesbury in 1991. Claimed an impressive 14 League tries last winter.

TAYLOR, Brett (Scrum-half)
Born 31.7.68. Career: Teacher. Heads a list of understudies to England's Matt Dawson that also includes Andy Gallagher and Dominic Malone. Formerly in the Army.

THORNEYCROFT, Harvey (Wing)
Born Northampton, 22.2.69. 6', 15st 11lb. Career: Surveyor. Rep hons: England A/B (9, N Otago92, 7t-32pts), Students, U21, Colts. Midlands (15, 2t-10pts). Barbarians (91-92). CLR: Nottingham (3t-12pts), Northampton (22t-103pts). Popular hard-running wing who burst on the representative scene in 1988 when he scored a hat-trick in England Colts' 32-12 win over Wales Youth. Toured New Zealand with England B in 1992. Was the mastermind behind the England XV Discovery tour of West Africa in

the summer which helped raise funds for the Max Brito fund by playing games against a Springbok XV in Accra and Ivory Coast in Abidjan.

TOWNSEND, Gregor Peter John (Centre/fly-half)
Born Edinburgh, 26.4.73. 6'1", 13st 7lb. Career: Trainee corporate banker. Rep hons: Scotland (19, Eng93, 4t, 3dg-29pts), A, Students, U21, 18 Group. Scotland 7s. Barbarians (93-94). CLR: 13t-65pts. Exhilarating high-risk attacker who finally came of age internationally in the 1995-96 Five Nations when he switched back to his preferred position of fly-half. Another graduate from Galashiels Academy, Gregor was one of the most talented schoolboy internationals ever produced by Scotland and went straight into the Scotland B team against France in 1992 when just 18. He also represented Scotland in the Students World Cup in Italy that year. Made his full debut against England as a replacement in 1993 and played throughout the 1994 Five Nations before enduring a less-than-happy tour of Argentina (1994). Recovered his poise to contribute fully in 1995, including that oft-replayed flip pass which allowed Gavin Hastings to score the winning try in Paris, but an untimely cruciate ligament injury prevented him competing in RWC95. Moved from Gala to Northampton in 1995, after playing club rugby in Australia, and is happy to play centre at club level. Represented Scotland in the Hong Kong 7s (1996) and scored a try against New Zealand in Dunedin this summer.

VOLLAND, Matthew James (Prop)
Born Peterborough, 30.6.74. 6', 16st 7lb. Career: Scaffolder. Rep hons: England U21, Midlands (1). Powerful prop learning his trade. Formerly with the Peterborough club.

REVIEW

Saints marched straight back into Division One, where they rightly belong, in the most emphatic style possible, boasting a 100 per cent record in League Two. Their new players – Gregor Townsend, John Bell and Michael Dods – settled quickly and made a huge contribution to the club's success and attractive playing style. And while captain Tim Rodber and Martin Bayfield may have struggled to retain their England places playing in League Two, it in no way affected the fortunes of Matt Dawson and Paul Grayson, who became England's regular half-backs. Other outstanding individuals included centre Matt Allen, who thrived in illustrious company, and young forwards Budge Pountney and Grant Seely who have the ability to challenge for high honours. Heartening, too, was the end-of-season return from injury of Ian Hunter.

NORTHAMPTON in the Courage League 1995-96

Sep	9	London Irish	A	Won	65	32	Allen(3T) Moir(2T) Dawson(T) Rodber(T) Seely(T) Thorneycroft(T) Grayson(7C, 2P)
	16	Moseley	H	Won	50	7	Dods(2T) Seely(2T) Allen(T) Bayfield(T) Grayson(T, 5C) Moir(T)
	23	Nottingham	A	Won	43	7	Allen(2T) Dawson(T) Dods(T) Moir(T) Seely(T) Thorneycroft(T) Grayson(4C)
	30	Wakefield	H	Won	23	0	Merlin(T) Pountney(T) Grayson(2C, 3P)

Oct	7	Bedford	A	Won	49	17	Seely(2T) Bell(T) Moir(T) Penalty(T) Townsend(T) Grayson(5C, 3P)
	14	Blackheath	H	Won	69	14	Seely(3T) Townsend(3T) Bell(2T) Allen(T) Dods(T, 7C) Phillips(T)
	21	Newcastle	A	Won	52	9	Allen(3T) Beddow(T) Dawson(T) Merlin(T) Penalty(T) Rodber(T) Grayson(6C)
	28	Waterloo	A	Won	69	3	Allen(3T) Dods(2T, C) Seely(2T) Townsend(2T) Merlin(T) Pountney(T) Grayson(6C)
Nov	4	London Scottish	H	Won	54	11	Townsend(3T) Thorneycroft(2T) Dawson(T) Phillips(T) Seely(T) Grayson(7C)
	11	London Irish	H	Won	52	24	Townsend(3T) Dods(T, 4C) Grayson(T, 2C) Pountney(T) Seely(T) Thorneycroft(T)
Jan	6	Nottingham	H	Won	35	5	Allen(T) Beal(T) Dawson(T) Penalty(T) Pountney(T) Grayson(5C)
Feb	24	Moseley	A	Won	46	16	Beal(2T) Dawson(2T) Allen(T) Bayfield(T) Grayson(T, 3C) Thorneycroft(T)
Mar	23	Bedford	H	Won	48	0	Bell(2T) Pountney(2T) Beal(T) Rodber(T) Seely(T) Townsend(T) Grayson(4C)
	30	Blackheath	A	Won	24	10	Bayfield(T) Clarke(T) Phillips(T) Pountney(T) Grayson(2C)
Apr	6	Newcastle	H	Won	26	5	Allen(T) Thorneycroft(T) Grayson(2C, 2D, 2P)
	13	Waterloo	H	Won	69	5	Moir(4T) Beal(2T) Pountney(2T) Allen(T) Dawson(T) Hunter(T) Grayson(7C)
	20	Wakefield	A	Won	34	21	Beal(T) Dawson(T) Morgan(T) Grayson(2C, D, 4P)
	27	London Scottish	H	Won	59	17	Allen(3T) Morgan(2T) Beal(T) Foale(T) Rodber(T) Seely(T) Grayson(7C)

ORRELL

Formation of Club: 1927
Ground: Edgehall Road, Orrell, WN5 8TL. Tel: 01695 623193
Capacity: 4,999
Colours: Amber and black
Honours: Courage League: runners-up 1991-92
Last season: CL1: 7th. Pilkington Cup: 4th round (lost 19-17 to Harlequins)
Most capped player: Dewi Morris (England) 26
Director of Rugby: Peter Williams
Coaches: Mike Slemen, Andy MacFarlane
Captain: TBA

ANGLESEA, Peter (Flanker)
Born 30.10.71. 6'4", 15st 8lb. Rep hons: Lancashire. CLR: 1t-5pts. Joined Orrell from local club Aspal. Spent the summer in South Africa playing for the Pirates club in Johannesburg. Has real pace and a useful sidestep for a flanker. One of the most improved players at the club.

BENNETT, Alex (Flanker)
Born 1.4.75. 6'3", 17st. Career: Student. Rep hons: England U21. Formerly with Otley. Powerful flanker and extremely fit, as befits a graduate of Carnegie College. Student at Manchester Met University and member of England squad at 1996 World Students Cup.

BIBBY, Steve (Lock)
Born Wigan, 7.7.69. 6'5", 18st. Career: Mechanic. Rep hons: Lancashire. CLR: 4t-19pts. Long-time servant of the club who, when fully fit, can compete with best and steal valuable lineout ball at number two.

BOTICA, Frano (Fly-half)
Born New Zealand, 3.8.63. 5'10", 14st. Career: PRP. Rep hons: New Zealand (7, Fr86, 2dg-6pts). ANZACS v British Lions 1989. New Zealand RL. Former Wigan and Castleford RL star who hopes to be available for Orrell from the autumn onwards. Started his career with North Harbour, Auckland, and made his international debut for the All Blacks against France in 1986. Turned professional with Wigan in 1989 and became the quickest player to reach 1000 points in rugby league history. Joined the Auckland Warriors after leaving Wigan, but his spell back home was plagued with injury problems. Has returned to England to play for Castleford, but still lives in nearby Wigan.

COOK, Steve (Scrum-half)
Born St Helens, 4.8.74. 5'9", 13st 2lb. CLR: West Hartlepool (4t-20pts). Educated at Liverpool College and Newcastle University. Played for Liverpool-St Helens as a 17-year-old before his studies took him to the north-east and the West Hartlepool club. Joins this season as a timely back-up at scrum-half following the departure of Austin Healey to Leicester, and the decision of Dewi Morris to come out of retirement with Sale.

CUNDICK, Jason (Prop)
Born 9.9.73. 6', 17st. Had established himself in the first team during an excellent 1994-95 but missed most of last season with a painful back injury.

CUSANI, Charles (Lock)
Born Wigan, 22.10.65. 6'6", 17st. Career: Catering. Rep hons: North (5). CLR: 1t-4pts. Mobile ball-handling lock who played rugby league for Wigan Schools before turning to union. Appeared for Lancashire and the North at Colts level before graduating to the senior sides at both county and divisional level. Has played in Italy for Roma Olympic. Is now the Orrell club steward looking after all the members' catering needs.

FARR, John Charles (Scrum-half)
Born Nantwich, 20.4.70. 5'10", 12st 12lb. Rep hons: Midlands (1, 1t-5pts). CLR: Bedford (3t-15pts). Former Winnington Park and Bedford player who made a big impression for Winnington Park in the Pilkington Cup last season and shone for the Midlands against the South West.

GASKELL, David (Backrow)
Born 30.4.75. 6'3", 16st 9lb. CLR: Liverpool (3t-15pts). Promising former St Helens backrow player who is looking to make the step up into League One rugby.

HAMER, Paul (Utility back)
Born St Helens, 12.11.66. 6', 13st 4lb. Career: Print manager. Rep hons: England 18 Group. British Police. CLR: Vale of Lune (2t, 1pg-11pts), Liverpool-St Helens (1t-4pts), Sale (3t, 1c, 5pg-29pts), Orrell (12t, 1c, 2dg-68pts). Educated at RGS Lancaster, Paul also played for England 16 Group. Versatile and valuable player equally at home on the wing or at fly-half. Has developed considerably in last two seasons and is good defensively.

HAYTER, Stuart (Backrow)
Born 5.7.65. 5'10", 13st 5lb. Combative all-purpose flanker who seems to revel in the role of super sub.

HESLOP, Nigel (Wing)
Born Hartlepool, 4.12. 63. 5'10", 13st. Career: Police officer. Rep hons: England (10, Arg90, 3t-12pts), A/B (3, Sp89), Colts. North (5, 1t-4pts). Lancashire. CLR: Waterloo (1t-4pts), Orrell (18t-72pts). Nigel returned from rugby league midway through last season and is looking forward to reappearing on the Orrell wing. Educated at Rainford HS, St Helens, he played for Liverpool-St Helens before joining Orrell. Made his international debut on tour in Argentina and was ever-present during England's 1991 Grand Slam, scoring a try against Scotland at Murrayfield. Last international appearance was against Wales as a replacement the following year.

HUXLEY, Jeff (Utility forward)
Born 28.6.63. 6'3", 16st 7lb. Career: Police officer. CLR: 1t-5pts. Evergreen backrow forward, fit and ready for another season in the club's cause.

LYON, David (Centre)
Born 3.9.65. 6'1", 14st 8lb. Experienced former Warrington and St Helens rugby league centre, who joined recently, David is the nephew of Billy Lyon, the RL player, and Eric Lyon, the former union stalwart.

MacFARLANE, Andy (Backrow and coach)
Born London, 15.4.61. 6'4", 16st. Career: Coach. Rep hons: England A/B (1, Sp88, 1t-4pts). North (17, 1t-4pts). Cumbria. Barbarians (86-87). CLR: Sale (4t-17pts). Experienced campaigner who 'retired' at Sale at the beginning of last season, but was persuaded his skills and experience could be fully utilised at Orrell. Played for the North in their 15-9 win over Australia in 1988 and has represented the Division on over 30 occasions. Last seen rolling back the years playing in the Middlesex Sevens in May.

MITCHELL, Peter (Prop)
Born Gloucestershire, 31.1.67. 6'1", 19st. Career: Farmer. Imposing forward who did well when pressed into service in 1995-96 when injuries badly affected front row availability.

MOFFATT, Alec (Hooker)
Born 29.6.68. 5'2", 13st. Reliable back-up hooker, particularly accurate throwing in. One of the smallest players in the League.

NAYLOR, James Richard (Wing)
Born Halifax, 6.2.74. 5'11", 14st. Career: Student. Rep hons: England A (5, S Aus95, 3t-15pts), U21, Colts. North (4, 3t-15pts). CLR: 11t-55pts. Sharp-witted wing who has been held back by niggling injuries. James attended Crossley Heath School and played for Old Crossleyans, whose other distinguished former pupils include former ex-England hooker Brian Moore and international referee Brian Campsall. James' talent was recognised first by Yorkshire Colts and he soon progressed into the England Colts squad, scoring four tries in four internationals in 1993. His form was such that England U21 then invited him on their tour of Australia (1993) when he was comfortably the youngest member of the party. On his return, he made a spectacular try-scoring debut for Orrell and played his first game for the North against Canada A at Fylde in March 1994. Toured Australia and Fiji with England A in 1995 and scored a try in 'Test' victory but aggravated an ankle strain which continued to flare up through the winter.

O'NEIL, Paddy (Lock)
Born 29.2.68. 6'7", 17st 9lb. Rep hons: Lancashire. Former Fylde lock who is now fulfilling his considerable potential.

PARR, Howard (Back five forward)
Born York, 1.1.72. 6'4", 16st. Career: Student. Rep hons: North U21. Versatile young forward who learned his rugby at Rossall School before joining Orrell. RAF training is likely to affect his availability.

PEACOCK, Alun (Fly-half)
Born 15.3.74. 5'10", 13st. Rep hons: England U21, Colts. CLR: 2c, 2pg-10pts. Represented Lancashire Colts for three consecutive seasons and is beginning to find his feet at senior level. Challenged Paul Hamer for the fly-half berth at the end of last season.

POVALL, Gary (Scrum-half)
Born 3.1.72. 5'8", 12st 4lb. Rep hons: Lancashire Schools. Ex-Merchant Taylors' schoolboy flanker who switched to scrum-half.

RAWLINSON, Rob (Prop)
Born 23.8.76. 6', 16st. Competitive prop who spent the summer with Peter Anglesea in Johannesburg playing for the Pirates club.

REES, Paul (Lock)
Born 3.5.75. 6'6", 17st. Career: Policeman. Former Winnington Park second row who joined Orrell in 1994-95.

SCOTT, Martin (Hooker)
Born Falkirk, 5.7.67. 6', 15st 10lb. Career: Civil servant. Rep hons: Scotland (1, Aus92), A, Development squad. CLR: 1t-5pts. A strong and mobile modern hooker, Martin was formerly with Edinburgh Academicals and Dunfermline from where he won his Scotland cap.

SMITH, Graham (Wing)
Born Paisley, 31.12.74. 6'2", 13st 9lb. Career: Student. Rep hons: Scotland U21. England Colts. CLR: 10t-50pts. Comfortably Orrell's top try scorer in 1995-96 with 10 Courage League tries, Graham also won Scotland U21 honours. Signed a summer contract to play for Wakefield Trinity.

TABERNER, Steve (Full-back)
Born Orrell, 15.9.62. 5'10", 13st. Career: Teacher. Rep hons: British Colleges. Lancashire. CLR: 14t, 1dg-65pts. Educated at Upholland GS and Chester College, Steve is a one-club man and a former Orrell captain. Enjoys triathlons and amateur dramatics.

TUIGAMALA, Lua (Utility back)
Born Western Samoa, 10.10.75. 6'2", 14st 8lb. CLR: 2t-10pts. Brother of Va'aiga Tuigamala, Lua travelled to England to live with the former All Black after he signed for Wigan. Can play wing and centre. Lacks the physical presence of his brother, but is a clever player who has worked hard on his pace.

WINSTANLEY, Phil (Prop)
Born Orrell, 16.9.68. 6', 16st. Career: Legal executive. Rep hons: North (3). Lancashire. CLR: 3t, 1pg-17pts. Goal-kicking prop who graduated into senior rugby via Orrell Colts having spent his early years playing in the backrow or even the wing. Remains extremely mobile and knowledgeable concerning the front-row laws, as befits the son-in-law of former international referee Alan Welsby. Played superbly for the North against South West in CIS Divisional game in 1995-96, with the official stats showing he made 12 tackles, but was injured in the next game against London and his chance of a team recognition went.

WOOD, Tim (Flanker)
Born 20.4.73. 6', 14st. Natural openside flanker from Liverpool-St Helens, Tim is improving all the time and could make a big impression this season.

WORMSLEY, Michael (Prop)
Born 1.12.76. 6'1", 17st. Rep hons: England 18 Group. Another product of St Anselm's College, Michael joins Orrell after a spell at Sale.

WYNN, Ian (Centre)
Born St Helens, 19.8.68. 6'2", 14st. Career: Draughtsman. Rep hons: Scottish Exiles, Development XV. CLR: 16t-80pts. Destructive ball-in-hand runner but can be inconsistent.

REVIEW

Orrell, as ever, confounded the critics and survived on seemingly slender resources. So there is no reason to suppose this season will be any different. The departures of Austin Healey and Simon Mason, and captain Paul Johnson to Leeds are, however, huge blows at a time when Orrell were looking to expand their game and make best use of useful backs such as Lua Tuigamala, Ian Wynn, Scotland U21 wing Graham Smith and Jim Naylor. The loss of Richard Webster to Bath will also be keenly felt as Orrell believed they had secured the services of the former Wales flanker from Salford RL. The arrival of Frano Botica on contract should give them the safety valve of a world-class goal-kicker and rugby league recruits David Lyon and Richard Webster will also bolster their challenge. The Lancastrians have the knack of remaining competitive whatever the circumstances.

ORRELL in the Courage League 1995-96

Sep	9	Harlequins	H	Lost	9	23	Mason(3P)
	16	Saracens	A	Lost	9	12	Mason(3P)
	23	Sale	H	Won	12	6	Mason(4P)
	30	Bath	A	Lost	20	55	Johnson(T) Scott(T) Mason(2C, 2P)
Oct	7	Gloucester	H	Won	21	3	Mason(T, C, 2P) Smith(T) Johnson(D)
	14	Leicester	A	Lost	3	22	Mason(P)
	21	West Hartlepool	H	Won	20	10	Bibby(T) Healey(T) Mason(2C, 2P)
	28	Wasps	H	Won	32	29	Smith(3T) Healey(T) Mason(3C, 2P)
Nov	4	Bristol	A	Lost	14	33	Wynn(T) Mason(3P)
	11	Harlequins	A	Won	25	21	Mason(T, 5P) Taberner(T)
Jan	6	Sale	A	Lost	13	39	Luger(T) Wynn(T) Mason(P)
	13	Saracens	H	Won	38	13	Smith(3T) Mason(T, 3C, 4P)
Feb	17	Gloucester	A	Lost	0	27	
Mar	30	Leicester	H	Lost	10	38	Smith(T) Mason(C, P)
Apr	6	West Hartlepool	A	Won	44	22	Wynn(2T) Anglesea(T) Huxley(T) Mason(T, 4C, 2P) Winstanley(T)
	13	Wasps	A	Lost	16	51	Hamer(T) Tuigamala(T) Mason(2P)
	20	Bath	H	Lost	11	44	Wynn(T) Healey(P) Mason(P)
	27	Bristol	H	Lost	26	29	Smith(2T) Healey(T, 2C) Tuigamala(T) Peacock(C)

SALE

Formation of Club: 1861
Ground: Heywood Road, Brooklands, Sale, Cheshire, M33 3WB.
 Tel: 0161 973 6348
Capacity: 5,000
Colours: Royal blue and white hoops
Honours: Courage League Two: Champions 1993-94
Last season: CL1: 5th. Pilkington Cup: 4th round (lost 18-9 to Wasps)
Most capped player: Fran Cotton (England) 31
Director of Rugby: Brian Wilkinson
Player/coach: John Mitchell
Captain: Jim Mallinder

ASHURST, Neil (Backrow)
Born St Helens, 12.5.69. 6'2". 16st 7lb. Career· Plasterer Rep hons: England U21, Colts.
North (12, 2t-10pts). CLR: Orrell (7t-31pts), Sale (7t-35pts). Underrated backrow
grafter who moved to Sale after a successful spell at Orrell. Began his career at West
Park, St Helens. Neil comes from a rugby league family in Thatlow Heath, with brother
Chris playing for St Helens.

BALDWIN, David Neil (Lock)
Born Ilkley, 3.9.65. 6'5", 17st 2lb. Career: Printer. Rep hons: England A/B (5, USSR89).
North (12, 1t-5pts). Yorkshire. Barbarians (94). CLR: Wakefield (2t-8pts), Sale (10t-
48pts). Much-respected front-of-the-line jumper, this former Bramley and Wakefield
lock, who made his Yorkshire county debut against Northumberland in 1985, toured
New Zealand with England B in 1992.

BAXENDELL, Jos (Centre)
Born Macclesfield, 13.5.71. 6'. 13st. Career: Surveyor. Rep hons: North (1, 2t-10pts).
CLR: Sheffield (1t-5pts), Sale (9t-45pts). Educated at King's Macclesfield, Jos played
first with Wilmslow and then moved to Heywood Road from Sheffield, where he
studied at the local university. Was Sale's leading try scorer in the League in 1995-96,
with six, and is possibly the most gifted back at the club. Jos is considering moving to
fly-half to further his representative career.

DEVEREUX, John (Wing/centre)
Born Pontycymmer, 30.3.66. 6'1", 15st. Career: PRP. Rep hons: Wales (21, Eng86,
5t-20pts), British Lions tourist (1989). Barbarians (85-86). Great Britain and Wales
RL. John has signed on a match-by-match contract, but a broken ankle could restrict
his availability. Educated at Ynysawdre Comprehensive and South Glamorgan Institute, John was plucked from the Students side to make his international debut against
England in 1986, having played just 17 minutes of senior rugby with Bridgend, against
Newport. A powerful centre, John won his last Welsh cap against Ireland in 1989 and
toured Australia with the Lions before signing for Widnes RL.

DIAMOND, Steve (Hooker)
Born Manchester, 3.2.68. 5'10", 14st. Career: Printer. Rep hons: North (1). CLR: 3t-15pts. Spent five years with the Metrovick club before joining Sale. Joker in the pack but an upbeat and inspiring character who captained the North on their tour of Italy in May.

ERSKINE, David (Lock)
Born Bexley, 14.10.69. 6'4", 16st. Career: Insurance inspector. Rep hons: Ulster. CLR: 7t-35pts. Versatile forward who is quick enough to deputise in the backrow. Appeared for Ulster in the Heineken European Cup last season. Works as an insurance inspector for club sponsors Independent Insurance. Formerly with CIYMS in Ulster and Boroughmuir.

FOWLER, John (Lock)
Born London, 6.2.69. 6'8", 17st 8lb. Career: Accountant. Rep hons: England A (6, S Aus95). North (6, 1t-5pts). CLR: Richmond (1t-4pts), Sale (3t-15pts). Former Richmond, Rosslyn Park and Newcastle Gosforth lock who has also enjoyed two spells in New Zealand, playing for King Country and Hawkes Bay, representing the latter against the 1993 British Lions. Toured Australia and Fiji with England A (1995) and made a significant contribution in the lineout during England's 27-19 win over Australia at Brisbane.

HADLEY, Adrian (Wing)
Born Cardiff, 1.3.63. 6'1", 14st. Career: Marketing/PRP. Rep hons: Wales (27, Rom83, 9t-36pts), B, Youth. Barbarians (84-85). Wales RL. Adrian was educated at Lady Mary HS, Cardiff, where he played full-back or centre and scored 26 tries in his debut season with Cardiff. Played in non-capped internationals against Spain and Japan before making his full debut in Wales' defeat in Romania (1983). Last appeared for Wales against France in 1988 before signing for Salford RL. Moved to Widnes RL in August 1992.

HEWSON, Luke (Hooker)
Born 6.12.69. 5'11", 17st. Reserve team hooker known affectionately as the 'Barn door' at Sale. Has a strong physical presence and certainly impressed against Leicester and Sale in 1995-96.

HIGGINBOTHAM, Graham (Centre)
Born 24.12.66. 6', 14st 8lb. Rep hons: Cheshire. CLR: Broughton Park (2t-9pts), Sale (1t-5pts). Former Broughton Park captain who switched to National League rugby late in his career, but has looked more than comfortable in his new environment. Very physical, he was seen at his best against Bath at the end of last season.

MALLINDER, Jim (Full-back/wing)
Born Halifax, 16.3.66. 6'3", 15st. Career: PE teacher. Rep hons: North (9, 4t-20pts). Yorkshire. CLR: Sale (28t, 2dg-134pts). Long-striding full-back and respected captain who has the pace to double up on the wing. Educated at Porter GS, Halifax, and Carnegie College. Formerly with Old Crossleyans and Roundhay.

MITCHELL, John (Backrow and coach)

Born New Zealand, 23.3.64. 6'3", 16st 8lb. Career: PRP. Rep hons: All Black tourist. Waikato. Helped Murray Kidd coach Ireland last season, but John Mitchell still has much to offer as a player. Signed originally as an assistant coach to Paul Turner but the latter's departure has catapulted him into the limelight. Made 136 provincial appearances for Waikato and captained them to their famous Ranfurly Shield win over Auckland in 1993, ending an eight-year winning sequence for Auckland. Also led Waikato to a crushing victory over the 1993 British Lions. Although never capped, John regularly captained the All-Blacks' midweek side on tour. Demands high levels of fitness, so Sale's training nights should be unusually strenuous this winter.

MORRIS, Andy (Flanker)

Born Blackburn, 1.9.71. 5'11", 12st 2lb. Career: Corporate finance. Rep hons: England U21. CLR: Former Nottingham and Sheffield openside with plenty of pace, Andy returned to his best form at the end of 1995-96.

MORRIS, Dewi (Scrum-half)

Born Crickhowell, 9.2.64. 6', 14st. Career: PRP. Rep hons: England (26, Aus88, 5t-21pts). British Lions (3, NZ93). North. CLR: 24t-106pts (Orrell), 2t-8pts (Liverpool-St Helens). Former Winnington Park and Orrell scrum-half who retired after RWC95 but has been tempted back to competitive action by Sale. Welsh born. Dewi made his England debut against Australia in 1988 but was surplus to requirements in RWC91. Was, however, outstanding during England's 1992 Grand Slam, and on the British Lions tour of New Zealand (1993). Lost his place to Kyran Bracken in the 1995 Five Nations but recovered to play in all but the Italian game in RWC95. Moto-cross enthusiast.

O'GRADY, Dylan (Backrow)

Born Manchester, 9.11.71. 6'1", 15st. Rep hons: Irish Exiles. Cheshire. CLR: 6t-30pts. Local lad and another who joined Sale from the Metrovick club. Reliable flanker who has also done well for the Irish Exiles.

REES, David (Wing)

Born London, 15.10.74. 5'9", 13st. Career: Student. Rep hons: England U21. Northumberland. CLR: 1t-5pts. Promising wing man who can also play centre, David finished last season in style, scoring a try during Sale's epic 38-38 draw with Bath and then scoring a brace for England U21 against Italy. A student at Manchester Metropolitan University, he travelled to South Africa in the summer with England for the World Students Cup. Educated at Gosforth HS and RGS Newcastle. He then studied graphic design and advertising at university. A sporting all-rounder, David has played soccer for Newcastle Boys, was a Northumberland schools sprint champion and county tennis player and a nationally ranked table tennis junior. Represented Northumberland in the 1995 CIS County final against Warwickshire.

RIDEHALGH, Mark (Prop)

Born 28.2.67. 6', 16st 5lb. Rep hons: North. Lancashire. Experienced prop who joined Sale from Orrell in 1994-95, having previously appeared for Fylde. Made his Sale debut against Saracens in November 1994.

RYAN, Neil (Utility back)
Born Wigan, 29.11.73. 5'9", 13st 4lb. Career: Student. Rep hons: England U21, 18 Group. North (3). Lancashire. CLR: Waterloo (4t, 5pg, 8dg-59pts), Sale (1t-5pts). Enigmatic talent who began his rugby at West Park School, moved to Mount St Mary's School in Sheffield before representing England 16 Group for two seasons. Moved to Waterloo and played for the North in South Africa (1994) before joining Sale. Toured Italy with the North in May 1996.

SAVERIMUTTO, Christian (Scrum-half)
Born Birkenhead, 8.8.71. 5'8", 13st. Career: Surveyor. Rep hons: Ireland (3, Fiji95). Ireland 7s. England Students. CLR: Waterloo (5t, 1dg-26pts), Sale (3t-15pts). Damaged cruciate knee ligaments playing for Ireland in the RWC Sevens in Lisbon in June 1996 and could struggle to play this season. Formerly with Waterloo, where he partnered Paul Grayson at half-back, Christian was educated at St Anselm's College, Birkenhead, and Sheffield's Hallam University where he completed a surveying degree. Qualifies for Ireland through his maternal grandparents. Younger brother Robin has played for Ireland U21. Full Ireland debut against Fiji in 1995 and also played against USA, and Scotland in the Five Nations before losing out to Niall Hogan.

SMITH, Andrew (Prop)
Born Nantwich, 28.3.69. 6'1", 17st 6lb. Career: Builder. Rep hons: North (4). Educated at Rossall School and member of Chester RFC before joining Sale. Toured South Africa with North (1994). Good ball-handler and sound scrummager, Andrew struggled for much of 1995-96 with a groin injury.

SMITH, Paul (Prop)
Born Nantwich, 28.3.69. 6', 17st. Career: Builder. Rep hons: North (2). Twin brother of Andrew and equally uncompromising in the front row. Also educated at Rossall, Paul was another to struggle with injury last season, being impeded with a sore back.

STOCKS, Gareth (Centre)
Born Rochdale, 17.12.69. 5'10", 14st. Career: Financial controller. Rep hons: England A. CLR: 7t, 1dg-38pts. Stocky centre capable of punching holes in the best organised defences.

VERBICKAS, Simon (Wing)
Born Manchester, 22.4.75. 6'1", 13st 7lb. Career: Sales. CLR: Broughton Park (1c-2pts), Sale (19t-95pts). Educated at St Anselm's College, Simon played for Broughton Park and enjoyed a sensational debut season for Sale, scoring 16 League tries, when the club were promoted from League Two in 1993-94, including five in Sale's remarkable 88-9 win over Otley. Damaged his spine and missed the following season but gradually returned to action with the Second XV in 1995-96. Still young and blessed with real pace.

VYVYAN, Charles Bovil (Back five forward)
Born Wimbledon, 1.9.65. 6'6", 17st 4lb. Career: Valuer. Rep hons: England Students. North (7, 2t-10pts). Yorkshire. Barbarians (94). CLR: Richmond (4t-16pts), Sale (8t-40pts). Educated at Downside and Cambridge, where he won Blues in 1987 and 1988, Charles is a former Richmond and Wharfedale member and made his Yorkshire debut against Alberta in 1991 before joining Sale in 1993. Renowned for his surging runs from tapped penalties. Keen fly-fisherman, he and his brothers, Richard, John, Simon, Paul, James and Hugh, have entered the Penryn Sevens for the last three years, winning twice and losing in the 1996 final.

WARR, Mark (Scrum-half)
Born Birmingham, 24.2.69. 5'9", 12st 12lb. Career: Social worker with Cheshire County Council. Rep hons: England Students, Universities. Warwickshire. CLR: 12t-60pts. Educated at Bablake School in Coventry where he won an England 16 Group cap, Mark studied psychology and PE at Birmingham University. Long-time member of Barker's Butt club before joining Sale. Has made three County final appearances for Warwickshire.

YATES, Alan (Prop)
Born 5.2.63. 6', 18st. Career: Mature student/Doorman. Rep hons: Cheshire. Enormously strong bodybuilder and soccer player with Oldham who only took up rugby five years ago and has learned the game almost exclusively in League One and Two. Makes up for lack of technique with sheer strength.

YATES, Chris (Wing)
Born Otahute, New Zealand, 13.5.71. 6', 16st. Career: PRP. Rep hons: England 7s. North (1). CLR: 8t-40pts. Powerful Anglo/Kiwi wing who represented England in 1995 Hong Kong 7s. Scored four League tries in 1995-96. Originally travelled to England with the intention of playing Rugby League but got diverted and played briefly for Old Aldwinians before joining Sale. A member of the Universities club in Auckland while in New Zealand.

REVIEW

The gloss was taken off a season of solid achievement by the parting of the ways with Paul Turner in the summer. Nobody has done more to drag the Cheshire club into the top flight and develop their game and, no matter what the views of some club members, he will be missed. The onus is now on John Mitchell to impose his own qualities on Sale and he arrives in England with a formidable reputation having transformed Waikato into one of the strongest provinces in New Zealand. Sale have steadily strengthened their squad over past seasons and could again trouble the best. Their pack grows in stature and young backs like Jos Baxendell, Chris Yates, Neil Ryan and David Rees are beginning to mature. Enticing Dewi Morris out of retirement is a major coup and the employment of contract RL professionals such as John Devereux is also an interesting development, although a nasty ankle injury could affect John's early-season availability.

SALE in the Courage League 1995-96

Sep	9	Gloucester	A	Won	22	17	Saverimutto(T) Vyvyan(T) C. Yates(T) Liley(2C, P)
	16	Leicester	H	Lost	12	16	Liley(D, 2P) Stocks(D)
	23	Orrell	A	Lost	6	12	Liley(D, P)
	30	Wasps	H	Lost	18	25	Liley(5P) Turner(D)
Oct	7	Bristol	A	Lost	6	30	Liley(2P)
	14	Harlequins	H	Won	29	11	Ashurst(T) Baldwin(T) Liley(2C, 5P)

21	Saracens	A	Won	24	9	Ashurst(T) Baxendell(T) Saverimutto(T) Liley(3C, P)
28	West Hartlepool	A	Won	29	11	Baldwin(T) Baxendell(T) Liley(T, 3P) C. Yates(T)
Nov 4	Bath	H	Lost	18	30	Baxendell(T) Mallinder(T) Liley(C, 2P)
11	Gloucester	H	Won	21	13	Liley(T, C, 2P) Rees(T) Turner(D)
Jan 6	Orrell	H	Won	39	13	Baldwin(T) Higginbotham(T) Warr(T) C. Yates(T) Liley(4C) Turner(2D)
Feb 17	Bristol	H	Won	15	6	Vyvyan(2T) Liley(C) Turner(P)
Mar 23	Wasps	A	Lost	16	25	Saverimutto(T) Liley(C, 3P)
30	Harlequins	A	Lost	0	55	
Apr 6	Saracens	H	Won	18	15	Liley(T, P) Ryan(T) Warr(T)
13	West Hartlepool	H	Won	44	13	Ashurst(T) Baxendell(T) Fowler(T) Hewitt(T) Mallinder(T) O'Grady(T) Liley(4C, 2P)
17	Leicester	A	Lost	10	32	Liley(C, P) Mallinder(T)
27	Bath	A	Drew	38	38	Baxendell(2T) Ashurst(T) O'Grady(T) C. Yates(T) Liley(2C, 3P)

SARACENS

Formation of Club: 1876
Clubhouse: Bramley Road, Southgate, London N14. Tel: 0181 449 3770
Ground: Enfield Football Club, Southbury Road, Enfield
Capacity: 8,000
Colours: Black, red star and crescent
Honours: Courage League Two: Champions: 1988-89, Runners-up: 1994-95
Last season: CL1: 11th. Pilkington Cup: 4th round (lost 40-16 at Leicester)
Most capped player: Philippe Sella (France) 111
Coach: Mark Evans
Captain: Tony Diprose

BOTTERMAN, Greg Richard (Hooker)
Born Welwyn Garden City, 3.3.68. 5'11", 15st 6lb. Career: Company manager. Rep hons: Emerging England, Colts. London (5). CLR: 2t-10pts. Former Datchworth and Bacavians hooker who was a bench reserve for England in their Grand Slam game against Scotland in 1995.

BRACKEN, Kyran Paul Patrick (Scrum-half)
Born Dublin, Ireland, 22.11.71. 5'11", 12st 10lb. Career: Solicitor. Rep hons: England (11, NZ93, 1t-5pts), A (4, B Col93, 1t-5pts), U21, Schools. South West. Barbarians (94). CLR: 7t-35pts (Bristol). A big summer signing from Bristol, Kyran burst on to the international scene with a courageous performance against New Zealand in 1993 when he overcame a painful ankle injury, courtesy of Jamie Joseph's reckless stamp. A regular for England throughout the 1995 Five Nations, he lost his place to Dewi Morris in RWC95, and then lost out to Matt Dawson last season after playing against South Africa in November. Educated at Stonyhurst, Lancashire, and originally capped by England 16 Group at fly-half, Kyran finished last season in excellent form and is determined to regain his England position.

BUCKTON, John Richard (Centre)
Born Hull, 22.12.61. 6'2", 12st 11lb. Career: Holiday company rep. Rep hons: England (3, A88), A/B (13, Sp88). North (10), London (7, 1t-4pts). Barbarians (87-88). CLR: 17t-83pts. Experienced centre who sets high standards in fitness and club loyalty. Made his international debut as a replacement in 1988 and started two Tests for England on tour in Argentina (1990). Formerly with Hull & East Riding and also enjoyed a spell with Marist Old Boys in New Zealand. Younger brother of Waterloo flanker Peter Buckton.

BURROW, Mark (Lock)
Born Chelmsford, 9.7.69. 6'6", 17st 8lb. Career: Student. Flame-haired former Ilford Wanderers lock who was a leading light in forming a Redheads XV to play occasional games in London.

CHESNEY, Kris (Wing)
Born Ilford, 2.3.74. 6'6", 16st 12lb. Career: Chef. Rep hons: England U21, London U21. CLR: 2t-10pts. Formerly with Barking, Kris is a frightening sight on the wing but has genuine pace and impressed many opponents in 1995-96. As recently as December 94 played for London U21 against New Zealand U21 at lock, but has made an impressive transition into the backs.

COPSEY, Anthony Hugh (Lock)
Born Romford, 25.1.65. 6'6", 17st 8lb. Career: Sales and marketing executive. Rep hons: Wales (16, Ire92). Barbarians (92-93). Londoner who studied at South Glamorgan Institute Cyncoed and eventually opted for Wales, making his international debut against Ireland at Lansdowne Road in 1992. Useful operator at international level, Tony was last capped, as a replacement, against Western Samoa on Wales' South Pacific tour in 1994. Played for Llanelli in Wales and fondly remembers his early career with Old Edwardians in London. Joined Saracens midway through 1995-96 season.

DAVIES, Brian (Scrum-half)
Born Nairobi, Kenya, 22.1.66. 5'10", 12st. Career: Systems analyst. Rep hons: London, Welsh Exiles. CLR: 7t-30pts. Brian stepped down after four years as captain in May during which time the club had experienced relegation, promotion and then a relegation that never was. Made the 400-mile trip from Barry three times a week to undertake his duties as captain. Formerly with Barry, Swansea University and Southend.

DIPROSE, Tony James (Backrow)
Born Orsett, 22.9.72. 6'5", 16st 10lb. Career: PRP/Promotions executive with Ebbswift. Rep hons: England A (15, Ire94, 3t-15pts), Emerging, Students, U21, 18 Group. London (8). CLR: 6t-30pts. Captained England A to a clean sweep of five victories last season. Tony again enhanced his reputation as the best ball-carrying No 8 in the Courage League. Educated at Campion School, Hornchurch, he graduated from Loughborough University with a Bsc in PE and Recreation Management and made his England A debut against Ireland in 1994, being voted the RFU Young Player of the Year that season. Toured Australia with England U21 in 1993 and Zimbabwe with London the following summer.

DOOLEY, Dan (Centre)
Born Romford, 18.10.68. 6'1", 15st. Career: Futures trader. Rep hons: Ireland A, Exiles. England U21, 18 Group. CLR: London Irish (1t-5pts), Saracens (5t-22pts). Robust centre who hails from Campion School and enjoyed a brief spell at London Irish before returning to Saracens.

EBONGALAME, Muna (Wing)
Born Cameroon, 9.6.73. 5'8", 12st. Career: Construction manager. Rep hons: Cumbria U18. Promising wing whose first team opportunities have been limited. Joined Saracens from Luton RFC.

EKE, Chris (Backrow)
Born Harpenden, 20.12.73. 6'3", 17st. Career: Trainee osteopath. Rep hons: Buckinghamshire. Powerful young backrow prospect who has joined the club from Wasps. Captained Bucks U21 against Yorkshire in CIS County final 1995.

FRIEL, Phillip (Scrum-half)
Born Romford, 14.1.73. 5'8", 12st 7lb. Career: Restaurateur student. Rep hons: London U21, Colts. Irish Exiles. Gutsy scrum-half who stepped into the fray when Davies broke his ankle last season. Formerly with Campion Old Boys.

GREEN, John (Back five)
Born Romford, 17.3.67. 6'4", 18st. Career: PE teacher. Rep hons: England Students, Schools. Irish Exiles. CLR: 9t-45pts. Yet another Campion Old Boy, John represented England in the 1988 World Students Cup. A powerful all-round forward, he also played for Bridgend while a student in Wales.

HALVEY, Eddie Oliver (Backrow)
Born Limerick, Ireland, 11.7.70. 6'4", 16st. Career: PRP. Rep hons: Ireland (6, Fr95, 2t-10pts), A. CLR: 1t-5pts. Dynamic Munster backrow forward who arrived at Saracens from Shannon midway through the 1995-96 season. Restricted initially by a nagging groin injury, Eddie looked back to his best form against Bath in April and his backrow partnership with Diprose and Hill should be worth watching. Educated at St Nessan's Community College, Limerick, he joined the local Thomond club before progressing to Shannon. Made his Munster debut in 1991, played for Ireland A in 1994 against Scotland and Wales and made his international debut against France at Lansdowne Road in 1995. Outstanding for Ireland against Wales (1995), he scored a try as a temporary replacement against the Welsh in RWC two months later. Played for an Ireland XV in the Peace International in May 1996.

HARRIES, Peter (Wing)
Born Romford, 10.9.70. 6'2", 13st 7lb. Career: Teacher. Rep hons: Welsh Students, U21, Exiles. England 18 Group. London Welsh (1t-4pts), Saracens (13t-65pts). Educated at Gaynes School, Upminster, played for England Schools in 1989 with Steve Ravenscroft.

HILL, Richard Anthony (Backrow)
Born Dormansland, 23.5.73. 6'2", 15st 8lb. Career: PRP. Rep hons: England A (6, 3t-15pts), Students, U21, Colts, 18 Group, England 7s. South West (5, 7t-35pts). Barbarians (94). CLR: 10t-50pts. Clever footballing flanker who was hampered by injury last season. Richard was educated at Stratford Castle Primary and Bishop Wordsworth School, where England namesake and scrum-half Richard Hill also attended. An outstanding Schools international, he completed his education at Brunel University, which now incorporates that well-known rugby nursery West London Institute. Represented England A against Western Samoa in December 1995 and New South Wales in January 1996.

HOLMES, Gary (Prop)
Born Hampstead, 7.7.65. 5'11", 16st. Career: Company director. Rep hons: England A/B (5, Nam90), Colts. London (6). CLR: Wasps (2t-9pts), Saracens (1t-5pts). Gary was educated at Queensbury School, Dunstable, and learned his trade at Wasps under the watchful eyes of Jeff Probyn and Paul Rendall. Served Wasps well for over a decade before moving to Bramley Road. Made his Saracens club debut against Shannon in August 1995 and made his League debut against his old colleagues at Wasps.

HUGHES, Gareth (Fly-half)
Born Wales, 25.7.66. 6', 14st Career: Teacher. Rep hons: British Polytechnic. Welsh Exiles. CLR: Askeans (1t, 8c, 3dg-53pts), Blackheath (1t-4pts), London Welsh (3t, 3c, 2pg-24pts), Saracens (3t, 2c, 3pg, 8dg-52pts). Much-travelled fly-half who also numbers Fylde among his former clubs. Devastating kicker when on form.

HUGHES, Paul (Wing/full-back)
Born Hitchin, 25.7.67. 5'8", 13st 7lb. Career: Construction. Rep hons: Hertfordshire. Formerly with Letchworth and Wasps.

JOHNS, Patrick Stephen (Lock)
Born Portadown, 19.2.68. 6'6", 16st 10lb. Career: Dental officer. Rep hons: Ireland (28, Arg90, 2t-10pts), B, U25, U21, Universities, Schools. Barbarians (93-94). Ulster. Educated at Trinity College, Dublin, he played for Ulster against the All Blacks in 1989-90 and made his debut for Ireland B that season. Made full international debut for Ireland against touring Argentina October 1990. Regular appearances for his country at lock or No 8. Superb performance against Wales to book Ireland's place in 1995 World Cup quarter-finals. Appeared in all four World Cup matches in South Africa. Played in last season's Five Nations Championship. Joined Saracens from Dungannon in the close season, having looked likely to go to Bedford. Enjoys painting and making wine.

LANGLEY, Mark (Lock)
Born Cardiff, 9.6.67. 6'4", 17st 10lb. Career: Regional sales manager. Rep hons: Wales Students, U21. London (1). CLR: 3t-15pts. Hard-working Welsh lock who played for Swansea University, Swansea, Penarth and Bridgend before joining Saracens.

LEE, Andy (Fly-half)
Born Woodford, 10.11.68. 5'9", 13st 7lb. Career: PE teacher. Rep hons: England Students, U21. London B. England U19 cricket. England Schools Football. CLR: 6t, 11c, 37pg, 15dg-207pts. Educated at Chigwell School, Andy is a supreme all-rounder, having represented his country at three sports. Played cricket with Nasser Hussain and Graham Thorpe for England U19 and still plays in the Essex League for Woodford. Also played for England Schools soccer and West Ham Youth despite 'not really liking football'. A former captain of West London Institute, where he was a longtime student, Andy's goalkicking was sorely missed towards the end of last season when he dislocated his shoulder against West Hartlepool and missed the last five games of their relegation struggle.

LYNAGH, Michael Patrick (Fly-half)
Born Queensland, Australia, 25.10.63. Career: PRP/Real estate consultant. Rep hons: Australia (72, Fiji84, 17t, 140c, 177pg, 9dg-911pts), Queensland. Barbarians (90-91). The world record points scorer in international rugby (911) joins Saracens on a three-year contract from Benetton Treviso in Italy, having stepped down from international duties after RWC95 when he captained Australia. Made his international debut as a centre against Fiji in Suva (84) before helping Australia to their Grand Slam in Britain and Ireland (84). Appeared in all three World Cups for Australia, directing affairs brilliantly from fly-half during their triumph in 1991.

METCALFE, Alastair (Backrow)
Born Ripon, 29.3.72. 6'3", 16st. Rep hons: England Students, U21, Colts. CLR: Wakefield (3t-15pts). Durable Yorkshireman who won Cambridge Blue in 1994.

RAVENSCROFT, Stephen (Centre)
Born Bradford, 2.11.70. 5'11", 14st 2lb. Career: Solicitor. Rep hons: England Students, U21, 18 Group. North (3). CLR: 2t-10pts. Educated at Bradford GS. Steve previously played for Otley and Bradford and Bingley before joining Saracens. Played Provincial U21 rugby for North Harbour during a prolonged stay in New Zealand and represented England in 1992 World Students Cup. Made his North debut against Northern Transvaal at Loftus Versveld in 1994.

SELLA, Philippe (Centre)
Born Cairac, France, 14.2.62. 5'11", 13st 8lb. Career: PRP/PR consultant. Rep hons: France (111, Rom82, 30t-125pts). Barbarians (91-92). The world's most capped player joins Saracens on a 12-month contract, his move to London also affording the opportunity to develop his business interests with Sella Communications. Sella spent his club career in France exclusively with Agen and made his international debut against Romania in 1982. Opened his try-scoring account with two in the next game, against Argentina, and played 45 consecutive internationals before missing the game against Romania in 1987 through injury. In 1986 he scored a try in every Five Nations game to equal the record of Johnny Wallace (Scotland, 1925), Patrick Esteve (France, 1923) and Carston Catcheside (England, 1924). Played in all three World Cup campaigns for France, finishing on a high note by helping France defeat England in the 1995 play-off game at Loftus Versveld. His retirement was honoured in the summer by Agen playing a World XV.

SINGER, Matt James (Full-back)
Born Bristol, 7.11.72. Rep hons: England Students. Educated at Wycliffe College, Stonehouse, Bristol University and Cambridge, Matt has also played for Neath and Racing Club Narbonne.

SORRELL, Kevin (Centre)
Born 6.3.77. 6', 12st 8lb. Career: Student. Rep hons: England 18 Group. Another product of Campion School. Formerly member of school barbershop singing group.

TRUELOVE, George (Wing)
Born 22.9.75. 6'4", 14st 4lb. Career: Student. Rep hons: England Colts, 18 Group. A promising wing, George was initially educated at Queen Elizabeth School, Barnet, before moving to Durham School where he was capped at Schools level.

TUNNINGLEY, Andrew (Full-back)
Born Harrogate, 29.3.67. 6'2", 14st. Career: Actuarial consultant. Rep hons: England A (1, Ire95), Emerging. London (4). CLR: 12t, 46c, 87pg, 1dg-415pts. Former Cambridge Blue (1988) who was sidelined at the end of last season with a neck injury. Toured Zimbabwe with London in 1994.

WALLACE, Paul Stephen (Prop)
Born Cork, Ireland, 30.12.71. 6'1", 16st. Career: PRP. Rep hons: Ireland (5, Jap95), A, Students, U21, Schools. Educated at Crescent College, Limerick, Paul was an exceptional Schools international in 1989 and 1990 and has made smooth progress towards a place in the full Ireland side. Made his senior debut against Japan in RWC95 and impressed during his two Five Nations appearances against Wales and England. Younger brother of Ireland international wing Richard.

WALLACE, Richard Michael (Wing)
Born Cork, Ireland, 16.1.68. 5'11", 14st. Career: Financial consultant/PRP Rep hons: Ireland (24, Nam91, 5t-23pts), U25, Students, U21. British Lions tourist (NZ1993). Elder brother of prop Paul, Richard began his rugby career with Cork Constitution before switching to Garryowen in Limerick. Holds a private flying licence and was formerly one of Ireland's most promising dinghy (Laser) sailors before concentrating on rugby. Powerful wing with deceptive pace, Richard made his international debut against Namibia in 1991 and was working in Moscow two years later when Ian Hunter was injured in New Zealand and he was called in to replace him.

WILSON, Stuart (Prop)
Born London, 27.3.64. 5'11", 15st 10lb. Career: Plasterer Rep hons: Middlesex, Hertfordshire. London Colts. CLR: 2t-10pts. Club stalwart and ultra-reliable member of the front row.

YANDELL, Craig (Lock)
Born Weston-Super-Mare, 16.8.72. 6'7", 17st 2lb. Career: Rep hons: England Students, U21, Colts. South West (6, 1t-5pts). Improving young lock who played for Llandovery and Narberth while completing a BSc in Business Studies at Swansea University.

REVIEW

Huge sighs of relief at Saracens on 24 May when EPRUC and RFU finally settled their differences and Saracens were spared relegation. Following the financial input of Nigel Wray, the arrival of Philippe Sella and Michael Lynagh and ambitious plans for a new ground, Saracens could ill afford to tread the minefield of League Two rugby. They deserved their reprieve for the decency and innovation they have brought to the game, but must now take full advantage of their stroke of luck. The goal-kicking of Lynagh should ensure a degree of success, and the arrival of Kyran Bracken is another major plus, but Saracens' backs lacked a try-scoring, cutting edge in 1995-96, a fault that needs to be addressed. The pack was mobile and solid but struggled occasionally for lineout possession. The popular Brian Davies, who epitomised the club's spirit, steps down as captain and his leadership will be hard to emulate.

SARACENS in the Courage League 1995-96

Sep 9	Leicester	A	Lost	3	31		Tunningley(P)
16	Orrell	H	Won	12	9		Tunningley(4P)
23	Wasps	A	Lost	16	38		Tunningley(T, C, 3P)
30	Bristol	H	Lost	11	24		Holmes(T) Tunningley(2P)
Oct 7	Harlequins	A	Lost	15	23		Gregory(T) Lee(T, C, P)
14	West Hartlepool	H	Won	31	30		Harries(T) Lee(C, 2D, 6P)
21	Sale	H	Lost	9	24		Lee(2P) Tunningley(D)
28	Bath	A	Lost	16	52		Harries(T) Tunningley(T) Lee(2P)
Nov 4	Gloucester	H	Won	19	16		Gregory(T) Lee(C, D, 3P)
11	Leicester	H	Won	25	21		Harries(T) Lee(C, D, 5P)
Jan 6	Wasps	H	Lost	20	24		Tunningley(T) Lee(5P)
13	Orrell	A	Lost	13	38		Chesney(T) Harries(T) Tunningley(P)
Feb 17	Harlequins	H	Lost	6	13		Lee(2P)
Mar 30	West Hartlepool	A	Won	41	31		Botterman(T) Diprose(T) Langley(T) Lee(T, 3C, D, 3P) Hughes(P)
Apr 6	Sale	A	Lost	15	18		Chesney(T) Hughes(T, C, P).
13	Bath	H	Lost	15	21		Diprose(T) Halvey(T) Hughes(C, P)
20	Bristol	A	Lost	7	21		Hill(T) Singer(C)
27	Gloucester	A	Lost	10	17		Hill(T) Singer(C, P)

WASPS

Formation of Club: 1867
Ground: Repton Avenue, Rugby Road, Sudbury, Middlesex, HA0 3DW.
    Tel: 0181 902 4220
Capacity: Currently 4,500, projected 7,500 for 1997-98
Colours: Black with gold Wasp on left breast
Honours: Pilkington Cup: Losing finalists: 1986, 87, 95
    Courage League: Champions: 1989-90, runners-up 1987-88, 90-91, 92-93
Last season: CL1: 4th. Pilkington Cup: Q/F (lost 22-9 to Gloucester)
Most capped player: Rob Andrew (England) 70
Director of Rugby: Nigel Melville
Coach: Rob Smith
Captain: Lawrence Dallaglio

CRONIN, Damian Francis (Lock)
Born Wegberg, West Germany, 17.4.63. 6'6", 17st 8lb. Career: Antiques reclamation/
PRP. Rep hons: Scotland (39, Ire88, 4t-18pts), A. British Lions tourist 1993 (NZ).
CLR: 3t-12pts (Bath), 4t-19pts (London Scottish). A welcome addition to Wasps'
pack, Damian returned to Scotland's senior side in New Zealand last summer, playing
in both Tests. Formerly with Bath and London Scottish, Damian has overcome serious
knee and spine injuries to pursue his rugby career. Was an outstanding member of
Scotland's Grand Slam-winning side in 1990, and although his appearances were
restricted in RWC91 he contributed fully to their World Cup campaign in 1995. Moves
to Wasps from Bourges, France.

DALLAGLIO, Lawrence Bruno Nero (Flanker)
Born Shepherd's Bush, London, 10.8.72. 6'4", 15st 7lb. Career: PRP. Rep hons: England (6, SA95, 1t-5pts), A/B (4, Fr94), Emerging, U21, Colts, England 7s. London (4,
2t-10pts). Barbarians (95-96). CLR: 11t-55pts. Voted 1995-96 RFU Player of the
Season, Lawrence enjoyed an exceptional Five Nations campaign, after making his full
debut against Western Samoa and appearing as a replacement against Scotland.
No less an achievement was to captain Wasps after the departure of Rob Andrew and
to help the club regroup. Educated at Ampleforth College, where he starred in their
Sevens team that won the Open and Festival tournaments at Rosslyn Park (1989),
Lawrence missed out on England Schools honours but has been capped at every other
age group level and represented England when they won the RWC Sevens at Murrayfield (1993). Toured South Africa with England in 1994 and was unlucky not to make
the RWC95 squad. Graduated from Kingston University in the summer.

DELANEY, Paul (Hooker)
Born London, 7.4.71. 5'8", 15st 7lb. Career: Quantity surveyor. Rep hons: England U21
and Colts. CLR: 2t-10pts. Educated at London Oratory School, Paul joined Wasps as a
Colt in 1988 and made his League debut against Bristol in 1992.

DUNN, Kevin Anthony (Hooker)
Born Gloucester, 5.6.65. 5'9", 14st 7lb. Career: Construction manager. Rep hons:
England A/B (17, Aus88, 4t-17pts). South West (10). CLR: Wasps (2t-10pts), Glouce-
ster (4t-16pts). Formerly with Spartans, Lydney, Gloucester and Waratahs RFC in
Australia, Kevin was educated at Churchdown Comp and made his England B debut
against Australia in 1988.

DUNSTON, Ian (Prop)
Born Essex, 11.6.68. 5'11", 17st. Career: Management Cost Accountant. Rep hons: England Colts. London (5). CLR: 4t-18pts. 'Paddy' Dunston was educated at Forest Lodge Comp and the City of London Polytechnic and joined Wasps in 1987, making his League debut two years later. Voted Wasps Young player of the Year in 1990, has toured Australia with London.

GOMARSALL, Andrew (Scrum-half)
Born Durham, 24.7.74. 5'10", 13st 8lb. Career: PRP. Rep hons: England A/B (5, S Aus95, 1t-5pts), Emerging, U21, Students, Colts, 18 Group. London (2). Barbarians (94-95). CLR: 6t-30pts. Andy has represented England at every level save full international and looks set to contest the scrum-half spot with Matt Dawson and Kyran Bracken over the coming years. A product of Bedford School, he captained England Schools to their first grand slam in 11 years in 1992 but had to wait patiently for regular first team rugby at Wasps while Steve Bates was in residence. Blessed with pace and strength, Andy was also a county and divisional hockey player of note.

GREENSTOCK, Nicholas James Jeremy (Centre/wing)
Born Dubai, UAE, 3.11.73. 6'3", 15st. Career: PR consultant. Rep hons: England A/B (4, Ire95), Emerging, U21 and 18 Group, England 7s. London (6, 2t-10pts). Barbarians (94). CLR: 10t-50pts. Suffered a dip in form and confidence before Christmas 1995 but finished the season strongly. Educated at Sherborne, where he won England Schools honours, Nick made a massive impact during the 1994-95 season when he was voted the RFU Young Player of the Season after figuring prominently for England A, U21 and Emerging England, the Barbarians and the England Seven at Hong Kong. No wonder he looked jaded at the start of last season. Graduated from Royal Holloway College with a BA (Hons) in Geography and now works as a PR consultant for Christow in London.

GREENWOOD, Matthew James (Back five forward)
Born Leeds, 25.9.64. 6'6", 17st. Career: Quantity surveyor. Rep hons: England A/B (13, Sp92, 1t-5pts), U21. North (10, 1t-5pts). London (5). Barbarians (93-94). CLR: Wasps (5t-25pts), Nottingham (1t-5pts). Ultra-reliable forward who joined Wasps from Nottingham, having started his career at Roundhay. Educated at Roundhay School and Trent Polytechnic, toured New Zealand with England B in 1992 and Canada the following summer with an England XV.

GREGORY, Guy Darren (Fly-half)
Born Chalfont St Giles, 13.1.69. 6', 13st 4lb. Career: Chartered surveyor. Rep hons: Emerging England, U21. London (8, 1t, 10c, 19pg-82pts). CLR: 3t, 23c, 24pg, 2dg-139pts. A product of Watford GS and Sheffield Polytechnic, Guy made his League debut in 1990 before joining Nottingham for four years while a student. A dropped goal specialist, he returned to Sudbury on completing his studies and shared the fly-half duties with Chris Braithwaite last season. Played for England in the World Students Cup (1992).

GRIFFITHS, Mike (Prop)
Born Tonypandy, 18.3.62. 5'11", 16st 8lb. Career: PRP. Rep hons: Wales (34, WS88), B, Lions tourist 1989. Barbarians (88-89). Powerful scrummager who has joined Wasps on a three-year contract from Cardiff, having previously played for Bridgend. Educated at Blaenclydach County School, Mike emerged from the Rhondda Youth and Mid District sides before joining Bridgend. Made his international debut against Western Samoa in 1988 and represented Wales in RWC91 and 95. Missed the 1993 Five Nations

after breaking a collarbone falling off a mountain bike while training with Wales at Club La Santa, Lanzarote.

HADLEY, Norman (Lock)

Born Winnipeg, Canada, 2.12.64. 6'6", 20st. Career: Broker. Rep hons: Canada (18, USA 87). Barbarians (92-93). Following an injury-plagued couple of seasons, 'Stormin' Norman' is probably best known for his headline grabbing eviction of troublemakers on the London Underground, but after recovering from a serious broken leg and a painful back operation Canada's former captain is anxious to resume playing. Educated at the University of British Columbia and the University of Victoria, Norman was first capped against USA in 1987 and played in all four games during Canada's excellent 1991 World Cup campaign. Fell out with the Canadian management prior to RWC95 although injury would have reduced his effectiveness. Has played club rugby in New Zealand and Japan, as well as England, and remains a formidable competitor.

HOPLEY, Damian Paul (Centre/wing)

Born London, 12.4.70. 6'2", 15st 2lb. Career: PRP. Rep hons: England (3, WS95), A/B (23, Aus90, 3t-14pts), England 7s, Students, Colts, 18 Group, Scottish Universities. London (7, 4t-18pts). Barbarians (94-95). CLR: 20t-96pts. Blockbusting centre/wing and famously good-natured tourist, having visited Australia, Fiji and South Africa with England and New Zealand with England B. Damian suffered torn cruciate knee ligaments while captaining England in Hong Kong in March and has spent the summer 'building up Western Samoan thighs' to stabilise the joint. After studying theology at St Andrew's University, he won a Blue at Cambridge and was an outstanding member of the England Seven which unexpectedly took the inaugural RWC crown at Murrayfield in 1993. Finally won a full England cap as a replacement against Western Samoa in RWC95. Brilliant pianist, look out also for his rendition of 'Flower of Scotland' using a bar stool as a bagpipe.

HOPLEY, Phil (Wing)

Born London, 6.10.66. 6'2", 14st 7lb. Career: Doctor. Rep hons: England Students, Irish Exiles. CLR: 17t, 1c, 2pg-92pts. Damian's elder brother, Phil went to St Benedict's College, Ealing, before training as a doctor at St Thomas' Hospital. Represented England throughout the 1988 World Students Cup in France but has subsequently used his Irish qualifications to play for Irish Exiles. A sevens specialist, Phil converted Buster White's winning try when Wasps beat Northampton 26-24 to take the 1993 Middlesex Sevens title.

JAMES, Aaron Gordon (Centre)

Born Otautan, New Zealand, 20.9.67. 6', 13st. Career: New Zealand Meat Products. Rep hons: Scottish Exiles. CLR: 1t-5pts. Former Southland utility back who played against England B (92) and the British Lions (93).

KING, Alexander David (Fly-half)

Born Brighton, 17.1.75. 6', 13st 4lb. Career: Student. Rep hons: England A/B (5, WS95, 1t, 8c, 9pg, 2dg-54pts), U21, Colts. South West. Barbarians (95-96). CLR: Rosslyn Park (2t, 12pg, 7c-60pts). The RFU's Young Player of the Year 1995-96 and deservedly so after a stunning rise to prominence via the South West divisional side and England U21, which led to him playing in all five England A internationals when he forged a fruitful partnership with Andy Gomarsall. Educated at Brighton College, Alex is a third-year Economics and Accountancy student at Bristol University and played no senior club rugby last season, having also missed most of the previous season with Rosslyn Park through a knee injury.

KINSEY, Richard (Lock)
Born Barnet, Middlesex, 5.2.64. 6'5", 18st. Career: Youth development officer for Bucks. Rep hons: Queensland. London (4). CLR: 4t-20pts. Educated at Fakenham School and Norfolk College of Agriculture, Richard played for Easts in Brisbane and appeared for Queensland against France, USSR and USA before returning to England.

LEWIS, Matthew (Fly-half)
Born Wales, 16.1.71. 5'10", 12st 4lb. Career: Trainee solicitor. Rep hohs: Wales A, U21, U18. Versatile Welsh utility back who arrives at Sudbury from Bridgend, where he formed a potent half-back partnership with Robert Howley. Educated at Llandovery College and University of Wales, Matt came third in the British Universities long jump.

MITCHELL, Simon John (Hooker)
Born Saltburn, 23.11.67. 5'10", 16st. Career: Bond trader. Rep hons: Emerging England. North (6). London (1). Yorkshire. Barbarians (94). CLR: West Hartlepool (5t-23pts), Harlequins (1t-5pts). Moved from West Hartlepool early in 1995 to successfully challenge Brian Moore at hooker. Educated at Sacred Heart Comprehensive, Redcar, Simon graduated to West Hartlepool via Yorkshire Colts and Acklam RFC. Joined Wasps in the summer of 1996.

MOLLOY, Darren (Prop)
Born Middlesex, 31.8.72. 6'2", 17st. Career: Student. Rep hons: Emerging England, Students, U21. London (3). CLR: 1t-5pts. Started at Old Gaytonians and also played for London Irish before joining Wasps. Toured Australia with England U21 in 1993.

POOLE-JONES, Richard (Flanker)
Born London, 22.10.69. 6'2", 15st. Rep hons: Barbarians, French Barbarians, Cambridge University, England 18 Group. Former student at King's Macclesfield and Toulouse University, Richard played for Biarritz and the French Barbarians against Australia but has been hampered by knee injury since joining Wasps.

REES, Gareth Lloyd (Utility back)
Born Duncan, Vancouver Island, Canada, 30.6.67. 6', 14st 8lb. Career: Teacher at Eton. Rep hons: Canada (34, USA86). British Columbia. Middlesex. Barbarians (92-93). Vastly experienced Canadian who rejoins Wasps after playing club rugby for Merignac in France, and spells with Oxford University and Newport. Educated at Harrow, Gareth represented Wasps in the 1986 Pilkington Cup final as a schoolboy and later that year made his Canadian debut at fly-half against USA. Has been fundamental to their cause ever since playing in all ten World Cup matches in RWC 87, 91, 95. Sent off against South Africa after the infamous brawl at Port Elizabeth, Gareth will prefer to remember career highlights such as kicking the decisive penalty when Canada defeated Wales 26-24 at Cardiff Arms Park (1993).

ROISER, Shane (Wing)
Born London, 7.6.73. 5'9", 13st. Career: Dental student. Rep hons: England Students, U21. London (5, 1t-5pts). CLR: Wasps (8t-40pts), Rosslyn Park (7t-35pts). One of the quickest wings around, Shane learned his rugby at Trinity Whitgift and played for Rosslyn Park before joining Wasps. Wasps' leading League try scorer in 1995-96 with 8.

SAMPSON, Paul (Full-back/wing)
Born Wakefield, 12.7.77. 5'10", 11st 10lb. Rep hons: England U21, Colts, 18 Group. President's 7. GBU20 Athletics. Probably the quickest player in British rugby, Paul posted a startling 10.48 secs to win the English Schools 100m Championship in Sheffield in July and intends to combine both athletics and rugby. Came to prominence with Woodhouse Grove School in 1994-95, playing in all six internationals for England 18 Group, including a famous 30-3 win over Australia at Kingsholm. Dramatically called into the full England training squad in February and subsequently played for England Colts, U21, and appeared for the English President's side at the Madrid Sevens.

SCRASE, Laurence (Wing/centre)
Born Dubai, UAE, 10.9.72. 6', 12st 7lb. Career: Student. Rep hons: London (1). CLR: 2t-10pts. Joined Wasps as a Colt in 1990 and has developed into a useful utility back. Pole vaulter and 200m specialist in the summer.

SCRIVENER, Peter (Backrow)
Born 27.10.73. 6'5", 16st. Rep hons: England Students, U21, 18 Group. England 7s. CLR: 3t-15pts. Educated at Coopers & Co, Coburn, and currently a student at Brunel University, Peter starred in the England Schools grand slam of 1992 and appeared for the England Seven in Hong Kong in 1995.

SHEASBY, Christopher Mark Andrew (Backrow)
Born Windsor, 30.11.66. 6'3", 16st. Career: Teacher. Rep hons: England A/B (6, 4t-20pts), Students, Colts. England 7s. London (4, 4t-20pts). Barbarians (89-90). CLR: 8t-39pts. Shed his reputation of being only a sevens specialist and became a model of consistency for Quins in recent seasons. Educated at Radley, London University and Hughes Hall, Cambridge, where he gained two Blues (90, 91), Chris is now a maths teacher at Pangbourne College. Still enjoys sevens and represented England at the Hong Kong tournament in March 1996. Joined Wasps in the summer of 1996.

UFTON, Jonathan (Full-back)
Born Dulwich, London, 31.1.74. 6'1", 12st 7lb. Career: Student. Rep hons: England Students, U21, Colts, 18 Group. London (2). CLR: 6t, 7c, 2pg, 2dg-56pts. Joined Wasps from Old Whitgiftians having previously been a member of the England Schools 18 Group squad that achieved the grand slam in 1992. Surrey schoolboy cricketer and fencer, father Derek was a distinguished former Charlton Athletic and England soccer player and Kent wicketkeeper.

WHITE, Michael (Flanker)
Born Poole, Hants, 30.3.66. 6'1", 14st 8lb. Career: Sales executive with sportswear company. Rep hons: London (4). CLR: 11t-52pts. Underrated by selectors, 'Buster' is a tough no-nonsense flanker who commands the respect of opponents. Attended Purbeck School and played for Swanage before joining Wasps in 1985.

WORSLEY, Joe (Backrow)
Born 14.6.77. 6'5", 17st. Career: Student. Rep hons: England U21, Colts, 18 Group. Educated at Hitchin Boys HS, played his early rugby at Welwyn RFC and an outstanding member of England 18 Group side that won grand slam in 1994-95. Capped by England Colts and U21 last winter. Talented saxophonist when given the opportunity.

REVIEW

Wasps, rocked by the departure of Rob Andrew, Dean Ryan, Nick Popplewell and later Steve Bates to Newcastle, regained their composure impressively and should again challenge for top honours this season. Much credit is due to Lawrence Dallaglio, whose appointment as captain in succession to Ryan was an inspired choice among a predominantly young squad. The arrival of Gareth Rees at centre, Alex King, Matt Lewis and sprint king Paul Sampson can only strengthen an already potent back division, and the return to fitness of Norman Hadley and the signing of Damian Cronin, Mike Griffiths and Simon Mitchell will bolster the pack. Off the pitch, after much consideration, Wasps, having initially opted to become a PLC, were boosted in July by the announcement of a £3.5m investment by Chris Wright of Chrysallis Records, and a merger with Queens Park Rangers is possible. Former England captain Nigel Melville has been appointed director of rugby, while Rob Smith continues as coach.

WASPS in the Courage League 1995-96

Sep	9	Bristol	H	Won	33	5	D.Hopley(2T) Roiser(2T) Ryan(T) Andrew(C, 2P)
	16	Harlequins	A	Lost	20	29	Dunston(T) Andrew(5P)
	23	Saracens	H	Won	38	16	D.Hopley(T) Ryan(T) Scrivener(T) White(T) Andrew(3C, 2P) Ufton(2D)
	30	Sale	A	Won	25	18	Ryan(T) Scrivener(T) Andrew(2D, 3P)
Oct	7	Bath	H	Lost	6	15	Andrew(D, P)
	14	Gloucester	A	Won	26	15	Dallaglio(2T) Ryan(T) Andrew(C, 3P)
	21	Leicester	H	Lost	11	21	Ufton(T, 2P)
	28	Orrell	A	Lost	29	32	Braithwaite(2T) Scrivener(T) Gomarsall(T) Ufton(2C) Kinsey(T)
Nov	11	Bristol	A	Won	17	9	Roiser(T) Gregory(4P)
Jan	6	Saracens	A	Won	24	20	Gomarsall(T) P.Hopley(T) Penalty(T) Gregory(3C, P)
Feb	17	Bath	A	Lost	12	36	Gomarsall(T) Penalty(T) Gregory(C)
Mar	9	Harlequins	H	Lost	3	34	Gregory(P)
	23	Sale	H	Won	25	10	Greenstock(T) Scrase(T) White(T) Gregory(2C, 2P)
	30	Gloucester	H	Won	21	10	Roiser(2T) White(T) Braithwaite(3C)
Apr	6	Leicester	A	Lost	12	15	Gregory(2D, 2P)
	13	Orrell	H	Won	51	16	Dallaglio(2T) Braithwaite(T) Greenstock(T) Gregory(T, 5C, 2P) Roiser(T) Scrase(T)
	20	West Hartlepool	H	Won	52	12	Gregory(2T, 6C) Roiser(2T) Gomarsall(T) Greenstock(T) Greenwood(T) Molloy(T)
	27	West Hartlepool	A	Won	34	3	Gomarsall(T) Greenwood(T) Penalty(T) Ufton(T, 3C) White(T) Braithwaite(D)

WEST HARTLEPOOL

Formation of club: 1881
Ground: Brierten Lane, Hartlepool, Cleveland TS25 3DR. Tel: 01429 272640
Capacity: 6,100
Colours: Red, green and white hoops
Honours: –
Last season: CL1: 10th. Pilkington Cup: Q/F (lost 11-10 to London Irish)
Most capped player: Mark Ring (Wales) 32
Director of Rugby: Mark Ring
Coaches: Kevin Moseley, Dave Stubbs
Captain: TBA

BEAL, Paul Andrew (Prop)
Born 10.2.68. 5'11", 16st 4lb. Career: Appliance fitter. Educated at Saltscar Comprehensive, Redcar, Paul joined Redcar as a schoolboy, later moving to West Hartlepool. Made his first team debut at Orrell in the Pilkington Cup, December 1994. Three weeks later rewarded with Courage League debut. 30 first team appearances, 13 in League with one try.

BENSON, Jonathan (Utility back)
Born 11.1.76. 5'10", 11st 10lb. Career: Student. Rep hons: England Schools. North U21. CLR: 1c, 2pg-8pts. Educated at Barnard Castle School, Jonathan played for Durham City before joining West Hartlepool in 1995-96. Ironically, he celebrated his debut that season with a try against his old club. Made his Courage League debut against Sale, October 1995.

BOTHAM, Liam James (Centre)
Born Doncaster, 26.8.77. 6'. Career: Professional cricketer (Hampshire). Rep hons: Northern Schools 18 Group. England U19 cricket. Son of former England Test cricketer Ian. Educated at Rossall School, Liam's gifted rugby talents as a schoolboy were admired by former England captain Bill Beaumont, who recommended him to West Hartlepool. A dedicated trainer, he was given first team squad experience on the replacements bench in 1995-96. Expected to have to decide between cricket and rugby over the next two years.

CONNOLLY, Jamie (Centre)
Born New Zealand, 6.2.73. 5'10", 14st. Career: Seeking work visa. Signed from leading New Zealand club Canterbury in July 1996. Solid defender with deft handling skills. Clever organiser and tactician. Exceptionally quick.

DeJONG, Wayne (Prop)
Born Sydney, Australia, 16.7.68. 5'10", 17st 7lb. Career: PRP. Rep hons: Sydney Districts. Arrived at West Hartlepool at the end of August. Ex-captain of Sydney Districts and the Sydney club.

EARNSHAW, Russell (Flanker)
Born Billingham, 8.4.75. 6'4", 15st 3lb. Career: Year out from university. Rep hons: England U21, Students. Represented Cambridge in the 1996 Varsity match and has

made West Hartlepool his first club. Long-striding athletic player, exciting on the burst with fine ball-handling skills. Squad man but expected to push hard for first team recognition.

EVANS, Owen (Wing)
Born 22.10.65. 5'10", 13st 8lb. Career: Pipe fitter. Rep hons: Durham. CLR: 32t-139pts. One of West Hartlepool's longest-serving players, Owen made his debut in 1984-85 after graduating from the club's junior ranks. Educated at Brinkburn Comprehensive, Hartlepool, he passed the 150-try milestone with a hat-trick against Wakefield, November 1995. Scored his 30th Courage League try against Saracens, October 1995.

HARTLAND, Virgil (Prop)
Born Cinderford, 23.4.77. 5'10", 17st 7lb. Career: Builder and decorator. Rep hons: England Colts. Typifies West Hartlepool's commitment to recruiting young, talented players rather than has-beens. Joined in close season from Gloucester. Party trick is to crush beer-cans in nightclubs and hand them to the barman before leaving.

HERBERT, Timothy James (Hooker)
Born 28.9.67. 6', 15st 4lb. Career: Commercial executive. Rep hons: North. CLR: 2t-10pts. Played for Northern and Sydney suburb club Manley before joining West Hartlepool. Debut at Orrell, Pilkington Cup, December 1994 and made Courage League debut on same ground three weeks later. Tim has made 33 first team appearances (18 League), scoring five tries. Educated at Hurstpierpoint College, Sussex, and Newcastle Polytechnic.

JOHN, Christopher (Fly-half)
Born 19.2.73. Career: PRP. Rep hons: Welsh Students, Schools. One of a clutch of new signings after making big impression at previous club, Cardiff. Gifted footballer who is expected to break into the full Welsh squad over the next two seasons. Mark Ring expects him to make 'great impact' on Courage League One this season.

JOHN, Stephan (Centre)
Born Cardiff, 11.10.73. 5'10", 13st. Career: Stockbroker in Newcastle. Rep hons: Wales Schools. Educated at Loughborough where he obtained an economics degree, Steve broke into the Cardiff first team last season and represented them in Europe. Strong tackler with blistering pace.

KNOWLES, Toby Jason Kelly (Fly-half)
Born 26.5.74. 5'10", 13st 4lb. Career: Student. Rep hons: England U21, Colts. Midlands U21 squad. Educated at Ellesmere College, Shropshire and now studying at Newcastle University, Toby made his debut for West Hartlepool against Leeds in 1994-95. Courage League debut at Orrell, October 1995.

LEE, Craig Philip (Centre)
Born 5.5.71. 5'10", 13st 5lb. Career: Fireman. Rep hons: England U21. Durham. North. Educated at Grange School, Stockton, Craig played for Stockton before joining West Hartlepool. He made his first team debut in 1991-92 and has scored 88 points.

74

MITCHELL, David Charles (No 8)
Born 19.10.71. 6'4", 15st 7lb. Career: Engineer. Rep hons: England Schools. North. CLR: 3t-15pts. A former Harrogate player, Dave made his first team debut in 1992-93. Has made 83 appearances (56 League), scoring 13 tries.

MORGAN, Ivan Edward (Backrow)
Born New Zealand, 30.1.76. Joined West Hartlepool summer 1996 from New Zealand club Canterbury, where his driving commitment and competitive attitude had made him a first team regular. Expected to start in the first team for 1996-97 season.

MOSELEY, Kevin (Lock)
Born Caerphilly, 2.7.65. 6'8", 17st. Rep hons: Wales (11, NZ88), B. One of the Welsh League's most competitive locks for the past decade, Kevin brings a wealth of experience to West Hartlepool after joining in summer 1996. The former Pontypool and Newport player graduated from making ten appearances for Wales B to gain the first of his Welsh caps against New Zealand in 1988. A fierce scrummager, his uncompromising style could add a new dimension to the pack in his first season although injury and fitness has been a problem in recent years. He has also played for New Zealand club Bay of Plenty.

MURPHY, Christopher Ian (Lock)
Born Hull, 2.2.76. 6'8", 19st 4lb. Career: Student. Rep hons: England A (1, Ire96), U21, Schools, Colts 18 Group. North. Educated at Hymers College, Hull, and Northumbria University. Chris made his first team debut at Orrell in Pilkington Cup, December 1994. Courage League debut three weeks later on same ground. 20 first team appearances, 11 in the League.

PARKER, Neil Ashley (Fly-half)
Born 30.4.71. 6'1", 12st 12lb. Career: Student. Rep hons: Durham. North U21. Educated at Brinkburn Comprehensive, Hartlepool, and Hallam University. Ashley progressed from the club's flourishing junior ranks to make his first team debut in 1990-91 and Courage League debut at Wakefield 1993-94. He has made 40 first team appearances scoring 113 points. 14 League appearances.

PEACOCK, Andrew (Hooker)
Born Newport, 3.12.68. Rep hons: Wales U19, U18. Monmouthshire. Educated at Gwent College of Higher Education, Hartlepool, and Newport. Powerfully built with superb control of the lineout throw, he is regarded as one of the best strikers in Wales and is highly mobile in the loose. Said to be 'relishing' the challenge of Courage League One action after joining West Hartlepool for the 1996-97 season.

RING, Mark (Fly-half)
Born 15.10.62. 6', 12st 10lb. Career: West Hartlepool's Director of Rugby. Rep hons: Wales (32, Eng83, 1t, 3c, 8pg-34pts). Barbarians (84-85). The former Wales, Cardiff and Pontypool player, Mark has joined West Hartlepool as player-coach. One of Wales' most impressive creative players and crowd pleasers in recent seasons. Eligible to play his first game for 'Wests' against London Irish. Plagued by various knee injuries over the years.

SILVA, Matthew (Full-back)
Born Cardiff, 15.3.70. 6'1", 14st 7lb. Career: PRP. Rep hons: Wales Rugby League. Wales B squad. One of the first rugby league players allowed back into union when he joined Newbridge from Halifax for 1995-96 season. Joined West Hartlepool from Newbridge in August. Strong, powerful, massive kicker Played junior rugby in Cardiff with Mark Ring.

STABLER, John (Fly-half)
Born Hartlepool, 5.2.63. Rep hons: North. CLR. 11t, 76c, 118pg, 8dg-579pts. John has played all his rugby at West Hartlepool. Returns this season after suffering injury and pleased coaches with his sharpness in pre-season training at Loughborough. Astute tactician with ability to control play and kick penalty goals with unruffled calm, John has represented the North since making his debut in 1986.

WESTGARTH, Kevin Michael (Lock)
Born Durham, 6.5.61. 6'7", 17st. Career: Sports development officer Rep hons. North-umberland (captain). North. CLR: 2t-8pts (Newcastle Gosforth). Former clubs Tynedale, Northern, Gosforth. Kevin made his first team debut in 1991-92. Made 102 appearances (57 League), scoring three tries.

WOOD, Michael Denis (Wing)
Born 15.7.76. 5'11", 12st 2lb. Career: Student. Rep hons: England 18 Group. CLR. 2t-10pts. Educated at Sedbergh School and Newcastle University, Mike made his debut against Newcastle Gosforth in February 1996. Courage League debut against Leicester away.

REVIEW

A season rich in optimism collapsed under strain imposed by the new professional era. Players left and the club came bottom of Courage League One with no points. The struggle was illustrated best by two meetings against Wasps. Of the team that played an abandoned match against them in November, only four survived to play the rearranged fixture five months later. The loss of Scotland's captain Rob Wainwright through a career move was another blow, and club pride in England A squad call-ups for Tim Stimpson, Andrew Blyth, Mike Shelley, Chris Murphy and Rob Leach was offset by the departure of four of them to new clubs. Murphy was 'best player' and hooker Tim Herbert the only ever-present. Stimpson, leading scorer with 110 points, narrowly missed a full England debut but his goal-kicking fallibility arguably cost the club wins at Saracens and Gloucester, after his brilliant running for tries had made victory possible. Welsh international Mark Ring joined as player and coaching director but a knee operation restricted his appearances.

WEST HARTLEPOOL in the Courage League 1995-96

Sep	9	Bath	H	Lost	15	20	Stimpson(4P) Hodder(D)
	16	Bristol	A	Lost	3	12	Stimpson(P)
	23	Gloucester	H	Lost	19	27	Brown(T) Stimpson(C, 4P)
	30	Harlequins	A	Lost	18	34	Hodder(T) Stimpson(T, C, P) Parker(P)

Oct	7	Leicester	H	Lost	12	19	Stimpson(4P)
	14	Saracens	A	Lost	30	31	Blyth(T) Evans(T) Shelley(T) Stimpson(T, 2C, 2P)
	21	Orrell	A	Lost	10	20	Mitchell(T) Stimpson(C, P)
	28	Sale	H	Lost	11	29	Wainwright(T) Stimpson(2P)
Nov	11	Bath	A	Lost	22	34	Evans(T) Evans(T) Shelley(T) Stimpson(2C, P)
Jan	6	Gloucester	A	Lost	16	17	Shelley(T) Stimpson(T, 2P)
Feb	17	Leicester	A	Lost	15	48	Stimpson(2T, C, P)
Mar	23	Harlequins	H	Lost	21	91	Evans(T) Herbert(T) Wood(T) Parker(2P)
	30	Saracens	H	Lost	31	41	Ions(T) Lee(T) Wood(T) Oliphant(2C, D, 3P)
Apr	6	Orrell	H	Lost	22	44	Blyth(T) Shelley(T) Thompson(T) Parker(2C, P)
	13	Sale	A	Lost	13	44	Penalty(T) Benson(C, 2P)
	20	Wasps	A	Lost	12	52	Patterson(T) Thompson(T) Oliphant(C)
	27	Wasps	H	Lost	3	34	Parker(P)
May	5	Bristol	H	Lost	15	37	Parker(T) Patterson(T) Oliphant(C, P)

Courage League Two

BEDFORD

Formation of Club: 1886
Ground: Goldington Road, Bedford MK40 3JY Tel. 01234 347511/354619
Capacity: 7,500
Colours: Oxford and Cambridge blue hoops
Honours: Pilkington Cup: Winners: 1975. Courage League. Division 3 champions
1994-95
Last season: CL2: 10th. Pilkington Cup: 5th Round (lost 37-0 to Bristol)
Most capped player: Jeff Probyn (England) 37
Director of Rugby: Geoff Cooke
Coach: Paul Turner
Captain: TBA

ALLEN, Paul (Wing)
Born Poole, 5.11.71. 5'11", 14st Career: Policeman. CLR 2t-10pts. Joined Bedford as a
colt in 1989-90. He has made 50 first team appearances and established a reputation for
solid defence.

BASRA, Singh (Prop)
Born Hitchin, 23.6.72. 5'8", 16st 7lb. Career: Shop manager CLR. 1t-5pts. Joined
Bedford 1993-94. Has made 53 first team appearances, six in the Courage League last
season where his scrummaging impressed.

BROWN, Simon (Prop)
Born Oxford, 31.10.72. 5'10", 16st. Career: Sports officer. Rep hons: England U21, 18
Group. London. CLR: 1t-5pts (Harlequins). Joined Bedford this summer from Harlequins where his progress was restricted by lack of opportunity. Expected to figure prominently at Bedford after joining an influx of new talent at Goldington Road for the 1996-97
season. Educated at Peers School and Radley, he is a hard-scrummaging young prop.

CHANDLER, Jim (Threequarter)
Born Cambridge, 4.1.67. 5'11", 15st. Career: Bricklayer. CLR. 5t-22pts. Joined Bedford
in 1984-85 as a colt. Played three Courage League games last season, scoring one try.
Has made 191 first team appearances. Considerable skill in attack and defence.

CLOUGH, Francis John (Centre)
Born Wigan, 1.11.62. 6'1", 14st 10lb. Career: Research engineer. Rep hons: England (4,
Ire86), XV (1, It90), B (4, It85, 3t-12pts), U23, 18 Group. Barbarians (85-86). London.
Lancashire. CLR: 10t-40pts (Wasps), 3t-15pts (Bedford). Fran was educated at St John
Rigby School and Durham University. Awarded four Blues at Cambridge University
(1984-87), once as captain. Orrell was his first club, where he was called up by Lancashire,
England Under-23 and England B before first appearing for England against Ireland in
1986. He went to Australia with England for the inaugural World Cup in 1987, playing
against the USA. He shared the dressing room at Cambridge University and Wasps with
Rob Andrew. He joined Bedford from Wasps, scoring try on debut. Two tries in six
Courage League games last season. Has made 32 appearances for Bedford.

78

COOK, Marcus (Full-back)
Born Cuckfield, 14.7.75. 6'4", 14st. Career: PE teacher CLR: 5t, 1dg-28pts. Joined Bedford from Burton-on-Trent in 1993-94. He made 25 appearances (16 Courage League) last season, scoring four tries, one dropped goal, two penalties (29pts). Landslide win in 'Player of Year' poll 1995-96 season. Needs four first team appearances to reach 50. Superb defence, especially when under a high ball.

DEANS, Matt (Flanker)
Born Zimbabwe, 27.5.71. 6'3", 15st. Career: Policeman. CLR: 5t-25pts. Joined Bedford from Cambridge in 1992-93. Played nine Courage League games last season, scoring one try. He has made 79 first team appearances. Polled third in 'Player of the Year' 1995-96 season. Strong-running powerhouse in the pack who attracted much interest from Courage League One clubs.

ELWINE, Anthony (Centre)
Born Hartlepool, 19.8.70. 6'1", 15st 7lb. Career: Transport manager CLR: 3t-15pts (West Hartlepool). Educated at Brierton Comprehensive, Hartlepool, Tony has joined Bedford from West Hartlepool. A product of 'Wests' junior system, he made his first team debut at Brierton Lane in the 1988-89 season. He was a Courage League ever-present in 1994-95 season.

ETHERIDGE, John (2nd Row)
Born Gloucester, 8.6.65. England B (2, It89). South West Division. Made a breakthrough in 1989 when making two appearances for England B. Also made the first of eight appearances for the South West Division in 1989. Joined Bedford in the summer from Northampton.

FARR, John (Scrum-half)
Born 20.4.70. 5'9", 12st 7lb. Career: PE teacher Rep hons. Cheshire, U21 Midlands. John returns to Bedford from Winnington Park He made three appearances for the Midland Division last season.

FINNIE, Andrew (Fly-half)
Born Luton, 22.10.64. 6', 13st 7lb. Career: Insurance broker. CLR: 4t, 84c, 200pg, 23dg-855pts. Club record points-scorer with 2,617. Broke Courage League points-scoring record in the 1994-95 season with 228 points, beating Simon Hogg's 222 for Division Four Clifton in 1993-94. Last season scored 122 points in 16 appearances with one try, 24 conversions, three dropped goals and 20 penalties. Courage League 1995-96, 12 appearances, one try, 16 conversions, three dropped goals, 13 penalties, 85 points. First played for Bedford as a colt in 1982-83. He has made 322 appearances.

HEWITT, Paul (Backrow)
Born Pontypool, 4.10.71. 6'2", 16st 5lb. Career· Biologist. Rep hons: Wales U19, Students. Monmouthshire. CLR: 1t-5pts. Paul, who studied Biological Sciences at Manchester Metro University, learned his rugby under Bobby Windsor, John Perkins et al at Pontypool and was probably the quickest forward at Sale. Sevens enthusiast, he represented Wales in the 1996 World Students Cup. Joined Bedford in August 1996.

HOWE, Mark (Hooker)
Born Bedford, 1.1.58. 5'10", 16st. Career: Farmer. Rep hons: England U23, Barbarians (87-88), Midlands. CLR: 8t-37pts. Has made the second highest number of appearances (478) for Bedford. Mark sprang to prominence in 1980 when he was offered an England trial. He made his first appearance for Bedford in 1976-77 while still a pupil at Bedford Modern School. Club's longest serving player.

HYDE, Ben (Scrum-half)
Born Cheltenham, 14.3.75. 5'6", 11st 7lb. Career: Student. Rep hons: England U16, U18 and Colts. Ben was a member of the South West Under-21 side that beat Leinster. He joined Bedford from Cheltenham in 1995-96 and made three Courage League appearances. Fast, elusive, good trainer, big tackler.

KEMBLE, Peter (Flanker)
Born Northampton, 16.6.70. 6', 14st. Career: Wholesaler. First played for the club in 1989-90 when making a large impression on junior rugby as a member of the Bedford School side. University commitments interrupted his Bedford career but he returned in 1993-94 as a ferocious tackler with plenty of pace.

MANSELL, Leigh (Prop)
Born 13.1.70. 6'2", 16st 3lb. Career: Salesman. CLR: 2t-10pts. First played for Bedford in 1989-90 when still a Colt. He played two seasons at Leicester before returning to Bedford where he has made 112 first team appearances, four in the Courage League last season, scoring one try. Powerful, outstanding in the loose.

OFFIAH, Martin (Wing)
Born London, 29.12.66. 6'2", 14st 4lb. Career: PRP. Rep hons: Great Britain Rugby League (33, Fr88, 26t-104pts). England (4, Wa92, 4t-16pts). Barbarians (87). Essex Second XI cricket. Joined Bedford and London Broncos in a sensational double move from Wigan early in August and has now set his sights on a full England rugby union cap. Educated at Wolverstone Hall, Martin was an outstanding young wing for Rosslyn Park and starred for the Londoners in two Middlesex Sevens tournaments before representing the Penguins at the Hong Kong Sevens. Had just scored a hat-trick for the Barbarians in their annual game against Cardiff in 1987 when Widnes RL swooped and the rest is history. Scored in 11 consecutive Division One fixtures in his opening season for Widnes and scored 44 tries in that campaign to lead the Division's scorers. By 1989 had completed a century of tries and passed the 200 mark in 1991 with a hat-trick against Wakefield. Transferred to Wigan in 1992 for a record £440,000. Reached 300 career tries in 1993 but suffered a nasty dislocated shoulder playing for Easts in Australia. Scored a sensational 100m try in the Challenge Cup final against Leeds in 1994, and claimed 400 career tries when playing against London Broncos last season. Finished the 1995-96 season as the League's highest try scorer for a sixth time.

OLIVER, Matthew (Centre)
Born Northampton, 30.11.76. 6'1", 13st 7lb. Career: Student. Rep hons: England Schools. East Midlands Colts. CLR: 8t-40pts. Another product of the prolific Bedford School nursery. Joined the club in 1994-95 while still featuring heavily in schools rugby. Matthew was a distinguished member of the 1995 East Midlands Colts Championship winning side. Played 16 Courage League games last season and was top try scorer.

PEPPER, Martin (Hooker/flanker)
Born Beverley, 14.12.67. 5'11", 15st 7lb. Career: Schoolmaster. Rep hons: England A, Students. North (2). CLR: Headingley (8t-32pts), Nottingham (5t-21pts). Switched to hooker last season with some success, Martin captained England in the 1992 World Students Cup from openside wing forward. Educated at Nunthorpe GS and Carnegie College, he made his Quins debut against Blackrock in September 1993. Joined Bedford in August 1996.

PROBYN, Jeffrey Alan (Prop)
Born London, 27.4.56. 5'10", 16st. Career: Director of Probros. Rep hons: England (37, Fr88, 3t-12pts), England B (4). London. Herts, Middlesex, Surrey. The prop who won't go away, Jeff joins Bedford at the age of 40 having previously done stalwart service with Old Albanians, Ilford Wanderers, Streatham/Croydon, Richmond, Askeans and Wasps. Unusual but hugely effective scrummager, Jeff made his international debut, aged 31, against France in 1988, and quickly became a key member of England's awesome pack of that era. Played a significant part in 1991 Grand Slam effort, appeared throughout RWC91 and was ever-present in the 1992 Grand Slam. England tried to retire him the following season but his form was such that he warranted selection for the 1993 Five Nations. A regular with Wasps IIs last season, as well as a committee man at Sudbury, Probyn's experience, on and off the field, should help.

RAYER, Michael Anthony (Full-back)
Born Cardiff, 21.7.65. 5'10", 13st 3lb. Career: Sales representative. Rep hons: Wales (21, WS91, 4t, 1pg-23pts), B (2, Fr87), Youth. A turbulent career marred by serious injury and ill-luck. Knee injury 1991 delayed entry to big time. Robbed of a British Lions tour chance when dropped by Wales in 1993. Played in two World Cup play-off qualifiers against Romania and Italy before breaking his leg for Cardiff and missing 1995 World Cup. Shared top Five Nations try-scoring honours 1994 with Nigel Walker and Philippe Saint-Andre. Played for Llandaff North, father Alec's old club, before joining Cardiff. Became first player to command a transfer fee for a switch between rugby union clubs when he joined Bedford from Cardiff in July 1996. The clubs agreed £15,000 fee after a lengthy wrangle.

RENNELL, Mark (No 8)
Born Stratford-on-Avon, 17.1.71. 6'3", 17st. Career: Self-employed builder Rep hons. England A (2, BCol93, 1t-5pts), U21 CLR: 11t-48pts. Mark first played for Bedford in 1990-91. Left to join Rugby Lions for one season but returned to Bedford in 1994-95. Tremendous ability but yet to come to terms with the demands of the new professional age and commitment to training. Has been given personal fitness trainer for 1996-97 campaign. Four Courage League games last season, scoring one try. He has made 87 first team appearances. Visionary, superb handling skills but one of the great enigmas of English rugby.

SHARP, Mark (Hooker)
Born Milton Keynes, 4.5.69. 5'8", 14st. Career: Engineer First played 1991-92 He has made 68 appearances. Travels from Milton Keynes. Mark made 15 Courage League appearances in 1995-96. Strong, powerful scrummager.

SIMPSON, Karl (Lock)
Born Stockton, 27.9.71. 6'6", 17st. Career Student CLR 2t-10pts. Has had experience of New Zealand's domestic rugby. He joined the club from Harlequins. Played 10 Courage League games last season. First-rate lineout jumper.

SKINGSLEY, Ian Richard (Flanker/No 8)
Born Swindon, 16.11.66. 6'4", 16st 7lb. Career: Sales rep for brick company. Rep hons:
East Midlands. CLR: 8t-37pts. Educated at Lincroft Junior (Oakley) and Sharnbrook
Upper Schools, Bedfordshire, Ian has represented the East Midlands for four years. He
has been a member of Bedford since the age of 12. Brief spells away from Bedford,
playing in New Zealand for Wellington, and for Selkirk (1989-90). An all-round
sportsman, Ian has rowed in the National Championships at Nottingham and Henley.
Played 11 Courage League games last season, scoring one try. He has made 225
appearances for the club.

SMITH, Simon (Fly-half)
Born 29.1.64. 5'8", 11st 5lb. Career: Sales executive. Rep hons: England B (2, 1t86, 2c,
1pg-7pts), 18 Group. London. CLR: 1t, 4c, 12pg, 4dg-60pts (Richmond), 1c, 5pg-17pts
(Bedford). Another talented product of Bedford School, Simon captained England
Schools. Took advantage of Bedford's youth policy, joining the club in 1981-82. Left to
play at Richmond and was forced to quit playing for three years because of a serious
elbow injury before returning to Bedford last season. Played three Courage League
games last season, scoring 17 points. He has made 66 first team appearances. Strong,
elusive, fast.

STONE, Richard (Scrum-half)
Born 4.11.72. 5'10", 13st 7lb. CLR: 2t-10pts. First played for Bedford in 1989-90 while
still a member of the Bedford School first team. Attended Loughborough University,
rejoining the club in 1995-96 and scoring eight tries in all competitions. He has made 20
appearances and improved with every match.

SUBBIANI, Robert (Wing)
Born Clun, 19.10.65. 5'11", 11st 4lb. Career: PE teacher. Rep hons: Wales U20, U21,
U23, Students. Barbarians (95-96). Pembrokeshire Students. Midlands. CLR: 1t-5pts
(Askeans); 10t-50pts (Bedford). Rob joined Bedford from Askeans in 1993-94 but he
first played senior rugby for Swansea from 1987-90, a period in which he began to
interest the Welsh selectors. Searing pace earned him a place in the Welsh Schools 100
metres team. He has made 55 appearances, 10 in the Courage League last season,
scoring four tries.

TAPPER, Ashley (Fly-half)
Born 31.8.69. 5'10", 12st 3lb. Career: PE teacher. Rep hons: Oxford Blue 1991. CLR: 1c,
6pg-20pts. Ashley joined Bedford from Bath in 1991-92. Made four Courage League
appearances last season. Twenty-one games for Bedford, scoring four tries, with one
conversion and four penalties. Superb defence built on speed and anticipation.

THOMPSON, Ross (Back five forward)
Born Bedford, 4.12.71. 6'4", 15st 7lb. Career: Computer operator. Rep hons: Midlands
Youth, U21. CLR: 1t-5pts. Formerly with Northampton, Ross joined Bedford in
1994-95. Ross played 14 Courage League games last season, scoring one try. He has
made 33 appearances showing versatility and reliability.

TURNER, Paul (Fly-half)
Born Newport, 16.2.59. 5'10", 11st 8lb. Career: Bedford player-coach. Rep hons: Wales
(3, Ire89). Barbarians (86-87). North. CLR: 3t, 53c, 47pg, 13dg-301 pts (Sale). Played
for Newbridge where he was first chosen for the Welsh squad. Picked as a replacement

in the Five Nations Championship match against Ireland in 1989, he gained full caps that season against France and England. Joined Sale in September 1992. Scored 144 Courage League points for Sale 1993-94 and 92 in 1994-95. Sale's record Courage League scorer with more than 300 points, Paul also holds the all-time club scoring records at Newbridge (2,296) and Newport (992). Drafted in to strengthen the North divisional side last season and produced outstanding performances for Sale as player-coach before receiving an injury. Bedford's player-coach for the 1996-97 season.

UPEX, Mark (Lock)
Born Dry Drayton, 1.4.66. 6'6", 16st 7lb. Career: Policeman. Played for Loughborough University before making his first senior appearance for Bedford in 1986-87 when still a Colt. He has made 220 appearances, 17 in the Courage League last season.

WHETSTONE, Benjamin Marcus (Centre/Wing)
Born Holbeach, 29.6.70. Career: Engineer. Rep hons: Midlands. CLR: 15t, 1dg-78pts. Ben played soccer until he was 18 and then joined Ely Rugby Club, for whom he played from 1988-91. He joined Bedford in 1992-93. Spent the summer of 1994 playing for the Belfast Club in Christchurch, New Zealand. Scored four tries in 20 matches in all competitions last season, three of them in the Courage League in 13 games. He has made 102 appearances.

WRIGHT, Chris (Lock)
Born Bedford, 20.11.69. 6'7", 18st. Career: Accountant. First played for Bedford in 1993-94. The elder brother of Matthew, another Bedford player, he has made a total of 13 appearances. Excellent number two jumper.

WRIGHT, Matthew (Flanker)
Born Bedford, 28.2.72. 6'4", 16st 1lb. Career: Executive. Rep hons: England Schools, Colts. Younger brother of Chris, Matthew joined Bedford in 1993-94. He has represented Northampton, Loughborough and Cambridge University where he failed to win a Blue. Played two Courage League games last season. He has made 14 appearances. Fierce tackler.

REVIEW

A season of turmoil and change left the club's 700 members anxious for the future. First team coach Mike Rafter became a casualty of the new professional era, resigning in November 1995 because he felt he could not give enough time to the job. Encouraging performances against Northampton, Newcastle, London Irish and London Scottish were offset by poor displays against Moseley, Nottingham and Wakefield. Beat Worcester to reach the Pilkington Cup fifth round before losing to Bristol. Full-back Marcus Cook won 'Best Player' award from Matthew Oliver and Matt Deans. Bedford became a private limited company in June 1996 when Sports Network Europe, owned by Frank Warren and Chris Roberts, offered £2.25m over five years. Ex-England manager Geoff Cooke was appointed for 1996-97 season to work closely with new player-coach Paul Turner. Made modern rugby history when signing Mike Rayer from Cardiff in July 1996 for £15,000, the first player to command a transfer fee for a switch between rugby union clubs, and then immediately went in pursuit of Wigan RL star Martin Offiah in a joint deal with London Broncos.

BEDFORD in the Courage League 1995-96

Sep	9	Wakefield	A	Lost	23	32	Oliver(T) Subbiani(T) Finnie(2C, 3P)
	16	Waterloo	H	Drew	10	10	Subbiani(T) Finnie(C, P)
	23	Blackheath	H	Won	21	18	Finnie(T, C, 3P) Oliver(T)
	30	Newcastle	A	Won	30	23	Oliver(T) Skingsley(T) Subbiani(T) Thompson(T) Finnie(2C, 2D)
Oct	7	Northampton	H	Lost	17	49	Whetstone(2T) Farr(T) Finnie(C)
	14	London Scottish	A	Lost	10	50	Farr(T) Finnie(C, D)
	21	London Irish	H	Lost	29	46	Alston(2T) Oliver(T) Whetstone(T) Finnie(3C, P)
	28	Moseley	A	Lost	18	27	Oliver(T) Subbiani(T) Finnie(C, 2P)
Nov	4	Nottingham	H	Won	20	12	Oliver(T) Roach(T) Finnie(2C, 2P)
	11	Wakefield	H	Won	20	13	Alston(T) Deans(T) Oliver(T) Stone(T)
Jan	6	Blackheath	A	Lost	8	23	Rennell(T) Finnie(P)
	13	Waterloo	A	Lost	24	48	Clough(2T) Goldsmith(T) Stone(T) Finnie(2C)
Mar	9	Newcastle	H	Lost	6	24	Tapper(2P)
	23	Northampton	A	Lost	0	48	
	30	London Scottish	H	Won	21	19	Allen(T) Cook(T, D) Tapper(C, 2P)
Apr	6	London Irish	A	Lost	13	25	Chandler(T) Smith(C, 2P)
	13	Moseley	H	Lost	8	23	Mansell(T) Smith(P)
	27	Nottingham	A	Lost	11	30	Oliver(T) Smith(2P)

BLACKHEATH

Formation of club: 1858
Ground: The Rectory Field, Charlton Road, Blackheath, London SE3 8SR.
  Tel: 0181 858 1578
Capacity: 3,000
Colours: Red and black hoops, blue collar
Honours: Middlesex Sevens: Winners: 1932, 58
Last season: CL2: 7th. Pilkington Cup: 4th round (lost 19-9 to Coventry)
Most capped player: C.N. Lowe (England) 25
Director of Rugby: Iain Exeter
Coach: Danny Vaughan
Captain: John Gallagher

ATKINSON, Andy (Centre)
Born Nairobi, Kenya, 25.6.64. 6', 13st 9lb. Career: Independent financial adviser. Strong lad. Stands the ball well up in the tackle. Reliable goal-kicker with a powerful and accurate left foot. Joined Blackheath 1995-96 from Wakefield where he was a first team regular, making more than 200 appearances. Second team 'Player of the Year' last season. Played a few first team matches.

BOOTH, Toby (Flanker)
Born 6.2.70. 5'11", 15st 6lb. CLR: 4t-20pts. Joined Blackheath in 1991. Club captain 1994-95. Missed most of last season with a bad knee injury. Expects to mount serious first team challenge 1996-97 after returning to full fitness. Fine sevens player. Mobile and quick, with good hands.

BRAITHWAITE, Chris (Fly-half)
Born 26.12.71. 5'11", 12st 10lb. Rep hons: London. CLR: 6t, 8c, 8pg, 2dg-76pts (Wasps). Joined Blackheath from Wasps in summer 1996. Quick and safe hands gained him London Division appearances in 1995. Playing prospects at Wasps suffered when they signed England A team player Alex King.

CAMPLIN, Paul (Scrum-half)
Chosen for the final England Colts trial in 1995-96. Member of England Colts squad. Starts 1996-97 season in Blackheath development squad.

CORLESS, Hadyn (Wing)
Born New Zealand, 1.4.62. 6'3", 15st 7lb. Rep hons: Kent. CLR: 2t-8pts (Askeans). Played for Askeans for five seasons before joining Blackheath midway through 1995-96 season. Badly injured cruciate ligaments playing for Askeans in 1994-95 season. Made unscheduled Blackheath debut against Cambridge University when half-fit, as late replacement for player taken ill en route to match. Fully recovered after surgery, expected to play leading first team role in 1996-97.

COYNE, Owen (Centre)
Born 24.8.70. 5'10", 14st. Career: Engineering company salesman. Rep hons: England U21. CLR: 2t-10pts. Club captain 1993-94. Joined Blackheath 1991. Sound in defence, he has sharp eye for 'the gap' on attack.

EKOKU, Abi (Wing)
Born London. 6'5", 17st 5lb. Career: PRP. Elder brother of Wimbledon soccer player Efan, Abi joined Blackheath in August 1996 from Halifax Rugby League club. He is a former London Broncos player and has thrown the discus for Great Britain. Superb tackler, keeping Martin Offiah scoreless when they met last season.

FRIDAY, Michael (Scrum-half)
Born 25.4.72. 5'9", 12st 11b. Career: Chartered surveyor. Rep hons: England Sevens. CLR: 15t-75pts. Club captain 1995-96 season. Joined Blackheath 1993. Represented Public School Wanderers at Safari Sevens, Nairobi, August 1996. Fastest sprinter in the club over first 15 metres. Devastating at the sevens game, making gaps for himself and others with electrifying pace. Restless, energetic, opinionated rugby enthusiast.

FURNEAUX, Gary (Second row)
Born 25.3.67. 6'5", 18st. Career: Garage owner in Folkestone. Sustained fractured eye socket from a raised elbow against Bedford in an acrimonious lineout incident at the start of 1995-96 and missed most of last season. Stalwart member of Blackheath's Courage League 3 promotion season 1994-95. Originally a hockey player, he was a late starter at rugby. Robust, fully committed.

GALLAGHER, John (Full-back)
Born Blackheath, 29.1.69. 6'1", 13st 2lb. Career: Teacher. Rep hons: New Zealand (18, It87, 13t-52pts). Barbarians (95-96). Ireland A 96. Kent. John first made his mark at St Joseph's Academy in south-east London. Emigrated to Wellington, New Zealand, and, like his father, became a policeman and outstanding full-back for the All Blacks, scoring 13 tries in 18 Tests. Returned to England to play rugby league for Leeds and London, but took advantage of RFU decision last season to ease ban on league players applying for reinstatement to union. Barred from competitive rugby in England before 1996-97 season. Played 'friendlies' for Harlequins 1995-96 and represented Irish Exiles to compensate for enforced absence. Joined Blackheath early 1996. Appointed Blackheath captain for 1996-97, giving coaching back-up for Danny Vaughan.

GRIFFIN, Jonathan (Fly-half/full-back)
Born 4.10.72. 5'9", 12st. Rep hons: Ireland Schools. Joined Blackheath from London Irish summer 1996. Played for London Irish development and second team 1995-96. One for the future, not expected to make first team squad at the start 1996-97.

GRIFFITHS, Matt (Wing)
Born 30.3.72. 5'8", 13st 4lb. Career: Journalist. Rep hons: England U21, Sevens. London. CLR: 10t-49pts. Began career at Blackheath and became established first team right winger before joining Wasps for 1995-96 season. Has returned to the Rectory Field for 1996-97 after failing to establish first team place at Sudbury. Fast, elusive, strong, sound in defence.

HANSLIP, Mark (Wing)
Born London 4.5.73. 5'10", 11st 7lb. Career: PE teacher. CLR: 7t-35pts. Joined Blackheath from Greenwich University three seasons ago. Fast over 50 metres. Needs to improve physique for modern game.

HARRIS, Michael (No 8)

Born 7.9.67. 6'4", 17st 1lb. Career: Printer. Rep hons: England U21, Colts, 18 Group, 16 Group, Schools. CLR: 9t, 7c, 15pg-100pts. Micky joined Blackheath from Wasps in 1993 and has become cornerstone of the pack. Elected 'Player of the Year' 1995-96 season. Strong, dynamic forward. Keen singer majoring in Elvis Presley impressions.

HOARE, Mitch (Full-back)

Born Coventry, 28.12.73. 5'10", 13st 7lb. Career: Media executive. Joined Blackheath 1995-96 from Coventry. Launched his career at Wasps. Struggled with injury last season. Yet to produce best form at Rectory Field. Expected to stake claim for regular first team place 1996-97.

HORROBIN, Ashley (Centre)

Born 5.1.70. 5'9", 14st 7lb. Rep hons: Welsh Students RL. Joined Blackheath midway through 1995-96 season but after playing a few midweek games for the club's development team was not available for selection. Returned for pre-season training summer 1996 and is rated good enough to mount first team challenge this season.

HOWARD, Sam (Fly-half)

Born 31.7.74. 6', 13st 7lb. Career: Teacher. Rep hons: England U21, Students, 16 Group. CLR: 5t, 29c, 67pg, 9dg-311pts. Educated at Brunel University, Sam joined Blackheath in 1993 and has been regular outside-half since arrival. Erratic form frustrates club coaches.

HOWE, Bobby (Hooker)

Born Beckenham, 12.4.63. 5'8", 14st. Career: Pipe fitter. Rep hons: Kent. Launched his career at Blackheath. Left to join Askeans for one season but returned to Rectory Field 1995-96, winning first team place in second half of season. Nominated 'Squad Player of the Year' 1995-96. Returned from honeymoon July 1996 for pre-season training.

JENSEN, Tim (Fly-half)

Born Australia. Graduate of the Australian Rugby Academy, he joined Blackheath from Wasps in summer 1996. First year at Oxford University will delay Tim's availability at Blackheath until December 1996. Spent two seasons at Wasps without becoming first team regular. Partly compensated for lack of opportunity by playing regularly for Public School Wanderers. Member of Oxford University's Malaysian tour party August 1996.

JOHNSON, Steven (Second row)

Born 10.10.73. 6'6", 15st 7lb. Rep hons: Wales U21, U20. Joined Blackheath from Swansea in summer 1996. Knee injury forced year out of the game 1995-96 season. An operation will delay start to his new Blackheath career but coaches expect him to mount first team challenge in second half 1996-97 season.

JOWETT, Dean (Full-back)

Born 10.10.74. 6'1", 13st. Rep hons: England Students, U21, Colts. CLR: 2t-10pts. Educated at St Mary's University, Twickenham, Dean captained England Students. Joined Blackheath 1995. Fast, reliable left foot, receiving considerable coaching assistance from John Gallagher.

McCORDUCK, Robert (Backrow/second row)
Born 9.1.72. 6'4", 16st. Rep hons: Welsh Universities. Played for Abertillery before agreeing to join Blackheath for 1995-96 season. Changed his mind, played one more season at The Park, and makes postponed start at the Rectory Field for the 1996-97 campaign.

NEIL-DWYER, Dominic (Centre)
Born 24.1.71. 5'10", 13st 11lb. Career: Advertising executive. Rep hons: England 16 Group. CLR: 1t-5pts. Joined Blackheath 1994 but broke an ankle badly in his first season. Recovered to gain first team place 1995-96 but has yet to show full potential.

PARK, Andy (Fly-half)
Career: Student. Rep hons: Ulster. Ireland Schools. Former captain of Ireland Schools, Andy joined Blackheath in summer 1996 from Northern Ireland Park Football Club. Student at Greenwich University. Blackheath coaches have 'great hopes' for early first team breakthrough.

PAWSON, Chris (Centre)
Born Exeter. 5'11", 13st 5lb. Career: Student. Rep hons: England U21, Colts, Schools. A student at Exeter University, Chris was added to the Blackheath squad in the close season. A charismatic leader, he has captained England Schools and England Colts. Powerful, strong, with quick hands.

POPE, Stephen (Prop)
Born 24.11.73. 5'11", 17st 2lb. Rep hons: England 16 Group. London U21. Joined Blackheath from Wasps for 1995-96 season and played several first team matches. Departures increase his first team hopes this season. Recommended to increase weight at the end of 1995-96, Steve's bulkier frame surprised coaches on return for pre-season training. Ordered to lose weight for 1996-97 start.

RIDGEWAY, Colin (Hooker)
Born Strood, 22.4.72. 5'11", 15st 7lb. Career: Engineering company financial controller. CLR: 5t-25pts. Joined Blackheath from school and first team regular for four seasons. Missed most of second half of last season with a knee injury. Surgery has cured problem. Worked hard pre-season to re-establish himself as first choice hooker for 1996-97.

SHADBOLT, Paul (Prop)
Born 1.10.73. 5'10", 17st 10lb. Career: Cleaning company owner. Rep hons: England U21, Development squad. CLR: 5t-25pts. Joined Blackheath from Saracens 1994-95. Dynamic prop in the new mould. Fast over 30 metres with safe ball-handling skills. Could become England possible but all-action style has caused catalogue of injury problems.

SHORTLAND, Steve (Second row)
Born 12.1.68. 6'7", 18st 6lb. Career: College lecturer. Rep hons: England Students, U21. CLR: 1t-4pts (Northampton); 1t-4pts (Harlequins); 3t-15pts (Wasps). Joined Blackheath from Wasps in summer 1996. Missed last season with serious knee injury received on tour to Australia. Survived punishing track and weight routines pre-season under

coach supervision. Said to be 'strong' and confident again. Trained with full England squad 1990-91.

SMITH, Richard (Centre)
Born 14.6.67. 6', 14st. Career: Lloyd's insurance executive. Rep hons: Kent. CLR: 3t-14pts. Strong tackler, determined on the break. Described by coaches as a 'forward centre' with remarkable ability to ride strong tackles.

TICEHURST, Russell (Second row)
Born 21.8.67. 6'6". CLR: 1t-5pts. Played for Sidcup before joining Blackheath for the 1995-96 season. Rapid progress has surprised Blackheath coaches. Clinched 'Most Improved Player' award 1995-96 season after becoming first team regular. The club 'comedian', he has worked hard at his game in an attempt to match the skills of opponents like Martin Bayfield. Steve Shortland's arrival could blunt first team chances 1996-97 season but seen as important squad member.

TIERNEY, John (Prop)
Born 21.2.62. 5'10", 16st 7lb. Rep hons: Kent. A Blackheath veteran, he is not expected to feature in the first team this season. Former 'Player of the Year' and still rated a formidable prop. A one-club player.

TUCKER, Ian (Centre)
Born New Zealand. Career: Student. Joined Blackheath in second half of 1995-96 season on arrival from South Africa. RFU qualification rule prevents him becoming available before November 1996. Begins first year studies at Oxford University autumn 1996. Hopes to play rugby in England short-term before returning to native New Zealand. Represented Blackheath at Middlesex Sevens 1996 and is a highly competent centre.

WALTON, Dominic (Flanker)
Born Farnborough, Kent, 16.11.70. 6'3", 17st. Career: Chartered surveyor. Rep hons: Kent, Schools. CLR: 3t-15pts. Spent summer 1996 playing rugby in New Zealand. Missed part of 1995-96 season with groin injury. Voted 1994-95 'Player of the Year'. Key member of the first team squad for 1996-97 season.

WELCH, Shaun (Scrum-half)
Born 18.12.70. 5'5", 11st. Rep hons: Kent. Joined Blackheath 1995-96 from Westcombe Park. Second team player with major first team potential as understudy to Mike Friday. Gained widespread approval last season when given first team chance as replacement for injured Friday.

WHITE, Leon (Flanker)
Born 19.8.67. 6', 15st 7lb. Career: Advertising executive. CLR: 2t-10pts. Joined Blackheath from Canterbury in April 1994 and established himself as first team regular 1995-96. Versatile openside and blindside. Key squad player for 1996-97 season.

WILKINS, Chris (Flanker)
Born 3.7.71. 6'3", 16st 2lb. Rep hons: England A (1, It95), U21, 18 Group, 16 Group, Schools. London. CLR: 1t-5pts (Wasps). Joined Blackheath from Wasps late 1995-96

season. Recovered rapidly from a serious neck injury to stake first team claim at Wasps last season, but Lawrence Dallaglio's progress forced Chris out of position on blindside to hasten departure from Wasps. Educated at Brentwood School and a useful Essex League cricketer.

REVIEW

Blackheath's approach to last season was merely to consolidate the foundations established in winning promotion from Courage League Three in 1994-95. A disappointing 1995-96 season left the players believing they should have led a more ambitious campaign. Blackheath started well and ended with a flourish, but with their pack decimated in mid-term by injuries to Gary Furneaux, Colin Ridgeway and Dominic Walton, the club under-achieved despite a fine home victory against Wakefield and another impressive performance at Moseley. The capture of ex-All Black John Gallagher early in 1996 illustrated the club's determination to embrace rugby's brave new world, and not even Matt Stewart's departure for Northampton could damage renewed club spirit and belief in the future, with Mick Harris celebrating the 'Player of the Year' award.

BLACKHEATH in the Courage League 1995-96

Sep 9	Nottingham	A	Lost	17	31	Codling(T) Harris(T) Howard(2C, P)
16	Wakefield	H	Won	20	16	Aldridge(T) Howard(D, 4P)
23	Bedford	A	Lost	18	21	Friday(T) Hanslip(T) Howard(C, 2P)
30	Waterloo	H	Won	21	9	Hanslip(T) Ridgeway(T) Howard(C, 3P)
Oct 7	Newcastle	H	Won	39	19	Barham(2T) Hanslip(2T) Griffiths(T) Ridgeway(T) White(T) Howard(2C)
14	Northampton	A	Lost	14	69	Hanslip(T) Howard(D, 2P)
21	London Scottish	H	Drew	16	16	Ticehurst(T) Howard(C, D, 2P)
28	London Irish	A	Lost	9	32	Howard(3P)
Nov 4	Moseley	A	Lost	9	27	Howard(D, 2P)
11	Nottingham	H	Won	25	16	Howard(2T, 2C, D, P) Stewart(T)
Jan 6	Bedford	H	Won	23	8	Coyne(T) Smith(T) Harris(2C, 3P)
13	Wakefield	A	Lost	0	17	
Feb 10	Waterloo	A	Lost	10	32	Harris(T) Howard(C, P)
17	Newcastle	A	Lost	10	25	Harris(T, C, P)
Mar 30	Northampton	H	Lost	10	24	Walton(T) Howard(C, P)
Apr 6	London Scottish	A	Lost	26	27	Friday(2T) Neil-Dwyer(T) Howard(C, 3P)
13	London Irish	H	Lost	23	46	Shadbolt(2T) Jowett(T) Howard(C, 2P)
27	Moseley	A	Won	51	36	Coyne(T) Essenhigh(T) Jowett(T) Shadbolt(T) Stewart(T) Walton(T) White(T) Howard(5C, 2P)

COVENTRY

Formation of club: 1874
Ground: Barker Butts Lane, Coundon, Coventry CV6 1DU.
  Tel: 01203 601174/591274
Capacity: 10,000
Colours: Navy blue and white hoops
Honours: Pilkington Cup: Winners: 1973, 74.
Last season: CL3: 1st. Pilkington Cup: 5th round (lost 16-6 to West Hartlepool)
Most capped player: David Duckham (England) 36
Director of Rugby: Derek Eves
Coaches: Jim Broderick, Lindsey Carver, Peter Rossborough, Darren Grewcock
Captain: Rob Hardwick

ADDLETON, David James (Hooker)
Born Coventry, 30.3.63. 5'9", 14st 2lb. Career: Water engineer. Rep hons: Midlands A. Irish Exiles. Warwickshire U21, U16, Schools. Educated at Park Hill Junior and Woodlands School, Dave made his Warwickshire debut in the CIS semi-final against Berkshire at Rugby last season. A product of Barkers' Butts, the club that nurtured Neil Back and Bill Gittings. Represented Irish Exiles in the Inter-Provincial Championship. Picked for Midlands A when team created two seasons ago to provide stepping stone between U21 and senior CIS Divisional team. Made more first team appearances (31, Julian Horrobin 28) than any other Coventry player last season.

BARDEN, Stuart (Centre/wing)
Born Coventry, 21.6.70. 5'10", 13st 3lb. Career: Electrical estimator. Rep hons: Warwickshire, U21, Colts. CLR: 5t-25pts. Nicknamed 'Jigger', made 12 first team appearances last season.

BLACKMORE, Andrew (Lock)
Born Bristol, 1.11.65. 6'7", 16st. Career: Sales executive. Rep hons: England A, 18 Group. Barbarians (94-95). Midlands. South West. Gloucestershire. CLR: 2t-9pts (Bristol). England A regular, Andrew is rated one of the country's best lineout specialists. Represented England XV against Canada. Keen Bristol City supporter. Colourful diet with strong preference for Indian Madras curry washed down with Courage Best. Developed handling skills playing basketball and is keen cricketer. Made 13 first team appearances last season. Once starred on TV's Generation Game.

BLUNDELL, Richard (Hooker)
Born Coventry, 8.9.77. 5'10", 15st. Career: Student. Rep hons: England Colts. One for the future, Richard played for England Colts last season and made six first team appearances.

BROWN, James (Fly-half)
Born Solihull, 8.12.77. 5'8", 10st 10lb. Career: Student. Rep hons: England Schools 18, 16 Group. Joined Coventry May 1996 from Millfield School. Reputed to be the best fly-half to emerge from the England Schools system for several seasons.

CHAPMAN, Stephan (Wing/centre)
Born Coventry, 27.3.70. 5'10", 12st 5lb. Rep hons: England U21 Warwickshire Colts. CLR:2t-9pts. 'Chappie' made 12 first team appearances last season.

CRANE, Mark (Prop)
Born Bristol, 10.10.71 6' 15st. Rep hons: England Schools. CLR. 1t-4pt (Bath). Played at Bath for six seasons. Courage League Four Clifton's top-scorer 1995-96. Joined Coventry May 1996.

CROFTS, Lee (Flanker)
Born Coventry, 7.9.68. 6'4", 17st 7lb. Career: Policeman. Rep hons: Warwickshire. CLR: 5t-25pts. Converted from second row to back row last season with remarkable results. Exceptional pace for a big man. Voted 'Most Improved Player' 1995-96 season. Joined police three years ago and became the British Police Heavyweight champion. A Coventry player for two seasons after joining from local club Broadstreet.

CURTIS, Michael (Centre)
Born Coventry, 27.6.72. 5'10", 15st 7lb. Career: Groundsman. Rep hons: Warwickshire, U21, Colts. CLR: 1t-5pts. Played for Warwickshire in the 1995-96 County Championship final. Nicknamed 'Mick the Munch' on the strength of his remarkable appetite. Powerful player with formidable physique. Appointed Coventry's groundsman on 1 August 1996.

DAWSON, Anthony (Scrum-half)
Born Crewe, 29.1.75. 5'10", 11st. Career: Teacher. Rep hons: E. Midlands. Educated at Crewe and Alsager University. 'Tigger' joined Coventry in January 1996 after making impression on coaches when playing for Stourbridge.

EVES, Derek (Flanker)
Born 7.1.66. 5'10", 15st 10lb. Career: Coventry Director of Rugby. Rep hons: England A (4, WS93, 2t-10pts), Sevens, Emerging, 18 Group. Barbarians (93-94). CLR: 17t-80pts (Bristol); 5t-25pts (Coventry). The former Bristol captain joined Coventry 1995-96 season after scoring club record of 17 Courage League tries for the League One club. Between 1987-88 and 1994-95 made club record 86 League appearances for Bristol. Captained England at Hong Kong Sevens.

GALLAGHER, Matthew David (Full-back/fly-half)
Born Solihull, 21.3.73. 6'1", 13st. Career: Student. Rep hons: Midlands U21. Warwickshire, U21, U16. English Universities. CLR: 4t, 8c, 26pg-114pts (Nottingham). Educated at Solihull School where he was a contemporary of new Coventry teammate Andy Smallwood, Matt is taking an HND in building at Sheffield Hallam University. Since his Warwickshire Schools 16-Group debut, he has gained Midlands U21 selection, played for English Universities and was a Courage League regular for Nottingham before joining Coventry. First club Birmingham Solihull, and he was member of the Warwickshire team beaten by Buckinghamshire in the Under-21s final at Twickenham. With Andy Smallwood, member of Warwickshire's County Championship-winning team against Northumberland in 1994-95. Joined Coventry May 1996.

GEE, Richard (Utility back)
5'9", 12st 10lb. Career: Land Rover employee. Rep hons: Midland U21 Warwickshire U21, Colts. CLR: 7t-35pts. Richard is an England U21 trialist.

GREWCOCK, Daniel Jonathan (Lock/no 8)
Born Coventry, 7.11.72. 6'6", 17st 7lb. Career: Service engineer. Rep hons: England Students. Warwickshire. Midlands. Educated at Templars Junior, Woodlands School, Crewe and Alsager Faculty of Manchester Metropolitan University where he studied for BA Honours degree in Business, Leisure and Education. Made his Warwickshire debut against East Midlands at Coventry last season and is a product of Barkers' Butts (1990-94). Member of the England Students squad. He made 10 Coventry first team appearances last season contributing 5 points.

GREWCOCK, Darren (Scrum-half)
Born Coventry, 10.9.65. 5'9", 12st 10lb. Career: Fitness instructor. Rep hons: Midlands U16. CLR: 2t-9pts (Leicester). Darren joined Coventry from Leicester in May 1996. Played for Leicestershire at junior level. Also divisional matches for Midland U16. Product of John Cleveland College, Hinckley Rugby Academy that produced Graham Rowntree and Dean Richards. Spent time in Australia, playing in Sydney for Southern Districts and Townsville. Appointed to Coventry coaching staff as fitness adviser for new season.

GULLIVER, Anthony (Second row)
Born Coventry, 4.3.60. 6'5", 17st. Career: Rugby coach. Rep hons: Midlands. Warwickshire. CLR: 2t-9pts. A Coventry player for 16 seasons. Recognised as one of the toughest players in the squad. 'Gully' has accepted the job of second team coach for 1996-97.

HANCOX, Simon Russell (Centre)
Born Coventry, 26.6.75. 6', 13st. Career: Student. Rep hons: Midlands U21 Warwickshire U21, Colts. CLR: 4t-20pts. Recently left Loughborough University and is taking a 'year out'. Fast and skilful.

HARDWICK, Robin John Kieran (Prop)
Born Kenilworth, 23.3.69. 6', 19st 12lb. Career: Computer engineer. Rep hons: England A, U21, Colts. Midlands. Warwickshire U21, Colts. CLR: 2t-9pts. Educated at Coundon Junior School, Coundon Court and Coventry Technical College, Rob has completed a remarkable comeback from injury after a two-and-a-half-year absence with knee ligament trouble that doctors feared could not be repaired. Returned to play in winning England A teams against France A (25-15) in Paris last January and Italy (22-19) in March. Former Barkers' Butts player, who can prop on either side of the scrum. Made 20 Coventry appearances last season, scoring one try.

HARRIS, Jeremy Charles (Outside-half)
Born Kettering, 22.2.65. 5' 6", 12st 6lb. Career: Narrow-boat builder. Rep hons: England A. Barbarians (95-96). Midlands, Colts, Schools. CLR: Leicester (4t, 37c, 86p, 37d-461pts). Educated at Welland Park and Robert Smyth Schools, Market Harborough. 'Jez' joined Coventry from Leicester in May 1996. Scored 32 points in two England A appearances. Joined the Tigers in 1985 and scored a club record of 37 dropped goals. Served a long apprenticeship as understudy to Les Cusworth, Brian Smith and Gerry Ainscough. Dropped 13 goals for Leicester in Courage League season

1994-95 to beat 11 scored in previous season. Kicked 7 penalties for Leicester against Bristol, December 1993. Scored 1,171 points in 225 games for Leicester.

HORROBIN, Julian (Back row)
6'3", 15st 4lb. Career: Engineer Rep hons: England U21, 18 Group. CLR:4t-16pts (Bristol); 13t-65pts (Coventry). The former Bristol player scored 100 points, including 20 tries, in 28 appearances for Coventry in all first team matches 1995-96. Voted 'Player of the Year' last season.

HYDE, Julian (Lock)
6'4", 18st. Career: Senior engineer Jaguar cars. Rep hons: England Colts. Midland A. Warwickshire 18 Group. CLR: 3t-13pts. Julian has played for the Public School Wanderers and Welsh Exiles. Made 23 first team appearances, scoring three tries, last season.

JOHN, David (Wing)
Born Trinidad, 23.9.65. 5'8", 13st. Career· Machine operator. Rep hons: Gloucestershire. CLR: 5t-25pts (Bristol). Discovered by Bristol on a pre-season tour to Holland five years ago. Broke his arm last season. Timed at 10.6 secs over 100m, he is one of the fastest wingers in the Courage League.

KILFORD, Wayne Ashley (Full-back)
Born Malvern, 25.9.68. 5'11", 13st. Career· Sales engineer. Rep hons: England U21, Colts. Midlands. CLR: 1t, 2c, 5pg-23pts (Nottingham); 4t, 1pg-23pts (Leicester). Former Nottingham and Leicester player, Wayne signed for Coventry in May 1996. An outstanding all-round sportsman, he has played cricket for Nottinghamshire seconds as a batsman.

LLOYD, Richard (Flanker)
Born Solihull, 1.12.77. 5'10" 14st. Career: Student. Rep hons: England 18 Group, 16 Group, Schools. Played for England Schools last season. Signed for Coventry May 1996 to be groomed as successor to Derek Eves.

LYDSTER, Paul (Scrum-half)
Born Coventry, 28.5.70. 6'1", 14st. Career· Fitter. Rep hons: Royal Navy U21 Warwickshire. CLR:5t-25pts. Joined Coventry two seasons ago from neighbouring junior club Broadstreet. First team regular last season and contender for Julian Horrobin's 'Player of the Year' award.

McADAM, Andrew (Wing)
Born Coventry, 23.3.71. 6'1", 13st 5lb. Career· Bank official. Rep hons: England Colts. Product of Barkers' Butts. Signed by Coventry from Leicester in May 1996. He made six first team appearances for Leicester last season.

PATTEN, Ian Stuart (Flanker/no 8)
Born Bristol, 31.8.70. 6'5", 16st. Career· Bank clerk. Rep hons: Midlands. Gloucester. South West. CLR: Bristol (3t-15pts); Coventry (1t-5pts). Regular member of Bristol back row before joining Coventry. Scored two tries against Leicester in Bristol's Courage League win 1993-94. Made nine first team appearances last season.

REAYER, Garrath (Centre)
Born Oxford, 11.3.69. 6'2", 14st 5lb. Career: Trainee solicitor. Rep hons: Southern Counties U21 Oxfordshire U21 CLR: 5t-25pts. Joined Coventry last season. Made delayed start until registration cleared January 1996. Fiercely competitive, strong tackler.

ROBINSON, Richie (Centre)
Born Kendal, 5.7.67. 6'1", 14st. Career: Accountant. CLR: 3t-15pts (Leicester). Regular in the Leicester team last season and played against Bath in the 1996 Pilkington Cup final. Signed for Coventry May 1996. He made 24 first team appearances for Leicester.

SHEPHERD, Ben (Wing)
Born Coventry, 14.10.72. 6', 14st. Career: Computer operator. Rep hons: England B Colts. Midlands Colts. Warwickshire U21, Colts. CLR: 11t-55pts. Second top try scorer last season with 16 in all matches.

SMALLWOOD, Andrew (Wing)
Born 13.6.72. Rep hons: Warwickshire. Midlands. CLR: 11t-55pts (Nottingham). Joined Coventry from Nottingham in May 1996. With Coventry's Matt Gallagher, member of Warwickshire's County Championship-winning team against Northumberland 1994-95. Exceptional speed, strong defensively.

THOMAS, Marc (Full-back)
Born Coventry, 7.2.61. Career: Teacher. CLR: 2t, 19c, 11pg-81pts. Gained first team place at 18. Left briefly to play for Harrogate where he was studying but returned to Coventry last season.

WOODMAN, Douglas (Wing)
Born Bristol, 7.3.62. 6', 14st 4lb. Career: Electrician. Rep hons: Somerset. CLR: 3t-12pts (Bristol); 12t-53pts (Clifton); 12t-60pts (Coventry). Coventry captain last season. Joined Coventry from Bristol four seasons ago.

REVIEW

Coventry captured their second Courage National League Three title in three seasons with some stylish and rugged performances. The club never looked back from October after beating Rotherham in the Pilkington Cup second round and celebrating consecutive home league victories over Rosslyn Park and Rotherham and success away at Fylde. Stourbridge were slaughtered 78-20 in the Pilkington Cup third round and the then league leaders Richmond were also well beaten. Blackheath received a 19-9 Pilkington Cup trouncing on their ground as the promotion bandwagon kept rolling with the arrival of new Director of Rugby Derek Eves and Andy Blackmore from Bristol. A Cup exit at West Hartlepool was followed by league defeat at promotion rivals Richmond but vital wins against Moseley and Reading clinched the title. Both first team and 'Extras' (Midlands-West Champions) scored more than 1,000 points in all games for the first time in the club's history.

COVENTRY in the Courage League 1995-96

Sep	9	Harrogate	A	Won	17	6	Hancox(T) Quick(4P)
	16	Rugby	H	Lost	6	13	Quick(2P)
	23	Reading	H	Won	32	20	Crofts(T) Hancox(T) Horrobin(T) Shepherd(T) Smith(T) Quick(2C, P)
	30	Morley	A	Lost	11	23	Quick(T, 2P)
Oct	14	Rosslyn Park	H	Won	32	10	Horrobin(T) Saverimutto(T) Shepherd(T) Quick(C, 5P)
	21	Fylde	A	Won	16	13	Saverimutto(T) Quick(C, 2P) Hart(D)
	28	Rotherham	H	Won	15	12	Quick(4P) Hart(D)
Nov	11	Richmond	H	Won	13	12	Penalty(T) Quick(C, P) Saverimutto(D)
Jan	6	Otley	A	Won	29	6	Eves(T) Gee(T) Horrobin(T) Lydster(T) Woodman(T) Quick(2C)
	13	Morley	A	Won	38	23	Morgan(2T) Shepherd(2T) Hancox(T) Hart(T, 3C) Quick(C)
Feb	17	Fylde	H	Won	42	7	Crofts(T) Hart(T, 2C, P) Hyde(T) Lydster(T) Shepherd(T) Smith(T) Woodman(T)
	24	Rotherham	A	Won	40	13	Crofts(T) Horrobin(T) Lydster(T) Reaver(T) Shepherd(T) Angell(3C, 3P)
Mar	2	Rosslyn Park	A	Won	46	17	Eves(2T) Barden(T) Crofts(T) Horrobin(T) Thomas(T, 5C, 2P)
	23	Richmond	A	Lost	10	15	Penalty(T) Thomas(C, P)
	30	Otley	H	Won	64	14	Horrobin(3T) Reaver(2T) Eves(T) Hardwick(T) Lydster(T) Thomas(T, 7C) Woodman(T)
Apr	6	Harrogate	H	Won	36	20	Woodman(2T) Barden(T) Lydster(T) Patten(T) Penalty(T) Thomas(3C)
	13	Rugby	A	Won	24	13	Barden(T) Horrobin(T) Thomas(C, 4P)
	27	Reading	A	Won	53	27	Horrobin(2T) Reaver(2T) Barden(T) Eves(T) Shepherd(T) Angell(2C, D, P) Thomas(C, 2P)

LONDON SCOTTISH

Formation of club: 1878
Ground: Richmond Athletic, Richmond, Surrey TW9 2SS. Tel: 0181 332 2473
Capacity: 6,200
Colours: Blue shirts, white shorts
Honours: Pilkington Cup: Losing finalists 1974. Middlesex Sevens:
  Winners: 1937, 60, 61, 62, 63, 65, 91
Last season: CL2: 3rd. Pilkington Cup: 4th round (lost 32-16 to Nottingham)
Most capped player: Gavin Hastings (Scotland) 56
Director of Rugby: Iain Russell
Coach: John Steele
Captain: Simon Holmes

BAIRD, James Edward (Prop)
Born 10.4.72. Career: City financial expert. Joined in October 1995 from Vancouver-Canada RFC. A former Harlequins player, James has nomadic tendencies with experience of rugby in Australia, Canada and Portugal. Enjoys running 'fly-half' style with the ball. Expected to struggle for inclusion in the Scottish front row this season.

BURNELL, Andrew Paul (Prop)
Born Edinburgh, 29.9.65. 6'1", 17st 2lb. Career: Sales director Leisure Enterprises. Rep hons: Scotland (41, Eng89). Lions (1, NZ93). Barbarians (89-90). CLR: 2t-10pts. Signed 31.8.89. Played all six games for Scotland in the 1991 World Cup. Won his first Scotland cap against England 1989. Played 23 consecutive Five Nations internationals until missing the 1995 Championship. One of eight Scots who played for the British Lions on the 1993 tour to New Zealand. Played in seven of the 13 matches, including the first Test. Scotland's Grand Slam tight-head 1990. Studied law and land management at Leicester Polytechnic. Played for Leicester for four seasons. Premier prop and ex-club captain, Paul has declined offers from several top clubs.

BURNELL, Simon (Second row)
Born 9.1.68. Signed 22.11.95. Marlow. Younger brother of Paul Burnell. Suffered from injury last season. Potential to become first team regular. Aggressive, competitive player.

BURNS, Stuart (Wing/full-back)
CLR: 4t, 7c, 23pg-103pts (Blackheath). Played on the wing for Cambridge in the 1992 Varsity match. Regular first teamer for Blackheath in 1994-95 but suffered long-term injury last season attempting flashy 'Offiah' shuffle in first match against a Northern Ireland touring team. Absent four months with hamstring problems and struggled to re-establish himself. Sound tackler. Moved to London Scottish in summer 1996.

CLARKE, Jonathan Drummond (Wing)
Born 6.3.73. CLR: 3t-15pts. Joined London Scottish from Havant January 1995. Regular first teamer last season after graduating from third team over two years. Trains hard. Fast and elusive. Club comedian, playing 'Eric Morecambe' to Euan Ferguson's 'Ernie Wise'.

DINGWALL, Gordon (Centre)
Born 17.7.66. Career: Pharmaceutical tester. Second team captain. Played several first team matches last season, his sixth at the club. Solid tackler expected to offer cover to first team squad. Has dry sense of humour.

DUTHIE, Maxwell Bryan (Flanker)
Born 22.1.70. Career: Solicitor in City. Rep hons: Cambridge University. CLR: Rosslyn Park (1t-5pts); London Scottish (2t-10pts). Won two Cambridge Blues (91 and 92). London Scottish coaches predict major progress this season after stepping up Max's personal fitness programme. Ready volunteer for rugby tours with well-thumbed passport. Regular tourist with Penguins.

ERIKSSON, Ronald (Centre)
Born 22.4.72. Career: PRP. Rep hons: Scotland (1, NZ96). CLR: 9t-45pts. Made debut for Scotland against New Zealand this year where he made a big impression. Hard-tackling centre with immense dedication. In his fifth year with London Scottish. Favours prison-style haircuts.

FERGUSON, Euan Gerald James (Wing)
Born 2.9.67. 6'1", 16st. Career: Building trade salesman. CLR: 2t-10pts. Became regular first teamer last season after graduating this season. Inspired by Jonah Lomu, models his game on All Black superstar in powerhouse touchline charges. Office girls invited to club function voted Euan 'best legs' in the squad.

FRASER, Gavin Gordon Angus (Full-back)
Born 23.2.72. Career: Sports industry. CLR. Waterloo (3t-15pts); London Scottish (2t-10pts). Joined the club from Waterloo last season. Promising attacking full-back but will have to fight hard for first team recognition this season.

HAMILTON, James Garth (Scrum-half)
Born Guildford, 1.7.70. 5'9", 12st 6lb. Career: Sales rep. Rep hons: Scottish Exiles. Midland Colts. CLR: Leicester (1t-5pts). Jamie made 15 Courage League appearances, six as replacement, for Leicester after making debut in December 1990 at Nuneaton. Frustrated by lack of opportunity, joined London Scottish for 1996-97 season. Represented victorious Leicester in 1995 Middlesex Sevens tournament. Former Lincoln and Linwood (New Zealand) player, broke shoulder blade at 17 and spent season on sidelines. Begins this season as threat to David Millard's place. Hobbies include snow-boarding.

HOLMES, Simon David (Flanker)
Born 12.12.66. Career: Works in communications industry. Rep hons: Barbarians (89-90). Anglo-Scottish. CLR: 3t-15pts. Captain this season. Won two Blues at Cambridge in 1989 and 1990. Openside flanker and one of the bravest in the Courage League. Leads from the front.

HUNTER, Robert Stuart (Flanker)
Born 23.5.72. Career: Army regular. Rep hons: Army. Former Saffron Walden player, Bob is a superb lineout jumper at four after training under direction of British high jump expert. Returns for new season with better physique, speed and stamina. Studied

Doddie Weir's lineout technique closely in match against Newcastle and claims his game has benefited.

JACKSON, David Thomas Hami (No 8)
Born 24.2.70. CLR: 2t-10pts. Has played for two seasons after joining from Edinburgh Academicals.

JANKOVICH-BESAN, Thomas (Flanker)
Born South Africa, 26.4.72. Career: Works for legal firm in City. Certain to mount challenge for first team place in his first season. Seen as long-term successor to Simon Holmes. Fast, determined, fine sevens player. Made mistake of telling teammates he took a passport on trip to Scotland.

JOHNSTON, David Nathaniel (Second row)
Born 7.6.72. 17st. Rep hons: Scotland U19. CLR: 1t-5pts. Has yet to fulfil potential after joining club from Twickenham five years ago. Lacks confidence but James Kelly's arrival is certain to spur more aggression from Dave after ex-Quin tossed him about like rag doll in pre-season training. 'Doesn't punch his weight,' say coaches.

KELLY, James Robert (Prop)
Born 16.2.76. Career: PRP. Rep hons: Scotland U21. Joined in January 1996 from Harlequins. Tremendous potential, tipped to gain full Scotland honours in next three seasons. Regrets angry exchange with teammate in first training session on arrival at Athletic Ground. Compensated by scoring two tries on debut against Watsonians. Exponent of controlled but fair aggression.

KEMP, Malcolm John (Wing)
Born 26.2.72. Career: Fitness instructor. Failed to gain regular first team place last season and could struggle for recognition again 1996-97. Formerly with Saracens.

McGAVIN, David Charles (Hooker)
Born 24.4.72. Career: Student. Rep hons: Scottish Exiles. Allegedly a sophisticated thinker, known as 'Mr Smooth' with his Sean Connery style. One of three hookers, with not much to choose between them. Flies regularly with family to Third World countries to work on irrigation projects. Spent summer 1996 in Africa.

McLELLAN, James William (Hooker)
Born 12.5.69. Rep hons: Anglo Scottish. CLR: 1t-5pts. Joined London Scottish five years ago and has fought hard for first team recognition. Expected to start season in first team squad. One of the club's fittest men, Jamie added extra stone in weight pre-season on coach's orders. Quiet man, skilled in one-line jokes delivered once a fortnight.

MILLARD, David Bruce (Scrum-half)
Born 19.9.64. 6'1". Career: Orthopaedic expert. Rep hons: Barbarians (93-94). Scotland Sevens. CLR: 22t, 1dg-103pts. Elected captain London Scottish Sevens team 1996-97. One of Courage League's tallest scrum-halves. Exceptionally fast with good control over forwards and eye for a break.

MORRISON, Iain Robert (Flanker)
Born 14.12.62. Rep hons: Scotland (15, Ire93). Cambridge University. Barbarians (95-96). CLR: 9t, 1c-40pts. Won two Blues in 1983 and 1984. Wonderful influence on team but not expected to offer himself for First XV inclusion this season. Club wants him to coach forwards. Notable Sevens specialist.

NISBET, Alan John (Second row)
Born 12.6.69. Career: RAF fitness instructor. Rep hons: RAF. Scottish Exiles. Ex Boroughmuir. Regular first teamer last season. Broad Scottish accent baffles Anglo teammates.

ORR EWING, David (Second row)
Born 8.9.69. Career: Army officer. CLR: 1t-5pts. Certain to feature in first team since loss of Scott and Cronin to Wasps and Bedford. Joined club four seasons ago.

ROBINSON, Anthony Paul (Prop)
Born 1.2.62. CLR: 2t-10pts. Unlikely to make first team 1996-97 Accepted coaching duties with development side. Made a few first team appearances last season. A popular clubman, two West Samoan friends looked him up for a drink at the Hong Kong Sevens. Played for Saracens before joining Scottish.

ROBINSON, Nicholas John (Full-back)
Born 7.12.68. Career: Brewery rep. Rep hons: Cambridge University. CLR: 1t-5pts. A Cambridge Blue in 1990, Nick is one of the tallest players in the squad.

ROWLANDS, Donald Martin (Flanker)
Born 16.12.70. Career: Works for firm of solicitors in City. Stalks opponents rather than flattens them. Clever ball stealer.

SIGNORINI, Oliver Douglas (Prop)
Born 21.3.65. CLR: 3t-14pts. A loose-head, Dougie is not the fittest, fastest or most skilled but makes the most of his competitive edge. Scored best try of the game against Northampton last season.

SLY, Mark Stuart (Centre)
Born 12.3.67. Career: Student. CLR: 3t-14pts. Squad man. Solid rather than spectacular.

STEELE, John David (Fly-half)
Born Cambridge, 9.8.64. Career: Estates management. Rep hons: England A. Barbarians. Midlands. CLR: Northampton (5t, 40c, 95pg, 11dg-419 pts); London Scottish (4t, 22c, 40pg, 5dg-199pts). Ex-Northampton, suffered broken jaw against Blackheath last season in violent incident described by one Scottish coach as the 'worst example of rugby thuggery' he'd seen. Recovered for March comeback but not at his best. Scottish hope to utilise John's experience in coaching role this season.

STENT, Ian Bowen (Fly-half)
Born Camberley, 22.12.72. Career: Rugby travel company representative. CLR: 2t, 8c, 29pg-113pts (Nottingham); 1c, 5pg-17pts (London Scottish). Joined London Scottish from Nottingham last season and made several first team appearances. Certain to run John Steele close for the fly-half berth with no selection guarantees in 1996-97.

TARBUCK, Christopher Richard (No 8/flanker)
Born Harlow, 20.8.68. 6'4", 15st 7lb. Career: Marketing manager Rep hons: England Students, Colts. Midlands. CLR: Saracens (3t-12pts); Leicester (4t-20pts). Played for Harlow, Southend and Saracens before joining Leicester where he made his debut in October 1993 at Newcastle Gosforth. Transferred to London Scottish for 1996-97 season, he will strengthen the No 8 position.

THOMPSON, Gavin (Centre)
Born Croydon, 20.8.69. Career: Insurance rep for Eagle Star. Rep hons: England A (10, Aus90). U21, 18 Group. London. CLR: 12t-53pts (Harlequins); 1t-5pts (London Scottish). Joined London Scottish from Harlequins last season but suffered long-term injury after Christmas. Unlikely to be fit for first month of 1996-97 season.

WALKER, Andrew Francis (No 8)
Born 14.11.65. Career: Financial trainer in City. CLR: 2t-10pts. A Sevens expert, nicknamed 'Chicken' for ability to run in all directions. Certain to push for first team place 1996-97.

WATSON, Toby (Wing)
Born 27.7.72. Career: Financial expert in City. Rep hons: Anglo-Scottish. Oxford University. CLR: 4t-20pts. Fastest player in first team squad. Won Oxford Blue 1993. Made rapid progress from third team to premier squad.

WISEMAN, Fraser Alasdair (Prop)
Born 26.3.73. Career: PE student, West London Institute. Can play loose-head or tight-head. Missed most of last season with injury.

WITHERS GREEN, Anthony (Scrum-half)
Born 20.2.68. Career: Car warehouse manager. Rep hons: Scottish Exiles. CLR: 3t-15pts. Challenged David Millard for first team place last season but could struggle to stake claim in 1996-97. Played for Harlequins before joining Scottish. Skilled exponent of 'Flaming Drambuie trick' in which flaming glasses are stuck to chest.

REVIEW

London Scottish enjoyed a more successful season than the management anticipated, with refereeing decisions going their way against Wakefield and Moseley. The players responded magnificently to the coaches' instruction to 'run your own campaign'. They relished the chance to break with stereotype. Good performances against Blackheath and Northampton compensated for a poor Pilkington Cup showing against Nottingham. Skipper Simon Holmes led by example to produce the best form of his career and John Steele, whose stirring form against Northampton won him the 'Man of the Match' award, ran Holmes close for best player of the season.

LONDON SCOTTISH in the Courage League 1995-96

Sep	9	Waterloo	A	Won	11	3	Rowland(T) Steele(2P)
	16	London Irish	H	Won	19	15	Millard(2T) Holmes(T) Steele(2C)
	23	Moseley	A	Won	21	19	Jackson(T) Millard(T) Steele(T, 3C)
	30	Nottingham	H	Won	17	9	Fraser(T) Steele(4P)
Oct	7	Wakefield	A	Won	20	16	Penalty(T) Watson(T) Withers-Green(T) Steele(C, P)
	14	Bedford	H	Won	50	10	Burnell(T) Fraser(T) Millard(T) Nisbet(T) Steele(T, 4C, D, 3P) Watson(T)
	21	Blackheath	A	Drew	16	16	Watson(T) Steele(C, D, 2P)
	28	Newcastle	H	Won	28	8	Eriksson(T) Harrold(T) Mair(T) Russell(2C, 3P)
Nov	4	Northampton	A	Lost	11	54	Signorini(T) Russell(2P)
	11	Waterloo	H	Drew	16	16	Withers-Green(T) Russell(C, 3P)
Jan	6	Moseley	H	Won	17	8	Withers-Green(T) Stent(4P)
	13	London Irish	A	Lost	20	21	Robinson(2T) Thompson(T) Stent(C, P)
Feb	17	Wakefield	H	Lost	22	31	Harrold(T) Steele(C, 5P)
Mar	9	Nottingham	A	Won	19	12	Orr-Ewing(T) Steele(C, 4P)
	30	Bedford	A	Lost	19	21	Duthie(T) Holmes(T) Robinson(T) Harrold(2C)
Apr	6	Blackheath	H	Won	27	26	Clarke(T) Millard(T) Walker(T) Steele(3C, 2P)
	13	Newcastle	A	Lost	11	45	Duthie(T) Steele(2P)
	27	Northampton	H	Lost	17	59	Steele(2T, 2C, P)

MOSELEY

Formation of club: 1873
Ground: The Reddings, Reddings Road, Moseley, Birmingham. Tel: 0121 449 2149
Capacity: 8,500
Colours: Red and black
Honours: Pilkington Cup: Losing finalists: 1972, 79, 82.
Last season: CL2: 6th. Pilkington Cup: 4th round (lost 26-5 to Newcastle Gosforth)
Most capped player: Mike Teague (England) 27
Director of Coaching: Mark Anscombe
Captain: Andy Houston

BALL, Dean John (Hooker)
Born 24.7.71 5'7", 14st 10lb. Career- Carpenter. Rep hons: Midlands, U21, Colts. CLR.
2t-10pts. Dean has made 124 first team appearances. Quick all-round player, good
skills, plays like a three-quarter. Impressed coaching staff by arranging wedding
summer 1996 to avoid missing pre-season training. Dressing-room character with
infectious humour.

BATEY, Gavin (Wing)
6'5", 16st 2lb. Joined Moseley 1995-96 from Old Hillsonians. Ex hockey player Quickest in squad over 15-50 metres. A 'Jonah Lomu' on the charge, dragging his bulk
through tackles. A former Royal Marine, Gavin played a few first team games end of
last season but is expected to challenge heavily for more recognition this season.

BONNEY, Jan (Centre)
Born 27.1.71. 6'1". 14st 10lb. Career: Student. Rep hons: England U21, Colts. CLR. 4t,
1dg-23pts. Jan has made 121 first team appearances. Big, aggressive, strong runner and
sound tackler.

BRIGHT, Martin Richard (Lock)
Born 15.1 70. 6'8", 18st 6lb. Career: Inland Revenue inspector. Rep hons: North
Midlands. Shropshire. CLR: 3t-15pts. Martin has made 64 first team appearances.
Nicknamed 'Tiny', he is a good middle jumper in the lineout and natural ball-winner.
Worked hard in pre-season training to lose two stone. Handicapped by back problems,
he was absent for more than two months last season. Joined from Shropshire club
Newport. He has been a regular first teamer for last two seasons.

BROOKS, Michael (Flanker)
Born 20.11 74. Career: Student. Rep hons: England 18 Group. Plays open-side. Former
Trent College student, now attending University of Central England, Birmingham.
Has made full recovery from operation to cruciate ligaments. Appearances 1995-96
curtailed by the injury. Member of England Schools' New Zealand tour squad in 1993.
Joined Moseley for 1995-96 but knee operation sidelined him for all but last two
months of season. Gained national design award honours for developing rucking and
tackling machine he is now trying to market.

103

CHUDLEIGH, Mark Anthony (Scrum-half)
Born Launceston, 31.1.74. 5'7", 12st. Career: Leisure centre supervisor. Rep hons: England U21, Colts. Second spell at the club after re-joining from Bristol. CLR: 1t-5pts (Bristol); 2t-10pts (Moseley). Mark has made 38 first team appearances. Regular first team player last season. Typical Cornish scrum-half, rough, tough, spends as much time with forwards as backs.

CORBETT, Liam Patrick (Full-back)
Born 4.9.70. 6'3", 14st 7lb. Career: Dentist. Rep hons: England Colts. Ireland Exiles. CLR: 2t, 1c, 2pg-18pts. Liam has made 55 first team appearances. Suffered depressed cheek fracture against Bedford last season, missed two months, and failed to regain first team place. Steady, sound defence, good kicker. Fully recovered from injury for 1996-97 season.

DOSSET, Christopher James (Full-back)
Born 8.1.69. 5'10", 12st. Career: Teacher. Rep hons: England Students. CLR: 2t, 1pg-13pts. Chris has made 70 first team appearances. Recognised as fittest player in the club. Teacher at King Edward's School, Aston. Educated at Loughborough University, Chris captained Moseley to title success in the 1996 Alnwick Sevens tournament. Then beat all-comers in post-Alnwick tourney 100 metre sprint challenge.

DOYLE, Phillip James (Hooker)
Born New Zealand, 15.1.68. 5'11", 16st. Career: Quantity surveyor. Rep hons: Manawatu (New Zealand). Phil has made 12 first team appearances. Qualified for last four Courage League games 1995-96. Highly experienced newcomer to the pack.

HANSON, David (Wing)
Born 16.5.66. 5'11", 11st 10lb. Career: Stores manager. Rep hons: North Midlands. CLR: 2t-10pts. David has made 66 first team appearances. Nicknamed 'Chicken' because of lean ribcage. Brother of Lorraine Hanson, Atlanta Olympics 400-metre runner. He is one of the quickest sprinters in the club.

HOUSTON, Andrew Brian (Fly-half)
Born 24.10.68. 5'8", 12st 7lb. Career: Stockbroker. Rep hons: England 18 Group. North Midlands. Andy has made 70 first team appearances and will captain Moseley for the 1996-97 season. Led the side several times last season after Neil Martin suffered long-term injury. Launched captaincy reign with five consecutive victories but broke bone in foot and missed two months.

JOHAL, Jag (Flanker)
Born 19.7.74. 5'10", 16st 10lb. Career: Student. CLR: 1t-5pts. Jag has made 26 first team appearances. Won 'Most Improved Player' award 1995-96. Son of former Olympic wrestler, Jag is in his third year at University of Central England, Birmingham. Strong and powerful, he became a first team regular last season after winning place just before Christmas.

JONES, Robert (Wing)
Born 8.6.73. 5'9", 12st. Career: Security officer. CLR: 1t-5pts. Bob has made 12 first team appearances. Educated at King Edward's School, Aston. Rejoined Moseley last half of 1995-96 season afer three years at Middlesbrough. Chosen 'Player of Tourna-

ment' at 1996 Alnwick Sevens, scoring eight tries in four matches. Sharp pace. Instinctive nose for try-line. Recognised as exciting prospect.

KERR, Alastair Douglas (Full-back/centre)
Born Douglas, Isle of Man, 8.1.71. 6'2", 13st 2lb. Career: Doctor. Rep hons: Anglo-Scots U21. UAU. England Students. Midlands. CLR: 9t, 38c, 76pg, 5dg-364pts. Educated at Plymouth College and Birmingham University where he studied medicine for five years, Alaistair represented England Students at the 1992 Students World Cup in Italy. He played for Plymouth Albion before joining Moseley where he has made 122 first team appearances. Played schools cricket for the West of England and was a member of the Devon U19 team in the season they became national champions. Unlikely to play this season after deciding to take year out working in New Zealand.

LANGLEY, Brandon Robert (Lock)
Born 11.3.71. 6'4", 17st 7lb. Career: Policeman. Rep hons: British Police. Staffordshire. Brandon has made 22 first team appearances. Fittest forward in the squad. Utility second row or back row player. Strong, good jumper, mobile.

MacKINNON, Stuart Donald (Prop)
Born 6.1.69. 6', 17st 7lb. Career: Shop fitter. Stuart has made 15 first team appearances. Joined from Stratford-upon-Avon, winning first team place just before Christmas 1995. Powerful scrummager. Converted by Moseley from tight to loose-head.

MILES, Philip Edward (Scrum-half)
Born Coventry, 7.11.68. 5'8", 11st 7lb. Career: Computer sales. CLR: 1t, 3pg-14pts (Moseley). Educated at Henry VIII School, Coventry, Phil has made 14 first team appearances since joining Moseley from Northampton. Played several matches at full-back as replacement last season. Well coached, cultured back-up.

MORGAN, Henry (Flanker/no 8)
Born New Zealand, 18.7.68. 6'3", 16st 7lb. Joined Moseley in December 1995 after playing full provincial season for King Country, New Zealand. Aggressive Wayne Shelford lookalike. Represented King Country for six seasons. Qualifies to play Courage League 1996-97. Scored three tries in five non-league appearances 1995-96. Hard trainer, Moseley anticipates major contribution from him this season.

NOBLE, James Adam (No 8)
Born 17.10.75. 6'11", 16st 7lb. Career: Student. Rep hons: North Midlands U21, Colts. Courage League debut against London Irish 1995-96, James has made seven first team appearances. Fine prospect, key member of Moseley's long-term development squad.

ORD, Michael John (Flanker)
Born 29.3.70. 6'2", 14st 7lb. Career: Physiotherapist. Rep hons: England Colts, 18 Group. Mike has made 41 first team appearances. Sound handler with astute linking skills. Doubled as Moseley's player/physio on 1996 summer tour to Holland.

POLL, Robin (Flanker)
Born 16.2.74. 6'4", 16st. Career: Student. Rep hons: England U21 CLR. 2t-10pts. Gained degree at Bristol University and has decided to continue his studies. Missed

most of last season with shoulder injury after gaining England U21 honours 1994-95. Robin has made 32 first team appearances. Versatile, can play No 8. Fully fit, will add depth to back row.

QUICK, Craig (Full-back)

6'2", 13st 7lb. Career: Policeman. Rep hons: Wales U18. Midlands U21 Warwickshire Colts. CLR: 1t, 9c, 24pg-95pts (Coventry). Tore hamstring at Coventry last season but was still top scorer in all matches with 163 points. Elected to join Moseley for 1996-97. Gained representative honours with Wales at youth level but opted to play for England. Rated best player Midlands U21 weekend training last season. Left-footed goal-kicker. Serious, dedicated player.

STUART, Robert Andrew (Centre)

Born Devizes, 29.9.72. 5'11", 13st. Career: Chartered surveyor. Rep hons: Scotland U21. Bob has made nine first team appearances. Joined Moseley from Bath where he made one Courage League appearance against Harlequins in 1994-95. Rated exciting prospect, and a natural footballer. Chances restricted by shoulder injury last season. Expected to make delayed start to 1996-97 season after summer operation. Set to forge dangerous midfield pairing with Jan Bonney. Hobbies include travel and carpentry from purpose-built workshop at home. Keen on athletics.

WEBBER, Nathan (Prop)

Born Stratford-upon-Avon, 20.6.74. 6'1", 16st 8lb. Career: Plasterer. Rep hons: England U21. Midlands. Warwickshire 18-Group, Colts. Educated at Stratford High School, Nathan made three appearances for the Midlands last season and has played 62 times for Moseley's first team. Rated an England prospect, he is a member of the RFU development squad under manager John Elliott. Good scrummager, gifted all-round skills. Mobile, safe handler at tight-head.

WILKINSON, David James (Wing)

Born 28.11.71. 6', 13st 2lb. Career: Teacher. Rep hons: Midland U21. CLR: 6t-30pts. David made Courage League debut against Newcastle Gosforth in 1994-95 season and has played 42 first team matches. Scored seven tries in run of eight first team games last season. Top try scorer 1995-96 with 11 in all matches.

WILLIAMS, Richard (Prop)

Born 10.2.69. 6', 16st 6lb. Career: Construction engineer. Joined Moseley from Waterloo. Understudies the regular front-row. Has made seven first team appearances.

WITHERS, James Alexander (Flanker/no 8)

Born Stratford-upon-Avon, 15.3.75. 6'2", 17st. Career: Student. Jamie made his first team debut last season and went on to play six games. Spent 1996 close season gaining match-play experience with a Brisbane, Australia club. Big, powerful, ambitious player with huge potential.

REVIEW

Moseley promised more than they delivered in 1995-96. Bottom of the Courage League after the first four matches, they recovered to celebrate five successive victories and rose to fourth place before Christmas. Disrupted by injuries and divisional calls on squad, they lost momentum and fell away in second half of the season. Beat Newcastle Gosforth twice in the League but lost to Rob Andrew's team in Pilkington Cup 4th round. Eleven players made their first team debuts, six later to become regulars. Jag Johal, Nathan Webber and several other youngsters established themselves. Consortium, including Aston Villa owner Doug Ellis, has given club £1m backing over next three seasons. Coaching director Barrie Corless was replaced in August by New Zealander Mark Anscombe, a former North Harbour forward who had been coaching Dublin club Old Wesley.

MOSELEY in the Courage League 1995-96

Sep	9	Newcastle	H Won	9	0	Kerr(3P)
	16	Northampton	A Lost	7	50	Purdy(T) Kerr(C)
	23	London Scottish	H Lost	19	21	Bonney(T) Kerr(T, D, 2P)
	30	London Irish	A Lost	8	49	Miles(T) Kerr(D)
Oct	7	Waterloo	A Lost	17	22	Corbett(T) Miles(3P) Houston(D)
	14	Nottingham	H Won	18	6	Bright(T) Houston(T) Corbett(C, 2P)
	21	Wakefield	A Won	11	9	Bonney(T) Kerr(2P)
	28	Bedford	H Won	27	18	Kerr(2T, 2C, P) Fuller(T) Owen(T)
Nov	4	Blackheath	A Won	27	9	Anderson(T) Kerr(T, C, 2P) Houston(2D) Bonney(D)
	11	Newcastle	A Won	9	8	Kerr(3P)
Jan	6	London Scottish	A Lost	8	17	Kerr(T) Dossett(P)
Feb	17	Waterloo	H Lost	24	30	Kerr(8P)
	24	Northampton	H Lost	16	46	Penalty(T) Kerr(C, 3P)
Mar	9	London Irish	H Lost	26	29	Ball(T) Chudleigh(T) Kerr(2C, 4P)
	30	Nottingham	A Lost	27	48	Bonney(T) Kerr(T, 3C, 2P) Penalty(T)
Apr	6	Wakefield	H Lost	15	26	Chudleigh(T) Jones(T) Kerr(C, P)
	13	Bedford	A Won	23	8	Binns(T, 2C, D, 2P) Smallcombe(T)
	27	Blackheath	H Lost	36	51	Hanson(T) Houston(T) Johal(T) Kerr(T, 2C, 4P)

NEWCASTLE

Formation of club: 1877
Ground: Kingston Park, Brunton Road, Kenton Bank Foot, Newcastle-upon-Tyne
NE13 8AF. Tel: 0191 214 0422
Capacity: 6,000
Colours: Green and white
Honours: Pilkington Cup: Winners 1976, 77
Last season: CL2: Pilkington Cup: 5th round (lost 44-22 to Harlequins)
Most capped player: Rob Andrew (England) 70
Director of Rugby: Rob Andrew
Coach: Steve Bates
Captain: TBA

ANDREW, Christoper Robert (Fly-half)
Born Richmond, Yorks. 18.2.63. 5'9", 12st 8lb. Career: Director of Rugby. Rep hons: England (70, Rom85, 2t, 33c, 86pg, 21dg-396pts), British Lions (5, Aus89, 1c, 1pg, 2dg-11pts). North (12, 3t, 11c, 15pg, 3dg-88pts), London (12, 2t, 20c, 28pg, 2dg-140pts). Barbarians (85-86). CLR: Wasps (16t, 82c, 161pg, 11dg-748pts), Newcastle (7c, 4pg-26pts). Record-breaking England fly-half whose signing last October heralded the beginning of modern professionalism. Educated at Barnard Castle School, Durham, and Cambridge University where he won rugby and cricket Blues – Rob has also played for Nottingham, Gordon in Sydney and Toulouse. First capped against Romania 1985 when he scored 24 points in a 54-3 win, Rob won 69 of his 70 caps at fly-half, a world record. He also holds the world record for dropped goals in internationals with 23, including two for the British Lions. Other individual highlights include a 30-point haul against Canada (December 94), with a 12 out of 12 kicking record, and 27 points against South Africa in Pretoria (94). A member of England's three World Cup squads, Rob shared in three Grand Slam triumphs and performed with distinction on British Lions tours to Australia (89) and New Zealand (93).

ARCHER, Garath Stuart (Lock)
Born South Shields, 15.12.74. 6'6", 18st. Career: PRP. Rep hons: England (2, Sc96), A (8), Emerging, U21, Colts, U18. South West (3), Army. CLR: Bristol (1t-5pts), Newcastle (2t-10pts). Aggressive lock who rejoined Newcastle from Bristol at the end of last season. Garath, the son of former Gosforth wing Stuart Archer, was educated at Biddick School and Durham School and was capped by England 16 Group a year early. A member of the England Schools 18 Group Grand Slam team in 1992 he has moved smoothly through the age group sides, toured Australia and Fiji with England A in 1995 and made his senior debut against Scotland at Murrayfield when he was preferred to Martin Bayfield. Formerly a radio telegraphist with the Royal Signals, Garath represented the Army in the 1995 Inter-Services Championship.

ARMSTRONG, Gary (Scrum-half)
Born Edinburgh, 30.9.66. 5'8", 13st 8lb. Career: PRP. Rep hons: Scotland (32, Aus88, 4t-16pts), A. Barbarians. CLR: 4t-20pts. Gary's outstanding career has been dogged by serious injury, notably knee ligaments and a damaged thumb, but he showed heartening signs of returning to his best form last season and was only denied a full Scotland recall by the exceptional displays of Bryan Redpath. Injuries to Redpath however saw him travel to New Zealand in the summer where he played in both Tests. Gary was educated at Jedburgh GS and Dunfermline HS and won Scotland recognition out of the Jedburgh club where he succeeded Roy Laidlaw at scrum-half. Made his international

debut against Australia in 1988. Gary played a massive part in Scotland's 1990 Grand Slam triumph and produced possibly the best rugby of his career the following year during RWC91. A British Lion in 1989, injuries and the pressure of playing top rugby took their toll in 1993 when Gary declined to tour New Zealand, but he is well capable of challenging for a place in South Africa in 1997.

ARNOLD, Richard (Backrow)
Born Taranaki, New Zealand, 16.8.65. 6'4", 15st 12lb. Career: PRP. Rep hons: North (3, 1t-5pts). CLR: 11t-49pts. Abrasive Kiwi forward who has played for Newcastle since arriving from New Zealand where he was a member of the Eltham club. Signed registration forms for West Hartlepool in 1995 but eventually decided to stay at Kingston Park.

BATES, Steven Michael (Scrum-half/development coach)
Born Merthyr Tydfil, 4.3.63. 5'10", 13st. Career: PRP/coach. Rep hons: England (1, Rom89), A/B (10, USSR89, 1t-5pts). London (29, 2t-9pts). Barbarians (88-89). CLR: Wasps (6t-28pts). Has given up a teaching job in Hampshire to join the Newcastle revolution. Educated at Welwyn and West London Institute, Steve joined Wasps in 1981 and was a key figure in their successes over the last decade. His one cap coincided with a runaway 58-3 victory for England over Romania, but, despite lengthy spells on the bench, he never made the starting line-up again.

BELGIAN, Philip (Utility back)
Born Gateshead, 31.10.75. 6'1", 14st 1lb. Career: Student. Rep hons: North U21. CLR: 1t, 4c, 5pg-28pts. Former RGS Newcastle schoolboy who kicked a huge dropped goal against Mount St Mary's in the 1994 *Daily Mail* U18 Cup final at Twickenham. Joined Newcastle from Bath, and was formerly with Gateshead Fell and West Hartlepool.

BLYTH, Andrew Awburn (Utility back)
Born Hexham, 2.10.75. 6', 13st 9lb. Career: Student. Rep hons: England A (3, WS95, 1t-5pts), U21, Colts, 18 Group. CLR: West Hartlepool (2t-10pts). Andrew transferred from West Hartlepool at the end of the 1995-96 season after a winter which saw him represent England A against Western Samoa and New South Wales. Educated at Mowden Hall, Stockfield, and Rugby School, he is a second-year student at Northumbria University taking geography and sports studies. Enjoys salmon fishing.

CHILDS, Graham Christopher (Centre)
Born Fareham, 3.4.68. 6', 13st 7lb. Career: Marketing executive. Rep hons: England A/B (6, Fr90, 1t-4pts), U21. North (4), London (4). CLR: Wasps (11t-50pts). Reliable centre who was voted Wasps player of the year in 94-95 before a job move brought him back to the north-east. Toured Argentina with England in 1990.

DIXON, John (Lock)
Born Middlesbrough, 5.10.61. 6'5", 19st. Career: Police officer. Rep hons: North (4). Durham. CLR: West Hartlepool (4t-18pts). Educated at Stainsby Comp and Houghall Agricultural College, John began his rugby with Durham City and Acklam and has been a rock for West Hartlepool and Durham county before moving to Newcastle.

DOUGLAS, Stephen Mark (Scrum-half)
Born Newcastle, 21.4.71. 6', 13st 8lb. Rep hons: England A (3, Sp92, 2t-9pts), Students, U21, Colts. CLR: 15t-67pts. Former RGS Newcastle schoolboy whose progress has

been badly hindered by knee surgery. Played for England in 1992 World Students Cup and is a former club captain.

FRANKLAND, Neil (Flanker/hooker)
Born Leeds, 16.2.63. Career: Pharmaceutical chemist. Rep hons: North (3). Yorkshire, Northumberland, British Police. CLR: 6t, 1dg-29pts. Educated at Ilkley GS and Aston University and a former Ilkley player, Neil is equally at home hooking or at wing forward.

METCALFE, Richard (Lock)
Born Leeds, 21.11.73. 7'1", 19st. Career: PRP. Rep hons: A/B (2, Vict95, 1t-5pts), U21, Yorkshire Colts. CLR: 2t-10pts. The only senior player in Britain currently topping 7ft, Richard is a talented all-round forward and a fine prospect. Educated at Rodillian School, Wakefield, he played for Sandal before joining Newcastle. Represented England U21 when they defeated New Zealand *Rugby News* U21 in 1994.

POPPLEWELL, Nicholas John (Prop)
Born Dublin, Ireland, 6.4.64. 5'10", 17st 3lb. Career: PRP. Rep hons: Ireland (39, NZ89, 3t-13pts), British Lions (3, NZ93). Barbarians (88-89). CLR: 3t-15pts. Immensely powerful prop who was first capped against New Zealand in 1989, although he only became a regular choice in 1991. Toured New Zealand with the 1993 British Lions and became the only non-English player in the Test pack. Missed Ireland's tour to Australia in 1994 to undergo surgery to a serious cruciate ligament injury to his knee and was visibly feeling the effects during the following Five Nations, although he was back to top form during RWC95. Educated at Newton Secondary School in Wexford, 'Poppy' was a schools hockey international and played for Greystones before venturing across the Irish Sea, first to join Wasps and then Newcastle.

ROBSON, George Henry (Scrum-half)
Born Alnwick, 24.1.65. 5'9", 12st 10lb. Career: Agricultural sales. Rep hons: Northumberland. CLR: 1t-5pts. Joined Newcastle from Alnwick. He is a county regular for Northumberland. Educated at Scarborough College and Harper Adams Agricultural College.

RYAN, Dean (Back five forward)
Born Tuxford, 22.6.66. 6'6", 17st. Career: PRP. Rep hons: England (3, Arg90, 1t-4pts), A/B (9, Aus88, 3t-13pts). London (15, 3t-14pts). Combined Services. Barbarians (88-89). CLR: Wasps (13t-61pts), Newcastle (2t-10pts). Experienced, aggressive back five forward who first came to national prominence in 1988 helping London to a memorable win over Australia. First capped on tour in Argentina in 1990, Dean left Saracens to join Wasps where he was the heart of their forward effort. Last capped at blindside wing forward against Canada, at Wembley in 1992, but was a hard-working tourist in South Africa (1994). Transferred to Newcastle soon after Rob Andrew's arrival in October 95. Has been bothered by a lingering calf problem over the last two seasons, which has required surgery.

STIMPSON, Tim Richard George (Full-back)
Born Liverpool, 10.9.73. 6'3", 15st 7lb. Career: Personnel officer with ICI. Rep hons: England A (5, Vic95, 2t, 12c, 6pg-58pts), Students, U21, 18 Group. England 7s. North (1). CLR: West Hartlepool (7t, 21c, 42pg-203pts). Powerful long-striding full-back who performed wonders in adversity with West Hartlepool last season. Educated at

Silcoates School, Wakefield, Tim earned England Schools caps at 16 and 18 Group and then moved to Durham University where he obtained a BA in Anthropology. Toured Australia with the England U21 team in 1993, became an A team regular in 1995-96 and moved to Newcastle in May.

UNDERWOOD, Tony (Wing)

Born Ipoh, Malaysia, 17.2.69. 5'9", 12st 10lb. Career: PRP. Rep hons: England (20, Can92, 10t-50pts), A/B (18, Fr89, 16t-58pts), Students, Colts. North (5, 2t-9pts), London (2, 1t-5pts). Barbarians (89-90). CLR: Leicester (24t-111pts), Newcastle (3t-15pts). Sidelined for much of last season following knee surgery after signing from Leicester. Tony was educated at Barnard Castle School and Cambridge University (Blues in 1990 and 1991) and played for England in the World Students Cup (1988), before touring Argentina with England (1990) where a troublesome knee injury again restricted his effectiveness. After an outstanding season for England B in 1992 he won his first senior cap against Canada at Wembley later that year. Shared in England's Grand Slam (95) and played in four games during RWC95, the last being the semi-final in Cape Town when opposite number Jonah Lomu scored four tries.

VAN ZANDVILET, Paul (Prop)

Born Newcastle, 14.10.66. 6', 17st. Career: PRP. CLR: 5t-25pts. Respected and experienced scrummager who joined Newcastle from Whitley Bay Rockcliff.

WALTON, Peter (Flanker)

Born Alnwick, 3.6.69. 6'3", 18st. Rep hons: Scotland (6, Eng94, 2t-10pts), A, Schools. England Colts. North (1). Barbarians (95-96). CLR: Newcastle (11t-45pts), Northampton (2t-10pts). Powerful Anglo/Scot who has played club rugby for Alnwick, Gosforth and Northampton before rejoining the newly constituted Newcastle club. Educated at Merchiston Castle School and the Royal Agriculture College, Cirencester.

WEIR, George 'Doddie' Wilson (Back five forward)

Born Edinburgh, 4.7.70. 6'6", 17st 7lb. Career: Sales executive. Rep hons: Scotland (39, Arg90, 3t-15pts), A, Students, U21, U18. Versatile, experienced and much-travelled Scottish forward who has moved to Newcastle from Melrose, where he was a member of five championship-winning teams. Doddie was educated at Stewart's Melville College and toured New Zealand with the Scottish Schools in 1988, when he played in seven of the eight games. Has subsequently toured New Zealand with the full Scottish squad, North America, Australia and the South Pacific. Enjoyed a particularly successful RWC95, where his ball-handling skills and athleticism were to the fore and has the distinction of scoring two tries against the All Blacks during Scotland's quarter-final defeat at Pretoria. His father played for Gala, as does brother Tom. Keen horse rider (one-day eventing) and enjoys clay pigeon shooting.

WILKINSON, Ross William (Centre)

Born Newcastle, 16.2.62. Career: Inland Revenue executive. Rep hons: Anglo/Scots, Durham, Northumberland. CLR: 21t-100pts. Educated at Lord Lawson Comp, Birtley, Ross played for North Durham RFC before embarking on a distinguished career with Newcastle.

REVIEW

Sir John Hall and Rob Andrew set the tone for the modern era with their big spending and aggressive recruitment, and took a lot of flak in the process. But Newcastle are now well poised to fight their way out of League Two and compete with Europe's best. Andrew has largely targeted seasoned internationals but the signings of Tim Stimpson and Andrew Blyth will surely pay dividends in the future. On the pitch Newcastle struggled until the New Year, and were thankful of the breathing space afforded by the RFU's temporary abolition of relegation, but results predictably improved when the big names became eligible.

NEWCASTLE in the Courage League 1995-96

Sep	9	Moseley	A	Lost	0	9	
	16	Nottingham	H	Won	31	24	Chandler(T) Holder(T) Robson(T) Clark(2C, 4P)
	23	Wakefield	A	Lost	7	26	Penalty(T) Clark(C)
	30	Bedford	H	Lost	23	30	Fletcher(T) Penn(T) Cramb(2C) Clark(2P) Frankland(D)
Oct	7	Blackheath	A	Lost	19	39	Fletcher(T) Cramb(C, 4P)
	14	Waterloo	H	Lost	26	29	Brummitt(2T) Wilkinson(T) Clark(C, 3P)
	21	Northampton	H	Lost	9	52	Cramb(3P)
	28	London Scottish	A	Lost	8	28	Wilkinson(T) Cramb(P)
Nov	4	London Irish	H	Lost	19	23	Wilkinson(T) Cramb(C, 4P)
	11	Moseley	H	Lost	8	9	Wilkinson(T) Chandler(P)
Jan	6	Wakefield	H	Lost	11	17	Metcalfe(T) Cramb(2P)
	13	Nottingham	A	Drew	24	24	Arnold(T) Frankland(T) Cramb(C, 4P)
Feb	17	Blackheath	H	Won	25	10	Cramb(T) Fletcher(T) Wilson(T) Andrew(2C, 2P)
Mar	9	Bedford	A	Won	24	6	Armstrong(T) Cassidy(T) Underwood(T) Andrew(3C, P)
	30	Waterloo	A	Won	36	13	Armstrong(3T) Popplewell(2T) Andrew(2C, P) Cramb(2C)
Apr	6	Northampton	A	Lost	5	26	Underwood(T)
	13	London Scottish	H	Won	45	11	Ryan(2T) Belgian(T, 2C, 2P) Popplewell(T) Underwood(T) Van Zandvilet(T) Walton(T)
	27	London Irish	A	Lost	28	29	Brummitt(2T) Penalty(T) Belgian(2C, 3P)

NOTTINGHAM

Formation of club: 1877
Ground: Ireland Avenue, Beeston, Nottingham. Tel: 0115 9254238
Capacity: 4,950
Colours: White and green
Honours: Middlesex Sevens: Winners 1945. Losing finalists: 1985, 1986
Last season: CL2: 9th. Pilkington Cup: 5th Round (lost 36-10 to Gloucester)
Most capped player: Rob Andrew (England 70)
Director of Rugby: Roger Whittaker
Director of Coaching: David Moss-Bowpit
Captain: TBA

ATKINSON, Peter Thomas (Flanker)
Born Wakefield, 18.9.70. 6'2", 14st. Career: Fitness teacher. Rep hons: N Div U18, Yorks U18, U16. Educated at Crossley Heath School, Halifax, and Loughborough University, Pete is a product of Old Crossleyans, Wakefield and Headingley. Joined Nottingham in September 1995 and has made four first team appearances. Quiet, efficient, workmanlike player.

BARLEY, Tim Peter (Scrum-half)
Born Manchester, 15.12.74. 5'11", 12st 7lb. Career: Student. Rep hons: N Yorks U18, U16. Notts, Lincs and Derbys U21. Educated at Ashville College, Harrogate, he studied maths and biology at Nottingham Trent University before joining Nottingham from Harrogate in September 1993. In his two first team appearances showed enormous potential.

BEESE, Gareth (Flanker)
Born Newport, Gwent, 14.11.72. 5'11", 14st 10lb. Career: Student. Rep hons: Wales U18, East Wales U18, Gwent Schools, Welsh Exiles U21. CLR: 4t-20pts. Educated at Fairwater Comprehensive, Cwmbran, and Nottingham University, Gareth played for Cwmbran and Newbridge before joining Nottingham in 1994. He represented Gwent Schools at all levels from U15-U19 and captained the Welsh Exiles U21 and Nottingham University sides. Joined Nottingham in 1994 and has made 19 first team appearances. Plenty of pace and fire.

BRADLEY, Mark (Flanker)
Born Derby, 21.12.69. 6'3", 15st 7lb. Career: Builder. Rep hons: Notts, Lincs and Derbys U16. CLR: 6t-30pts. Joined Nottingham from Belper in 1990 and has made 109 first team appearances. Made rapid progress last season.

BRENNAN, Jonathan Michael (Flanker)
Born Birmingham, 20.12.71. 5'11", 14st. Career: Purchasing officer. Rep hons: Great Britain Students (Amateur Rugby League). Midlands U18, Warwicks U21, N Midlands U18. CLR: 1t-5pts. Educated at St Peter's RC School, Solihull, Jonathan gained a business studies BSc at Leeds Metropolitan University. He played for Birmingham and Solihull before joining Nottingham in 1994. He has made 27 first team appearances. Has understudied Gary Rees and is regarded as possible successor.

BYGRAVE, Richard James (Centre)
Born Rotherham, 2.5.71. 5'9", 13st 7lb. Career: Warranty administrator. Rep hons: Midland U19, Notts, Lincs and Derbys U21. CLR: 2t-10pts. 'Noggin' attended Chesterfield Boys School and played for the town club before joining Nottingham in 1992. He was a member of the Midlands U19 squad that toured Canada in 1989 Joined Nottingham 1992 and has made five first team appearances. One of the fastest sprinters in the squad.

CARROLL, Nicholas (Centre)
Born Liverpool, 9.1.70. 5'11", 12st 7lb. Career: Teacher. Rep hons: Notts, Lincs and Derbys U21. CLR: 1t, 1dg-8pts. Educated at Cardinal Newman Comprehensive, Pontypridd, Nottingham Polytechnic and Loughborough University. Nick played for Moderns and Llantwit Farore before joining Nottingham in 1993. Suffered injury problems last season but recovered to play in the final weeks.

CLAYDON, Charles (Hooker)
Born Somerset, 24.7.68. 5'10", 13st 10lb. Career: Teacher. Rep hons: Scotland North. Midland U18. CLR: 1t-5pts. Educated at Queen Victoria School, Dunblane, Perthshire, Loughborough University, gaining a BSc in PE, sports science and recreational management. Charlie joined Nottingham in September 1994 and has made 19 first team appearances. Disciplined, reliable workhorse.

DAWSON, Alex (Full-back)
Born Amersham, 22.2.76. 5'10", 12st. Career: Student. Rep hons: Hawkes Bay Colts. South West Div U21. Bucks, Schools. Educated at Aylesbury Grammar School and Nottingham Trent University. A former Northampton player, he joined Nottingham in September 1995 and has made three first team appearances. Plenty of pace but inexperienced.

DOWNEY, Martin Christopher (Prop)
Born Uxbridge, 20.4.65. 6'3", 16st 7lb. Career: Quarry manager. Rep hons: Kent, Norfolk U21, Warwickshire U18, U16. Educated at King Edward V1, Stratford-upon-Avon and Leicester Polytechnic where he gained a BEng (Technology). Married with three sons, he has played for Leicester, Stratford-upon-Avon, Lowestoft and Yarmouth, Maidstone NRFC. Joined Nottingham September 1993 and has made 26 first team appearances. Known as the 'Bonecrusher', a powerful scrummager.

FREER, Martin Trevor (Prop)
Born Chatham, 15.10.63. 5'11", 15st 7lb. Career: Ergonomist. Rep hons: Kent, Kent U21, London Counties U19, Midlands. CLR: 3t-14pts. Educated at Judd School, Tonbridge, and Loughborough University where he gained a BSc (Hons), 'Freeway' has played for Old Juddians and Blackheath. Member of Nottingham's 'World' tour party 1988. Joined Nottingham 1986 and has made 230 first team appearances.

GABRIEL, Brian John (Scrum-half)
Born Dunstable, 25.9.66. 5'11", 14st. Career: Trainee building society manager. Rep hons: Midlands. CLR: 8t, 1c, 3pg-43pts (Bedford). Educated at Manshead Upper School, Dunstable, 'Gabs' has had three spells at Nottingham. He played for Bedford

and Dunstable before joining Nottingham in 1989. He returned to Bedford 1991-92, rejoined Nottingham 1992-93, joined Leicester 1993-94, rejoining Nottingham 1994-95. Needs one match to complete 100 first team appearances. Nearing the end of a long and distinguished career.

HODGKINSON, Simon David (Full-back)
Born Bristol, 15.12.62. 5'10", 12st. Career: Owns sports supply business. Rep hons: England (14, Rom89, 1t, 35c, 43pg-203pts), B (3, Fr88, 2t, 10c, 7pg-49pts), U23, Students. Barbarians. Midlands. Educated at Stamford School and Trent Polytechnic where he gained BA in business studies, 'Hodgie' joined Nottingham in 1981. Appointed captain 1987-88, leading club on 'World' tour 1988, he has achieved remarkable feat of playing 313 first team matches over 13 seasons despite international and divisional calls. Has joined Nottingham's coaching staff and was being talked into playing one more season at pre-season training.

IRELAND, Mark Winston (Prop)
Born Kendal, 5.10.66. 5'10", 15st 7lb. Career: Medical rep. Rep hons: Northern Division Colts, London Division U21, Cumbria Colts (captain). CLR: 1t-5pts. Educated at Heversham Grammar School, Cumbria and Loughborough University where he gained BSc in sports studies and geography, 'Irish' joined Nottingham in 1990. He has made 48 first team appearances. Inspirational motivator both on the pitch and in the dressing room.

JACKSON, Andrew Lee (Prop)
Born Lancaster, 8.1.67. 5'10", 14st 7lb. Career: Electrical engineer. Rep hons: Staffs Colts. CLR: 2t-10pts. Educated at Chasetown High School, 'Jacko' joined Nottingham from Lichfield 1991. He has made 114 first team appearances. Solid technique compensates for lack of stature. Hard scrummager.

JONES, Lee (Prop)
Born Ilkeston, 16.6.71. 6'4", 17st. Career: Computer programmer. Rep hons: Notts, Lincs and Derbys, U21. Educated at Kirk Hallam Comprehensive and SE Derbys College, he joined Nottingham from Ilkeston 1994-95 and has made 20 appearances. Sprang from junior rugby to become one of the most exciting talents in the squad. Useful lineout jumper.

LAKE, Richard John (Fly-half)
Born Dewsbury, 13.10.73. 6', 14st. Career: Student. Rep hons: England B U16, Scottish Exiles U21, U17, North Div U16, Yorkshire U21. Educated at Abbey Grange High School, Leeds and Nottingham Trent University, he joined Nottingham from Leicester in 1995, making one first team appearance last season.

MALIK, Nigel (Flanker)
Born Nottingham, 19.8.66. 6'3", 15st 8lb. Career: Policeman. Rep hons: Notts, Lincs and Derbys, and U21. Educated at West Bridgford High School and Ealing College, he played for Paviors, Ealing and Richmond before joining Nottingham 1983. Left 1986, rejoined 1993 and has made 30 first team appearances. Methodical, workmanlike player.

REED, Steven (Wing)
Born Stockton-on-Tees, 20.2.75. 5'11", 14st 2lb. Career: Student. Rep hons: Scotland U21, England U19, Schools, Midlands U21. CLR: 5t-25pts. Educated at Solihull School and Nottingham Trent University studying law, he joined Nottingham from Leicester in 1994 and has made 17 first team appearances. The most charismatic squad member when breaking off either foot to launch an attack. Reliable finisher.

REES, Gary William (Flanker)
Born Long Eaton, 2.5.60. 6', 14st 7lb. Career: Financial consultant director. Rep hons: England (23, SA84, 2t-8pts). Barbarians. Midlands. Educated at Trent College, Long Eaton, he joined Nottingham 1978. Captained Midlands Championship winners 1994-95 which led to England recall. Appointed Nottingham coach 1993-94. He has made 302 first team appearances over 16 consecutive seasons. Vastly experienced and respected flanker whose international caps were restricted by Peter Winterbottom's excellence.

ROBINSON, Wayne Andrew (Full-back)
Born Mansfield, 6.8.75. 6'3", 13st 8lb. Career: Student. Rep hons: Midlands U21, Colts. Notts, Lincs and Derbys Colts. Educated at Manor School and Clarendon College, he joined Nottingham from Mansfield in 1992. Learned a lot on his tour to Canada with the Midland Under-21 side but yet to realise full potential. He has made two first team appearances.

ROYER, Alan Richard (Scrum-half)
Born Leicester, 1.12.70. 6', 12st 7lb. Career: NRFC administrator. Rep hons: England Schools, U18. CLR:8t-40pts. Educated at Lutterworth Grammar School and Loughborough College, he played for Leicester, Leicester Vipers and made guest appearance for Fylde before joining Nottingham 1993. He has made 60 first team appearances. Starts the new season with an invitation to join the Midland squad. Potential match-winner.

RUTTER, Bradley Jonathan (Fly-half)
Born Sutton-in-Ashfield, 5.6.74. 5'11", 13st 5lb. Career: Student. Rep hons: Midland Division Colts, Notts, Lincs and Derbys U21. Educated at Clarendon College, he joined Nottingham from Mansfield in 1991. He has made four first team appearances.

SMITH, Damian (Centre)
Born Nottingham, 21.11.71. 6'2", 14st 2lb. Career: Hospital physiotherapist. Rep hons: Notts, Lincs and Derbys, U21. Educated at Redhill Comprehensive and Birmingham University, gaining BA in physiotherapy. Joined Nottingham from Moderns 1995 and has made only two first team appearances after an administrative error caused confusion over his registration. Tipped to become a key player with enough pace to burn-off opponents.

SUSSUM, Robert Brian William (No 8)
Born Limaoady, N Ireland, 12.9.70. Rep hons: Irish Exiles U21. London Schools, Midland Universities. Educated at The Leys School, Cambridge, and Nottingham University. Joined Nottingham from London Irish 1994. Returned to Irish in September 1995, re-joining Nottingham later in 1995-96. Has made 14 first team appearances but his form has suffered through changing clubs.

TOMLINSON, Richard George (Centre)
Born Worcester, 25.11.71. 5'10", 13st 9lb. Career: Surveyor. Rep hons: England Schools U18 group, Midland Division U21, North Midlands U21. Educated at Kings School, Worcester, Loughborough University, Sheffield Hallam University, joined Nottingham from Rugby 1994. He has made 13 first team appearances but is likely to become first choice centre this season. Plenty of pace with sound handling technique.

VELDHUIZEN, Albert Dirk Willem (2nd row)
Born Leicester, 30.11.70. 6'4", 17st 7lb. Career: Sales adviser. Rep hons: Notts basketball U16. Educated at Lancaster Boys School, Rugby School, and Strathclyde University, played for Vipers (Leics), Glasgow High Kelvinside, Brussels British and Strathclyde University before joining Nottingham in 1993. Has made 12 first team appearances.

WEBSTER, John Andrew (Centre)
Born Fulford, 3.10.69. 5'11", 14st. Career: Accountant. Rep hons: England Students, U21, Universities, Schools. N England Schools. Notts, Lincs and Derbys U21. Educated at Pocklington, York, and Nottingham University, played for Selby before joining Nottingham 1990. He has made 40 first team appearances. Progress in business has blunted initial rugby sparkle but intelligent and gifted performer.

REVIEW

Nottingham finished second from bottom of Courage League Two, losing 12 of their 18 fixtures. They beat London Scottish 32-16 to reach the fifth round of the Pilkington Cup only to lose 36-10 at home to Gloucester. President John Drapkin commented: 'Not a great season. Despite some impressive talent, performances did not live up to expectations until the last month of the season.' Results suffered chiefly through a loss of dressing-room morale in the early stages which was addressed and rectified in the second half of the season. Simon Hodgkinson and Gary Rees each completed 300 first team appearances. Richard Byrom, who has joined Worksop, and Chris Gray each completed 100 Courage League appearances. The transfers of Matt Gallagher and Andy Smallwood to Coventry in May brought the curtain down on a season's struggle at Beeston as the 119-year-old club fought to come to terms with rugby's revolution.

NOTTINGHAM in the Courage League 1995-96

Sep	9	Blackheath	H	Won	31	17	Beese(T) Reed(T) Royer(T) Stent(2C, 4P)
	16	Newcastle	A	Lost	24	31	Beese(2T) Parsonage(T) Hodgkinson(3C, P)
	23	Northampton	H	Lost	7	43	Smallwood(T) Gallagher(C)
	30	London Scottish	A	Lost	9	17	Hodgkinson(D, 2P)
Oct	7	London Irish	H	Lost	9	22	Hodgkinson(3P)
	14	Moseley	A	Lost	6	18	Hodgkinson(2P)
	21	Waterloo	H	Lost	12	18	Hodgkinson(4P)
	28	Wakefield	H	Won	22	18	Reed(T) Hodgkinson(C, 5P)

Nov	4	Bedford	A	Lost	12	20	Ireland(T) Royer(T) Hodgkinson(C)
	11	Blackheath	A	Lost	16	25	Claydon(T) Hodgkinson(C, 3P)
Jan	6	Northampton	A	Lost	5	35	Gallagher(T)
	13	Newcastle	H	Drew	24	24	Penalty(T) Reed(T) Hodgkinson(C, 4P)
Feb	17	London Irish	A	Lost	27	39	Bygrave(T) Byrom(T) Hodgkinson(C, 2D, 3P)
Mar	9	London Scottish	H	Lost	12	19	Hodgkinson(4P)
	30	Moseley	H	Won	48	27	Royer(3T) Reed(2T) Carroll(T) Gallagher(T, C) Hodgkinson(4C, P)
Apr	6	Waterloo	A	Won	24	13	Brennan(T) Hodgkinson(T, 3C, P) Smallwood(T)
	13	Wakefield	A	Lost	15	36	Gallagher(T) Smallwood(T) Hodgkinson(C, D)
	27	Bedford	H	Won	30	11	Royer(2T) Bradley(T) Byrom(T) Hodgkinson(2C, 2P)

RICHMOND

Formation of club: 1861
Ground: The Athletic Ground, Kew Foot Road, Richmond, Surrey TW9 2SS.
 Tel: 0181 940 0397
Capacity: 5,000
Colours: Old gold, red and black
Honours: Middlesex Sevens: Winners: 1951, 53, 55, 74, 75, 77, 79, 80, 83
Last season: CL3: 3rd. Pilkington Cup: 3rd round (lost 27-12 to London Welsh)
Most capped player: Brian Moore (England) 64
Director of Rugby: John Kingston
Coaches: John Kingston, Rob Lozowski
Captain: Ben Clarke

BOYD, Adrian (Fly-half)
Born Enfield, 9.8.72. 5'10", 11st 9lb. Career: Accountant. Rep hons: England Students,
U21. CLR: 16t-80pts. Educated at St Olave's GS, Adrian played for Orpington and
Westcombe Park and won a Blue at Cambridge (1993) before joining Richmond.
Leading League try scorer in 1995-96 with 11.

BROWN, Spencer 'Buster' (Wing)
Born Eton, 11.7.73. 5'10", 13st. Career: Royal Marines musician. Rep hons: Navy,
Combined Services. Strong-running wing who trained at the Marines School of Music
in Deal where he played for Deal RFC. Educated at Weavers School, Wellingborough.

CARR, Paul (Lock)
Born London, 25.3.68. 6'7", 15st 2lb. Career: Graphic designer. Rep hons: Hampshire
U21. CLR: 1t-5pts. Product of Lancashire Poly and Fylde RFC.

CLARKE, Andrew (Wing)
Born London, 14.8.74. 5'7", 12st 13lb. Career: Student. Rep hons: England U21,
Students. CLR: 5t-25pts.

CLARKE, Benjamin Bevan (Backrow)
Born Bishop's Stortford, 15.4.68. 6'5", 17st 7lb. Career: PRP. Rep hons: England (28,
SA92, 2t-10pts), A (11, Sp91, 2t-8pts), Students. British Lions (3, NZ93). Barbarians
(90-91). CLR: Saracens (8t-32pts), Bath (14t-68pts). Assumes the captaincy at Richmond after signing from Bath in May. Ben remains one of the most talented and
versatile backrow players in the game and the dual challenge of helping Richmond and
gaining a place in the Lions touring party to South Africa should give an extra edge to
his game this season. Educated at Bishop's Stortford College and the Royal Agricultural College, Cirencester, Ben was another to benefit from the coaching of Tony Russ
at Saracens and was already poised for England honours when he joined Bath. After a
satisfactory debut against South Africa in 1992, he impressed during a poorish Five
Nations season for England and was outstanding at blindside wing forward for the
Lions in New Zealand in 1993. Intends to retain a working connection with National
Power.

119

CLARKE, Christopher John (Prop)
Born Poole, 1.9.71. 6', 16st. Career: Accountant. Rep hons: England A (7, It93), U21, 18 Group. South West (8). Barbarians (94). Educated at Marlborough College, Swansea University and Oxford University, Chris moved smoothly through the England age groups but was unable to establish himself at senior level with Bath, so moved to Richmond in the summer of 1996.

COTTRELL, Stephen Richard (Centre)
Born Christchurch, New Zealand, 22.10.67. 6'1", 14st 7lb. Career: Lawyer. Rep hons: New Zealand Development XV, Universities. Otago. Wellington. Rock-solid Kiwi centre who captained New Zealand in the 1992 World Students Cup. Also led Cambridge University to victory in the 1995 Varsity match having missed the previous year's game through injury. Graduated from Cambridge with an M.Phil. (Criminology) and joins Richmond as an amateur.

CROMPTON, Darren (Prop)
Born Exeter, 12.9.72. 6'1", 17st. Career: PRP. Rep hons: England A (2, S Aus95, 1t-5pts), Emerging, U21, 18 Group. South West (5). CLR: 5t-25pts. Educated at Exeter College, Darren captained England 18 Group in 1991 and is a former England U21 captain. Represented England in the 1992 World Students Cup and toured Australia and Fiji with England A in 1995. Moved to Richmond in May from Bath, where first team rugby often proved elusive. Don't pick an arguement with his father who represented GB at judo and Ireland at shooting.

CUTHBERT, Andy Simon Jonathan (Hooker)
Born 11.2.68. 5'10", 14st 7lb. Rep hons: England U21, Students. CLR: 12t-60pts.

DAVIES, Adrian (Fly-half)
Born Bridgend, 9.2.69. 5'9", 12st. Career: PRP. Rep hons: Wales (9, Barbarians90, 2c, 3pg, 3dg-22pts), A/B, U21, Schools. Adrian signed for Richmond from Cardiff in May, having amassed 846 points for Cardiff in the last four seasons of Heineken League rugby. After learning his rugby at Pencoed and Neath, he won four rugby Blues at Cambridge, where he also represented the University at soccer. Sporadic international career since making his debut as a replacement against the Barbarians in 1990, but has been a member of Wales' RWC91 and 95 squads and toured Australia (91), Zimbabwe and Namibia (92), Canada and the South Pacific (94) with the national team. Former member of the Mid Glamorgan Youth Orchestra and choir.

FALLON, Jim (Wing)
Born Devon, 27.3.66. 6'1", 14st 4lb. Career: PRP. Rep hons: England A/B (5, Fr90, 3t-12pts). South West (6, 5t-20pts). Barbarians (90-91). CLR: Richmond (8t-32pts), Bath (8t-32pts). Jim returns from a four-year spell with Leeds RL with the proud boast of being the only player to appear in both a Pilkington Cup final at Twickenham, with Bath, and a Silk Cut Challenge Cup final at Wembley, with Leeds in 1995. Powerful, deceptively quick and a fierce tackler, Jim had joined Bath from Richmond and was seemingly on the verge of a full England rugby union cap in 1992 when he went to rugby league.

FOSTER, James (Prop)
Born 24.3.67. 6'1", 16st 10lb. Career: Oil analyst. CLR: 3t-13pts. Cambridge Blue in 1988 and a former member of Chinnor RFC.

GOODBURN, Giles Andrew (Centre)
Born Worthing. 11.11.72. 5'11", 13st. Career: Trainee accountant.

GREGORY, Jonathan (Full-back)
Born Chertsey, 2.6.73. 6'1", 13st 8lb. Career: Student. Rep hons: England Colleges and Universities. Middlesex. CLR: 5t, 43c, 69pg-318pts. Educated at St Mary's Catholic School, Bishop's Stortford.

HARRISON, Harry (Lock)
Born Wegburg, West Germany, 27.4.71. 6'8", 19st. Career: Royal Navy officer. Rep hons: Royal Navy, Combined Services. Educated at the Read School, Drax.

HARVEY, Ben (Scrum-half)
Born Redruth, 26.6.74. 5'9", 13st. Career: Student. Rep hons: South West U21. Educated at St Thomas's, Exmouth, Ben was Kyran Bracken's understudy at Bristol.

HUTTON, Michael James (Centre/wing)
Born London, 9.4.70. 6', 15st 7lb. Career: Doctor. Rep hons: England U21, Middlesex. CLR: 21t-95pts. Mike captained Richmond to promotion in 1995-96 and is vice-captain this season. Educated at St Benedict's, Ealing, and the Charing Cross and Westminster Medical School.

HUTTON, Robert John (Flanker)
Born London, 11.9.72. 6', 15st 10lb. Career: Student. Rep hons: England 18 Group. Younger brother of Michael and another product of St Benedict's, Ealing. Played rugby league at Nottingham University and has experimented playing hooker.

JONES Adam (Full-back/wing)
Born Basingstoke, 7.11.74. 5'11", 12st 7lb. Career: Student. Rep hons: Wales Youth. Educated at Millfield and Kingston University, Adam arrives from Harlequins having made his Quins debut against Cambridge University in November 94. Represented Wales in World Students Cup this summer.

JONES, Luke Evan (Flanker)
Born Suffolk, 6.11.70. 6'3", 14st 7lb. Career: Trainee accountant. Rep hons: London U21. CLR: 4t-20pts. A former Surrey Schools cricketer, Luke was educated at RGS Guildford and Oxford University where he studied experimental psychology.

KOTTLER, James (Wing/centre)
Born Huddersfield, 10.1.72. 6'1", 14st 7lb. Career: Accountant. CLR: 2t-10pts. Graduate of Newcastle University, he played previously for Northampton U21 and Harlequins U19.

MARTIN, Neil Frederick Clay (Backrow)
Born Birmingham, 19.10.69. 6'3", 15st 4lb. Career: PRP. Rep hons: England Students. Midlands. CLR: 7t-28pts. Former Moseley captain and Oxford's best forward in the 1994 Varsity match. Educated at King Edward's School, Birmingham, and Birmingham University, Neil is also a cricket Blue.

MASON, Simon John Peter (Full-back/wing)
Born Birkenhead, 22.10.73. Career: PRP. Rep hons: Ireland (2, Wal96, 2c, 6pg-22pts),
A, Students, U21. North of England U21. CLR: Newcastle (1t, 22c, 46pg, 2dg-193pts).
Orrell (4t, 16c, 38pg-166pts). Arrives at Richmond via Liverpool-St Helens, Newcastle
Gosforth and Orrell, where his all-round play impressed all-comers last season. Edu-
cated at St Anselm's College, alongside Leicester's Austin Healey, Simon narrowly
missed out on England Schools and England U21 honours and, with three Irish
grandparents in Dublin, happily answered the call from Ireland. Made his A team
debut on the wing against Scotland and was called into the full side against Wales after
Jim Staples was concussed against France. Retained his place ahead of Staples for the
visit to Twickenham and also played for the Ireland XV against the Barbarians in the
Peace International.

MOORE, Andrew Phillip (Scrum-half)
Born Cardiff, 6.9.68. 5'10", 12st 10lb. Career: PRP. Rep hons: Wales (4, Jap95,
2t-10pts), Students, U20, U19. Former Bridgend and Cardiff scrum-half who has
joined Richmond in tandem with his Cardiff half-back colleague Adrian Davies.
Andrew was a pupil at Llanishen HS, Cardiff, and played for various Welsh age group
teams before captaining Wales U20. Scored the winning try for Oxford in the 1990
Varsity match while studying for a diploma in social studies and played one season for
Bridgend before rejoining Cardiff, where he had played his youth rugby. Nominated as
the Man of the Match after Cardiff's SWALEC Cup final victory over Llanelli (1994),
Andrew scored a try on his international debut against Japan in Bloemfontein during
RWC95. Played against South Africa in September 95 and against Fiji and Italy, but
lost his international place to Robert Howley.

MOORE, Brian Christopher (Hooker)
Born Birmingham, 11.1.62. 5'9", 14st 8lb. Career: Lawyer. Rep hons: England (64,
Sc87, 1t-4pts), A/B (3, It85, 1t-4pts), Students, U23. British Lions (5, Aus89). Midlands
(10), London (11). Barbarians (87-88). CLR: Nottingham (1t-4pts), Harlequins (2t-
9pts). Comes out of retirement to join Richmond as an amateur. Won the last of his 64
England caps against France in the RWC95 play-off game in Pretoria and finally
stepped aside at Harlequins in December 1995. Educated at Crossley and Porter GS
and Nottingham University, Brian is England's most-capped hooker and was an
integral member of three World Cup squads and three Grand Slam-winning teams.
Captained Nottingham, where he was a club member for ten years, and also led
England Students before making his international debut against Australia in RWC87.
His experience could prove important in a vital season for Richmond.

QUINNELL, Craig (Back five)
Born Swansea, 9.7.75. 6'6", 18st. Career: PRP. Rep hons: Wales (1, Fiji95), U21, U19,
Schools. Strapping forward who arrives at Richmond from Llanelli with an impressive
family pedigree that includes brother Scott, father Derek and uncle Barry John.
Educated at Llandovery College, where he won schoolboy honours, Craig rocketed
through the age group levels and made his senior debut against Fiji last November at
the age of 20.

QUINNELL, Scott Leon (Backrow)
Born Swansea, 2.8.72. 6'4", 16st 8lb. Career: PRP. Rep hons: Wales (9, Can93,
3t-15pts), A/B, Youth, U18. Barbarians (93-94). Wales RL. Scott returns to Union
from Wigan RL where he was developing into one of the best all-round forwards in the
13-man code. The son of Derek and nephew of Barry John, Scott played for Wales at all
age group levels, touring New Zealand in 1990 with the Schools and Canada in 1991

with the Youth before turning to senior rugby with Llanelli. Made his international debut against Canada (November 93) and played a starring role in the Welsh team that won the 1994 Five Nations, including the try of the tournament against France at Cardiff Arms Park. Last played for Wales against Western Samoa that summer, Scott also represented his country in the 1995 Rugby League World Cup, reaching the semi-final before losing to England.

SHORT, Ben Mark (Scrum-half/fly-half)
Born London, 18.2.71. 5'10", 13st 12lb. Career: Advertising. Rep hons: England Colts, Schools. CLR: 5t-25pts. Educated at King's, Winchester, and Kingston University, Ben has previously played for Harlequins and Queensland University.

SHORT, Cameron James (Centre)
Born London, 18.2.71. 6', 14st. Rep hons: England Colts. Educated at Montgomery of Alamein School, Winchester, Cameron is Ben's twin brother and joins Richmond from London Irish.

TAYLOR, Will (Centre)
Born Roehampton, 7.11.72. 6', 13st 9lb. Career: Student. Rep hons: England Schools. Educated at Gunnersbury School and Richmond Sixth Form College. Will has played for Exeter University and Florida State while studying USA. Has switched from flanker to centre.

WEST, Richard John (Lock)
Born Hereford, 28.3.71. 6'8", 20st. Career: PRP. Rep hons: England (1, WS95), A (2, Natal95), Emerging, Students, U21. Midlands (5), South West (1). Barbarians (93-94). Educated at Hillside School in Malvern and Old Swinford School in Stourbridge. Played for Ledbury and Longlevens before joining Gloucester.

YELDHAM, Matthew (Prop)
Born London, 29.1.69. 5'11", 17st. Career: Insurance underwriter. Rep hons: England Students. CLR: 1t-5pts. Educated at Uppingham School and Southampton University. Matt has also played for Haywards Heath and Harlequins U21.

REVIEW

A tumultuous season for one of England's oldest clubs which saw Richmond promoted from League Three and a rash of sensational signings, courtesy of Ashley Levett who invested £2.5m in the club. First came the Cardiff and Wales half-backs Andrew Moore and Adrian Davies and then, in one fell swoop at the Cafe Royal, Ben Clarke, rugby league stars Scott Quinnell and Jim Fallon, and Darren Crompton and Richard West were unveiled. By way of a curtain call, Orrell and Ireland full-back Simon Mason signed up two weeks later. All fitted Levett's criteria that they should be at the peak of their careers. His five-year plan now is to win promotion from League Two at the first attempt and to become Europe's top side.

RICHMOND in the Courage League 1995-96

Sep	9	Morley	H	Won	27	24	Boyd(T) Cuthbert(T) Fitzgerald(T) Gregory(4P)
	16	Rosslyn Park	A	Won	16	11	Luger(T) Gregory(C, 3P)
	23	Fylde	H	Won	47	11	Boyd(2T) Cuthbert(T) Fitzgerald(T) Hutton(T) Penalty(T) Gregory(4C, 3P)
	30	Rotherham	A	Won	43	6	Elliott(2T) Boyd(T) Fitzgerald(T) Gregory(T, 3C, 4P)
Oct	14	Rugby	A	Won	21	20	Luger(T) Short(T) Gregory(C, 3P)
	21	Otley	H	Won	46	3	Boyd(2T) Jones(2T) Della-savina(T) Gregory(T, 4C, P) Kottler(T)
	28	Harrogate	A	Won	48	19	Cuthbert(T) Elliott(T) Fitzgerald(T) Hutton(T) Jones(T) Luger(T) Short(T) Gregory(5C, P)
Nov	11	Coventry	A	Lost	12	13	Gregory(4P)
Jan	6	Reading	A	Won	5	3	Short(T)
	13	Rotherham	H	Lost	9	16	Gregory(3P)
Feb	10	Rugby	H	Drew	13	13	Cuthbert(T) Gregory(C, 2P)
	17	Otley	A	Won	41	17	Boyd(2T) Hutton(2T) Elliott(T) Palmer(T) Gregory(4C, P)
	24	Harrogate	H	Won	24	7	Greenwood(T) Gregory(T, C, 4P)
Mar	23	Coventry	H	Won	15	10	Boyd(T) Cuthbert(T) Gregory(C, P)
	30	Reading	H	Won	28	17	Clarke(2T) Elliott(T) Hutton(T) Gregory(C, 2P)
Apr	6	Morley	A	Lost	21	24	Boyd(T) Gregory(T, 2P) Roblin(T)
	13	Rosslyn Park	H	Won	35	26	Clarke(3T) Cuthbert(T) Roblin(3C, 3P)
	27	Fylde	A	Lost	25	26	Boyd(2T) Cuthbert(T) Gregory(2C, 2P)

ROTHERHAM

Formation of club: 1923
Ground: Clifton Lane, Badsley Moor Lane, Rotherham, S Yorks S65 2AA.
  Tel: 01709 370763
Capacity: 1,520
Colours: Maroon and sky hoops
Honours: Courage League: Division 4 champions 1994-95
Last season: CL3: 4th. Pilkington Cup: 2nd Round (lost 24-15 to Coventry)
Most capped player: –
Coaches: Ged Glynn, Geoff Wappett
Captain: TBA

BARRATT, Chris (Hooker)
Born London. 5'11", 15st 7lb. Career: Engineering sales manager. Educated at Sheffield
University, Chris played for Blackheath before joining Rotherham in 1993. Has yet to
become a regular first teamer.

BAYSTON, Tom (Hooker)
Born Goole, 9.11.66. 5'10", 15st 7lb. Career: Farmer. CLR: 5t-25pts. Joined Rotherham
from Selby in 1993. Lacks physical stature but is incredibly strong. Regular first teamer
before 1995-96 season when appearances were limited.

BINNS, Simon James (Fly-half)
Born 20.9.74. 5'11", 13st 7lb. Career: Student. Rep hons: England U21, Students,
Schools. Yorkshire. CLR: 1t, 2c, 2pg, 1dg-18pts. Simon, tipped to extend his representative honours, has been signed from Moseley where he made six first team appearances. Yorkshire and England Under-21 stand-off last year, he has just completed
studies at Birmingham University. A former Bradford GS pupil, he is reunited with
assistant coach Geoff Wappett, who enjoyed such success coaching at the school.

BRACKENBURY, Russell Andrew (Backrow)
Born Dronfield, 21.2.64. 6'1", 16st 7lb. Career: Local government officer. CLR: 1t-5pts
(Nottingham). Joined Rotherham from Nottingham in 1994. Utterly reliable when
given a first team chance. Squad member.

BUNTING, Simon (Prop)
Born Rotherham, 17.9.70. 6'1", 16st 7lb. Career: Construction worker. CLR: 1t-5pts.
Graduated from Rotherham Colts to make first team debut in 1991. Mobile but trying
to improve strength with weight training.

BURNHILL, Steve (Centre)
Born Cleckheaton. 5'11", 13st. Career: Agricultural representative. Rep hons: Barbarians (94). North. Yorkshire (captain). CLR: 1t-4pts (Leicester); 9t-36pts (Sale); 1t-5pts
(Rotherham). Educated at Loughborough University, Steve toured South Africa in
1984 with England as a student. Former Sale and Leicester player, returned to his first
club Cleckheaton before joining Rotherham in 1995. Made Courage League debut for
Rotherham last season.

CARR, Jeremy (Second row)
Born Sheffield. 6'7", 19st. Jeremy moved to South Africa with his family as a youngster and played a good standard of rugby there. Joined Rotherham in 1994 but missed all of last season with a broken leg. Trained hard in the close season to recover full fitness for the 1996-97 season.

CHALLINOR, Andrew (Backrow)
Born Rotherham, 23.8.69. 6'3", 18st. Career: Local government officer. Rep hons: Yorkshire Colts. CLR: 3t-15pts. Joined Rotherham in 1992. Tremendous physique. Missed part of last season studying for exams. A surveyor for Rotherham Council.

COY, Sam (Prop)
Born Rotherham, 19.1.66. 5'11", 18st 7lb. Career: Farmer. CLR: 4t-20pts. Ex-Rotherham Colts. Made Rotherham first team debut 1985. Superb scrummager. Works on the family farm just outside Rotherham.

DAWSON, Martin (Full-back)
Born Nottingham. 6', 12st 6lb. Career: Sports goods salesman. CLR: 2t-10pts. Educated at Mount St Mary's School, Sheffield, and Loughborough University. Martin joined Rotherham in 1995, One of the club's fastest sprinters after developing his pace in track work at Loughborough.

DUDLEY, John (Backrow)
Born Sheffield, 16.7.66. 6'4", 18st. Career: Builder and nightclub bouncer. CLR: 9t-45pts. John has played more than 250 games for the club, 98 in local and national Courage League, scoring 28 tries. A product of Rotherham Colts, he made his first team debut in 1984. As Rotherham have moved up the leagues, so John has adapted to the demands at higher level. Aggressive forward. Dangerous on the charge from tapped penalties.

HARPER, Jon (Centre)
Born London, 9.9.74. 6', 13st 7lb. Career: Student. Rep hons: London Colts. CLR: 9t-45pts. Joined Rotherham 1993. Immaculate handler, tackling compensates for lack of real pace. Studying for a Masters at Sheffield University.

HARRIS, Nick (Backrow)
Born Newcastle-upon-Tyne. 6'5", 16st. Career: Surgeon. CLR: 3t-15pts. Joined Rotherham from Sheffield in 1994. Impeccable manners in the clubhouse but the subject of close scrutiny by referees during matches.

HEASELGRAVE, Richard (Wing)
Born Birmingham. 5'11", 13st. Career: Student. Rep hons: England Students. Yorkshire, Students. CLR: 8t-40pts. Joined Rotherham 1994 and was an ever-present in 1995-96 season. Studying for Masters at Sheffield University. Utility back. Represented Yorkshire in the County Championship last season.

McINTYRE, Darren (Scrum-half)
Born Hull. 5'11", 13st 7lb. Career: Agricultural representative. CLR: 2t, 1dg-13pts.
Played for Hull Lomans before joining Rotherham in 1995. Powerful on the break,
Darren works closely with the backrow.

MILLS, Matthew (Second row)
Born Selby, 29.12.73. 6'6", 16st. Career: Student. A student at Sheffield Hallam
University, Matt joined Rotherham in 1994. Became first team regular towards the end
of last season. Exceptionally fit. Lives for rugby.

PASCOE, Ashley (Scrum-half)
Born Gwent. 5'7", 12st 7lb. Career: Teacher. CLR: 1t-5pts. Educated at Loughborough
University before taking a teaching job in South Yorkshire. Made a few first team
appearances as third choice scrum-half.

PINDER, Mark (Backrow)
Born Rotherham, 18.12.70. 6', 16st 7lb. Career: Teacher. Joined Rotherham in 1991 as a
Colt. Yet to become first team regular.

RICHARDSON, Brian (Second row)
Born Edinburgh, 8.6.59. 6'7", 17st. Career: RAF. Rep hons: Scotland B. Joined Rotherham from Boroughmuir in 1991. Captained Boroughmuir to the Scottish First Division
title. Works in the RAF careers office in Sheffield. Eldest squad member. Excellent
motivator.

RICK, Lee (Prop)
Born Rotherham, 20.3.69. 6'2", 17st 7lb. Career: Engineer. Rep hons: England Colts.
North Colts. CLR: 1t-5pts. Made his first team debut in 1987. Lost ground as a player
when he was made redundant and worked abroad. Returned in 1995. Solid, strong
prop.

SCOTT, Paul (Wing)
Born Rotherham, 18.10.65. 5'11", 13st 7lb. Career: Company director. Rep hons:
Northumberland, Students. CLR: 12t, 2c, 2pg, 1dg-73pts. Graduated from junior
ranks at Gosforth, as Newcastle University student, and Rotherham to become a first
team regular. Has caught the eye of statisticians at the start of 1996-97 season with 299
first team appearances, 99 in local and national Courage League matches. Played
County Championship for Northumberland when competition was stronger. Unlucky
not to receive Yorkshire call-up.

SELKIRK, Richard (No 8)
Born Sheffield, 19.6.62. 6'1", 17st. Career: Teacher. CLR: 11t-55pts. Joined Rotherham
in 1986 after playing for Sheffield and Headingley. Richard has made more than 250
appearances for Rotherham, 103 in national and local Courage League matches, with
44 tries. Captained first team 1988-93. Wields massive influence over Rotherham. Made
national news in 1994-95 when broke his ever-present League record to attend a family
wedding in the West Indies. Organising brains of the pack. Slight lack of height has
probably cost him higher honours. Hobby: basketball.

TURNER, Tim (Centre)
Born Rotherham, 16.6.68. 6'2", 14st. Career: Male model. CLR: 5t-25pts. Graduated from Rotherham's junior sides. Made his first team debut in 1987. Tim has overcome a series of injuries after breaking his leg on elevation to the first team. Leicester tried to recruit him three years ago.

WAREHAM, Richard (Hooker)
Born Wakefield. 5'11", 16st 7lb. Career: South Yorkshire's RFU youth development officer. CLR: 1t-5pts. Educated at Loughborough University, Richard played for Leicester and Moseley before joining Rotherham in 1994. Prop converted to hooker.

WEST, Craig (Backrow)
Born Rotherham, 8.2.64. 6'2", 17st. Career: Electrician. Rep hons: North. CLR: 9t-45pts. Joined Rotherham in 1988 from local club Dinnington. He toured Italy with the North Division in summer 1996 after bringing appearance tally in local and national Courage League matches to 86 with 21 tries. Rejected many offers to play at higher level to remain loyal to Rotherham. Hopes to return to Dinnington to complete playing career.

WILSON, Scott (Prop)
Born Rotherham, 14.1.72. 5'11", 16st. Career: Engineer. Graduated from Rotherham Colts to make first team debut 1993. Incredible body strength but not first choice. Weights and training fanatic.

WOOD, Matt (Backrow)
Born Sheffield, 5.6.72. 6'2", 16st 7lb. Career: Construction worker. Former Rotherham Colts, he made his first team debut in 1992. Irregular first team appearances but reliable when promoted.

REVIEW

Rotherham struggled to come to terms with the pace of Courage National League Three after clinching the League Four title in 1994-95. Three of the first four League matches were lost and a battle for survival seemed inevitable when they crashed out of the second round of the Pilkington Cup in early October, losing 15-24 at home to Coventry. By the half-way stage, Rotherham's performances had shown a marked improvement with narrow losses at Otley and Coventry followed by wins against Harrogate and Reading. The transformation in the New Year was staggering. Players returned from injury, new players were recruited, and the club stormed to nine wins in ten matches to clinch promotion by finishing fourth behind Coventry, Richmond and Rugby. Martin Dawson, Steve Burnhill, Ashley Pascoe, Darren McIntyre and Cambridge University captain Steve Cottrell made their League debuts for the club. Cottrell's decision to join Richmond, however, is a blow. Ged Glynn now leads the coaching team, helped by England 18 Group coach Geoff Wappett.

ROTHERHAM in the Courage League 1995-96

Sep 9	Rosslyn Park	A	Lost	14	29	Dudley(T) Heaselgrave(T) Plant(2C)
16	Fylde	A	Won	19	16	Harper(T) Plant(C, 4P)
23	Rugby	A	Lost	18	30	Penalty(T) Turner(T) Plant(C, 2P)
30	Richmond	H	Lost	6	43	Plant(2P)
Oct 14	Otley	A	Lost	25	27	Askwith(2T) Harper(T) Heaselgrave(T) Plant(C, P)
21	Harrogate	H	Won	35	3	Scott(2T) Pascoe(T) Selkirk(T) Sorby(T) Plant(2C, 2P)
28	Coventry	A	Lost	12	15	Plant(2D, 2P)
Nov 11	Reading	H	Won	25	22	Bayston(T) Breakwell(T, C) Coy(T) Scott(T) Plant(P)
Jan 6	Morley	A	Won	11	10	Rick(T) Plant(2P)
13	Richmond	A	Won	16	9	Dudley(T) Hough(T) Breakwell(2P)
Feb 10	Otley	H	Won	36	22	Hough(T) Selkirk(T) Turner(T) Worrall(T, C) Plant(C, D, 3P)
17	Harrogate	A	Won	26	20	Harper(2T) Plant(2C, D, 3P)
24	Coventry	H	Lost	13	40	McIntyre(T) Scott(T) Plant(P)
Mar 23	Reading	A	Won	17	15	Dawson(T) Heaselgrave(T) Scott(T) Plant(C)
30	Morley	H	Won	29	21	Selkirk(2T) Burnhill(T) Plant(C, 4P)
Apr 6	Rosslyn Park	H	Won	24	9	Dawson(T) Heaselgrave(T) McIntyre(T, D) Plant(C)
13	Fylde	H	Won	29	19	West(2T) Selkirk(T) Plant(C, D, 3P)
27	Rugby	H	Won	29	18	Harper(T) Heaselgrave(T) Plant(2C, 5P)

RUGBY LIONS

Formation of Club: Reconstituted in 1994
Ground: 9 Webb Ellis Road, Rugby, CV22 7AW. Tel: 01788 542433
Capacity: 4,000
Colours: Orange, black and white
Honours: CL2: Winners 1990-91 CL3: Runners-up 1988-89
Last season: CL3: 3rd. Pilkington Cup: 3rd round (lost 27-7 at Saracens)
Most capped player: Geoffrey Conway (England) 18
Director of Rugby: Mal Malik
Coach: Paul Williams
Captain: David Bishop

ASHMEAD, Paul (Flanker)
Born 3.1.66. 6'1", 15st 2lb. Rep hons: South West (2). Gloucestershire. CLR. Gloucester (10t-42pts), Rugby (2t-10pts). Tough flanker and former first team regular at Gloucester whose experience is proving invaluable for Rugby.

BAKER, Simon (Scrum-half)
Born 1.2.75. 5'7", 12st 8lb. Career: Student. Rep hons: Warwickshire. Coventry-born trainee teacher who has been studying at Liverpool University. Has proved an able deputy to Bishop.

BISHOP, David (Scrum-half)
Born Westminster, 5.1.65. 5'10", 13st 8lb. Career: Sales manager. Rep hons: Midlands (1). Irish Exiles, Warwickshire. CLR: 29t-130pts. Inspirational captain who missed just one League game last season. Educated at Skinners School, Tunbridge Wells, and Leicester University, David works for Paramount Press in London.

BOWMAN, Philip John (Lock)
Born Burton-on-Trent, 16.2.65. 6'5", 17st 10lb. Career: Financial consultant. Rep hons: England Colts. Warwickshire. CLR: 7t-29pts. Has enjoyed a long and successful second-row partnership with Steve Smith for club and county. Educated at Redmor HS and John Cleveland College, Hinkley, Phil joined Rugby in 1986 from the Hinkley club and is the longest-serving member of the first team squad.

BROADY, James (Prop)
Born 3.5.74. 5'9", 16st 2lb. Gloucester second team player before he moved to Rugby. Voted Newcomer of the Year 1995-96. Robust, mobile and aggressive, James is expected to make a big impact this season.

BURDETT, Robert Leslie (Hooker)
Born Rugby, 26.7.73. 5'11", 14st 7lb. Career PE teacher. Rep hons: Warwickshire. CLR: 4t-20pts. Promising young hooker who was educated at Lawrence Sheriff School, Rugby, and Loughborough University. Rob became a regular in the Warwickshire county side in 95-96 at the expense of Coventry's Dave Addleton, having made his

debut against Notts, Lincs and Derby in 94-95. His arrival heralded a run of 11 consecutive victories which ended only when they lost to Gloucestershire in the 1996 final. Rob is a physical education teacher at Nicholas Chamberlaine School in Bedworth.

CHAPMAN, Richard (Centre)
Born 12.2.74. 6', 14st. Rep hons: Warwickshire, Midlands U21 Outstanding prospect though he was held back by injury in 1995-96.

ELLIS, Mark Richard (Lock)
Born Kirby Muxloe, 23.12.68. 5'11", 14st 12lb. Career: Builder. Rep hons: Warwickshire, Leicestershire, Midlands U21. CLR: 2t-9pts. Represented Warwickshire in the 1995-96 CIS County final. Mark was educated at Mount Grace High, John Cleveland College and Hinkley College. Was a member of Hinkley RFC before joining Rugby in 1988. Subsequently moved to Kenilworth, but returned for the 1995-96 season.

EVANS, Denzil (Fly-half)
Born Rugby, 1.12.74. 5'9", 12st 3lb. CLR: 8c, 10pg, 1dg-49pts. Hails from a Welsh family, but Rugby born and bred, and an exciting talent. Denzil is an outstanding product of Rugby's Colts squad.

EVANS, Steve (Prop)
Born 10.2.75. 5'11", 16st 7lb. Rep hons: Midlands U21 Warwickshire. CLR: 1t-5pts. Steve is another of Rugby's impressive array of props. He likes the ball in hand and his scrummaging has improved steadily.

GARDNER, John (Flanker)
Born 15.2.70. 6'1", 15st 3lb. Career: Gas fitter. Rep hons: Warwickshire. CLR: Nuneaton (2t-8pts), Rugby (3t-15pts). Uncompromising former Nuneaton and Broadstreet flanker.

GILLOOLY, Adrian Michael (Wing/Centre)
Born Rugby, 6.4.70. 6', 14st 1lb. Career: Accountant. Rep hons: Warwickshire, Irish Exiles U21. CLR: 5t-25pts. A versatile back, Adrian was educated at Lawrence Sheriff School and Loughborough University and came up through the youth system at Webb Ellis Road. Enjoyed one season with Dundas Valley in NSW (1993).

GLOVER, Stuart (Centre)
Born 3.11.69. 6', 14st. Career: Student. Rep hons: England Students. Warwickshire. CLR: Bedford (1t-4pts), Rugby (3t-15pts). Quality centre who arrived from Bedford. Mature student at Exeter University.

MEE, Richard (Prop)
Born 25.5.67. 6', 18st 7lb. Rep hons: Warwickshire. CLR: 2t-10pts. Formerly with Leicester. Toured France with Warwickshsire in May 1996.

MILNER, Robert (Hooker)
Born Coventry, 5.6.68. 5'11", 14st 9lb. Career: Farmer. Rep hons: Warwickshire. Reliable squad member who joined Rugby from Nuneaton. Educated at Nicholas Chamberlaine Senior, Bedworth, and Warwickshire College of Agriculture.

NICHOLLS, Mark (No 8)
Born 7.7.71. 6'4", 15st 4lb. CLR: 1t-5pts. Son of Gloucester stalwart Mike Nicholls, Mark still lives at Kingsholm Road. Suffered from a stress fracture to his ankle last season, but should challenge hard in 1996-97.

ORAM, Dave Edward (Flanker)
Born Sutton Coldfield, 25.2.68. 6'2", 14st 4lb. Career: Welder. Rep hons: Warwickshire. CLR: 3t-15pts. Lively former Moseley flanker, Dave also enjoyed a year working and playing in Sweden before joining Rugby. Educated at Alderbrook Comprehensive and Solihull College.

PALMER, Mark William (Centre)
Born Great Yarmouth, 23.3.67. 6', 13st. Career: Accountant. Rep hons: Warwickshire. CLR: 9t, 3c, 1pg-52pts. Club stalwart Mark works in Coventry and played for Warwickshire in the CIS County final in 1995-96. Educated at Reading School and Leicester University, he joined Rugby from the Abbey Club in Reading.

PELL, Richard (Fly-half)
Born 2.10.60. 5'10", 13st. Rep hons: Midlands. Warwickshire. CLR: 14t, 3c, 5pg, 14dg-126pts. A talented veteran, Richard tried to give up last year to coach but the promising Jack McLeod was lured north of the border and Pell again answered the call. Noted dropped goal specialist.

QUANTRILL, Jim (Full-back)
Born Poole, 30.5.69. 6'2", 15st. Career: Bank employee. Rep hons: Midlands (4, 5c, 8pg-34pts). English Universities, UAU. Warwickshire. Barbarians (95-96). CLR: 6t, 40c, 69pg-316pts. Impressed for the Midlands during 1995-96 CIS Divisional Championship. Jim also represented the Barbarians against Newport and scored 183 League points in 17 games for Rugby in 1995-96. Formerly with Old Silhillians and Birmingham & Solihull, he was educated at Solihull School and Nottingham University.

REVAN, Trevor Samuel (Prop)
Born Moseley, Birmingham, 5.12.63. 6'2", 17st 7lb. Career: Warehouse assistant. Rep hons: England A/B (1, Ire91). Midlands (6, 1t-4pts). Warwickshire. CLR: 7t-31pts. A renowned scrummager, Trevor was educated at Hartfield Crescent Comprehensive. A former member of Birmingham Welsh, he has represented Warwickshire for ten years.

SAUNDERS, Eddie (Wing)
Born 2.11.60. 6'. 12st 7lb. Rep hons: Midlands (10, 2t-9pts), Barbarians (96), Warwickshire. CLR: 51t-232pts. Lightning quick wing who has proved a magnificent servant for Coventry and Rugby. Was finally selected for the Barbarians against Cardiff over

Easter 96 and celebrated with a try, but England honours have always eluded him. Has scored a record 51 Courage League tries – Tony Swift is the nearest on 43 – Eddie crossed for nine League scores in 1995-96. Received a special award for his services to rugby from the Rugby Writers' Club in 1996 and Rugby organised a testimonial game at the end of the season. Intends to play one more season.

SMITH, Steven Davis (Lock)
Born Solihull, 20.6.68. 6'6", 17st 3lb. Career: Company accountant. Rep hons: Midlands, U21. Warwickshire. Irish Exiles. CLR: 1t-5pts. Powerful lock who joined Rugby after spells with Old Silhillians, Solihull, Coventry and Tukapa in Taranaki. Educated at Lode Heath secondary and Solihull College.

THOMPSON, Paul (No 8)
Born 24.9.74. 6'4", 15st 7lb. Career: Student. Rep hons: Midlands U21, Warwickshire. Emerging backrow player. Paul is a student at Hull University.

UNDERHILL, Neil (Lock)
Born 23.6.72. 6'10", 17st. Rep hons: Warwickshire. Lineout expert Neil is a graduate of Loughborough University and spent the summer playing club rugby in Canterbury, New Zealand, and is beginning to fulfil his enormous lineout potential.

WATSON, Dean (Wing)
Born Coventry, 8.11.65. 5'9", 13st. Career: Fireman. Rep hons: Warwickshire. CLR: 4t-18pts. Reliable wing, joined Rugby from Stoke Old Boys in 1989. Educated at Coventry Boarding School in Shropshire, Dean works as a fireman in Coventry.

WRAITH, David (Centre)
Born 18.1.69. 5'10", 12st 8lb. Career: Post office employee. Rep hons: Warwickshire. CLR: 1t-5pts. Talented all-rounder, played cricket for Warwickshire U21

REVIEW

It was an enjoyable season at Webb Ellis Road where Rugby Lions have now become a PLC in preparation for professional rugby, although the vast majority of their squad remain uncontracted amateurs. As ever, a strong pack laid the foundations for success and many of the same personnel helped Warwickshire to another CIS County final where they eventually lost to Gloucestershire. Ever-green scrum-half David Bishop missed just one game and fly-half Richard Pell was again a mainstay, despite threatening to retire the previous summer. Eddie Saunders, another 'veteran', helped himself to nine League tries and received the biggest cheer of the season when he captained Rugby against an Invitation XV in an end-of-season testimonial. Saunders, still one of the fittest wings around, has promised to continue for this season at least. Rugby have retained virtually the same squad for the last three years and are hoping that an excellent team spirit can help them retain a place in League Two.

RUGBY in the Courage League 1995-96

Sep	9	Fylde	H	Won	36	9	Bishop(2T) Ellis(T) Quantrill(3C, 5P)
	16	Coventry	A	Won	13	6	Quantrill(T, C, 2P)
	23	Rotherham	H	Won	30	18	Saunders(3T) Pell(T) Evans(2C, D, P)
	30	Reading	A	Won	23	13	Quantrill(T, 2C, 3P) Saunders(T)
Oct	14	Richmond	H	Lost	20	21	Gillooly(T) Penalty(T) Quantrill(2C, 2P)
	21	Morley	A	Lost	13	21	Pell(T) Quantrill(C, 2P)
	28	Otley	A	Lost	12	13	Quantrill(4P)
Nov	11	Rosslyn Park	H	Won	22	13	Quantrill(T, 3P) Saunders(T) Pell(D)
Jan	6	Harrogate	H	Won	25	19	Jenkins(T) Pell(T) Revan(T) Saunders(T) Quantrill(C, P)
	13	Reading	H	Won	37	19	Glover(T) Jenkins(T) Palmer(T) Saunders(T) Quantrill(4C, 3P)
Feb	10	Richmond	A	Drew	13	13	Saunders(T) Quantrill(C, 2P)
	17	Morley	H	Won	27	16	Glover(2T) Quantrill(C, 5P)
	24	Otley	H	Won	22	11	Burdett(2T) Mee(T) Quantrill(2C P)
Mar	30	Harrogate	A	Won	8	3	Saunders(T) Quantrill(P)
Apr	6	Fylde	A	Won	16	13	Palmer(T) Quantrill(C, 3P)
	13	Coventry	H	Lost	13	24	Ashmead(T) Quantrill(C, 2P)
	27	Rotherham	A	Lost	18	29	Bishop(T) Pell(T) Quantrill(C 2P)
May	4	Rosslyn Park	A	Won	47	23	Oram(2T) Ashmead(T) Bishop(T) Evans(T) Nicholls(T) Wraith(T) Evans(3C, P) Quantrill(P)

WAKEFIELD

Formation of club: 1901
Ground: Pinderfields Road, College Grove, Wakefield WF1 3RR. Tel: 01924 374801
Capacity: 2,450
Colours: Black and gold quarters
Honours: Yorkshire Cup: Winners 1968-69, 77-78, 81-82, 85-86, 89-90, 93-94
Last season: CL2: 4th. Pilkington Cup: 5th Round (lost 16-12 to Bath)
Most capped player: Mike Harrison (England) 15
Manager: Andy Gomersal
Coaches: Jim Kilfoyle, Roger Burman, Steve Townend, Clive Harris
Captain: Simon Croft

ADAMS, John (Flanker)
Born Wakefield, 2.9.65. Career: Student teacher. CLR: 1t-5pts. Joined Wakefield from
neighbouring Sandal. Has had to live in first-team regular Jon Griffiths' shadow, but
should get his break during Jon's year at Cambridge University.

BAILEY, Alistair (Lock)
Born 27.6.73. Career: Student. Recently graduated with a music degree, Ally shows
cultural depths rarely seen in the scrum. He has patiently developed his undoubted
talent and should become a cornerstone of the pack.

BARTLE, Jamie (Wing)
Born Leeds. Career: Student. Rep hons: England Schools. Made his first team debut
when still at school. Progress last season wrecked by a serious knee injury received in a
Colts trial. He has made a full recovery and the coaches expect rapid development this
season. Formerly a pupil at Mount St Mary's School, Jamie scored a superb try in the
1994 *Daily Mail* U18 Cup final against RGS Newcastle.

BIRKBY, Alex (Scrum-half)
Born 21.7.77. Long and successful club career is predicted for Alex after dramatic
progress last season.

CROFT, Simon (Lock)
Born Harrogate, 22.3.65. Career: Estate agent. CLR: 1t-5pts. Imported from Harrogate
in 1993, Simon has been chosen to captain the team this season, a reward, the coaches
say, for his selfless commitment and rapid all-round improvement to his game.

FALKINGHAM, Derek (Lock)
Born Leeds, 9.12.64. Career: Policeman. Rep hons: Yorkshire. CLR: 3t-15pts. Joined
Wakefield from Morley three seasons ago with a reputation for jumping power in the
lineout. Achieved his ambition of playing for Yorkshire and is a regular choice for the
Police.

FLINT, Jonathan (Centre)
Born Harrogate, 6.6.71. CLR: 6t, 1pg-33pts (Otley). Joined this season from Otley.
Played for Otley and Yorkshire.

GARNETT, Terry (Hooker)
Born Hull, 10.5.67. 5'11", 16st 9lb. Career: Chartered surveyor. Rep hons: England Colts. North. CLR: 10t-42pts. Launched playing career at Hull Ionians and later played for Hull and East Riding before joining Wakefield. Made his mark as a flanker for England Colts. Named in that position as replacement for Northern Division against Australia 1987. Senior debut for North in France 1993. Terry's switch to hooker has given his rugby career a boost. Vital member of Wakefield's fiery front row last season, resulting in occasional brushes with referees. Lives in Hull. One of youngest ever to win judo black belt. Enjoys fishing.

GLEN, Michael (Wing)
Born 6.11.76. Career: Student. Rep hons: Scotland U21 Recommended to the club by Moseley officials and studying in Leeds, Mike is expected to push hard for regular first team service this season.

HENDRY, Derek (Backrow forward)
Born South Africa, 15.5.71. Career: Insurance agent. Joined the club in November 1995 after arriving from South Africa. 'Dixie' received limited opportunities during his qualifying period last season but has shown tremendous determination and dedication in summer training to suggest he will become a valuable asset in Courage League matches this season.

JACKSON, Michael (Full-back)
Born Manchester, 21.1.67. 6'1", 13st 10lb. Career: Bank official. Rep hons: North. Lancashire, Colts. CLR: 4t, 44c, 124pg-480pts (Fylde). Launched career at Old Aldwinians, Manchester, before moving to Fylde where he became captain. Joined Wakefield 1995-96. Mike was first team captain for two of his first three seasons with the club. Versatile, he played on the wing for the North on tour to Zimbabwe two years ago and has played also at centre and fly-half. Capable goal-kicker.

JONES, Stephen (Wing)
Born Hartlepool, 9.6.75. 6', 12st 9lb. Rep hons: England U21 CLR: 2t-10pts (West Hartlepool). Joined Wakefield from West Hartlepool in the close season.

LANCASTER, Phil (Prop)
Born Hartlepool, 15.1.64. 6'1", 16st 7lb. Career: Leading fire fighter. Rep hons: North. Durham. England Fire Services. CLR: 3t-13pts (West Hartlepool). Has captained the Durham county side. Joined Wakefield from West Hartlepool, where he was a former captain, in the close season.

LATHAM, Rod (Prop)
Born Ghana, West Africa, 1.8.69. Career: Between jobs. Rep hons: North. Yorkshire, U21, Schools, Colts. Northern Division replacement last season. Rod's career began with Yorkshire club Selby. Brought up in Ghana where his father, a mining engineer, played rugby. Ability to play on either side of the scrum has solved many selection problems when players injured. Experience of playing county rugby added a new dimension to his game last season. He has become more mobile with greater try-scoring potential. Lists 'wine, women and song' and angling (32lb pike biggest catch) as hobbies. Lost job in dripping factory during summer beef scare.

McCLARRON, Alisdair (Wing)
Born Driffield, 19.6.73. 6'3", 14st. Signed in the summer from East Yorkshire Courage North East One club Driffield, Alisdair is reputed to be one of the finest young prospects in the region. Tall and very quick, he has been a prolific try scorer in junior rugby and is hoping to repeat that success in League Two.

MANLEY, Paul (Flanker)
Born Stockport, 26.1.68. 6'1", 15st 7lb. Career: Civil engineer. Rep hons: England Colts. North. Lancashire. CLR: 7t-29pts (Orrell). Made his mark at Burnage before moving to Orrell where he became a stalwart member of the club. Played many times for Lancashire and made his debut for the North in 1990. Joined Wakefield in the close season.

MASSEY, Peter (Full-back)
Born Pontefract, 3.4.75. 5'11", 13st 7lb. Career: Student. Rep hons: England U21, Colts. North U21. Yorkshire U18. U19. CLR: 6t-30pts (Morley). Member of the North Under-21 Championship winning team 1995-96. Toured Italy this year with North Development squad before leaving neighbouring Morley to join Wakefield in the close season. Enjoys music and travel and is an accomplished cricketer.

MAYNARD, Philip (Centre)
Born 8.1.70. Career: Salesman. Rep hons: England Colts. CLR: 10t-47pts. Phil is one of Wakefield's longest serving players with a record stretching back 10 years. Under-rated strong running centre. Most appearances (31) last season.

PETYT, Richard (Fly-half)
Born Keighley, 4.7.67. 6', 13st 7lb. Career: Chartered surveyor. Rep hons: Yorkshire 18 Group. Northumberland. CLR: 3pg-9pts (Newcastle Gosforth); 3t, 9c, 14pg, 9dg-101pts (Otley); 3t, 1dg-18pts (Wakefield). Educated at Bradford Grammar School, Richard first played for Rugby when still at school. Later studied at Newcastle University, joining Newcastle Gosforth where he gained a place in the Northumberland team. Joined Otley and moved to Wakefield in the close season. He was on the replacement bench for the North against Canada A last season, but has yet to make his senior Divisional debut.

RUSHWORTH, Christopher (Flanker)
Born 27.2.69. Career: Engineer. Rep hons: Army. CLR: 3t-15pts. Joined the club three seasons ago when serving as an Army regular. Now rated an uncompromising blindside flanker after establishing his credentials as a first teamer last season.

SCULLY, David Andrew (Scrum half)
Born Doncaster, 7.8.65. 5'8", 12st. Career: Fire fighter. Rep hons: England B (4, It92, 1t-4pts), Sevens. North. Yorkshire, Colts. CLR: 37t, 2pg-166pts. Debut for England B 1992, touring New Zealand with them that year. Captained Northern Division against the All Blacks at Liverpool RFC 1993. Member of England's World Cup Sevens winning team in 1993, receiving 'Best Moment' award for cover tackle. Represented England in the 1995 and 1996 Cathay Pacific-Hong Kong Bank Sevens tournaments. Wakefield's most experienced player and former captain. Remains loyal to the club despite receiving many offers to play for League One clubs.

STEWART, Paul (Lock)
Born Halifax, 9.10.62. 6'6", 16st 9lb. Career: HGV driver. Rep hons: North. Yorkshire.
CLR: 5t-24pts. Wakefield's second-longest serving player, Paul first played at 14 for
Halifax junior club Heath. Stayed at that club for 15 seasons. Unlucky not to gain
representative honours, but fulfilled that ambition when joining Wakefield. Played for
Yorkshire and established himself at Divisional level, playing twice for North on their
challenging tour to France 1993. Member of the North team that beat Western Samoa
1995-96. Competitive and works hard at his game.

SZABO, Richard (Prop)
Born Leeds, 13.7.66. 6', 16st 10lb. Career: Policeman. Rep hons: Yorkshire. British
Police. Joined Wakefield from Morley in 1993. Injuries have curtailed his appearances
but his powerful scrummaging has gained him Yorkshire county and British Police
honours.

THOMPSON, Richard (Wing)
Born Leeds, 3.12.69. 6', 13st 7lb. Career: Bank official. Rep hons: England 16 and 18
Group. North, 16 and 18 Group. Yorkshire. CLR: 19t-93pts. Missed two seasons with a
broken leg received playing for England 18 Group against France at La Rochelle, 1988.
Later played for Yorkshire and the North at Under-21 level, making his senior Yorkshire debut 1992-93. Left College Grove briefly to play for West Hartlepool. Richard
became Wakefield's main strike force when Jon Sleightholme joined Bath. Switched
from full-back to wing last season. Wakefield's 1995-96 'Player of the Year'. Ambitions
to join the West Yorkshire Police Force.

WHITE, Paul (Wing/Centre)
Born 15.12.64. Career: Dentist. Rep hons: Irish Exiles. CLR: 5t-25pts. Joined Wakefield from Morley where he gained experience at centre but has developed into a
match-winning wing. Described by Wakefield coaches as a quiet, thoughtful player.

WILBY, John (No 8)
Born 19.1.66. Played for Loughborough University, Nottingham and Leeds before
joining Wakefield after a 'year out' through lost interest. Re-established his game last
season before a broken leg, in a match at his old club Nottingham, terminated his
season. Trained hard in the close season and was expected to make a full recovery for
1996-97.

WYNN, Ian (Centre)
Born St Helens, 19.8.68. 6'2", 14st. Career: Draughtsman. Rep hons: Scottish Exiles.
Development XV. CLR: 16t-80pts. Destructive runner with the ball in hand who joins
Wakefield from Orrell.

REVIEW

League Two runners-up to Saracens in 1994-95 but not promoted, Wakefield failed to
reproduce their form of the previous season with disappointing results, despite a late
flourish to clinch fourth place. Injuries, suspensions and non-availability of players
depleted the squad for the first half of the season and loss of concentration in the

final stages of matches against London Scottish, Moseley and Nottingham resulted in defeats in games they should have won. Wakefield's 16-12 home defeat by Bath in the Pilkington Cup fifth round was their best performance and hinted at their true potential. Regular first teamers Gavin Baldwin and Nick Green departed for Leeds at the end of the season, but several players were recruited in the summer with loyal supporters making generous donations to keep the club competitive. Outstanding openside flanker Jonathan Griffiths played rugby league for Paris St Germain in the summer and will be attending Cambridge University in the autumn, but will be available thereafter.

WAKEFIELD in the Courage League 1995-96

Sep 9	Bedford	H	Won	32	23	Maynard(T) Metcalfe(T) White(T) Yates(T) Jackson(3C, 2P)
16	Blackheath	A	Lost	16	20	Penalty(T) Jackson(C, 3P)
23	Newcastle	H	Won	26	7	Green(T) Petyt(T) Jackson(2C, 4P)
30	Northampton	A	Lost	0	23	
Oct 7	London Scottish	H	Lost	16	20	Rushworth(T) Jackson(C, 3P)
14	London Irish	A	Lost	7	31	Miller(T) Jackson(C)
21	Moseley	H	Lost	9	11	Jackson(2P) Shuttleworth(D)
28	Nottingham	A	Lost	18	22	Maynard(T) Shuttleworth(T) Jackson(C, 2P)
Nov 4	Waterloo	H	Won	14	6	Falkingham(T) Jackson(3P)
11	Bedford	A	Lost	13	20	Scully(T) Jackson(C, 2P)
Jan 6	Newcastle	A	Won	17	11	Green(T) Jackson(4P)
13	Blackheath	H	Won	17	0	Petyt(T) Scully(T) Jackson(2C) Metcalfe(D)
Feb 17	London Scottish	A	Won	31	22	Green(T) Scully(T) Stewart(T) White(T) Jackson(C, 3P)
Mar 30	London Irish	H	Lost	19	31	Metcalfe(T) Jackson(C, 4P)
Apr 6	Moseley	A	Won	26	15	Rushworth(T) Scully(T) Jackson(2C, 4P)
13	Nottingham	H	Won	36	15	Scully(2T) Jackson(T, C, 3P) Maynard(T) Rushworth(T)
20	Northampton	A	Lost	21	34	Jackson(T, C, 3P) Scully(T)
27	Waterloo	A	Lost	10	20	Adams(T) Jackson(C, P)

WATERLOO

Formation of club: 1882
Ground: St Anthony's Road, Blundellsands, Liverpool L23 8TW.
 Tel: 0151 924 4552
Capacity: 8,900
Colours: Green, red, white
Honours: Pilkington Cup: Runners-up 1977
Last season: CL2: 5th. Pilkington Cup: 4th round (lost 20-15 at Leeds)
Most capped player: H.G. Periton (England) 21
Chairman of rugby: Richard Greenwood
Manager: Ian Aitchison
Coaches: Tosh Askew, Gareth Hopkin
Captain: Nick Allott

ALLOTT, Nicholas (Flanker)
Born Southport, 2.2.64. 6'5", 17st, 4lb. Career: Computer sales executive. Rep hons:
North. Lancashire. CLR: 4t-19pts. Joined Waterloo from Southport. Good club man
who played one season at Liverpool-St Helens before returning to Waterloo. Chosen to
captain the side in 1996-97 after successful stint as skipper in 1990-91. Great motivator
generating enormous respect from players and club officials. One of northern rugby's
most underrated players. Hard, strong man.

BECKETT, Mark Douglas (Prop)
Born Hartlepool, 16.10.65. 6'2", 19st 7lb. Career: Financial services sales executive. Rep
hons: North. Lancashire. CLR: 2t-9pts. Known as 'Onslow' because of his resemblance
to a television character, Mark joined Waterloo from West Hartlepool. Started his
career as a No 8 but is employed as a prop by Waterloo. Coaches working on increased
mobility to utilise his skills in rucks and mauls after two seasons of unsatisfactory
performances. Hoping to prove a point to critics this season. Buys shirts with 19.5 inch
collars.

BLYTH, David (Back row forward)
Born Liverpool, 14.3.71. 6'3", 17st. Career: Leisure industry. Rep hons: England U21,
Colts. Scottish Exiles. North. Lancashire. CLR: 2t-10pts. Yet to fulfil full potential, he
was a member of the North of England's 1996 summer tour to Italy. Works with Dick
Greenwood offering corporate hospitality: Euro 96, British Grand Prix, British Open
golf among successful campaigns in summer 1996. Powerful on the burst and uses his
height to telling effect at the back of the lineout. In his mid-20s, much depends on
players like David this season.

BRUCE, Ian (Wing)
Born Colombo, Sri Lanka. 5'10", 14st. Career: Medical student. Rep hons: Scotland
U21. Scottish Exiles. North Schools. Lancashire. Schools. CLR: 1t-5pts (Orrell),
3t-15pts (Waterloo). Has spent 1996 in New Zealand on medical exchange trip.
Expected to return for club duty in October 1996. A former Orrell player, Ian has relied
heavily on pace to burn-off opponents since playing representative schools rugby.

BUCKTON, Peter (Flanker)
Born Hull, 24.11.60. 6'2", 14st. Career: Waterloo youth development officer. Rep hons:
England A (3, It95), U23, Students. Barbarians. North. Yorkshire. CLR: 6t-24pts

(Liverpool-St Helens), 11t-54pts (Waterloo). The 'Old Fox' is one of the best uncapped players of his generation. Missed full England cap because considered too fragile. Played for Liverpool and Orrell before joining Waterloo four years ago. Outstanding individualist, extremely mobile. Light, quick, supportive player. Has captained Waterloo for the past two seasons and is club's former rugby director. Has led North of England and Yorkshire.

COAST, Marcus (Centre)
Born 14.5.76. 6'1", 14st. Career: Student. Rep hons: North U21. Cheshire U21. New arrival from New Brighton. Rugged centre, performances for North U21 squad have impressed Dick Greenwood for past two years. First spotted at Merseyside and Waterloo schools level. Closely resembles style of ex-Waterloo star Andy Northy, now playing at St Helens.

DICKINSON, Jamie (Wing)
Born 26.7.76. 5'9", 11st. Career: Student. Rep hons: Herts U21, Colts. A student on three-year course at Edge Hill College, Ormskirk. Jamie broke into the first team towards the end of last season. Quick, elusive, balanced runner. He can also play full-back. Tipped for stardom. Represented former club St Alban's in Pilkington Shield 1994-95. Keen athlete.

EMMETT, Martin (Fly-half)
Born 4.5.71. 5'10", 12st 2lb. Career: Computer technician. CLR: 1t, 14c, 34pg-135pts. Steady, first team regular at full-back in 1995-96 but prefers fly-half. Grabbed his chance when Chris Thompson was injured last season. Martin, a dressing-room wag, is nicknamed 'Oko', 'Scapegoat' and 'Big Fella'.

EVANS, Damion (Back row forward)
Born 29.11.74. 6'3", 15st 7lb. Career: Student. Rep hons: Ireland U21. Midlands U21, Colts. Joined midway through 1995-96 season but was hardly seen at Waterloo through Ireland U21 commitments. Sound, strong tackler, he attends Sir John Moores University. Travelled from Midlands for pre-season training. One of the most promising youngsters in the club.

GREEN, Jason (Wing)
Born 19.1.72. 5'6", 13st 3lb. Career: PRP. Rep hons: Lancashire Colts. Fast and elusive. Signed from Widnes rugby league club in the close season. Waterloo scouts pounced on hearing Jason wanted to play rugby union. Certain to become first team regular and should inject much needed experience and excitement on touchline.

HACKETT, Paul (Hooker)
Born 28.2.64. 5'11", 15st 4lb. Rep hons: England Colts. North. Cheshire. CLR: 5t-21pts. Former Waterloo captain. Made debut for North of England 1987. Paul is a skilful all-rounder, and Dick Greenwood first coached him playing for England Colts 1983. Left Waterloo briefly for Crewe and Nantwich but returned last season when he became bored with retirement.

HANDLEY, Anthony (Fly-half)
Born Manchester, 18.11.73. 5'10", 13st. Career: Student. Rep hons: England U21, Students, Colts. Lancashire. CLR: 1t, 1c, 7pg, 1dg-31pts. Tipped to fulfil his potential

this season after restless period as rugby under-achiever. Played at centre for two seasons when Neil Ryan occupied fly-half berth. Attends Liverpool University and represented Lancashire in a County Championship final. Known as 'Biff'. Avid cross-word puzzler on away trips.

HILL, Michael (Prop)
Born Skegness, 5.6.71. 6'2", 17st 7lb. Career: Teacher. Rep hons: Cheshire. Joined Waterloo from Manchester at the end of 1995-96 season. Qualifies to play start 1996-97 season.

HILL, Nigel (Centre)
Born Johannesburg, South Africa, 4.12.67. 6', 13st 6lb. Career: Teacher. Rep hons: South West U21. Oxfordshire. CLR: 1t-5pts. Joined Waterloo on qualifying for sports science course at Liverpool Polytechnic. Steady inside-centre tackling well above his weight. Spent a season at Moseley but returned to command a regular first team place. Teaches at Meole Brace School, Shrewsbury. Can also play at fly-half.

KAY, Ben (Back row)
Born Bootle, 14.12.75. 6'6", 17st. Career: Student. Rep hons: England U21, Colts, Students. North. Lancashire. CLR: 1t-5pts. Son of Waterloo president and High Court Judge John Kay, Ben is regarded as a high-flier. Known as 'M'lud', he is one of Waterloo's great hopes. Represented England Students at 1996 World Students Cup in South Africa. Talented athlete, big, quick, highly regarded by the England hierarchy. Dismissed allegations he lacks power with powerhouse performances on North of England's Italy tour June 1996.

McCAUGHREAN, Philip (Centre)
Born Liverpool, 2.12.69. 5'10", 15st 3lb. Career: Timber merchant. Rep hons: England Colts, Schools. CLR: 4t, 2pg-26pts. Nicknamed 'Corky', shed two stones weight pre-season on orders of coaches. Converted scrum-half. Talented footballer accused of lacking commitment for modern game. Dressing-room livewire, told to tighten his game to become regular first teamer.

MONAGHAN, Gareth (Wing)
Born Manchester, 22.6.71. 5'10", 11st 7lb. Rep hons: North. Lancashire. U21, Colts. Signed from Sale in summer 1996 following successful Italy tour with the North of England in June. Lancashire 'Player of Season' 1995-96. Elusive runner. Hobbies include reading and cinema.

PETERS, Stephen (Prop)
Born 8.11.60. 6'1", 19st 1lb. Career: Youth development officer, Cheshire. Rep hons: England Students. North. Lancashire. Natal. CLR: 1t-4pts. Steve is England Women's rugby team coach with girlfriend Gill Burns a squad member. Expected to make impact after two indifferent seasons.

PILECKI, Bartholomew (Prop)
Born Brisbane, Australia. 6'3", 18st 7lb. Career: PRP. Rep hons: Lancashire. Queensland. Ineligible to play Courage League and Pilkington Cup matches 1995-96 but qualifies for debut 1996-97 season. 'Bart Man' expected to feature heavily in Waterloo first team action after regular second team appearances last season. Son of ex-Australia international S.J. Pilecki, capped regularly 1978-83.

STEVENSON, Mark (Centre)
Born Durham, 6.11.74. 6'. 12st 2lb. Career: Student. Rep hons: Durham. North Colts. Elusive, balanced runner, excellent in open play.

TEMMEN, Carl (Second row)
Born Preston. 6'7". 17st 7lb. Career: British Leyland engineer. Rep hons: North U21. Joins Waterloo from Preston Grasshoppers for the 1996-97 season. Needs hardness of competition to fulfil promise. Squad man but expected to make regular outings in long season.

THOMPSON, Christopher (Full-back)
Born 13.11.71. 6'. 11st 7lb. Career: Lawyer. Rep hons: England U21, Students. North. Cheshire. CLR. 3c. 6pg-24pts. Educated Millfield and graduate of Sheffield Polytechnic. Chris is one of the most gifted runners in northern rugby. Recovering from broken leg suffered on North's 1993 Zimbabwe tour. Worked hard pre-season to regain full fitness. String of injuries have seriously disrupted playing schedule for past two seasons. Nicknamed 'Physio' for obvious reasons. Versatile full-back, wing or centre.

TOPPING, David (Scrum-half)
Born 14.1.74. 5'7". 11st 7lb. Rep hons: England U21, Students. English Universities. Lancashire U21. Colts. Joined from Orrell for 1995-96 season but debut delayed by qualification regulations. Lively, extrovert scrum-half.

WHALLEY, Andrew (Wing)
Born Merthyr Tydfil, 21.9.74. 5'10". 12st. Career: Student. Rep hons: North U18. Cheshire. Joined Waterloo for 1995-96 season but had his new club career seriously disrupted by knee injury. Two operations pre-season but fully fit for 1996-97 after tortuous self-imposed summer training schedule. Expected to stake early claim for first team action.

WHITE, Paul (Second row)
Born 8.5.70. 6'4". 17st 7lb. Career: Policeman. Rep hons: British Polytechnics, London Division U21. U19. CLR. 2t-10pts. Best lineout jumper in the club. Ex-Liverpool Polytechnic where he studied sports science. Paul is known as the 'Duke'

WILKINSON, Nigel (Second row)
Born 25.5.60. 6'5". 17st. Rep hons: England U23. North. Lancashire. Dick Greenwood first coached Nigel at England Under-23 level in 1981. Makes few first team appearances but always in the frame for recall. Made more than 500 appearances for the club.

WOLFENDON, Christopher (Flanker)
Born Liverpool. 6'3". 16st 3lb. Career: Runs tyre business. Rep hons: Anti Assassins. CLR. 1t-5pts. Loyal, ever-present at training, great club man. Played first team but not regular. Known as 'Mizumo' for clumsily treading on teammates in training.

WRIGHT, Simon (Scrum-half)
Born 15.2.65. 5'8". 12st 7lb. Career: Financial services consultant. Rep hons: Cheshire. CLR. 7t, 1dg-38pts. Missed two seasons with serious ankle injury but back to best form in past two seasons, winning 'Player of the Year' award 1995-96. Simon comes from a

rugby-playing family containing brothers Chris (Harlequins), Paul (New Brighton) and Mike, who makes occasional appearances for Waterloo.

YOUNG, Patrick (Scrum-half)
Born 14.8.73. 5'10", 12st 7lb. Career· Architect. Expected to mount big challenge for Simon Wright's first team place this season.

REVIEW

A poor start, with three Courage League defeats, gave Waterloo uphill task for the remainder of the season. They were bitterly disappointed to lose their Pilkington Cup fourth round tie at Leeds in December after producing their worst team performance of the season, but recovered well in the second half of the year to finish fifth behind Northampton, London Irish, London Scottish and Wakefield. Nick Allott, veteran captain Peter Buckton, Stuart Beeley, Tony Handley, Ben Kay and the outstanding Simon Wright were the pick of the squad. Waterloo have no millionaire benefactor for 1996-97 in a pro-soccer area, so will rely heavily on TV money to meet player payroll demands. Club secretary Keith Alderson forecasts a 'hard and very long season' but adds: 'We will survive the challenge.'

WATERLOO in the Courage League 1995-96

Sep	9	London Scottish	H	Lost	3 11	Emmett(P)
	16	Bedford	A	Drew	10 10	Buckton(T) Wright(T)
	23	London Irish	H	Lost	16 50	Smith(T) Aitchison(C, 3P)
	30	Blackheath	A	Lost	9 21	Ryan(3P)
Oct	7	Moseley	H	Won	22 17	Wright(T) Emmett(C, 4P) Ryan(D)
	14	Newcastle	A	Won	29 26	Wolfenden(T) Wright(T) Emmett(2C, 3P) Ryan(2D)
	21	Nottingham	A	Won	18 12	Emmett(5P) Aitchison(P)
	28	Northampton	H	Lost	3 69	Ryan(D)
Nov	4	Wakefield	A	Lost	6 14	Emmett(2P)
	11	London Scottish	A	Drew	16 16	Buckton(T) Emmett(C, 3P)
Jan	6	London Irish	A	Lost	16 39	Beckett(T) Smith(T) Handley(D, P)
	13	Bedford	H	Won	48 24	Buckton(2T) Bruce(T) Emmett(T, 3C, 4P) Kay(T) McCaughrean(T)
Feb	10	Blackheath	H	Won	32 10	Allott(T) Blyth(T) Bruce(2T) Emmett(3C, 2P)
	17	Moseley	A	Won	30 24	Blyth(T) McCaughrean(T) Emmett(C, 6P)
Mar	30	Newcastle	H	Lost	13 36	McCaughrean(T) Emmett(C, 2P)
Apr	6	Nottingham	H	Lost	13 24	White(T) Thompson(C, 2P)
	13	Northampton	A	Lost	5 69	Fletcher(T)
	27	Wakefield	H	Won	20 10	Hackett(T) McCaughrean(T) Thompson(2C, 2P)

Rugby in England 1995-96

Courage League

Bath claimed their sixth Courage League title in nine seasons, with Leicester only one point behind in a titanic climax to the domestic season. The situation at the top of League One could not have been more delicately poised when Bath played Sale at the Recreation Ground and Leicester met Harlequins at Welford Road on the final Saturday, 27 April 1996.

Bath needed to lose for only the third time all season, while Leicester needed nothing less than victory to take the title. In the end, both matches see-sawed so crazily that spectators absorbed by the cut-and-thrust on both grounds spent most of their time watching one game while tuned in to proceedings at the other match.

For most of the afternoon, Bath seemed to be coasting to victory, with events at Leicester a mere sideshow to the stranglehold they had placed on Sale. Then Bath almost blew it! Their 27-5 advantage was demolished by Sale in an amazing recovery which resulted in the northern club scoring 26 points in the second half, which included three sparkling tries. At the final whistle, the scoreboard had adopted American basketball characteristics, bearing 38-38 statistics.

Meanwhile, Leicester, favourites to beat Harlequins, relinquished the title by going down 19-21 to the London club after their full-back John Liley had missed a 40-yard penalty in the second minute of injury time.

They were not to know it at the time but the two Liley brothers, Robert of Bath and John of Leicester, were to give the final moments of both matches a storybook finale. Robert kicked the face-saving penalty that earned Bath the draw; John missed his kick, only to discover the horrific ramifications of the family shoot-out when a sombre Leicester captain Dean Richards broke the news in the dressing room later.

Typically, there were no recriminations, Richards reminding his players of the collective responsibility they shared in defeat. No one could have done more than the underrated Liley to sustain Leicester's challenge last season. He contributed 272 points in 17 League games. And his try and three penalties against Quins on that heartbreaking final Saturday also took him to 441 points for the season in all matches, breaking his own club record.

Harlequins, eighth in 1994-95, came third and Wasps, led by Lawrence Dallaglio, recovered from the defection of key players to Newcastle Gosforth before Christmas to come fourth. The Courage League top four – Bath, Leicester, Harlequins, Wasps – all qualified to compete in the Heineken European Cup 1996-97 season.

Ian McGeechan, mastermind coach behind Northampton's rampage to promotion, declined an offer from Wales to direct their World Cup salvage operation at the height of his club's League Two charge. He said he would remain loyal to Northampton, with the League One title his ultimate aim. 'My goal at Northampton is to win the First Division and get into Europe. We will have every chance provided we keep this squad together over the next three to four years. I am happy where I am,' he said.

Led by Tim Rodber, the Saints averaged 47 points a game to accumulate more points (867) than any other leading Courage League club. At one stage McGeechan said: 'I honestly believe we would be in the top three of the First Division playing as we are. In terms of fitness and tactics, we have moved on with the result that we're playing high-quality rugby.' The arrival of Jonathan Bell, Gregor Townsend and Michael Dods gave them a rich Celtic mix to the delight of their average 5,000 gate, an attendance often higher than that of the local Football League club.

Second-placed London Irish also relied heavily on the strategy of their coach, Clive Woodward. A member of Bill Beaumont's Grand Slam side in 1980, Woodward put his version of total rugby to full effect at Sunbury in a side captained magnificently by Gary Halpin. The big Irishman was so committed to the promotion compaign that he took a year out from international rugby to concentrate on his domestic role.

'This is a sleeping giant,' confessed Woodward after clinching promotion. 'It's a big club as wealthy as any in the country. A lot of people associated with it are captains of industry, prepared to back our League One campaign.'

Coventry, promoted from League Three with Richmond, Rugby and Rotherham, stormed to their second League Three title in three seasons with a brand of stylish and rugged rugby. Their first and second teams amassed more than 1,000 points in all games for the first time in the club's history. Richmond's promotion season and ambition convinced millionaire businessman Ashley Levett to back his belief that the club can become a Courage League giant. A string of big-name signings, including Ben Clarke, Scott Quinnell and Ireland's new full-back Simon Mason, were recruited for the London club's campaign to reach Courage League One.

Exeter's storming run to the League Four title, with London Welsh second, was inevitable after they became the first club to win at London Welsh for two seasons. Jason Thomas, their 24-year-old centre, played so well in his second term with the club that the Welsh selectors see him as a possible for their 1999 World Cup squad. Welsh, skippered by Andy Tucker, had set a Courage National League record of 25 matches without defeat before visiting Exeter spoiled the party.

Courage League Tables

DIVISION ONE

	P	W	D	L	F	A	Pts
Bath	18	15	1	2	575	276	31
Leicester	18	15	0	3	475	242	30
Harlequins	18	13	0	5	524	314	26
Wasps	18	11	0	7	439	322	22
Sale	18	9	1	8	365	371	19
Bristol	18	8	0	10	329	421	16
Orrell	18	7	0	11	323	477	14
Gloucester	18	6	0	12	275	370	12
Saracens	18	5	0	13	284	451	10
West Hartlepool	18	0	0	18	288	634	0

DIVISION TWO

	P	W	D	L	F	A	Pts
Northampton	18	18	0	0	867	203	36
London Irish	18	15	0	3	584	405	30
London Scottish	18	10	2	6	361	389	22
Wakefield	18	8	0	10	328	331	16
Waterloo	18	7	2	9	309	483	16
Moseley	18	7	0	11	327	447	14
Blackheath	18	6	1	11	341	469	13
Newcastle	18	5	1	12	348	405	11
Nottingham	18	5	1	12	333	433	11
Bedford	18	5	1	12	287	520	11

DIVISION THREE

	P	W	D	L	F	A	Pts
Coventry	18	15	0	3	524	264	30
Richmond	18	13	1	4	476	266	27
Rugby	18	12	1	5	395	284	25
Rotherham	18	12	0	6	384	368	24
Morley	18	9	2	7	336	328	20
Harrogate	18	6	3	9	333	387	15
Otley	18	6	1	11	278	441	13
Reading	18	5	1	12	397	484	11
Rosslyn Park	18	3	2	13	290	426	8
Fylde	18	3	1	14	283	448	7

DIVISION FOUR

	P	W	D	L	F	A	Pts
Exeter	18	14	0	4	448	230	28
London Welsh	18	12	0	6	424	269	24
Liverpool-St Helens	18	11	1	6	471	343	23
Walsall	18	10	0	8	406	324	20
Leeds	18	9	1	8	311	345	19
Clifton	18	7	2	9	283	298	16
Redruth	18	7	2	9	358	391	16
Havant	18	7	1	10	287	368	15
Aspatria	18	5	1	12	356	497	11
Plymouth Albion	18	4	0	14	266	545	8

DIVISION FIVE (NORTH)

	P	W	D	L	F	A	Pts
Wharfedale	12	12	0	0	331	146	24
Worcester	12	9	0	3	317	187	18
Birmingham Solihull	12	8	1	3	202	160	17
Winnington Park	12	8	0	4	225	215	16
Sheffield	12	7	0	5	205	190	14
Sandal	12	6	0	6	244	198	12
Stourbridge	12	6	0	6	200	177	12
Preston Grasshoppers	12	5	1	6	167	209	11
Kendal	12	5	0	7	215	227	10
Nuneaton	12	4	1	7	178	329	9
Stoke-on-Trent	12	3	0	9	184	204	6
Lichfield	12	3	0	9	165	284	6
Broughton Park	12	0	1	11	127	234	1

DIVISION FIVE (SOUTH)

	P	W	D	L	F	A	Pts
Lydney	12	11	1	0	320	132	23
Weston-super-Mare	12	10	0	2	207	123	20
Henley	12	8	0	4	349	192	16
Barking	12	8	0	4	243	187	16
Berry Hill	12	7	0	5	203	195	14
Cheltenham	12	6	0	6	194	173	12
Camberley	12	5	1	6	151	212	11
Askeans	12	5	0	7	187	275	10
Tabard	12	4	1	7	195	244	9
High Wycombe	12	4	1	7	161	244	9
North Walsham	12	3	1	8	149	212	7
Met Police	12	2	1	9	130	204	5
Camborne	12	2	0	10	146	241	4

Courage Clubs Championship 1996-97

National League One
Bath, Bristol, Gloucester, Harlequins, Leicester, London Irish, Northampton, Orrell, Sale, Saracens, Wasps, West Hartlepool.

National League Two
Bedford, Blackheath, Coventry, London Scottish, Moseley, Newcastle, Nottingham, Richmond, Rotherham, Rugby, Wakefield, Waterloo.

National League Three
Clifton, Exeter, Fylde, Harrogate, Havant, Leeds, Liverpool St Helens, London Welsh, Lydney, Morley, Otley, Reading, Redruth, Rosslyn Park, Walsall, Wharfedale.

National League Four South
Askeans, Barking, Berry Hill, Camberley, Charlton Park, Cheltenham, Henley, High Wycombe, Metropolitan Police, Newbury, North Walsham, Plymouth Albion, Tabard, Weston-super-Mare.

National League Four North
Aspatria, Birmingham Solihull, Hereford, Kendal, Lichfield, Manchester, Nuneaton, Preston Grasshoppers, Sandal, Sheffield, Stoke-on-Trent, Stourbridge, Winnington Park, Worcester.

Courage Trophy Winners

	Winners	Runners-up
1987-88	Leicester	Wasps
1988-89	Bath	Gloucester
1989-90	Wasps	Gloucester
1990-91	Bath	Wasps
1991-92	Bath	Orrell
1992-93	Bath	Wasps
1993-94	Bath	Leicester
1994-95	Leicester	Bath
1995-96	Bath	Leicester

Pilkington Cup 1995-96

Final

Bath 16 Leicester 15 (Twickenham, 4 May 1996)

Bath won the Pilkington Cup for the tenth time in a frenzied and controversial finish to an epic Twickenham battle between two old foes on Saturday 4 May 1996. Bath's glory in completing the League and Cup 'double' was overshadowed by Leicester's embarrassment over the behaviour of their abrasive England flanker, Neil Back, in a stormy incident at the final whistle.

Incensed, like the rest of his team, by the last-minute penalty try decision which cost the Tigers the Pilkington Cup, Back gave international referee Steve Lander a two-handed push in the back which caused the official to stumble and fall over another player. Back's shove, seen by millions on television, cost him a six-month ban by the RFU disciplinary panel for 'conduct which was prejudicial to the interest of the game'. He was banned from playing all rugby until Monday 4 November 1996.

Leicester were so furious over what they claimed was daylight robbery that they threatened to boycott the presentation ceremony after their 16-15 defeat. But captain Dean Richards persuaded all but one – Neil Back, taking an early bath – of his players to collect their losers' medals from the Royal Box.

Leicester deservedly paid a heavy price for killing the ball in the face of Bath's onslaught in the final minutes. They gave away three penalties in just over a minute and then came a fourth, under the posts, which persuaded Lander to dish out the ultimate punishment.

The storm of booing that followed Bath on their victory march to the Royal Box suggested a widespread perception that Leicester were robbed, but Bath's director of rugby Jon Hall observed: 'It's almost criminal to have 70 per cent of possession as Leicester did and do nothing with it. Bath played all the rugby and the penalty try was the right decision.'

Leicester, playing most of the attacking football in the opening 20 minutes of each half, scored two excellent tries through fly-half Niall Malone and lock Matt Poole, the former one of the better tries seen at Twickenham in recent seasons. Indeed, had John Liley's unerring kicking not wavered – he failed with four kickable penalties from five attempts – Leicester could have taken an unassailable lead.

Bath, badly missing the drive of their injured No 8 Ben Clarke, relied on crumbs of occasional comfort with a general lack of conviction in the Leicester 22. Jon Callard landed two penalties successfully and Mike Catt planted a dropped goal between the Leicester posts, yet their hopes appeared to be irretrievably dashed six minutes from the end when Poole stole a throw-in by Graham Dawe and followed Back's clever grubbing kick for a try.

Moments later Bath's controversial penalty try enabled Jon Callard to kick the winning conversion from under the posts.

Bath: J. Callard; A. Lumsden, P. de Glanville (capt), A. Adebayo, J. Sleightholme; M. Catt, A. Nicol; D. Hilton, G. Dawe, J. Mallett, M. Haag, N. Redman, S. Ojomoh, A. Robinson, E. Peters.

Scorers: T: Penalty try. C: Callard. PG: Callard (2). DG: Catt.

Leicester: J. Liley; S. Hackney, S. Potter, R. Robinson, R. Underwood; N. Malone, A. Kardooni; G. Rowntree, R. Cockerill, D. Garforth, M. Johnson, M. Poole, J. Wells, N. Back, D. Richards (capt).

Scorers: T: Malone, Poole. C: Liley. PG: Liley.

HT: 9-7. Att: 75,000.

Referee: S. Lander (RFU).

Pilkington Cup Winners

1972 GLOUCESTER 17 Moseley 6
1973 COVENTRY 27 Bristol 15
1974 COVENTRY 26 London Scottish 6
1975 BEDFORD 28 Rosslyn Park 12
1976 GOSFORTH 23 Rosslyn Park 14
1977 GOSFORTH 27 Waterloo 11
1978 GLOUCESTER 6 Leicester 3
1979 LEICESTER 15 Moseley 12
1980 LEICESTER 21 London Irish 9
1981 LEICESTER 22 Gosforth 15
1982 GLOUCESTER 12 MOSELEY 12 (shared title)
1983 BRISTOL 28 Leicester 22
1984 BATH 10 Bristol 9
1985 BATH 24 London Welsh 15
1986 BATH 25 Wasps 17
1987 BATH 19 Wasps 12
1988 HARLEQUINS 28 Bristol 22
1989 BATH 10 Leicester 6
1990 BATH 48 Gloucester 6
1991 HARLEQUINS 25 Northampton 13 (aet)
1992 BATH 15 Harlequins 12 (aet)
1993 LEICESTER 23 Harlequins 16
1994 BATH 21 Leicester 9
1995 BATH 36 Wasps 16
1996 BATH 16 Leicester 15

Pilkington Cup Results 1995-96

Round 1:

Askeans 30 Brixham 18; Basingstoke 20 Berry Hill 11; Bridlington 34 Syston 10; Broadstreet 26 Wharfedale 21; Camberley 26 Barking 24; Ealing 8 Weston-s-Mare 26; Gloucester OB 25 Camborne 8; Harlow 41 Abbey 6; Henley 30 Ruislip 8; High Wycombe 0 Cheltenham 15; Hornets 34 Bournemouth 23; Hull Ionians 52 Selly Oak 8; Launceston 10 Met Police 16; Leighton Buzzard 11 Birmingham and Solihull 29; Lewes 24 Oxford 17; Macclesfield 47 Sandal 17; Manchester 15 Scunthorpe 22; N. Walsham 23 Letchworth 12; Northern 22 Sheffield 10; Nuneaton 26 Winnington Park 32; Old Blues 5 Tabard 11; Olney 0 Westcombe Park 23; Preston Grasshoppers 19 Stourbridge 44; Stafford 13 Netherall 18; Stockton 13 Broughton Park 11; Stoke-on-Trent 13 Lichfield 11; Sudbury 6 Lydney 28; Worcester 30 Kendal 17.

Round 2:

Basingstoke 19 Lewes 28; Birmingham and Solihull 14 Worcester 19; Bridlington 50 Aspatria 10; Cheltenham 11 Weston-s-Mare 13; Clifton 11 Met Police 12; Gloucester OB 7 London Welsh 16; Harrogate 6 Fylde 23; Havant 11 Exeter 20; Henley 33 Hornets 8; Liverpool St Helens 15 Hull Ionians 8; Lydney 37 Harlow 7; Macclesfield 18 Morley 6; Netherall 7 Winnington Park 17; Northern 21 Stourbridge 22; Otley 16 Stoke-on-Trent 11; Plymouth Albion 18 Camberley 39; Redruth 19 N. Walsham 15; Rosslyn Park 14 Richmond 22; Rotherham 15 Coventry 24; Scunthorpe 18 Walsall 49; Stockton 8 Leeds 27; Tabard 28 Askeans 15; Westcombe Park 9 Reading 32.

150

Round 3:

Bridlington 13 Winnington Park 17; Coventry 78 Stourbridge 20; Exeter 17 Redruth 15; Leeds 12 Fylde 6; Lewes 10 Camberley 40; London Welsh 27 Richmond 12; Macclesfield 35 Walsall 36; Met Police 10 Reading 27; Otley 31 Rugby 40; Tabard 17 Lydney 19; Weston-s-Mare 19 Henley 18; Worcester 24 Liverpool St Helens 8.

Round 4:

Nottingham 32 London Scottish 16; Camberley 0 Wakefield 18; Gloucester 47 Walsall 0; Newcastle Gosforth 26 Moseley 5; Orrell 17 Harlequins 19; Winnington Park 26 Lydney 11; Bedford 27 Worcester 12; Weston-s-Mare 9 West Hartlepool 25; Sale 9 Wasps 18; Reading 7 Bristol 44; Exeter 0 Leicester 27; Bath 12 Northampton 3; Blackheath 9 Coventry 19; Leeds 20 Waterloo 15; London Irish 21 London Welsh 3; Saracens 27 Rugby 7.

Round 5:

Bedford 0 Bristol 37; Leeds 13 London Irish 29; Leicester 40 Saracens 16; Newcastle Gosforth 22 Harlequins 44; Nottingham 10 Gloucester 36; Wakefield 12 Bath 16; West Hartlepool 16 Coventry 6; Winnington Park 0 Wasps 57.

Quarter-finals:

Bristol 12 Bath 19; Gloucester 22 Wasps 9; Leicester 24 Harlequins 9; London Irish 11 West Hartlepool 10.

Semi-finals:

London Irish 21 Leicester 46; Bath 19 Gloucester 10.

Final: Leicester 15 Bath 16.

Rugby in Wales 1995-96

Heineken League

Division One

Neath, shrugging off the disappointment of defeat in the SWALEC Cup final just 11 days earlier, clinched the last Heineken Division One title on the final evening of an exhausting season by defeating the same opponents amid much excitement at the Gnoll. Neath won 45-25 and, vitally, scored seven tries in the process to gain maximum bonus points. Just over 40 miles away, Cardiff trounced Llanelli 65-13 to claim maximum bonus points also and finish level on 72 with Neath. But the Welsh All-Blacks took the title by virtue of their 121 tries in the season, as opposed to 119 for Cardiff, who reluctantly had to settle for second place.

The purists were left shaking their heads. Cardiff had, after all, won 18 games to Neath's 17 and not lost once to either of the other top four finishers. But there's no denying the new system made for exciting running rugby and Neath were worthy champions. Under the enlightened coaching of Darryl Jones and Lyn Jones, the Welsh All-Blacks produced many passages of breath-taking rugby and their triumph was a fitting send-off for brothers Glyn and Gareth Llewellyn, club stalwarts who moved on to Harlequins at the end of the season.

In contrast to the previous season, when they scored just 33 tries, Neath opted for the running game throughout. Their four defeats were all incurred in the thirteen games before Christmas, but they finished the season with nine straight victories, scoring 70 tries in the process. Perhaps the highlight was a 95-17, 15-try demolition of Aberavon, who Darryl Jones had coached to the Division Two title the previous season. That memorable final evening against Pontypridd started badly for Neath with Steele Lewis silencing the 9,000 crowd with an early try but Ian Boobyer settled frayed nerves in the 23rd minute, scoring from a tapped penalty. Tries followed at regular intervals thereafter from John Davies, Chris Bridges, Chris Higgs, Patrick Horgan, Huw Woodland and finally Steve Williams.

Pontypridd, for whom Neil Jenkins again led the points-scoring chart with 285, were good value for their third place – their total of 98 tries was also the third highest in the division. Llanelli were inconsistent but their fourth place secured a place in Europe and was a distinct improvement from seventh the previous season. Bridgend flattered to deceive on occasions but equalled their fifth place of 1994-95 and Swansea were again sixth. At the other end of the table Abertillery and Aberavon struggled all season and were duly relegated, while Treorchy recovered enough to avoid the drop. Above the Rhondda club, Gwent teams packed the next three places Newbridge, Newport and Ebbw Vale, who showed signs of promise in winning 50 per cent of their 22 games.

Division Two

Dunvant's ability to score tries and secure bonus points paid handsome dividends in Division Two where they finished ten points clear of Caerphilly, despite both clubs winning 18 games apiece. Under the captaincy of full-back Dean Evans, Dunvant made a flying start to win eight of their opening nine games and, despite a slight mid-season dip in form, they finished with a flourish to record five straight wins, including revenge triumphs over Llandovery and Ystradgynlais. Caerphilly made a miserable start, losing their opening three games to Llandovery, Dunvant and Pontypool, but recovered superbly to win 18 of their remaining 19 games. As

Caerphilly, like Dunvant, also reached the SWALEC Cup quarter-finals they can reflect on a fine season. A gulf in class existed behind Dunvant and Caerphilly, with third-placed Cross Keys winning just 11 of their 22 games. Gwent neighbours Pontypool started promisingly with five victories but trailed off disappointingly. Abercynon, who narrowly missed out on promotion the previous season, had to fight hard to stave off relegation, a fate which awaited Llanharan and Tenby United who recorded just four wins all season.

Division Three

Blackwood took the Division Three title at a canter, recording four more wins than second-placed Cardiff Institute and finishing 17 points clear of the students. Forward strength was, as ever, the key to Blackwood's success, as illustrated by No 8 Jamie Sims' total of 13 tries. Cardiff Institute were slow out of the blocks, with just two wins in their first seven games, but thereafter played with much more consistency, although third-placed Kenfig Hill did complete the double over them. Kenfig had made a poor start but finished strongly, emerging with a win over Blackwood in their final game. The previous season Pyle had accompanied the students out of Division Four and, after incurring just one defeat in their opening nine games, promotion again looked a possibility. Unfortunately, they fell away dramatically and with only one win in the last 11 games Pyle were left fighting relegation. Tondu, in fourth place, were competitive and No 8 Karl Hocking enjoyed an impressive season to lead the division in try-scoring on 14. At the other end, Mountain Ash and Builth Wells both flirted with relegation, but ultimately Blaina and Glamorgan Wanderers made the drop.

Division Four

Merthyr ran in 85 tries to secure 25 bonus points en route to the Division Four Championship, with Rumney finishing the season strongly to claim second place. Controversially, though, Tumble won more games than any team – 18 – yet their inability to maximise bonus points saw them trail home in fourth. Merthyr began with impressive victories over Whitland and Llantrisant, but defeats against Carmarthen Quins and Tumble acted as a timely reminder that Division Four boasted strength in depth. No 8 Len Owen emerged as Merthyr's top try-scorer with 11, while for Rumney Wales full-back Jonathan Mason contributed 187 points. Third-placed Carmarthen Quins were always entertaining to watch, with Anthony Dragone and Nick Jackson both claiming 11 tries apiece. Life became no easier for Pontypool United who, having been relegated from Division Three the previous season, again made the drop, managing just one win throughout a long and bitter winter. Aberavons Quins will accompany them.

Division Five

Despite losing their first two games, Kidwelly were undisputed champions of Division Five, winning 18 games and scoring 94 tries, a total only bettered in Division One. Wing Marc Evans led the try-scoring blitz with 20, including seven against Hendy, and Craig Thomas and Les Mathias both clocked up ten apiece. Second place was keenly contested between Oakdale and Ystrad Rhondda, with the issue eventually being decided on the final afternoon of the season with Oakdale defeating Ystrad 11-7. Oakdale had lost six of their first seven games but sprinted to promotion with a 14-match winning streak.

Heineken League Tables

DIVISION ONE

	P	W	D	L	Bonus Pts	Tr	Pts
Neath	22	17	1	4	37	121	72
Cardiff	22	18	1	3	35	119	72
Pontypridd	22	16	1	5	28	98	61
Llanelli	22	15	0	7	29	88	59
Bridgend	22	12	1	9	22	73	47
Swansea	22	11	0	11	22	83	44
Ebbw Vale	22	11	0	11	8	44	30
Newport	22	10	1	11	9	43	30
Newbridge	22	9	0	13	11	47	29
Treorchy	22	5	1	16	10	45	21
Aberavon	22	3	0	19	8	38	14
Abertillery	22	2	0	20	8	43	12

DIVISION TWO

	P	W	D	L	Bonus Pts	Tr	Pts
Dunvant	22	18	0	4	24	78	60
Caerphilly	22	18	0	4	14	57	50
Cross Keys	22	11	0	11	18	68	40
Pontypool	22	12	0	10	15	63	39
Bonymaen	22	10	0	12	14	55	34
Llandovery	22	11	2	9	5	37	29
Maesteg	22	10	1	11	7	38	28
Abercynon	22	10	0	12	6	39	26
Ystradgynlais	22	10	1	11	5	38	26
SW Police	22	7	0	15	11	49	25
Llanharan	22	9	0	13	6	41	24
Tenby Utd	22	4	0	18	4	33	12

DIVISION THREE

	P	W	D	L	Bonus Pts	Tr	Pts
Blackwood	22	18	2	2	23	78	61
Cardiff Inst	22	14	1	7	15	60	44
Kenfig Hill	22	13	0	9	13	58	39
Tondu	22	14	0	8	11	48	39
Penarth	22	10	1	11	9	47	30
Tredegar	22	10	0	12	7	47	27
Narberth	22	9	1	12	8	45	27
Builth Wells	22	9	2	11	6	41	26
Pyle	22	9	1	12	7	35	26
Mountain Ash	22	9	2	11	5	30	25
Blaina	22	8	2	12	6	35	24
Glam Wanderers	22	3	0	19	5	35	11

DIVISION FOUR

	P	W	D	L	Bonus Pts	Tr	Pts
Merthyr	22	17	0	5	25	85	59
Rumney	22	15	1	6	21	79	52
Carmarthen Quins	22	15	1	6	20	69	51
Tumble	22	18	0	4	12	51	48
Llantrisant	22	16	1	5	11	48	44
Whitland	22	11	1	10	17	57	40
Glynneath	22	12	0	10	11	48	35
Rhymney	22	8	0	14	11	54	27
Vardre	22	7	1	14	6	42	21
St Peter's	22	5	0	17	9	39	19
Aberavon Quins	22	4	1	17	5	34	14
Pontypool Utd	22	1	0	21	4	25	6

DIVISION FIVE

	P	W	D	L	Bonus Pts	Tr	Pts
Kidwelly	22	18	0	4	29	94	65
Oakdale	22	15	1	6	21	69	52
Ystrad Rhondda	22	15	0	7	17	71	47
Seven Sisters	22	14	0	8	18	64	46
Abergavenny	22	13	0	9	14	52	40
Felinfoel	22	13	0	9	11	49	37
Tonmawr	22	10	1	11	4	30	25
Garndiffaith	22	7	0	15	10	47	24
Cardiff Quins	22	7	0	15	8	42	22
Abercarn	22	6	1	15	9	41	22
Pontyberem	22	7	0	15	5	36	17*
Hendy	22	5	1	16	5	29	16

* Two points deducted.

Division Six. Promoted: Bedwas (East), Waunarlwydd (West), Resolven (Central).

Top scorers 1995-96

285 Neil Jenkins (Pontypridd); 282 Gareth Rees (Newport); 222 Kevin Thomas (Felinfoel); 220 Jason Williams (Pontypool); 219 Stuart Hancox (Tumble); 205 Byron Hayward (Ebbw Vale); 198 Aled Williams (Swansea); 187 Jonathan Mason (Rumney), Jason Davies (Hendy); 183 Wayne Jervis (Llanharan), Anthony Dragone (Carmarthen Quins); 176 Kevin Williams (Merthyr).

Top try-scorers 1995-96

21 Steve Ford (Cardiff); 20 Marc Evans (Kidwelly); 17 Wayne Proctor (Llanelli); 15 Chris Higgs (Neath); 14 Karl Hocking (Tondu), Paul John (Pontypridd); 13 Jeremy Banyon (Vardre), Jamie Sims (Blackwood), Gareth Jones (2 Bridgend, 11 Cardiff); 12

Alan Harris (Swansea), David Manley (Pontypridd); 11 Gafyn Stiff (Cardiff Institute), Richard Lewis (Seven Sisters), Richard Dixon (Abergavenny), Simon Davies (Swansea), Anthony Dragone (Carmarthen Quins), Nick Jackson (Carmarthen Quins), Len Owen (Merthyr), Neil Jenkins (Pontypridd).

Leading team try-scorers 1995-96

121 Neath; 119 Cardiff; 98 Pontypridd; 94 Kidwelly; 88 Llanelli; 85 Merthyr; 83 Swansea; 79 Rumney; 78 Dunvant, Blackwood; 73 Bridgend.

Leading team bonus points 1995-96

37 Neath; 35 Cardiff; 29 Kidwelly, Llanelli; 28 Pontypridd; 25 Merthyr; 24 Dunvant; 23 Blackwood; 22 Swansea, Bridgend; 21 Rumney, Oakdale; 20 Carmarthen Quins.

All-time Welsh League records (1990-96)

Leading aggregate points

1311 Neil Jenkins (Pontypridd) 127, 173, 203, 285, 249, 285
1019 Aled Williams (Swansea) 120, 132, 195, 176, 198, 198
 852 Adrian Davies (Cardiff) 6, 0, 264, 209, 207, 166
 771 Jimmy Morris (Llanelli) 189, 161, 204, 97, 109, 11
 737 Byron Hayward (Ebbw Vale) 28, 121, 82, 236, 65, 205
 714 Paul Parry (Builth Wells) 0, 0, 222, 199, 149, 144
 709 Jonathan Mason (Rumney) 46, 16, 221, 101, 138, 187

Leading aggregate tries

66 Steve Ford (Cardiff) 8, 7, 4, 7, 19, 21
60 Ieuan Evans (Llanelli) 7, 11, 20, 4, 8, 10
60 Wayne Proctor (Llanelli) 0, 7, 20, 4, 12, 17
48 Gareth Snook (St Peter's) 9, 9, 11, 12, 3, 4
48 Simon Davies (Swansea) 2, 9, 10, 9, 7, 11
44 Neil Jenkins (Pontypridd) 5, 5, 11, 7, 5, 11

SWALEC CUP 1995-96

Final

Neath 22 Pontypridd 29 (Arms Park, Cardiff, 4 May 1996)

Pontypridd, a friendly small-town club who refuse to be overawed by wealthier, more fashionable rivals, deservedly took the honours in an entertaining 25th anniversary SWALEC Cup final played at Cardiff Arms Park in perfect conditions. There were mistakes aplenty, notably in the first half when Neath pounced twice to take advantage of Pontypridd slips, but the same spirit of adventure that induced such errors also enabled Ponty to overturn a 22-10 deficit to claim a famous victory. Geraint Lewis scored two dramatic late tries to add to Paul John's earlier effort and Neil Jenkins, atoning for a number of missed kicks in the 1995 final against Swansea, kicked 14 points.

Pontypridd's captain Nigel Bezani, who didn't even play senior rugby until he was 32, could hardly contain his excitement. At the age of 39, he retired two weeks later, after Ponty's final Heineken League fixture, and had feared that last season's disappointing Cup final defeat against Swansea was his last chance to lift a major trophy. Despite advancing years, he led by example and was going stronger than most at the end. His side had moved confidently through to the final with a 35-17 win over Llanelli, David Manley scoring two tries, with Paul John and Geraint Lewis scoring one apiece at the Brewery Field, Bridgend. Neath advanced in more frenetic fashion, escaping with a 24-22 win over Newport at Cardiff. Pontypridd, like Neath, lack a millionaire patron or wealthy corporate sponsors and occasionally fret about their long-term ability to compete in Wales, let alone in Europe. Their sense of community and willingness to trust in youth should serve them well, though.

Neath's Heineken League victory soon made up for their Cup disappointment and their talented youngsters will continue to improve and benefit from the painful experience of losing, when the immaturity of youth and the lack of a goal-kicker cost them dear. The situation was further compounded when an injury to Paul Williams also denied them the option of tactical kicking at fly-half. Despite scoring four tries, they often lacked focus or direction, particularly in the final quarter.

More disappointed than most was Neath's openside flanker Ian Boobyer, who was looking to complete a notable fraternal hat-trick by gaining a winners' medal to put alongside those of brothers Neil and Roddy, who have tasted Cup final success with Llanelli and Swansea respectively. Neath flourished all season, despite their kicking deficiencies, but always feared they might be found out. 'Today the devil vomited on our laps,' was the memorable but apt comment of assistant coach Lyn Jones, borrowing his favourite catchphrase from BBC's *Blackadder* comedy series. Jones may have been 'as sick as a parrot' but his sense of humour and the Neath spirit remained intact, as they were to show nine days later when they clinched the Heineken trophy.

Neath: R Jones; C Higgs, L Davies, J Funnell, G Evans; P Williams, P Horgan; D Morris, B Williams, J Davies, Glyn Llewellyn, Gareth Llewellyn (capt), R Jones, I Boobyer, S Williams.

Scorers: T: Horgan (2), Davies, Richard Jones. C: Horgan

Pontypridd: C Cormack; D Manley, J Lewis, S Lewis, G Lewis; N Jenkins, Paul John; N Bezani (capt), Phil John, N Eynon, G Prosser, M Rowley, M Lloyd, R Collins, D McIntosh.

Scorers: T: G Lewis (2), Paul John. C: Jenkins. PG: Jenkins (3). DG: Jenkins.

Referee: D Bevan (Clydach).

Round 5:

Abergavenny 8 Cardiff Institute 23, Abertillery 3 Bridgend 32, Builth Wells 7 Rumney 25, Caerphilly 32 Rhymney 5, Dunvant 16 Glamorgan Wanderers 8, Merthyr 17 Llanelli 30, Neath 76 Heol-y-Cyw 8, Newbridge 24 Cross Keys 8, Newport 49 Ystradgynlais 5, Penarth 6 Cardiff 62, Penygraig 9 Llandovery 10, Pontypridd 41 Treorchy 5, South Wales Police 26 Abercynon 16, Swansea 17 Tonmawr 8, Whitland 19 Blackwood 17 (aet), Ynysddu 15 Maesteg 36.

Round 6:

Llandovery 5 Newport 25, Llanelli 18 Bridgend 15, Neath 64 Whitland 17, Newbridge 13 Rumney 10, Pontypridd 41 Maesteg 13, Swansea 9 Cardiff 20, Caerphilly 29 South Wales Police 13, Cardiff Institute 13 Dunvant 41.

Quarter-finals:

Llanelli 11 Cardiff 10, Neath 44 Dunvant 17, Newbridge 15 Pontypridd 20, Newport 16 Caerphilly 10.

Semi-finals:

Llanelli 17 Pontypridd 35 (Bridgend), Neath 24 Newport 22 (Cardiff).

Past Finals

	Winners		Runners-up		Loyd Lewis MOM Award	
1972	Neath	15	Llanelli	9		
1973	Llanelli	30	Cardiff	7		
1974	Llanelli	12	Aberavon	10		
1975	Llanelli	15	Aberavon	6	Phil Bennett	(Llanelli)
1976	Llanelli	16	Swansea	4	Phil Bennett	(Llanelli)
1977	Newport	16	Cardiff	15	Ian Barnard	(Newport)
1978	Swansea	13	Newport	9	David Richards	(Swansea)
1979	Bridgend	18	Pontypridd	12	Steve Fenwick	(Bridgend)
1980	Bridgend	15	Swansea	9	Gareth Williams	(Bridgend)
1981	Cardiff	14	Bridgend	6	Rob Lakin	(Cardiff)
1982	Cardiff	12	Bridgend	12	Mark Titley	(Bridgend)
	(Cardiff win by scoring try)					
1983	Pontypool	16	Swansea	6	David Bishop	(Pontypool)
1984	Cardiff	24	Neath	19	Gareth Jones	(Neath)
1985	Llanelli	15	Cardiff	14	Gary Pearce	(Llanelli)
1986	Cardiff	28	Newport	21	Adrian Hadley	(Cardiff)
1987	Cardiff	16	Swansea	15	Anthony Clement	(Swansea)
1988	Llanelli	28	Neath	13	Jonathan Davies	(Llanelli)
1989	Neath	14	Llanelli	13	Chris Bridges	(Neath)
1990	Neath	16	Bridgend	10	Kevin Ellis	(Bridgend)
1991	Llanelli	24	Pontypool	9	Rupert Moon	(Llanelli)
1992	Llanelli	10	Swansea	7	Rupert Moon	(Llanelli)
1993	Llanelli	21	Neath	18	Gareth Llewellyn	(Neath)
1994	Cardiff	15	Llanelli	8	Andy Moore	(Cardiff)
1995	Swansea	17	Pontypridd	12	Paul Arnold	(Swansea)
1996	Pontypridd	29	Neath	22	Paul John	(Pontypridd)

WRU League One Club Directory

BRIDGEND

Formation of club: 1878
Ground: Brewery Field, Tondu Road, Bridgend, Mid Glamorgan.
  Tel: 01656 659032
Capacity: 11,000
Colours: Blue and white stripes
Honours: WRU Cup: Winners: 1979, 80. Runners-up: 1981, 82, 90
Last season: Heineken Division One: 5th
Most capped player: JPR Williams (Wales) 55
Coach: Gerald Williams
Captain: Ian Greenslade

CAERPHILLY

Formation of club:1886
Ground: Virginia Park, Pontygwindy Road, Caerphilly. Tel: 01222 882573
Capacity: 3,000
Colours: Green and white hoops
Honours: Heineken Division Four: Runners-up 1993-94. Division Three:
  Runners-up 1994-95. Division Two: Runners-up 1995-96

st season: Heineken Division Two: Runners-up
Most capped player: None
Coach: Chris Davey
Captain: TBA

CARDIFF

(*See* Heineken European Cup Club Directory, page 184-5)

DUNVANT

Formation of club: 1888
Ground: Broadacre, Killay, Swansea SA2 7RU. Tel: 01792 207291
Capacity: 3,500
Colours: Red and green hoops
Honours: Heineken Division Three: Champions 1990-91 Division Two: Champions
  1992-93, 95-96
Last season: Heineken Division Two: Champions
Most capped player: None
Director of Rugby: Andrew Beer
Coaches: Malcolm Jones, Mark Perdue, Bleddyn Taylor
Captain: TBA

EBBW VALE

Formation of club: 1880
Ground: Eugene Cross Park, Ebbw Vale, Gwent. Tel: 01495 302995
Capacity: 8,000
Colours: Red, white and green
Honours: Welsh Club champions: 1951-52, 53-54, 56-57, 59-60
Last season: Heineken Division One: 7th
Most capped player: Denzil Williams (Wales) 36
Coach: Nigel Way
Captain: Kingsley Jones

LLANELLI

(*See* Heineken European Cup Club Directory, page 186-7)

NEATH

(*See* Heineken European Cup Club Directory, page 188)

NEWBRIDGE

Formation of club: 1888
Ground: The Welfare Ground, Bridge Street, Newbridge. Tel: 01495 243247
Capacity: 7,000
Colours: Blue and black hoops

Honours: Welsh Club champions: 1964-65
Last season: Heineken Division One: 9th
Most capped player: Don Hayward (Wales) 15
Coaching Coordinator: Roger Powell
Captain: TBA

NEWPORT

Formation of club: 1874
Ground: Rodney Parade, Rodney Road, Newport. Tel: 01633 258193
Capacity: 16,000
Colours: Black and amber
Honours: Heineken Division Two: Champions 1990-91. WRU Cup: Winners
   1976-77. Runners-up 1977-78, 85-86.
Last season: Heineken Division One: 8th
Most capped player: Ken Jones (Wales) 44
Coaches: Steve Jones, Stan Liptrot
Captain: Richard Goodey

PONTYPRIDD

(*See* Heineken European Cup Club Directory, page 189-90)

SWANSEA

Formation of club: 1873
Ground: St Helen's, Bryn Road, Swansea. Tel: 01792 466872
Capacity: 14,000
Colours: All white
Honours: Heineken Division One: Champions 1991-92, 93-94. WRU Cup: Winners:
   1977-78, 94-95. Runners-up 1975-76, 79-80, 82-83, 86-87, 91-92.
Last season: Heineken Division One: 6th
Most capped player: Robert Jones (Wales) 54
Director of Coaching: Mike Ruddock
Captain: Garin Jenkins

TREORCHY

Formation of club: 1886
Ground: The Oval, Treorchy, Rhondda. Tel: 01443 434671
Capacity: 6,000
Colours: Black and white hoops
Honours: Heineken Division Three: Champions 1992-93. Division Two: Champions
   1993-94.
Last season: Heineken Division One: 10th
Most capped player: David Jenkins, William Cummins (Wales) 4
Coach: Clive Jones
Captain: TBA

Rugby in Scotland 1995-96

Tennents League

It promised to be the tensest finale to the tightest league campaign for years. Stirling County, reigning champions from the old set-up, needed to win the last game of the competition by 43 points to claim the first Scottish Tennents Premiership title. Their opponents were Heriot's FP, who had just escaped the relegation drop, and the venue was historic Goldenacre. It was a daunting task, but one Stirling felt they could pull off if everything went their way. But, stunningly, the underdogs raced into an 11-0 lead, inflicting a severe body-blow to the contenders' ambitions and, although Stirling recovered to win the match 34-14, the title had slipped from their grasp.

It went instead to Melrose, Scotland's premier club for the fifth time in seven seasons. On their record, the best all-round side in the country, the Greenyards outfit were worthy winners of a reshaped competition which brought heightened levels of entertainment, drama and tension to the club scene.

The Tennents Premiership set a fierce challenge. Four divisions of only eight teams, playing home and away for the first time, with two sides to be relegated and two promoted, ensured every encounter would have a sharp competitive edge. A couple of bad results and relegation loomed; a few successes and the title beckoned. It would be, said Peter Gallagher, the experienced Watsonians coach, 'dog eat dog all the way'.

The major argument that competition would focus playing resources and hone skills and performance under pressure – essential if Scotland, a country of limited numbers, was to hold its head up on the international stage – certainly was reinforced, if clubs could hold on to their players. Those who lost out to the lure of English cash in a newly professional environment, also slumped on the home front.

Melrose, with the greatest roll of talent – Craig Chalmers, Bryan Redpath, Graham Shiel, Doddie Weir, Craig Joiner, all full internationals spearheading a powerful squad – were the obvious pre-championship favourites, with Stirling County, Watsonians and Boroughmuir thought to provide the chasing bunch and the other four, Hawick, Gala, Heriot's and Edinburgh Academicals, scrapping to avoid the drop.

But predictions have to be proved on the park and have an embarrassing tendency to rebound on the prophets. The opening day of the new order turned the calendar back some years as Hawick, champions 10 times from the start of the leagues, turned over the reigning holders at Stirling to suggest a Greens revival that ultimately bore fruit with victory in the first Tennents Scottish Cup final. It was a day, too, when Scott Welsh, the Hawick stand-off, launched a run of sparkling individual performances which took him to the fringes of the national side.

Sean Lineen, the New Zealand-bred former Scotland centre, drew on his international pedigree to score a glorious winning try at Melrose and throw down the gauntlet for Boroughmuir, champions five years earlier and a side who, on their day, can be brilliant. That day does not always dawn.

Watsonians, with Gavin and Scott Hastings leading a richly talented back division and a mobile, if not too rugged, pack, played some glorious running rugby but their carefree challenge ran into the brick wall of Melrose ambition when, in their own Myreside backyard, they came a massive 41-16 cropper. Craig Chalmers unveiled a new goal-kicking style which brought him a tally of 21 points. But this extra accomplishment was not, it seemed, enough to recapture his Scotland stand-off berth.

Stirling County, scrambling into form after a poor start, made up valuable ground when Kenny Logan scored two tries in a 27-26 win at Melrose, a highlight of an otherwise frustrating season for the left winger. A subsequent defeat at a Boroughmuir side inspired by a powerhouse display from No 8 Stuart Reid left the Melrose challenge jaded. The unfortunate Reid was to be struck down by injury just as he seemed set to fulfil his early promise with a regular national berth.

Boroughmuir then lost the services of their captain, Peter Wright, the Scotland and Bristol Lions prop, sent off at Gala for swearing at international referee Ken McCartney and the Edinburgh club's challenge immediately subsided. Mr McCartney then ruled out a match-winning 'try' by Gavin Hastings, which meant Watsonians lost at Melrose and another Edinburgh contender bit the dust.

A storm errupted after Melrose captain Bryan Redpath had scored an injury-time try to beat Edinburgh Academicals at Raeburn Place. Coach David Sole virtually accused Kelso referee Colin Henderson of cheating, an allegation which earned the Scotland Grand Slam captain a lengthy suspension after an unseemly wrangle with the SRU authorities. But the result put Melrose back in the title driving seat. A try by Scotland winger Craig Joiner tightened their grip in earning a draw at Stirling County and a hat-trick of tries by the young winger in a 31-11 victory over Gala set the final target. Stirling would have to beat Heriot's in a postponed match by 43 points. They didn't.

At the other end of the table, Gala, who had lost the glittering talents of Gregor Townsend and Michael Dods to Northampton before the campaign started, were soon detached at the foot. Between the other three strugglers the battle was tight and bitterly fought. The showdown came on an early November afternoon, when Heriot's beat Edinburgh Academicals 34-21 and Hawick scraped a vital 19-18 win at Meggetland as the Boroughmuir title challenge disintegrated. It doomed Academicals to relegation alongside Gala.

Attractive Currie always set a hot pace in Division 2 and emerged worthy champions, while Gary Armstrong did just enough to ensure success for Jed-Forest's promotion drive before crossing the Border to enlist in Sir John Hall's mercenary forces at Newcastle. Stewart's Melville and Selkirk, clubs who had contributed much to the game over the years through open, attractive rugby, continued to decline, sliding down to Division 3. But the first season of the Tennents Premiership emphasised that Scottish club rugby is now a hard competitive world with little room for sentiment. Dog eat dog indeed.

Tennents League Tables

DIVISION ONE

	P	W	D	L	F	A	Pts
Melrose	14	9	1	4	326	199	19
Stirling County	14	9	1	4	320	215	19
Watsonians	14	8	1	5	393	270	17
Boroughmuir	14	7	2	5	327	301	16
Hawick	14	7	0	7	243	288	14
Heriot's FP	13	5	1	7	278	360	11
Edinburgh Academicals	14	4	1	9	243	282	9
Gala	13	2	1	10	179	394	5

DIVISION TWO

	P	W	D	L	F	A	Pts
Currie	14	11	0	3	357	266	22
Jed-Forest	14	10	0	4	302	185	20
Glasgow High/Kelvinside	14	8	0	6	379	239	16
West of Scotland	14	7	0	7	268	258	14
Dundee HSFP	14	6	0	8	259	239	12
Kelso	14	6	0	8	275	260	12
Selkirk	14	5	0	9	215	307	10
Stewart's-Melville	14	3	0	11	193	490	6

DIVISION THREE

	P	W	D	L	F	A	Pts
Glasgow Academicals	14	12	0	2	461	132	24
Biggar	14	11	0	3	324	181	20
Kirkcaldy	14	10	0	4	316	182	18
Preston Lodge	14	6	0	8	245	246	12
Peebles	14	6	0	8	200	237	12
Musselburgh	14	6	0	8	229	336	12
Grangemouth	14	5	0	9	201	273	8
Corstorphine	14	0	0	14	154	543	0

DIVISION FOUR

	P	W	D	L	F	A	Pts
Kilmarnock	14	12	1	1	418	130	25
Glasgow S	14	10	1	3	415	172	21
Gordonians	14	10	0	4	381	163	20
Ayr	14	7	1	6	343	218	15
Langholm	14	6	1	7	183	217	13
Haddington	14	5	0	9	263	471	10
Edinburgh Wanderers	14	4	0	10	252	349	8
Wigtownshire	14	0	0	14	123	558	0

Ross High and Aberdeenshire were promoted from Division 5.

Previous Champions

1973-74	Hawick	1985-86	Hawick
1974-75	Hawick	1986-87	Hawick
1975-76	Hawick	1987-88	Kelso
1976-77	Hawick	1988-89	Kelso
1977-78	Hawick	1989-90	Melrose
1978-79	Heriot's FP	1990-91	Boroughmuir
1979-80	Gala	1991-92	Melrose
1980-81	Gala	1992-93	Melrose
1981-82	Hawick	1993-94	Melrose
1982-83	Gala	1994-95	Stirling County
1983-84	Hawick	1995-96	Melrose
1984-85	Hawick		

SRU TENNENTS CUP 1995-96

Final

Hawick 17 Watsonians 15 (Murrayfield, 11 May 1996)

Hawick established an historic treble when they became the first holders of Scottish rugby's first national cup competition. They were the first winners of the Border League competition in 1902; they clinched the National League title in its inaugural year 1974; and produced a thrilling finale at Murrayfield to snatch a famous victory last May.

Brian Renwick's team were trailing Watsonians by 15 points when they began to mount their fightback. Full-back Colin Turnbull scored a dramatic try late in the second half to capitalise on lock forward Alistair Imray's early try, and when Scott Welsh converted that effort Hawick established enough pressure to crack the Watsonians defence again.

Hawick ran a penalty for Welsh to seize an opening for a match-winning try that cancelled all the early optimism built on the strength of tries by Scott Hastings and Duncan Hodge.

Hawick: C. Turnbull; G. Sharp, C. Murray, A. Stanger, K. Suddon; W. Welsh, K. Reid; B. McDonnell, J. Hay, A. Johnstone, A. Imray, I. Elliot, J. Graham, B. Renwick (capt), G. Harris.

Replacement: A. Barnes for Graham.

Scorers: T: Imray, Turnbull, Welsh. C: Welsh.

Watsonians: D. Lee; F. Henderson (capt), S. Hastings, A. Garry, J. Kerr; D. Hodge, E. Weston; T. Smith, G. McKelvie, J. Waddell, S. Grimes, C. Mather, G. Hannah, C Browne, I. Sinclair.

Scorers T: Hastings, Hodge. C: Hodge. PG: Hodge.

Referee J M Fleming (Boroughmuir)

SRU Tennents Cup Results 1995-96

Round 3:

Aberdeen GSFP 11, Dundee HSFP 12; Biggar 14, Ayr 6; Cambuslang 19, Glenrothes 28; Dumfermline 5, Melrose 72; Duns 30, Peebles 19; GHK 59, Annan 15; Glasgow Academicals 44, Cartha Queen's Park 10; Hawick 46, East Kilbride 6; Hillhead/ Jordanhill 20, Gordonians 25 (*aet*); Kirkcaldy 54, Edinburgh Wanderers 0; Portobello FP 32, Haddington 10; Selkirk 10, Gala 21; Stewartry 18, Livingston 10; Trinity Academicals 57, Perthshire 22; Watsonians 33, Edinburgh Academicals 6; Waysiders/ Drumpellier 8, Hutchesons'/Aloysians 21.

Round 4:

Boroughmuir 25, GHK 15; Corstorphine 23, Trinity Academicals 8; Dundee HSFP 5, Stirling County 3; Duns 3, Hawick 22; Glasgow Academicals 17, Currie 12; Glasgow Southern 8, Jedforest 25; Glenrothes 10, Musselburgh 20; Gordonians 16, Gala 18; Grangemouth 16, Kilmarnock 22; Heriot's FP 18, Kirkcaldy 12; Langholm 20, Portobello FP 16; Melrose 89, West of Scotland 12; Preston Lodge FP 29, Kelso 26; Stewartry 3, Watsonians 62; Stewart's-Melville FP 70, Hutchesons'/Aloysians 0; Wigtownshire 9, Biggar 21.

Dundee HSFP 17, Jedforest 6; Glasgow Academicals 29, Gala 6; Hawick 52, Biggar 17; Kilmarnock 27, Corstorphine 8; Melrose 50, Boroughmuir 22; Musselburgh 17, Preston Lodge FP 20; Stewart's-Melville FP 20, Heriot's FP 25; Watsonians 98, Langholm 3.

Quarter-finals:

Glasgow Academicals 8, Melrose 14; Hawick 26, Preston Lodge FP 11; Heriot's FP 6, Watsonians 23; Kilmarnock 13, Dundee HSFP 37

Semi-finals:

Dundee HSFP 7, Watsonians 57 (*at Myreside*); Hawick 28, Melrose 15 (*at Netherdale*).

Scottish Inter-District Championship 1995-96

Exiles 17 Edinburgh 6; North and Midlands 53 Glasgow 18; Glasgow 27 Exiles 28; South 18 North and Midlands 12; Edinburgh 31 South 30; North and Midlands 8 Exiles 21; South 23 Glasgow 5; Edinburgh 57 Glasgow 13; Exiles 34 South 9; Edinburgh 15 North and Midlands 22:

	P	W	D	L	F	A	Pts
Scottish Exiles	4	4	0	0	100	50	8
Edinburgh	4	2	0	2	109	82	4
North and Midlands	4	2	0	2	95	72	4
South	4	2	0	2	80	82	4
Glasgow	4	0	0	4	63	161	0

Scottish Tennents League Club Directory

LEAGUE ONE

BOROUGHMUIR

Formation of club: 1919
Ground: Meggetland, Colinton Road, Edinburgh EH14 1AS. Tel: 0131 443 7571
Colours: Blue and green
Last season: League One: 4th
Most capped player: Sean Lineen (Scotland) 29
Coach: Henry Edwards
Captain: Stuart Reid

CURRIE

Formation of club: 1970
Ground: Malleny Park, Balerno, Edinburgh EH14 5HA. Tel: 0131 449 2432
Colours: Amber and black
Last season: League Two: Champions
Most capped player: –
Coaches: Bruce McNaughton, Paul Matthews
Captain: Clem Boyd

HAWICK

Formation of club: 1873
Ground: Mansfield Park, Mansfield Road, Hawick, Roxburghshire.
  Tel: 01450 374291
Colours: Dark green
Last season: League One: 5th
Most capped player: Jim Renwick (Scotland) and Colin Deans (Scotland) both 52
Coach: Bill Murray
Captain: Brian Renwick

HERIOT'S FP

Formation of club: 1890
Ground: Goldenacre, Bangsholm Terrace, Edinburgh EH3 5QN. Tel: 0131 552 5925
Colours: Blue and white horizontal stripes
Last season: League One: 6th
Most capped player: Andy Irvine (Scotland) 51
Coaches: Kenny Milne, Donald McDonald
Captain: Cameron Glasgow

JED-FOREST

Formation of club: 1885
Ground: Riverside Park, Jedburgh. Tel: 01835 862855
Colours: Royal blue
Last season: League Two: Runners-up
Most capped player: Roy Laidlaw (Scotland) 47
Coaches: Donald Millar, Alistair Christie
Captain: Kevin Armstrong

MELROSE

Formation of club: 1877
Ground: The Greenyards, Melrose, Roxburghshire. Tel: 01896 822993
Colours: Yellow and black hoops
Last season: League One: Champions
Most capped player: Keith Robertson (Scotland) 44
Coach: Rob Moffatt
Captain: Bryan Redpath

STIRLING COUNTY

Formation of club: 1904
Ground: Bridgehaugh Park, Causeway Head Road, Stirling.
  Tel: 01786 474827
Colours: Red, white and black
Last season: League One: Runners-up
Most capped player: Kenny Logan (Scotland) 24
Coaches: Peter Dods, Muff Scobie
Captain: Ian Jardine

WATSONIANS

Formation of club: 1875
Ground: Myreside, Myreside Road, Edinburgh EH10 5DB. Tel: 0131 447 5200
Colours: Maroon and white hoops
Last season: League One: 3rd
Most capped player: Gavin Hastings (Scotland) 61
Coaches: Peter Gallagher, Andrew Ker
Captain: Grant McKelvey

LEAGUE TWO

BIGGAR

Formation of club: 1975
Ground: Hartree Mill, Biggar. Tel: 01899 21219
Colours: Black with red collar and cuffs
Last season: League Three: Runners-up
Most capped player: –
Coach: TBA
Captain: TBA

DUNDEE HSFP

Formation of club: 1880
Ground: Mayfield, Arbroath Road, Dundee. Tel: 01382 451045
Colours: Blue and red
Last season: League Two: 5th
Most capped player: David Leslie (Scotland) 32
Coach: Jon Phillips
Captain: David Hamilton

EDINBURGH ACADEMICALS

Formation of club: 1857
Ground: Raeburn Place, Stockbridge, Edinburgh EH4 1HQ. Tel: 0131 332 1070
Colours: Blue and white hoops
Last season: League One: 7th
Most capped player: David Sole (Scotland) 44
Coach: Bob Easson, David Sole
Captain: Rob Hoole

GALA

Formation of club: 1875
Ground: Netherdale, Nether Road, Galashiels TD1 3HE. Tel: 01896 755145
Colours: Navy blue, green and white
Last season: League One: 8th
Most capped player: Peter Brown (Scotland) 27
Coach: Gary Callander
Captain: Ian Corcoran

GLASGOW ACADEMICALS

Formation of club: 1867
Ground: New Anniesland, Helensburgh Drive, Glasgow. Tel: 0141 959 1101
Colours: Navy blue and white hoops
Last season: League Three: Champions
Most capped player: William Simmers (Scotland) 28
Coach: TBA
Captain: TBA

GLASGOW HIGH/KELVINSIDE

Formation of club: 1982 (amalgamation of Glasgow High and Kelvinside
  Academicals)
Ground: Old Anniesland, 637 Crow Road, Glasgow. Tel: 0141 959 1154
Colours: Navy blue, green and white
Last season: League Two: 3rd
Most capped player: Duncan Munroe (Scotland) 6
Coach: Walter Malcolm
Captain: Murray Wallace

KELSO

Formation of club: 1876
Ground: Poynder Park, Bowmont Street, Kelso, Roxburghshire. Tel: 01573 224 300
Colours: Black and white
Last season: League Two: 6th
Most capped player: John Jeffrey (Scotland) 40
Coach: TBA
Captain: TBA

WEST OF SCOTLAND

Formation of club: 1865
Ground: Burnbrae, Glasgow Road, Milngavie, Glasgow G62 6HX.
  Tel: 0141 956 3116
Colours: Red and yellow hoops
Last season: League Two: 4th
Most capped player: Sandy Carmichael (Scotland) 50
Coach: TBA
Captain: TBA

Rugby in Ireland 1995-96

Insurance Corporation League

The Insurance Corporation All-Ireland League could hardly have ended in more dramatic fashion when on the final afternoon of the season Garryowen lost 37-12 at home to Young Munster and thereby gifted the title to great Munster rivals Shannon. Garryowen had gone into the game equal on points with Shannon but Young Munster, celebrating their centenary season, had their own agenda and produced their best performance of the season to finish fourth overall.

There was no inkling of the upset in store when the two sides reached half-time at 9-9 with fly-half Aidan O'Halloran kicking two dropped goals and a penalty for Young Munster and Kenny Smith replying with three penalties for Garryowen. After the break O'Halloran kicked a third dropped goal and Smith added a fourth penalty before Young Munster's driving forwards took over and laid the foundations for victory. First came a converted try from Des Clohessy, after a powerful surge from David Walsh, before Mick Fitzgerald added a second and Walsh a third. O'Halloran kicked a second conversion and two further penalties and Young Munster were home and dry.

Meanwhile in Cork, Shannon were completing a 31-17 victory over University College, Cork, in a Munster Senior Cup quarter-final at Musgrave Park when they heard the news. 'An unusual end to the season but no less welcome for that,' was the remarkably restrained reaction of Shannon coach Niall O'Donovan. Third-placed Cork Constitution were the only side to top 200 League points but for all their attacking power lacked consistency. Young Munster will be well pleased with fourth as a launching pad for this season but the major disappointment lay with St Mary's, who looked genuine championship contenders with four games remaining, but contrived to win just once more. There was much relief for those at the bottom end, with a reorganisation this season meaning there was no relegation.

DIVISION ONE

	P	W	D	L	F	A	Pts
Shannon	10	8	0	2	156	78	16
Garryowen	10	8	0	2	171	78	16
Cork Constitution	10	7	0	3	208	149	14
Young Munster	10	7	0	3	170	127	14
St Mary's College	10	5	1	4	147	119	11
Lansdowne	10	4	1	5	180	172	9
Ballymena	10	4	1	5	157	181	9
Old Wesley	10	3	1	6	156	164	7
Blackrock College	10	3	0	7	160	208	6
Old Belvedere	10	3	0	7	135	189	6
Instonians	10	1	0	9	145	233	2

DIVISION TWO*

	P	W	D	L	F	A	Pts
Old Crescent	10	9	1	0	246	103	19
Dungannon	10	7	1	2	254	171	15
Terenure College	10	7	1	2	191	118	15
Bective Rangers	10	6	0	4	186	147	12
Greystones	10	5	1	4	164	173	11
Sunday's Well	10	4	2	4	223	194	10
Malone	10	5	0	5	205	220	10
Wanderers	10	4	0	6	167	206	8
Clontarf	10	3	0	7	130	212	6
Dolphin	10	1	0	9	165	245	2
NIFC	10	1	0	9	157	299	2

*Top three promoted, no relegation from Division Two.

DIVISION THREE*

	P	W	D	L	F	A	Pts
Monkstown	11	9	1	1	186	137	19
City of Derry	11	8	1	2	169	117	17
Highfield	11	6	3	2	182	163	15
DLS Palmerston	11	6	1	4	177	198	13
Skerries	11	5	3	3	169	153	13
UC Cork	11	5	2	4	211	130	12
Bohemians	11	5	1	5	139	149	11
Buccaneers	11	4	1	6	148	129	9
Waterpark	11	3	2	6	121	252	8
Bangor	11	3	0	8	153	185	6
UC Dublin	11	3	0	8	145	197	6
Galwegians	11	1	1	9	127	207	3

*Top six promoted to Division Two. Divisions Three and Four to be reconstituted.

DIVISION FOUR

	P	W	D	L	F	A	Pts
Portadown	9	8	0	1	211	81	16
Dublin Univ	9	7	0	2	254	105	14
Collegians	9	7	0	2	183	101	14
Queen's Univ	9	6	0	3	176	92	12
Galway Corinthians	9	6	0	3	127	81	12
CIYMS	9	3	0	6	145	203	6
Ards	9	3	0	6	139	244	6
Ballina	9	2	1	6	129	178	5
Sligo	9	1	1	7	79	211	3
City of Armagh	9	1	0	8	86	233	2

UCG withdrew from competition

Smithwicks Interprovincial Championship 1995-96

The 1995-96 Smithwicks Interprovincial Championship was all about the re-emergence of Leinster, who took their first title since 1983. Undoubtedly the strongest Irish province, their manner of victory reflected much credit on manager Jim Glennon, coach Ciaran Callan and captain Chris Pim.

The campaign started with a free-flowing 42-26 win over Irish Exiles at Sale, the start of a very testing week that included a midweek Heineken Cup game against Pontypridd and a convincing 41-3 victory over Connacht. Next up was the big one, a 19-15 win over Munster at Thomond Park, a victory the Leinster front row particularly enjoyed after a pushover try against the home pack. The championship was clinched in emphatic style with a 31-3 win over Ulster, Leinster racing into a 22-0 lead in as many minutes.

'It was an excellent series of wins but we had a good feeling about this tournament from an early stage,' said Glennon. 'Before it all began we travelled to Milan in the European Cup and came away with a win. That was an outstanding result, as a number of clubs will discover this season when they play there. Shortly after that, we took a young team to St Helen's for a friendly against Swansea and again came away with a good result. It was then I realised what a strong squad we had.'

The front row is a case in point, with the trio of Henry Hurley, Shane Byrne and Paul Wallace dominating all-comers. This is regardless of the fact that British Lions Nick Popplewell was unavailable while completing his move to Newcastle. Reserves Paul Flavin and Angus Mckeen couldn't make the Leinster side, but both propped for Ireland A.

Elsewhere in the pack Steve Jamieson packed down alongside Neil Francis in the second row, Chris Pim was an inspiring blindside wing forward and captain and Stephen Rooney impressed on the openside. But the revelation was Victor Costello at No 8, whose power and athleticism soon resulted in a call-up to the national team.

Behind the scrum Alain Rolland showed such good form at scrum-half that national captain Niall Hogan could only watch from the bench, although in 'mitigation Hogan's medical duties had seen the Terenure scrum-half make a slow start to the season. Centre Kurt McQuilken and wing Niall Woods were others whose form for Leinster attracted national attention.

SMITHWICKS INTERPROVINCIAL CHAMPIONSHIP 1995-96

	P	W	D	L	F	A	Pts
Leinster	4	4	0	0	133	53	8
Ulster	4	3	0	1	73	63	6
Munster	4	2	0	2	91	68	4
Exiles	4	1	0	3	71	113	2
Connacht	4	0	0	4	51	132	0

Results: 25 November: Exiles 28 Connacht 22, Ulster 14 Munster 10. 2 December: Exiles 26 Leinster 42, Connacht 9 Ulster 27. 9 December: Munster 20 Exiles 14, Leinster 41 Connacht 9. 16 December: Munster 15 Leinster 19, Ulster 29 Exiles 3. 23 December: Leinster 31 Ulster 3, Connacht 11 Munster 46.

PAST CHAMPIONSHIPS

1946 Ulster	1972 Leinster-Munster-Ulster
1947 Munster	1973 Munster
1948 Leinster	1974 Ulster
1949 Leinster	1975 Leinster-Ulster-Munster
1950 Ulster	1976 Ulster
1951 Ulster	1977 Leinster-Munster-Ulster
1952 Munster	1978 Munster
1953 Ulster	1979 Leinster
1954 Leinster-Munster	1980 Leinster
1955 Ulster-Connacht	1981 Leinster
1956 Leinster-Ulster-Connacht	1982 Leinster-Ulster-Munster
1957 Munster	1983 Leinster-Ulster-Munster
1958 Leinster	1984 Ulster
1959 Munster	1985 Ulster
1960 Leinster	1986 Ulster
1961 Leinster	1987 Ulster
1962 Munster	1988 Ulster
1963 Leinster	1989 Ulster
1964 Leinster	1990 Ulster
1965 Munster	1991 Ulster
1966 Ulster-Munster	1992 Ulster
1967 Ulster	1993 Ulster
1968 Munster	1994 Ulster
1969 Ulster	1995 Munster
1970 Ulster	1996 Leinster
1971 Leinster	

Branch Competitions 1995-96

LEINSTER

Senior Cup Winners: Terenure
Kitty O'Shea Leinster Championship: Terenure
Metropolitan: Greystones
Smithwick's Provincial Towns Cup: Carlow
Junior League Div One: Suttonians

Schools:

Senior Cup (Coca-Cola): Blackrock College
Junior Cup (Coca-Cola): Blackrock College

ULSTER

Senior Cup Winners: Dungannon
Senior League: Portadown
Junior Cup: Dungannon
Qualifying league: Ballynahinch

Schools:

Schools Cup: Methodist College, Belfast/Regent House (shared trophy)
Medallion Shield: Methodist College, Belfast

MUNSTER

Senior Cup Winners: Shannon
Development League: Young Munster
Junior Cup: Shannon
Junior League Division One: Richmond

Schools:

Munster Senior Cup: PBC Cork
Munster Junior Cup: CBC Cork

CONNACHT

Smithwicks Senior Cup Winners: Galwegians
Senior League: Corinthians
Rank Xerox Junior Cup: Monivea
Rank Xerox Junior League Div One: Creggs

Schools:

Statoil Senior Cup: Garbally College
Statoil Junior Cup: Garbally College

Insurance Corporation League One Club Directory

BALLYMENA

Formation of club: 1887
Ground: Eaton Park, 209 Raceview Road, Ballymena BT42 4HV.
  Tel: Ballymena 656746
Capacity: 3,000
Colours: Black
Honours: IC League Two: Runners-up 1994-95
Last season: IC League One: 7th
Most capped player: Willie John McBride (Ireland) 63
Coach: Davey Smyth
Captain: Colin Wallace

BLACKROCK

Formation of club: 1882
Ground: Stradbrook Road, Blackrock, Dublin. Tel: 003531 2805967
Capacity: 5,000
Colours: Royal blue and white hoops
Honours: IC League One: Runners-up 1994-95
Last season: IC League One: 9th
Most capped player: Fergus Slattery (Ireland) 61
Coach: Tony Smeeth
Captain: Mike Brewer

CORK CONSTITUTION

Formation of club: 1892
Ground: Temple Hill, Ballin Temple, Cork. Tel: 0035321 292563
Capacity: 7,000
Colours: White
Honours: IC League One: Champions 1990-91
Last season: IC Ireland League One: 3rd
Most capped player: Tom Kiernan (Ireland) 54
Coach: Christy Cantillon
Captain: TBA

DUNGANNON

Formation of club: 1873
Ground: Stevenson Park, Dungannon. Tel: Dungannon 22387
Capacity: 4,500
Colours: Blue and white hoops
Honours: IC League Two: Runners-up 1995-96
Last season: IC League Two: Runners-up
Most capped player: Willie Anderson (Ireland) 27
Director of Rugby: Willie Anderson
Coach: Davey Haslett
Captain: Michael Patton

GARRYOWEN

Formation of club: 1884
Ground: Dooradoyle, Limerick. Tel: Limerick 227672
Capacity: 11,000
Colours: Navy blue, yellow and white
Honours: IC League One: Champions: 1991-92, 93-94
Last season: IC League One: Runners-up
Most capped player: Gordon Wood (Ireland) 29
Coach: Phil Danaher, Declan Madden
Captain: Paul Hogan

INSTONIANS

Formation of club: 1919
Ground: Shane Park, Stockmans Lane, Belfast. Tel: Belfast 660629
Capacity: 3,000
Colours: Purple, yellow and black
Honours: IC League Two: Champions 1993-94
Last season: IC League One: 11th
Most capped player: Keith Crossan (Ireland) 41
Coach: Brian McLoughlin
Captain: Andy Adair

LANSDOWNE

Formation of club: 1872
Ground: Lansdowne Road, Dublin 4. Tel: 003531 6689300
Capacity: 40,000 (non international games)
Colours: Red, yellow and black
Honours: –
Last season: IC League One: 6th
Most capped player: Moss Keane (Ireland) 51
Coaches: Donal Spring, Paul Clinch, Mano Ryan
Captain: Mark McDermott

OLD BELVEDERE

Formation of club: 1930
Ground: Anglesea Road, Ballsbridge, Dublin. Tel: 003531 6689748
Capacity: 2,500
Colours: Black and white hoops
Honours: IC League Two: Runners-up 1994-95
Last season: IC League One: 10th
Most capped player: Tony O'Reilly (Ireland) 29
Coach: TBA
Captain: Steve Tormey

OLD CRESCENT

Formation of club: 1947
Ground: Rosbrien, Limerick. Tel: Limerick 228083
Capacity: 5,000
Colours: Navy, blue and white stripes
Honours: IC League Two: Winners 1995-96
Last season: IC League Two: Winners
Most capped player: P. Lane (Ireland) 1
Coach: Jed O'Dwyer
Captain: Liam Toland

OLD WESLEY

Formation of club: 1891
Ground: Donnybrook, Dublin. Tel: 003531 6609893
Capacity: 12,000
Colours: White with blue and red band
Honours: IC League Two: Champions 1990-91
Last season: IC League One: 8th
Most capped player: Paddy Orr (Ireland) 58
Coach: Mark Duffey
Captain: Conor Howey

ST MARY'S COLLEGE

Formation of club: 1900
Ground: Templeville Road, Templeogue, Dublin Tel: 003531 4900440
Capacity: 9,000
Colours: Royal Blue with white star
Honours: –
Last season: IC League One: 5th
Most capped player: Paul Dean (Ireland) 32
Coach: Ciaran Fitzgerald
Captain: Brian Keane

SHANNON

Formation of club: 1884
Ground: Thomond Park, Limerick Tel: Limerick 452350
Capacity: 12,000
Colours: Black and blue hoops
Honours: IC League One: Champions: 1994-95, 95-96
Last season: IC League One: Champions
Most capped player: Ginger McLoughlin (Ireland) 18
Coach: Niall O'Donovan
Captain: Conor McDermott

TERENURE COLLEGE

Formation of club: 1940
Ground: Lakelands Park, Greenlea, Terenure, Dublin. Tel: 003531 4907572
Capacity: 3,000
Colours: Purple, black and white
Honours: –
Last season: IC League Two: 3rd
Most capped player: Mike Hipwell (Ireland) 12
Coach: Gerry Murphy
Captain: James Blaney

YOUNG MUNSTER

Formation of club: 1895
Ground: Tom Clifford Park, Greenfields, Limerick Tel: Limerick 228433
Capacity: 10,000
Colours: Black and amber
Honours: IC League One: Champions 1992-93. IC League Two: Runners-up 1990-91
Last season: IC League One: 4th
Most capped player: Peter Clohessy (Ireland) 16
Coach: Dan Mooney
Captain: Declan Edwards

Heineken European Cup 1995-96

The sceptics scoffed and those without ambition or foresight were quick to find fault, but the Heineken European Cup hit the ground running in its inaugural season and will provide the highlight of the domestic season in Europe this year, a remarkable achievement for a fledgling competition. Nobody can pretend there weren't problems. Scheduling, in a busy season, was a nightmare, the English clubs were notable absentees though not by choice, and press coverage was sporadic. But starting from scratch the organisers made it happen and the joint sponsors, ITV and Heineken, will be well rewarded for their £20 million investment over three years.

This season the competition has been expanded from 12 to 20 teams which allows the top four clubs in England to compete, along with three Scottish Districts and the winners of a play-off between Benetton Treviso and Dinamo Bucharest, from which Treviso emerged. The four pools have been expanded from three to five clubs, with the winners again progressing to the semi-finals.

The final took place at Cardiff Arms Park on a mild Sunday afternoon in January when an encouraging crowd of 20,000 watched Toulouse become Europe's first champion club by beating Cardiff 21-18 after 30 exhausting minutes of extra time. On an ideal day for rugby, Toulouse briefly threatened to demolish Cardiff in spectacular fashion, scoring excellent tries in the opening ten minutes through Thomas Castaignede and Jerome Cazalbou. Castaignede, who has rapidly emerged as the most exciting young back in France, crossed after six minutes following a powerful break by Stephane Ougier, a full-back that most countries would kill for but is apparently surplus to requirements for France. Christophe Deylaud and Cazalbou carried on the movement with quick passing for Castaignede to deliver the *coup de grâce*.

Next up was Cazalbou, who sprinted over after purposeful runs from Castaignede and David Berty. Cardiff looked shell-shocked but regrouped around the lineout domination of Derwyn Jones and John Wakeford and the driving play of captain Hemi Taylor at No 8. Davies reduced the deficit to six points at half-time and a third penalty after the break further improved the situation before Castaignede potted a 40-yard dropped goal. The momentum, however, was with Cardiff and justice was done when Davies landed two penalties to force extra time, the last a tremendous 45-yard effort three minutes into injury time. Extra time was tense and dramatic, as all extra-time duels should be, but was eventually settled by Deylaud, enjoying one of his calmer less eccentric afternoons, who kicked a simple penalty in front of the posts after he had earlier swapped kicks with Davies.

Final

Cardiff 18, Toulouse 21 (aet) (Arms Park, Cardiff, 7 January 1996)

Cardiff: M Rayer; S Ford, M Hall, M Ring, S Hill; A Davies, A Moore; A Lewis, J Humphries, L Mustoe, D Jones, J Wakeford, E Lewis, H Taylor (capt), O Williams.

Replacements: J Davies for Ring (40), N Walker for Ford (90).

Scorer: PG: Davies (6).

Toulouse: S Ougier; E Ntamack (capt), P Carbonneau, T Castaignede, D Berty; C Deylaud, J Cazalbou; C Califano, P Soula, C Portolan, H Miorin, F Belot, D Lacroix, S Dispagne, H Manent.

Replacements: R Castel for Lacroix (57), H Mola for Berty (70), E Artiguste for Castaignede (93).

Scorers: T: Castaignede, Cazalbou. C: Deylaud. PG: Deylaud (2). DG: Castaignede.

Referee: D McHugh (Ireland).

Earlier rounds

The competition, as far as the wider public was concerned, had taken off the previous week when two high-quality semi-finals were televised live on a rare quiet weekend of sport. In dry conditions at the Stade des Sept-Deniers in Toulouse, the home side proved much too strong for a spirited but limited Swansea who, in partial mitigation, also suffered badly from injuries. Toulouse scored three tries in their 30-3 victory and could have scored more.

Toulouse had qualified from Pool A having disposed of Farul Constanta 54-10 in Romania and then defeating Michael Lynagh's Benetton Treviso 18-9 in a tight tactical encounter. Treviso had previously destroyed Constanta 86-8, scoring 12 tries in the process. Swansea had qualified from the much tighter Pool D amid chaotic scenes at St Helen's when they defeated Castres 22-10 in a torrid game, which finished with Scottish referee Chris Muir needing a police escort off the pitch as protection against angry French fans. Munster had contributed fully to the excitement in this group, defeating Swansea 17-13 at Thomond Park and going down bravely 19-12 away to Castres.

Meanwhile in the Dublin semi-final, icy driving rain may have made the conditions miserable at Lansdowne Road but Leinster and Cardiff produced a marvellous spectacle, with Cardiff playing superbly into the wind in the second half to claim a 23-14 victory. Hemi Taylor and Mike Hall scored valuable tries, Adrian Davies added two conversions and a penalty, and Davies and Andrew Moore kicked a dropped goal apiece. Leinster's driving forward play impressed all-comers but they failed to capitalise on their first-half domination and had to be content with a try from captain Chris Pim and three penalties from fly-half Alan McGowan.

Cardiff had qualified on points difference from Pool B, a thumping 46-6 win over Ulster helping their cause as Begles Bordeaux could only manage a 29-16 win at Ravenhill. The high spot of this group, and indeed of all the qualifying games, was a tremendous 14-14 draw between Cardiff and Begles in front of a packed 10,000 crowd at the Stade Andre-Moga. A game featuring 14 internationals was played with a near international intensity and included classic tries by Begles' wing Phillipe Bernat-Salles and Cardiff flanker Mark Bennett. Leinster, the Irish inter-provincial champions, had also enjoyed a dramatic campaign, securing an invaluable 24-12 win away to Milan before winning a mid-week shoot-out against Pontypridd 23-22 at Lansdowne Road.

European Cup 1995-96 Results

POOL A

Constanza 10 Toulouse 54 (31 October 1995)

Constanza: V Brici; C Saua, A Tinca, N Fulina (capt), E Florea; V Bezarau, M Focat; C Pinghert, N Lupu, D Manole, N Marin, N Branescu, C Florea, T Oroian, A Girbu.

Replacements: T Cabala for E Florea (38), A Seciuiu for Lupu (51), R Ruxanda for C Florea (55), N Coman for Foca (75).

Scorers: T: Foca. C: Florea. PG: Florea.

Toulouse: S Ougier; E Ntamack (capt), T Castaignede, P Carbonneau, D Berty; C Deylaud, J Cazalbou; C Califano, P Soula, C Portolan, H Miorin, F Belot, J-L Cester, S Dispagne, R Castel.

Replacements: O Carbonneau for Castaignede (5), E Artiguste for Cazalbou, Lacroix for Castel (60), P Lasserre for Portolan (68).

Scorers: T: Cester, Ntamack (2), Berty (2), Castaignede, Ougier, penalty try. C: Deylaud (7).

Referee: D Davies (Wales).

Treviso 86 Constanza 8 (7 November 1995)

Treviso: P Dotto; M Perziano, I Francescato, T Visentin, L Manteri; M Lynagh, A Troncon; G Grespan (capt), N Giulato, M Trevisiol, M Giacheri, D Scaglia, S Rigo, C Checchinato, J Gardner.

Replacement: L Perziano for M Perziano (40).

Scorers: T: Manteri (2), M Perziano (2), L Perziano (2), Dotto (2), Checchinato, Troncon, Giulato, Gardner C: Lynagh (10). PG: Lynagh (2).

Constanza: E Florea; C Sasu, A Tinca, N Fulina (capt), D Talaba; V Bezarau, T Coman; C Pinghert, N Lupu, D Manole, N Branescu, C Florea, T Oroian, A Girbu, I Ruxanda.

Scorers: T: Talaba. PG: Florea.

Referee: B Stirling (Ireland).

Toulouse 18 Treviso 9 (12 December 1995)

Toulouse: S Ougier; E Ntamack (capt), P Carbonneau, T Castaignede, D Berty; D Deylaud, J Cazalbou; C Califano, P Soula, C Portolan, F Belot, H Miorin, D Lacroix, S Dispagne, H Manent.

Replacement: H Mola for Berty (77).

Scorers: PG: Deylaud (5). DG: Deylaud.

Treviso: P Dotto; M Perziano, I Francescato, F Mazzariol, L Manteri; M Lynagh, A Troncon; G Grespan (capt), M Trevisiol, G Rossi, M Giacheri, D Scaglia, S Rigo, C Checchinato, J Gardner.

Replacement: W Cristofoleto for Checchinato (7).

Scorers: PG: Lynagh (2). DG: Lynagh.

Referee: J Bacigalupo (Scotland).

Pool winners: **Toulouse**

POOL B

Begles 14 Cardiff 14 (21 November 1995)

Begles: P Fauthoux; P Bernat-Salles, E Darritchon, L Lafforgue, P Tauzin; V Etcheto, G Accoceberry (capt); L Verge, S Morizot, O Sourguens, C Mougeot, A Berthozat, M Barrague, J-J Alibert, P Farner.

Replacements: S Conchy for Barrague (67), P Eyhartz for Berthozat (74).

Scorers: T: Bernat-Salles. PG: Etcheto (3).

Cardiff: M Rayer; S Hill, M Hall, M Ring, N Walker; A Davies, A Moore; A Lewis J Humphreys, L Mustoe, D Jones, J Wakeford, E Lewis, M Bennett, H Taylor (capt).

Replacement: C Mills for Lewis (35).

Scorers: T: Bennett. PG: Davies (3).

Referee: D McHugh (Ireland).

Ulster 16 Begles 29 (13 December 1995)

Ulster: J Bell; J Topping, W Harbison (capt), M Field, A Park; M McCall, A Matchett; R Mackey, A Clarke, G Leslie, J Davidson, D Tweed, D McBride, P Johns, S Duncan.

Scorers: T: McBride, Matchett. PG: McCall (2).

Begles: P Fauthoux; P Bernat-Salles, S Loubsens, E Darritchon, P Tauzin; J Berthe, X Pierre; L Dehez, S Morizot, O Sourgens, S Mougeot, A Berthozat (capt), S Conchy, J-J Alibert, P Farner.

Replacements: P Eyhartz for Mougeot (16), V Chamboulives for Morizot (51), F Garcia for Dehez (55).

Scorers: T: Loubsens (2), Bernat-Salles, Fauthoux (2). C: Berthe, Fauthoux.

Referee: D Bevan (Wales).

Cardiff 46 Ulster 6 (28 November 1995)

Cardiff: M Rayer; S Ford, S John, M Hall, N Walker; A Davies, A Moore; A Lewis, J Humphreys, L Mustoe, D Jones, J Wakeford, E Lewis, H Taylor (capt), O Williams.

Replacement: M Bennett for Lewis (78).

Scorers: T: Moore (2), Davies, Taylor, Hall. C: Davies (3). PG: Davies (5).

Ulster: J Bell; J Topping, W Harbison (capt), M Field, J Cunningham; M McCall, N Doak; R Mackey, A Clarke, G Leslie, J Davidson, G Longwell, S Duncan, D Erskine, D McBride.

Replacement: R Wilson for McBride (78).

Scorer: PG: McCall (2).

Referee: G Borreani (France).

Pool winners: Cardiff

POOL C

Milan 21 Leinster 24 (31 October 1995)

Milan: F Williams; R Crotti, M Platania, M Tommasi, Marcello Cuttitta; D Dominguez, M Bonomi; S Cerioni, C Orlandi, F Properzi, F Berni, G Croci, D Beretta, G Milano (capt), T Cicco.

Replacement: M Giovanelli for Milano (52).

Scorers: T: Crotti, Platania. C: Bonomi. PG: Dominguez (3).

Leinster: C O'Shea; P Gavin, V Cunningham, K McQuilkin, N Woods; A McGowan, A Rolland; H Hurley, S Byrne, P Wallace, M O'Kelly, B Rigney, V Costello, D Oswald, C Pim (capt).

Scorers: T: O'Shea, Woods. C: McGowan. PG: McGowan (4).

Referee: M Maciello (France).

Pontypridd 31 Milan 12 (22 November 1995)

Pontypridd: C Cormack; D Manley, S Lewis, S McIntosh, G Jones; N Jenkins, Paul John; N Bezani (capt), Phil John, N Eynon, M Rowley, G Prosser, M Spiller, M Lloyd, P Thomas.

Scorers: T: Manley. C: Jenkins. PG: Jenkins (8).

Milan: F Williams; M Platania, M Bonomi, M Tommasi, Marcello Cuttitta; D Dominguez, F Gomez; Massimo Cuttitta, A Marengoni, F Properzi, F Berni, P Pedroni, D Beretta, G Milano (capt), M Giovannelli.

Scorer: PG: Dominguez (4).

Referee: B Campsall (England).

Leinster 23 Pontypridd 22 (6 December 1995)

Leinster: C O'Shea; P Gavin, V Cunningham, K McQuilkin, N Woods; A McGowan, A Rolland; H Hurley, S Byrne, P Wallace, N Francis, B Rigney, S Rooney, V Costello, C Pim (capt).

Replacements: N Hogan for Rolland (31), A McKeen for Wallace (temp), E Miller for Costello (temp).

Scorers: T: McGowan, O'Shea. C: McGowan (2). PG: McGowan (3).

Pontypridd: C Cormack; D Manley, J Lewis, S McIntosh, S Enoch; L Jarvis, Paul John; N Bezani (capt), Phil John, A Metcalfe, M Rowley, G Prosser, R Collins, M Lloyd, P Thomas.

Scorers: T: Cormack. C: Jarvis. PG: Jarvis (5).

Referee: D Gillet (France).

Pool winners: **Leinster**

POOL D

Munster 17 Swansea 13 (1 November 1995)

Munster: P Murray (capt); R Wallace, S McCahill, D Larkin, K Smith; P Burke, D O'Mahoney; J Fitzgerald, T Kingston, P Clohessy, G Fulcher, M Galwey, D Corkery, A Foley, E Halvey.

Replacement: B Toland for Halvey (32).

Scorers: T: Wallace, Murray. C: Smith (2). PG: Murray.

Swansea: G Thomas; A Harris, R Boobyer, D Weatherley, Simon Davies; A Williams, R Jones; C Loader, G Jenkins, C Anthony, S Moore, A Moore, Stuart Davies (capt), R Appleyard, A Reynolds.

Scorers: T: Harris. C: Williams. PG: Williams (2).

Referee: E Morrison (England).

Castres 19 Munster 12 (8 November 1995)

Castres: L Labit; C Savy, N Combes, J-M Aue, P Garrigue; F Rui (capt), F Seguier; L Toussaint, C Urios, T Lafforgue, J-F Gourragne, T Bourdet, G Pages, A Cigagna, N Hallinger.

Replacement: S Bristow for Toussaint (70).

Scorers: T: Combes. C: Labit. PG: Labit (4).

Munster: P Murray (capt); R Wallace, S McCahill, S Larkin, K Smith; P Burke, D O'Mahoney; J Fitzgerald, T Kingston, P Clohessy, P O'Connor, G Fulcher, M Galwey, A Foley, D Corkery.

Replacements: B Toland for Galwey (32), B Walsh for Burke (58).

Scorer: PG: Smith (4).

Referee: D Davies (Wales).

Swansea 22 Castres 10 (5 December 1995)

Swansea: A Flowers; A Harris, D Weatherley, M Taylor, Simon Davies; A Williams, R Jones; K Colclough, G Jenkins, C Anthony, S Moore, A Moore, A Reynolds, Stuart Davies (capt), R Appleyard.

Scorers: T: Harris, Jenkins. PG: Williams (4).

Castres: C Savy; J-M Aue, A Hyardet, N Combes, P Garrigues; F Rui, F Seguier (capt); S Bristow, C Urios, T Lafforgue, J-F Gourragne, T Bourdet, G Pages, A Cigagna, N Hallinger.

Replacement: G Jeannard for Gourragne (64).

Scorers: T: Aue. C: Savy. PG: Savy.

Referee: C Muir (Scotland).

Pool winners: Swansea

Semi-finals

Leinster 14 Cardiff 23 (Lansdowne Road, Dublin, 30 December 1995)

Leinster: C Clarke; P Gavin, V Cunningham, K McQuilkin, C O'Shea; A McGowan, A Rolland; H Hurley, S Byrne, P Wallace, N Francis, S Jamieson, S Rooney, V Costello, C Pim (capt).

Replacement: R Hennessy for Clarke (55).

Scorers: T: Pim. PG: McGowan (3).

Cardiff: M Rayer; S Ford, M Hall, M Ring, S Hill; A Davies, A Moore; A Lewis, J Humphreys, L Mustoe, D Jones, J Wakeford, E Lewis, O Williams, H Taylor (capt).

Scorers: T: Taylor, Hall. C: Davies (2). PG: Davies. DG: Davies, Moore.

Referee: B Campsall (England).

Toulouse 30 Swansea 3 (Toulouse, 30 December 1995)

Toulouse: S Ougier; E Ntamack (capt), E Artiguste, T Castaignede, D Berty; C Deylaud, J Cazalbou; C Califano, P Soula, C Portolan, F Belot, H Miorin, D Lacroix, S Dispagne, H Manent.

Replacements: R Castel for Lacroix (57), H Mola for Berty (63), P Lasserre for Califano (67), O Carbonneau for Castaignede (71).

Scorers: T: penalty try, Manent, Artiguste. C: Deylaud (3). PG: Deylaud (3).

Swansea: R Boobyer; A Harris, M Taylor, D Weatherley, Simon Davies; A Williams, R Jones; C Loader, G Jenkins, K Colclough, S Moore, A Moore, A Reynolds, Stuart Davies (capt), R Appleyard.

Replacements: M Evans for Reynolds (29), M Thomas for A Moore (38).

Scorer: PG: Williams.

Referee: J Fleming (Scotland).

Heineken European Cup 1996-97

Group A: Pontypridd, Treviso, Bath, Edinburgh, Dax
Group B: Llanelli, Leinster, Pau, South of Scotland, Leicester
Group C: North & Midlands, Ulster, Brive, Neath, Harlequins
Group D: Munster, Milan, Wasps, Cardiff, Toulouse

Fixtures 1996-97

12 October

Pool A: Pontypridd v Treviso, Bath v Edinburgh
Pool B: Llanelli v Leinster, Pau v South of Scotland
Pool C: North & Midlands v Ulster, Brive v Neath
Pool D: Munster v Milan, Wasps v Cardiff

16 October

Pool A: Treviso v Dax, Edinburgh v Pontypridd
Pool B: Leinster v Leicester, South of Scotland v Llanelli
Pool C: Ulster v Harlequins, Neath v North & Midlands
Pool D: Milan v Toulouse, Cardiff v Munster

19 October

Pool A: Dax v Edinburgh, Pontypridd v Bath
Pool B: Leicester v South of Scotland, Llanelli v Pau
Pool C: Harlequins v Neath, North & Midlands v Brive
Pool D: Toulouse v Cardiff, Munster v Wasps

26 October

Pool A: Bath v Dax, Edinburgh v Treviso
Pool B: Pau v Leicester, South of Scotland v Leinster
Pool C: Brive v Harlequins, Neath v Ulster
Pool D: Wasps v Toulouse, Cardiff v Milan

2 November

Pool A: Dax v Pontypridd, Treviso v Bath
Pool B: Leicester v Llanelli, Leinster v Pau
Pool C: Harlequins v North & Midlands, Ulster v Brive
Pool D: Toulouse v Munster, Milan v Wasps

16 November

Semi-finals

4 January

Final

Heineken European Cup Club Directory

BATH (*see* pages 7-13)

BRIVE

Founded: 1907
Ground: Parc Municipal des Sports, 116 Avenue du 11 Novembre, 1900 Brive,
    France. Tel: 0033 55742014
Capacity: 15,000
Honours: French Club championship: Runners-up: 1965, 72, 75, 96
Colours: Black and white
Coaches: Laurent Seigne, Didier Faugeron

Brive were beaten by Toulouse in last season's French Championship final, the fourth occasion they have fallen at the last hurdle. Brive nonetheless experienced their best ever season, winning their first major title, the Challenge du Manoir. Coaches Laurent Seigne and Didier Faugeron did a fine job, assisted by former Australia captain Nick Farr-Jones who acted as coaching adviser. Brive's recent success has been based on a powerful pack led by No 8 Thierry Labrousse, who scored two tries on his France debut against Romania in April 1996, while enjoying a new lease of life with his former France hooker Vincent Moscato, who last made the headlines by being sent off against England in 1992. Brive are captained by Alain Penaud who regained the France outside-half berth on the summer tour of Argentina, now that Toulouse's Thomas Castaignede insists his international future lies at centre. One youngster to watch is teenage wing Jerome Carrat, whose brother Sebastien is one of the top sprinters in France. The arrival from Bourgoin of the newly capped wing David Venditti will add further to a pacy backline that also includes former international full-back Sebastien Viars. One disappointment has been the departure of wing Alexandre Bouyssie, who starred for France in the 1996 Hong Kong Sevens, to Begles.

CARDIFF

Founded: 1876
Address: Cardiff RFC, Cardiff Arms Park, Cardiff CF1 1JA. Tel: 01222 383546
Ground: Cardiff Arms Park
Capacity 12,000
Colours: Cambridge blue and black
Honours: Welsh Club champions: 1947-48, 48-49, 53-54, 54-55, 57-58, 81-82.
    Heineken League Champions: 1994-95. Welsh Cup Winners: 1980-81, 82-83,
    83-84, 85-86, 86-87, 93-94
Chief Executive: Gareth Davies
Coaches: Terry Holmes, Charlie Faulkner

Cardiff have always ranked as one of the world's great clubs and despite just missing out on the Heineken League in Wales last season, they performed wonderfully well in the Heineken Cup. A tenacious 14-14 draw in Begles was the key to qualification from their group, along with a convincing win over Ulster. Leinster were dispatched in impressive style in the snow and wind of Lansdowne Road and although Toulouse threatened to run away with the final, scoring two tries in the opening ten minutes, Cardiff recovered their poise only to be squeezed out in extra time. The mid-summer signings of scrum-half Robert Howley from Bridgend, Neath centre Leigh Davies, the

Llanelli duo of full-back Justin Thomas and flanker Gwyn Jones and the return of prop David Young from Rugby League has greatly strengthened a squad already blessed with the likes of Hemi Taylor, Emyr Lewis, Jonathan Humphreys, Derwyn Jones and Simon Hill. That's just as well because the draw has not been particularly kind with Cardiff entertaining Munster and Milan and facing difficult away trips to Wasps and their old rivals Toulouse.

DAX

Founded: 1904
Ground: Parc Municipal des Sports, Boulevard des Sports, 40100 Dax, France.
  Tel: 0033 58741402
Capacity: 18,000
Honours: French Club championship: Runners-up: 1956, 61, 63, 66, 73
Colours: Blue and white

Dax qualified for this season's Heineken Cup by finishing fourth in the French Club championship. Despite reaching the finals five times they have never won that title and they rather lost interest last season after losing to Toulouse in the semi-final, a 50-17 play-off defeat against Pau not being one of the club's better days. Missing this winter will be the prolific Thierry Lacroix, who spent his summer playing for Natal and is likely to play for Racing Club de France on his return. Former French captain Olivier Roumat has also been the subject of speculation, but has confirmed he will be staying with the club. On a more positive note the versatile Richard Dourthe, son of former French international Claude, enjoyed an outstanding domestic season despite his two-match international ban after kicking Ben Clarke in the Five Nations. Dourthe can play both full-back and centre, is developing into a reliable kicker and regained his Test place on tour in Argentina in June. Another important figure will be No 8 Fabien Pelous who is already being tipped as a future France captain. Dax have a fine reputation for producing international No 8s, notably Jean-Pierre Bastiat. The signing of the eccentric but talented Hugo Mola from Toulouse should strengthen their back division and excite the famous Dax band.

EDINBURGH

Grounds: Goldenacre (Heriot's FP), Meggetland (Boroughmuir),
  Myreside (Watsonians)
Colours: Royal blue
Honours: District champions: eight occasions
Coaches: Grecco Hogg, Iain Barnes
Manager: Rob Flockhart

Gavin Hastings suggested three seasons ago that Scottish rugby's most rewarding road forward might be for Edinburgh and other Districts to take on the best in Britain. It would, he argued, expand players' horizons, improve their skills and stimulate public interest, attracting possible five-figure crowds. His vision will become a reality when Edinburgh take on Bath, arguably the world's top club. Gavin is an improbable starter but younger brother Scott, now Scotland's most capped player, is still hungry for the fray and will provide the focal point for Edinburgh's backs. Edinburgh's golden era was probably in the late 1980s when the brothers Hastings, Milne and Calder swept them to three consecutive District titles but the new generation are keen to prove their worth. Up front lineout specialist Scott Murray will have benefited from a tour of New Zealand, in the back five Darren Burns and Stuart Reid could be influential figures, while behind the scrum look out for captain and scrum-half Ally Donaldson, a prolific goal kicker. Scotland's capital may currently be short of big-name players but there is a genuine depth, with the District drawing from half the clubs in the Premiership's top division. Teamwork will be a crucial element as they tackle Pontypridd, Treviso, Dax and Bath but Edinburgh have the potential to surprise.

HARLEQUINS *(see pages 25-31)*

LEICESTER *(see pages 32-7)*

LEINSTER

Founded: 1879
Address: Leinster Branch, Donnybrook, Dublin 4, Ireland. Tel: 003531 6685999
Ground: Lansdowne Road
Capacity: 40,000 (for non-internationals)
Colours: Dark blue and white
Honours: Interprovincial champions: 1949, 50, 59, 61, 62, 64, 65, 72, 80, 81, 82, 84, 96
Manager: Jim Glennon
Coach: Ciaran Callan

Leinster, who greatly enjoyed their first taste of European rugby, have looked on helplessly as many of their more experienced players departed across the water, and wondered exactly what it meant in terms of their Heineken Cup prospects. There is no reason, however, to suppose that the London Irish trio of Conor O'Shea, Vic Costello and Niall Woods won't be available, and with Saracens having no European commitments, Paul Wallace could also be on call. Another factor is that the Heineken Cup comes after the Interprovincial series when the English-based players certainly won't be available. Do Leinster stick with their Interprovincial squad or call in the Anglos? Leinster built up an excellent team spirit last winter, when they lost just twice in 12 games, so manager Jim Glennon will probably operate a squad in the broadest sense. The fixture list has been kind with Leinster travelling to Llanelli and South of Scotland – sides they have visited on a regular basis and who hold no fears. Leinster's strength last season was in the pack and nothing will change in that respect but they must make better use of their backs. Scrum-half Niall Hogan's availability is uncertain as he undertakes medical studies at Oxford.

LLANELLI

Founded: 1872
Address: Stradey Park, Llanelli, Dyfed SA15 4BT. Tel: 01554 775963
Ground: Stradey Park
Capacity: 13,500
Colours: Scarlet
Honours: Welsh Club champions: 1967-68, 73-74, 76-77, 90-91.
    Heineken League champions: 1992-93. Welsh Cup winners: 1972-73, 73-74, 74-75, 75-76, 84-85, 87-88, 90-91, 91-92, 92-93
Manager: Anthony Buchanan
Coach: Gareth Jenkins

Llanelli's form has fluctuated dramatically over the last decade but they remain one of the biggest names in British rugby and the Heineken Cup will be better for their presence. Few clubs have a more glorious past and the prospect of a packed house at Stradey watching an important European Cup clash is one to set the pulse racing. Not that the Scarlets exactly finished in a blaze of glory last season, qualifying in fourth position despite losing their last Heineken League game 65-13 at Cardiff. The summer has brought a number of problems to grapple with. The departure of inspirational captain Phil Davies to Leeds was well broadcast in advance but the loss of Wales full-back Justin Thomas and exciting young flanker Gwyn Jones to Cardiff is a blow. Llanelli have been working hard to improve their strength in depth but again much will depend on the performance of club stalwarts such as Ieuan Evans, Rupert Moon, Nigel Davies, and wing/full-back Wayne Proctor. The latter bagged 17 League tries last season to take his career total to 60, equalling that of Evans.

MILAN

Founded: 1928
Address: Residenza Portici 8, Milano 2, 20090 Segrate, Italy. Tel: 70602642
Ground: Camp Comunale, M Giurati, Via Pasca
Colours: Red, white and black
Honours: Palmares Serie A: 1929, 30, 31, 32, 33, 34, 36, 38, 39, 40, 41, 42, 43, 46, 91, 93, 95, 96. Runners-up: 52, 55, 58, 63, 87
Coach: Gustavo Milano

Milan were disappointed with their showing in the 1995-96 Heineken Cup, their campaign faltering at the first hurdle when they lost 24-21 at home to Leinster. They failed to do themselves justice at Sardis Road against Pontypridd, which developed into a shoot-out between Neil Jenkins and Diego Dominguez, the Welshman winning conclusively. The Milan squad is littered with established Italian internationals, especially in the front five. South African-reared prop Massimo Cuttita is an international-class scrummager and veteran of two World Cups and is often joined in the Italian front row by two club colleagues – hooker Carlo Orlandi and fellow prop Franco Properzi-Curti. Orlandi scored against Australia in Sydney in 1994, while the Indian-born Properzi-Curti was ever present for Italy in RWC91 and RWC95. At lock Pierpaulo Pedroni is an Italy regular. Argentinian-born half-backs Diego Dominguez and Fabio Gomez are capable of controlling a contest – Dominguez actually toured France with the Pumas as Hugo Porta's deputy in 1986 but three years later made his Italian debut in a memorable 15-9 win over France in Rome and played a prominent role in both RWC91 and RWC95.

MUNSTER

Founded: 1880
Address: Munster Branch, Penrose House, Penrose Quay, Cork, Ireland.
  Tel: 0135321 501533
Grounds: Thomond Park (Limerick), Musgrave Park (Cork)
Colours: Red and white
Honours: Interprovincial champions: 1948, 58, 60, 63, 66, 69, 74, 79, 95
Manager: Colm Tucker
Coach: Jerry Holland

Nobody will relish a visit to Munster, who are formidable opponents on their own patch. Three times they have beaten Australia (1966, 81 and 92) and who can forget their epic 12-0 win over New Zealand in 1978? They also drew 3-3 with the 1972 All Blacks. Munster find themselves in a really tough group and although they may well contest the Interprovincials with an inexperienced squad they would prefer to face the might of Toulouse, Cardiff, Wasps and Milan with all their top English-based players such as Paul Burke, David Corkery, Gabriel Fulcher, Keith Wood and Eddie Halvey. But that's always making the massive assumption that their English paymasters are agreeable. Munster know already that Peter Clohessy, who now seems destined for Australia, will be unavailable but they can usually be relied on to field a competitive pack. Interestingly Mick Galway has been recalled to the national training squad and the motivation of European rugby may yet see him recapture his form of 1993 when he won selection for the British Lions. Munster did not perform well in the Interprovincials last season, when they finished third due mainly to a sub-standard performance away to Ulster, but they have always played superbly well against the odds.

NEATH

Founded: 1871
Address: The Gnoll, Gnoll Park Road, Neath, West Glamorgan. Tel: 01639 636547
Ground: The Gnoll
Capacity: 8,000
Colours: Black
Honours: Welsh Club champions: 1956-57, 66-67, 86-87, 88-89, 89-90.
  Heineken League champions: 1990-91, 95-96. Welsh Cup winners: 1971-72, 88-89, 89-90
Director of Rugby: Brian Thomas
Coaches: Darryl Jones, Lyn Jones

Neath's all-singing, all-dancing style of running rugby won them a host of friends last season, not to mention the Heineken League championship and a place in the SWA-LEC Cup final. Whether such an approach can successfully be adapted to the European arena remains to be seen, especially after a summer which has seen the departure of key personnel such as locks Gareth and Glyn Llewellyn, to Harlequins and Wasps respectively, and blockbusting centre Leigh Davies to Cardiff. Neath have a proud record of developing their own talent so there is no reason to suppose other top players won't emerge. Former Wales Schools coach Darryl Jones, who has enjoyed great success with Neath Tertiary College, has an encyclopedic knowledge of young players in Wales and has formed a formidable partnership with Lyn Jones, the dynamic former Wales flanker who would have relished playing in the current Neath side. The Welsh All Blacks scored 121 tries in 22 games en route to the Heineken Championship but their defeat against Pontypridd in the SWALEC Cup final underlined their lack of a reliable goal kicker, a deficiency that needs to be addressed.

NORTH & MIDLANDS

Ground: McDiarmid Park, Perth (St Johnston FC)
Capacity: 10,000
Colours: Light blue and white
Honours: District champions: twice (shared)
Coach: Iain Rankin, Brian Edwards
Team manager: John Methven

The Cinderella District, North & Midlands won their place in Europe in an emotion-charged play-off with Glasgow, crowning their most successful ever season, which also brought victories over Edinburgh and Western Samoa – their first ever against major tourists. This success was due, in no small measure, to the inspiring leadership of former Scotland flanker David McIvor and all is now set for a European adventure with St Johnston FC offering the use of their ground in Perth. North & Midlands have long had to export their best players but now have a solid core of talent packed around McIvor. The brightest star has been none other than Scotland captain Rob Wainwright. Rowen Shepherd, Gavin Hastings' successor as Scotland's full-back, is another wandering star in their ranks, while a switch of allegiance inside the Stirling County camp brought in Scotland hooker Kevin McKenzie and his younger brother Mark, a richly talented fly-half. Up front a solid front row is built around McKenzie senior, while Scotland lock Stewart Campbell is a powerhouse in the second row and McIvor, Wainwright and Gareth Flockhart constitute a well-balanced backrow. With such a small player base, consistency is always the problem but that 43-9 triumph over Western Samoa last November showed exactly what they can achieve when everybody is available.

PAU

Founded: 1902
Ground: Stade du Hameau, Boulevard de L'Aviation, 64010 Pau, France.
  Tel: 0033 590224774
Capacity: 15,000
Honours: French Club championship: 1928, 46, 64
Colours: Green and white

Pau, who finished third in the 1996 French Championship after losing narrowly to Brive in the semi-finals, have been French champions on three occasions, the last being in 1964 when they defeated Beziers in the final. Led last season by No 8 Philippe Ebel, Pau also reached the final of the Challenge du Manoir before losing to Brive. Early-season inconsistency meant they finished only sixth in their pool in the French Championship but this was good enough to qualify for the knockout stages. They then secured victories over 1993 champions Castres and the 1995 semi-finalists Bourgoin en route to the semi-finals and, although losing out to Brive, they bounced back to thrash Dax 50-17 in the third-fourth place championship play-off, scoring eight tries. The basis of their success was a solid scrum, a strong defence, indomitable team spirit and the goal-kicking of outside-half David Aucagne. A major plus for Pau has been the return of France wing Philippe Bernat-Salles to his home-town club from Begles. Disappointingly though, outstanding young prop Jean-Louis Jordana has taken the well-worn path to Toulouse. Away visits to Pau could become some of the most popular on the European circuit. The university town lies in the shadow of the Pyrenees, on the edge of Basque country and close to the Atlantic coast.

PONTYPRIDD

Founded: 1876
Address: The Clubhouse, Sardis Road, Pwllgwaun, Pontypridd. Tel: 01443 405006
Ground: Sardis Road
Capacity: 10,000
Colours: Black and white hoops
Honours: Welsh Club champions: 1962-63, 75-76, 77-78. Welsh Cup winners: 1996.
  Heineken League: Runners-up: 1994-95
Coach: Dennis John

One of the great success stories of Welsh club rugby, Pontypridd responded to the modern-day challenge of league rugby to successfully contest and then overcome the established clubs in the Principality, so much so that they themselves have become members of the elite. All this has been achieved without compromising their close community spirit, friendliness and ethos of club loyalty. Last season they celebrated the retirement of revered club captain Nigel Bezani by defeating Neath to take the SWALEC Cup after losing in the final in 1995 to Swansea. To finally land a major trophy will have done wonders for their self-confidence. They also finished a highly respectable third in the league after being runners-up the previous winter. In Europe they comprehensively defeated Milan and narrowly lost to Leinster in an exciting contest. Though lacking the financial clout of some, Pontypridd have successfully kept the majority of their squad together, with the exception of promising fly-half Lee Jarvis, who has left for Cardiff. The signing of Wales wing/centre Gareth Thomas from Bridgend is a major coup, however, and with new captain Neil Jenkins at the helm Ponty will be a force to be reckoned with.

SOUTH OF SCOTLAND

Grounds: Netherdale (Galashiels), Mansfield Park (Hawick), The Greenyards (Melrose)
Honours: District champions on 17 occasions
Coach: Eric Paxton
Team manager: George Murray

Historically the strongest of the Scottish Districts, South have a powerful sense of local identity, enhanced by many memorable encounters with all the major touring teams. Border rugby has long been the bedrock of the game in Scotland, reflected in success at District and club level. But the advent of professionalism has presented a massive threat to the South, who traditionally confine selection to the Border clubs only. In the last 12 months their ranks have been harshly stripped as Gregor Townsend, Michael Dods, Gary Armstrong, Doddie Weir and Craig Joiner – all established internationals – have taken the road south. The exodus will test the District's strength in depth but with Premiership champions Melrose and a resurgent Hawick to call on, the South will remain highly competitive for a campaign which starts in the foothills of the Pyrenees at Pau. The key figure will surely be Craig Chalmers, last season's captain, who could revive his international prospects on the testing European stage. Alongside Chalmers will be scrum-half Bryan Redpath who enjoyed an excellent 1996 Five Nations but missed the summer tour of New Zealand through injury. Up front the South lack the physical presence of many sides and will, as ever, have to rely on their mobility and versatility, as epitomised by New Zealand-reared flanker Nick Broughton.

TOULOUSE

Founded: 1908
Ground: Les Sept-Deniers, 114 rue des Troenes, 31200 Toulouse, France.
 Tel: 0033 61570505
Capacity: 12,000
Colours: Red and dark blue
Honours: French Club championship: 1912, 22, 23, 24, 26, 27, 47, 85, 86, 89, 94, 95, 96.
Coaches: Guy Noves, Serge Laire

Toulouse, the reigning Heineken Cup champions, beat Brive 20-13 in Parc des Princes last June to clinch their third successive French championship and 13th title in all. The Haute-Garonne club lies in the rugby heartland of south-west France and includes captain and wing Emile Ntamack, prop Christian Califano and dazzling centre Thomas Castaignede among their stars. The French champions have a big mobile pack but despite the undoubted quality of their forwards, the Toulouse philosophy, started by Pierre Villepreux and continued by current first-team coaches Guy Noves and Serge Laire, is to play expansive rugby. Christophe Deylaud is an outstanding playmaker at club level, bringing out the best in Castaignede and a formidable trio of strike runners in wings Ntamack and David Berty and full-back Stephane Ougier. Richard Castel, the international flanker who scored two tries against Ireland in last season's Five Nations

Championship, could not win a regular place in the Toulouse pack last winter and has moved to Beziers to ensure regular first-team rugby. Talented wing Hugo Mola is another who was often confined to the bench and has moved to Dax but the squad has been strengthened by the arrival of new France prop Jean-Louis Jordana from Pau.

TREVISO

Founded: 1932
Ground: Stadio Comunale, Campo di Monigo, Via Olimpia, Treviso, Italy.
 Tel: 0422 324242
Colours: White, blue and green
Honours: Palmares Serie A: 1956, 78, 83, 89, 92. Runners-up: 1982, 83, 84, 90, 92

Benetton Treviso, with Michael Lynagh at the helm, made an immediate impact on the Heineken Cup last season despite not progressing beyond the pool stages. They scored 12 tries to defeat Farul Constanta 86-8 before travelling to France to tackle Toulouse, who scraped through 18-9. Lynagh will be missed but Treviso are more than a one-man team. They qualified for this year's tournament by defeating Dinamo Bucharest in a play-off in June. Leading their effort will be two Australian-born players, lock Mark Giacheri and flanker Julian Gardner, who have become international regulars with Italy. Giacheri is a formidable lineout operator, while Gardner is an experienced flanker, having first tasted international rugby in 1987 for Australia against Argentina. Lock Robert Favoro has won over 40 caps, while prop Giovanni Grespan and No 8 Carlo Checchinato are international-class forwards. A back division containing Italy's first-choice scrum-half Alessandro Troncon and centres Ivan Francescato and Tomas Visentin should not be underrated. Francescato, first capped as a scrum-half against Romania in 1990, is the fourth in line of brothers Rino, Nello and Bruno to represent Italy. A clever runner, he scored a memorable try against USA at RWC91 and has also scored twice against Wales at Cardiff Arms Park in 1992 and 1994.

ULSTER

Founded: 1880
Address: Ulster Branch, Ravenhill Grounds, 85 Ravenhill Park, Belfast BT6 0DG.
 Tel: 01232 235677
Ground: Ravenhill
Capacity: 12,000
Colours: White with red socks
Honours: Interprovincial champions: 1947, 51, 52, 54, 68, 70, 71, 75, 77, 85, 86, 87, 88, 89, 90, 91, 92, 93
Director of Rugby: Tony Russ

After a glorious decade of success Ulster have been knocked off their perch as top dogs in Ireland by Munster and Leinster in the past two years, but they remain a powerful unit, especially in front of a packed Ravenhill crowd, preferably under lights on a wet Wednesday evening. Outstanding results against tourists have included draws with New Zealand in 1935 and 1953, a draw with Australia in 1967 and a famous 15-13 victory in 1984, and victories over Argentina (1973), Fiji (1985) and Western Samoa (1988). Ulster made an inauspicious European debut last season, suffering a drubbing at Cardiff before performing better, in defeat, at home to Begles. Much more encouraging was the David Humphreys-inspired victory over New South Wales in a friendly. This season they begin afresh with the arrival of Tony Russ, formerly with Leicester, as director of rugby on a five-year contract. Like the other provinces, Ulster will be awaiting news on the availability of the English-based stars such as Jonathan Bell, Allen

Clarke, Paddy Johns, Jeremy Davidson and Humphreys. With evergreens such as Mark McCall and Maurie Fields still playing well, Ulster have the potential to be competitive and could cause an upset.

WASPS (*see* pages 67-72)

EUROPEAN CONFERENCE

Group A: Newbridge, Glasgow, Agen, Newport, Sale, Montferrand
Group B: Bristol, Treorchy, Narbonne, Dinamo Bucharest, Bridgend, Castres
Group C: Orrell, Dunvant, Toulon, Northampton, Connacht, Padova
Group D: Swansea, London Irish, Gloucester, Ebbw Vale, Bourgoin, Begles

Fixtures 1996-97

12 October

Pool A: Newbridge v Glasgow, Agen v Newport, Sale v Montferrand
Pool B: Bristol v Treorchy, Narbonne v Dinamo Bucharest, Bridgend v Castres
Pool C: Orrell v Dunvant, Toulon v Northampton, Connacht v Padova
Pool D: Swansea v London Irish, Gloucester v Ebbw Vale, Bourgoin v Begles

16 October

Pool A: Glasgow v Sale, Newport v Newbridge, Agen v Montferrand
Pool B: Treorchy v Bridgend, Narbonne v Castres, Dinamo Bucharest v Bristol
Pool C: Dunvant v Connacht, Northampton v Orrell, Toulon v Padova
Pool D: London Irish v Bourgoin, Ebbw Vale v Swansea, Gloucester v Begles

19 October

Pool A: Sale v Newport, Newbridge v Agen, Montferrand v Glasgow
Pool B: Bridgend v Dinamo Bucharest, Bristol v Narbonne, Castres v Treorchy
Pool C: Connacht v Northampton, Orrell v Toulon, Padova v Dunvant
Pool D: Bourgoin v Ebbw Vale, Swansea v Gloucester, Begles v London Irish

26 October

Pool A: Agen v Sale, Newport v Glasgow, Newbridge v Montferrand
Pool B: Narbonne v Bridgend, Dinamo Bucharest v Treorchy, Bristol v Castres
Pool C: Toulon v Connacht, Northampton v Dunvant, Orrell v Padova
Pool D: Gloucester v Bourgoin, Ebbw Vale v London Irish, Swansea v Begles

2 November

Pool A: Sale v Newbridge, Glasgow v Agen, Montferrand v Newport
Pool B: Bridgend v Bristol, Treorchy v Narbonne, Castres v Dinamo Bucharest
Pool C: Connacht v Orrell, Dunvant v Toulon, Padova v Northampton
Pool D: Bourgoin v Swansea, London Irish v Gloucester, Begles v Ebbw Vale

16 November

Semi-finals

4 January

Final

Five Nations Championship 1995-96

Only an author of the most compelling work of fiction could have constructed the plot for the climactic finale that evolved to decide the 1996 Five Nations Championship. The England supporters went to Twickenham to give Will Carling a rousing send-off on his 59th and final appearance over eight seasons as England captain. The French followers invaded Cardiff for the prospect of watching their rejuvenated team clinch the title and commit Wales to another dose from the wooden spoon.

At around 4.30 pm on that Saturday afternoon of 16 March, the Welsh ruined the script. England stormed to an emphatic 28-15 victory over Ireland; while Wales, against all the forecasts, beat France 16-15 in one of the biggest formbook upsets for years.

Welsh captain John Humphreys had hardly completed an extravagant display of post-match euphoria in a jubilant jig of joy around the Arms Park than a WRU official was leaving the stadium with a security parcel for dispatch to London on a train leaving the Principality at 5.30. It contained the Five Nations Trophy, marked for delivery to London's Hilton Hotel, where Carling and his team were celebrating a Championship-winning performance that had seemed beyond their capabilities in a faltering start to the campaign after South Africa had given them the runaround at Twickenham back in November.

Not since Scotland in 1933 had a team scored so few tries – three – as England to claim the Triple Crown. Carling, England's 'Captain Courageous', knew that Saturday would become a red-letter day in his calendar of achievement, but even he could not have anticipated the events that were about to unfold when he limped off in the first half with a twisted ankle after handing the responsibilities of leadership for the rest of the match to Dean Richards.

England manager Jack Rowell and his triumphant captain are thought not always to have enjoyed the closest relationship. But Rowell needed little persuasion to find the right words to describe Carling's retirement from the captaincy. Asked what England will look like without Will Carling at the helm, he replied: 'Like Trafalgar Square without Nelson's Column!'

England re-discovered the art of try-scoring just in time to give their 'Swing Low' anthem the conviction it needed. In a season when the team talked of lessons learned from the World Cup, there was little evidence until that final Championship match that England had been doing their homework.

But if England had been labelled a stereotyped, functional unit, unable to deliver an acceptable quota of entertainment, Bath's flying wing Jon Sleightholme blew away the pessimism with a try against Ireland that he colourfully called 'The Pizza'.

Neither Sleightholme – dropped by Bath at the start of the season – nor Paul Grayson had been contenders when England played so disappointingly against South Africa four months earlier. But, come the final whistle on the season at Twickenham, both 'unknowns' had made an indelible mark on the Championship, with Grayson's 22 goals representing 80 per cent of England's points.

Carling, limping on crutches, said: 'As I drove away from Twickenham, it slowly sunk in that it was over and then I allowed myself to be a little proud of my time as captain.'

Elsewhere, the vanquished were counting the cost of Championship failure. Scotland, who started the campaign having to adjust to life after Gavin Hastings, beat Ireland in Dublin and then produced the finest performance of the season to destroy the French at Murrayfield. Afterwards, Philippe Saint-Andre admitted Wainwright's side had beaten them at their own game. They scraped a narrow win in Cardiff to leave the stage set for a possible Grand Slam victory over England in Edinburgh. But Scotland could not deliver the ultimate prize their supporters expected as England, whose pack averaged a stone a man heavier, strangled tartan hopes to bring the curtain down on a season that had promised so much.

Ireland, responding well to the leadership of new coach Murray Kidd, took credit from a decisive victory against Wales at Lansdowne Road and gave England a fright at

Twickenham. Kidd employed 26 players during the campaign to end the season more optimistic than he had been at the start.

Wales, fourth in the table, ended an eight-match Championship losing sequence against France to cast off the sackcloth and ashes and offer new coach Kevin Bowring hope that his long-term plans for the 1999 World Cup finals will be rewarded sooner rather than later. New scrum-half Robert Howley evoked memories of Gareth Edwards in his prime and new centre Leigh Davies, who once had soccer trials for Birmingham, Justin Thomas, Gwyn Jones and Arwel Thomas showed immense promise under the inspired leadership of Cardiff's John Humphreys.

If France could have clung to the 15-13 lead they had established against Wales, they would have won the competition for the first time since 1993. Their captain Philippe Saint-Andre pinpointed his team's defeat in Scotland as a crucial turning point in French fortunes. 'Of course we were disappointed with our performance in Cardiff but looking at the season as a whole it was the defeat in Edinburgh that was the hardest to take.'

For some, the Five Nations had been a minefield of lost opportunity. For others, like Will Carling, the campaign had got better and better.

FINAL TABLE

	P	W	D	L	F	A	Pts
England	4	3	0	1	79	54	6
Scotland	4	3	0	1	60	56	6
France	4	2	0	2	89	57	4
Wales	4	1	0	3	62	82	2
Ireland	4	1	0	3	65	106	2

FRANCE 15 ENGLAND 12 (Parc des Princes, Paris, 20 January 1996)

A coolly delivered dropped goal by Thomas Castaignede less than a minute from the start of injury time destroyed England's hopes. The French centre-three quarter had come of age just 24 hours before his 21st birthday.

It was a workmanlike rather than flair performance by the French in a game which started controversially when Rory Underwood thought he had scored a try in the opening minute. He insisted afterwards that he got a touch in a frantic tussle with Emile Ntamack and Philippe Saint-Andre.

The disputed 'try' set the standard for the siege mentality France adopted in deciding to abandon their traditional running game in preference for an attritional war. The match became a goal-kicking contest between the trusty boots of Thierry Lacroix and Paul Grayson.

France trailed for long periods, Lacroix missing three of his six penalty attempts at goal and was twice wide with drop kicks. But successful penalties in the 34th, 63rd and 75th minutes, followed by a dropped goal in the 54th minute matched the outstanding forward contribution of flanker Abdelatif Benazzi. Grayson, unnerved by two missed goal-kicks in the first half, put England ahead twice with penalty goals and twice brought them level with dropped goals, but France deserved their narrow win.

France's 21-year-old centre Richard Dourthe was banned for one month after admitting kicking England No 8 Ben Clarke in the head. 'No excuses, I was stupid,' was his candid reaction.

France: J-L Sadourny (Colomiers); E. Ntamack (Toulouse), R. Dourthe (Dax), T. Castaignede (Toulouse), P. Saint-Andre (Montferrand, capt); T. Lacroix (Dax), P. Carbonneau (Toulouse); M. Perie (Toulon), J-M. Gonzalez (Bayonne), C. Califano (Toulouse), O. Roumat (Dax), O. Merle (Montferrand), A. Benazzi (Agen), L. Cabannes (Racing), F. Pelous (Dax).

Replacement: P. Bernat-Salles (Begles-Bordeaux) for Sadourny (55).

Scorers: PG: Lacroix (3). DG: Lacroix, Castaignede.

England: M Catt; J. Sleightholme (Bath), W. Carling (Harlequins, capt), J. Guscott (Bath), R. Underwood (Leicester); P. Grayson, M. Dawson (Northampton); G. Rowntree (Leicester), M. Regan (Bristol), J. Leonard (Harlequins), M. Johnson (Leicester), M. Bayfield (Northampton), S. Ojomoh (Bath), L. Dallaglio (Wasps), B. Clarke (Bath).

Replacement: D. Richards (Leicester) for Clarke (17-25).

Scorers: PG: Grayson (2). DG: Grayson (2).

Referee: D.T.M. McHugh (Ireland).

IRELAND 10 SCOTLAND 16 (Lansdowne Road, Dublin, 20 January 1996)

Favourites Ireland, who last triumphed over the Scots in 1988, were disappointing again, despite impressive pre-match preparation. With the wind and rain at their backs, Scotland began at blinding speed to stretch the Irish defence to the limits and offer their new coach Murray Kidd a rough baptism.

The Scots played with a genuine self-belief after their demoralising defeat by Italy. Their discipline and legitimate aggression in the tackle swept aside an Irish team who flattered to deceive. Bryan Redpath, Gregor Townsend and captain Rob Wainwright gave heroic performances for Scotland, with Eric Peters and Ian Smith playing well in an outstanding back-row.

Scotland raced to a 16-3 lead with tries from Kevin McKenzie and Michael Dods, and a penalty by Dods and towering dropped goal by Townsend. Ireland had chopped the deficit to 10-16 at the interval but, despite lengthy periods of possession and territorial advantage after the break, failed to capitalise on their advantage. Ireland produced only one passage of sustained pressure for Peter Clohessy to score a fine try.

Ireland: J. Staples (Harlequins, capt); R. Wallace (Garryowen), J. Bell (Northampton), K. McQuilkin (Bective Rangers), S. Geoghegan (Bath); E. Elwood (Lansdowne), C. Saverimutto (Sale); N. Popplewell (Newcastle), T. Kingston (Dolphin), P. Clohessy (Young Munster), G. Fulcher (Cork Constitution), N. Francis (Old Belvedere), J. Davidson (Dungannon), D. Corkery (Cork Constitution), P. Johns (Dungannon).

Scorers: T: Clohessy. C: Elwood. PG: Elwood.

Scotland: R. Shepherd; C. Joiner (Melrose), S. Hastings (Watsonians), I. Jardine (Stirling County), M. Dods; G. Townsend (Northampton), B. Redpath (Melrose); D. Hilton (Bath), K. McKenzie (Stirling County), P. Wright (Boroughmuir), S. Campbell (Dundee HSFP), G. Weir (Melrose), R. Wainwright (Watsonians), I. Smith (Gloucester), E. Peters (Bath).

Scorers: T: Dods, McKenzie. PG: Dods. DG: Townsend.

Referee: B. Campsall (England).

ENGLAND 21 WALES 15 (Twickenham, 3 February 1996)

England's superior forward power stole victory, but Wales took most of the glory from a disappointing match. Will Carling, Tim Rodber and Lawrence Dallaglio were the pick of an England team that struggled in the lineouts and relied heavily on the 21-7 penalty count in their favour.

Paul Grayson had a poor match at fly-half, landing only four of his nine place kicks, with three first-half penalty attempts and a dropped goal attempt early in the second half squandered. England had to rely on desperate defensive measures to maintain their points advantage when Robert Howley crowned an excellent debut for Wales with a late try.

Earlier, Mike Catt put Rory Underwood over for his 49th England try and his 50th in international rugby and, seven minutes into the second half, Jeremy Guscott charged down Justin Thomas's clearance for his 18th try to place him joint-second (with Cyril Lowe) on the all-time England scorers' list.

Grayson converted from wide out and then recovered his composure to kick three penalties before Howley became the first Welsh scrum-half to score a try at Twickenham on his international debut since Chico Hopkins in 1970.

England: M. Catt; J. Sleightholme (Bath), W. Carling (Harlequins, capt), J. Guscott (Bath), R. Underwood (Leicester); P. Grayson, M. Dawson (Northampton); G. Rowntree (Leicester), M. Regan (Bristol), J. Leonard (Harlequins), M. Johnson (Leicester), M. Bayfield (Northampton), T. Rodber (Northampton), B. Clarke (Bath), L. Dallaglio (Wasps).

Replacement: P. de Glanville (Bath) for Carling (52).

Scorers: T: Underwood, Guscott. C: Grayson. PG: Grayson (3).

Wales: J. Thomas; I. Evans (Llanelli), L. Davies (Neath), N. Davies, W. Proctor (Llanelli); A. Thomas (Bristol), R. Howley (Bridgend); A. Lewis (Cardiff), J. Humphreys (Cardiff, capt), J. Davies (Neath), G. Llewellyn (Neath), D. Jones, E. Lewis, H Taylor (Cardiff), G. Jones (Llanelli).

Replacements: S. Williams (Neath) for Lewis (35-42) and for G. Jones (42-5); G. Jenkins (Swansea) for Humphreys (56).

Scorers: T: Taylor, Howley. C: A. Thomas. PG: A. Thomas

Referee: K. McCartney (Scotland).

SCOTLAND 19 FRANCE 14 (Murrayfield, Edinburgh, 3 February 1996)

The all-round talent of Michael Dods steered Scotland into contention for their first Grand Slam in six years. Two tries and three penalty goals from the Northampton utility back had the Scottish crowd offering repeated renditions of 'Flower of Scotland' long before Rob Wainwright led his team from the scene of their triumph.

With three minutes left, and with only two points separating the teams, Dods faced up to the challenge of kicking one of the most crucial penalties of his life with the game depending on his success. But from the moment he swung his right boot it was clearly a case of *bonne nuit* for France as the ball split the uprights with unerring accuracy.

If Dods' eye for a half-chance and his kicking ability sealed the result, the combined talents of Bryan Redpath and Gregor Townsend cut such a swathe through the fragile ranks of blue shirts that the French had no answer to their wizardry.

Dods' match-winning 19 points were a new individual record for a player in this fixture, beating Gavin Hastings, who twice scored 18 against France.

Thierry Lacroix became France's leading points-scorer (357), ahead of Didier Camberabero (354), on landing his second successful penalty.

Scotland: R. Shepherd (Edinburgh Academicals); C Joiner (Melrose), S. Hastings (Watsonians), I. Jardine (Stirling County), M. Dods (Northampton); G. Townsend (Northampton), B. Redpath (Melrose); D. Hilton (Bath), K. McKenzie (Stirling County), P. Wright (Boroughmuir), D. Weir (Melrose), S. Campbell (Dundee HSFP), R. Wainwright (Watsonians, capt), E. Peters (Bath), I Smith (Gloucester).

Scorers: T: Dods (2). PG: Dods (3).

France: J-L Sadourny (Colomiers); E. Ntamack (Toulouse), A. Penaud (Brive), T. Castaignede (Toulouse), P. Saint-Andre (Montferrand, capt); T. Lacroix (Dax), P. Carbonneau (Toulouse); M. Perie (Toulon), J.-M. Gonzalez (Bayonne), C Califano (Toulouse), O. Roumat (Dax), O. Merle (Montferrand), A. Benazzi (Agen), L. Cabannes (Racing), F. Pelous (Dax).

Replacement: S. Glas (Bourgoin) for Lacroix (13-23).

Scorers: T: Benazzi. PG: Lacroix (2), Castaignede.

Referee: C. Thomas (Wales).

FRANCE 45 IRELAND 10 (Parc des Princes, Paris, 17 February 1996)

Ireland were crushed by seven tries and further humiliated after a one-sided encounter when their prop Peter Clohessy was found guilty of an act of thuggery in trial-by-video after the match. The Irish Rugby Union and the French Rugby Federation cited the 17-stone forward for dangerous play after film evidence had condemned him of stamping on Olivier Roumat's face early in the second half.

Clohessy was informed of his 26 playing weeks' ban on his return to Dublin. Against a vibrant young French side, Ireland were completely outclassed, slipping to defeat by a record margin against the French, their 12th consecutive reverse in Paris.

Victor Costello and John Bell both battled bravely, but the front row performed poorly and scrum-half Niall Hogan hardly gave a pass worthy of note. In sharp contrast to the limp performances of a host of Irish players, young outside-half Thomas Castaignede put on a show that guarantees a bright future at international level. Stephane Glas was a revelation when he replaced the injured Thierry Lacroix and Abdelatif Benazzi produced another fine performance, this time at lock.

France: J-L. Sadourny (Colomiers); E. Ntamack (Toulouse), O. Campan (Agen), T. Lacroix (Dax), P. Saint-Andre (Montferrand); T Castaignede (Toulouse), G. Accoceberry (Begles); C. Califano (Toulouse), J.-M. Gonzalez (Bayonne), F. Tournaire (Narbonne), A. Benazzi (Agen), O. Roumat (Dax), R. Castel (Toulouse), L Cabannes (Racing), F. Pelous (Dax).

Replacements: S. Glas (Bourgoin) for Lacroix (21); M Perie (Toulon) for Califano (50); S. Dispagne (Toulouse) for Roumat (55); M. de Rougemont (Toulon) for Gonzalez (67).

Scorers: T: Ntamack (2), Castel (2), Saint-Andre, Campan, Accoceberry. C: Castaignede (5).

Ireland: J. Staples (Harlequins, capt); N. Woods (Blackrock), J. Bell (Northampton), K. McQuilkin (Bective Rangers), R. Wallace (Garryowen); D. Humphreys (London Irish), N. Hogan (Terenure); N. Popplewell (Newcastle), T. Kingston (Dolphin), P. Clohessy (Young Munster), P. Johns (Dungannon), G. Fulcher (Cork Constitution), J. Davidson (Dungannon), D. Corkery (Cork Constitution), V Costello (St Mary's).

Replacement: M. Field (Malone) for Staples (40).

Scorers: T: penalty try. C: Humphreys. PG: Humphreys.

Referee: E. Morrison (England).

WALES 14 SCOTLAND 16 (Arms Park, Cardiff, 17 February 1996)

This match will be remembered for Arwel Thomas's brave attempt to land a conversion from near the touchline in the last minute that would have snatched a draw for Wales. The young Welsh fly-half was given the awesome responsibility after Wayne Proctor had scored an excellent try following good approach work by Gwyn Jones and Justin Thomas. He placed the ball five metres in from touch, 22 metres out, struck the ball confidently, but at the last moment it curved narrowly wide of the upright to leave the huge Scottish following relishing the prospect of a Grand Slam encounter with England.

The two sides fought a thrilling battle, with both back divisions prepared to use their pace at every opportunity. The ever-promising Thomas never quite managed to impose himself on the game but the Bridgend scrum-half Robert Howley had another splendid match.

For Scotland, their captain Rob Wainwright again looked one of the players of the tournament, and Ian Jardine and Scott Hastings ran with the freedom so often denied them in previous Scottish line-ups. The match level 9-9, Scotland launched Ian Smith and Bryan Redpath at the Welsh and Townsend stretched over the line. Michael Dods's conversion flew straight to give Scotland a points margin that was beyond Arwel Thomas's kicking powers.

Wales: J. Thomas; I. Evans (Llanelli), L. Davies (Neath), N. Davies, W. Proctor (Llanelli); A. Thomas (Bristol), R. Howley (Bridgend); A. Lewis, J. Humphreys (Cardiff, capt), J. Davies, G. Llewellyn (Neath), D. Jones, E. Lewis (Cardiff), R. Jones (Llanelli), H. Taylor (Cardiff).

Scorers: T: Proctor. PG: A. Thomas (3).

Scotland: R. Shepherd; C. Joiner (Melrose), S. Hastings (Watsonians), I. Jardine (Stirling County), M. Dods; G. Townsend (Northampton), B. Redpath (Melrose); D. Hilton (Bath), K. McKenzie (Stirling County), P. Wright (Boroughmuir), S. Campbell (Dundee HSFP), G. Weir (Newcastle), R. Wainwright (Watsonians, capt), I. Smith (Gloucester), E. Peters (Bath).

Replacements: K. Logan (Stirling County) for Joiner (39).

Scorers: T: Townsend. C: Dods. PG: Dods (3).

Referee: J. Dumé (France).

IRELAND 30 WALES 17 (Lansdowne Road, Dublin, 2 March 1996)

Two weeks after suffering their heaviest defeat in the Championship, Ireland hit the 30-point mark for the first time in the Five Nations in an exciting match. The Irish celebrated their first hat-trick of consecutive wins over Wales for 30 years, scoring four tries against them for only the second time in this 100th match between the two nations.

Ireland announced their intentions from the start, hoisting a series of high balls that fell like a bomb among the Welsh backs. From one of these aerial bombardments, Arwel Thomas faltered, Ireland won the ruck and Simon Geoghegan ran onto David Humphreys's chip to sneak in for an opening try.

Leigh Davies, Wales' best back, then put Ieuan Evans in for a try under the posts which Arwel Thomas converted. But Niall Woods punished Arwel Thomas's poor clearance for a second try, and Thomas's nightmare continued when he missed an easy penalty to leave Wales facing a 15-7 deficit at the interval. Evans scored a second try after 65 minutes, but Irish tries by Gabriel Fulcher and David Corkery drew verses of 'Alive, Alive O' from a jubilant crowd.

Ireland: S. Mason (Orrell); S. Geoghegan (Bath), J. Bell (Northampton), M. Field (Malone), N. Woods (Blackrock College); D. Humphreys (London Irish), N. Hogan (Terenure College, capt); N. Popplewell (Newcastle), A. Clarke (Northampton), P. Wallace (Blackrock College), G. Fulcher (Cork Constitution), J. Davidson (Dungannon), D. Corkery (Cork Constitution), V. Costello (St Mary's College), D. McBride (Malone).

Scorers: T: Geoghegan, Woods, Fulcher, Corkery. C: Mason (2). PG: Mason (2).

Wales: J. Thomas; I. Evans (Llanelli), L. Davies (Neath), N. Davies, W. Proctor (Llanelli); A. Thomas (Bristol), R. Howley (Bridgend); A. Lewis, J. Humphreys (Cardiff, capt), J. Davies, G. Llewellyn (Neath), D. Jones, E. Lewis (Cardiff), G. Jones (Llanelli), H. Taylor (Cardiff).

Scorers: T: Evans (2). C: A. Thomas (2). PG: A. Thomas.

Referee: D. Méné (France).

SCOTLAND 9 ENGLAND 18 (Murrayfield, Edinburgh, 2 March 1996)

England denied Scotland the Grand Slam with a performance of ruthless efficiency and awesome control that left some critics claiming them to be the most negative side in international rugby. Away victories at Murrayfield, however, should not be sneezed at.

Jason Leonard, England's tight-head prop, was cited by the Scottish Rugby Union for an act of foul play undetected by the match officials. The flashpoint came in a punching incident which left Scotland's captain, Rob Wainwright, heavily concussed and a virtual passenger for the rest of the match. Later, a disciplinary hearing in London ruled that video evidence presented was inconclusive, leaving a relieved Leonard available for England's final Five Nations match against Ireland.

For the third successive time, no tries were scored in a Calcutta Cup game. Only the enterprising Gregor Townsend looked like ending that dismal run with a 60-metre break ended by Will Carling's tackle.

Dean Richards, recalled from the wilderness, played a blinder before limping off after 77 minutes. Paul Grayson's six successful penalties for England were from nine attempts at goal. Twice he missed with drop kicks at goal in the second half. Meanwhile, Michael Dods landed three of his six place kicks for Scotland.

Rory Underwood established a fixture record, playing his 12th match of the series to pass the record of 11 matches held jointly by Sandy Carmichael and Alastair McHarg.

Scotland: R. Shepherd; C. Joiner (Melrose), S. Hastings (Watsonians), I. Jardine (Stirling County), M. Dods; G. Townsend (Northampton), B. Redpath (Melrose); D. Hilton (Bath), K. McKenzie (Stirling County), P. Wright (Boroughmuir), S. Campbell (Dundee HSFP), G. Weir (Newcastle), R. Wainwright (Watsonians, capt), I Smith (Gloucester), E. Peters (Bath).

Scorers: PG: Dods (3).

England: M. Catt; J. Sleightholme (Bath), W. Carling (Harlequins, capt), J. Guscott (Bath), R. Underwood (Leicester); P. Grayson, M. Dawson (Northampton); G. Rowntree (Leicester), M. Regan (Bristol), J. Leonard (Harlequins), M. Johnson (Leicester), G. Archer (Bristol), B. Clarke (Bath), L. Dallaglio (Wasps), D. Richards (Leicester).

Replacement: T. Rodber (Northampton) for Richards (77).

Scorers: PG: Grayson (6).

Referee: W.D. Bevan (Wales).

ENGLAND 28 IRELAND 15 (Twickenham, 16 March 1996)

England clinched the Five Nations Championship and Will Carling completed his reign as captain after 59 matches. Later, when asked what his team would look like without Carling's leadership, England manager Jack Rowell replied in a flash: 'Like Trafalgar Square without Nelson's Column.'

Carling left the stage of his last match in charge horizontally, having gone down like a shot stag in the 35th minute without an opponent in the vicinity. He tore ankle ligaments after stumbling awkwardly and his premature departure meant that Dean Richards was given the responsibility of leading England to the title.

All the pre-match pundits had got it wrong, believing that France would beat Wales in Cardiff and take the trophy. And once again England defied their critics to snatch the match. The contest turned on Jon Sleightholme's splendid try, only the third time all season that an England player had crossed the line.

England had to haul back Ireland's six-point lead built on David Humphreys' sweetly taken dropped goal after 80 seconds. Orrell full-back Simon Mason kicked four penalty goals from four attempts, but the result was never in doubt once Paul Grayson and Matt Dawson began searching for breaks and Martin Johnson started to make an impact in the lineouts.

Grayson's dropped goal on the hour and his sixth penalty seven minutes later tightened England's grip on the Triple Crown before Sleightholme's thrilling burst through tired Irish ranks.

England: M. Catt; J. Sleightholme, J. Guscott (Bath), W. Carling (Harlequins, capt), R. Underwood (Leicester); P. Grayson, M. Dawson (Northampton); G. Rowntree (Leicester), M. Regan (Bristol), J. Leonard (Harlequins), M. Johnson (Leicester), G. Archer (Bristol), B. Clarke (Bath), L. Dallaglio (Wasps), D. Richards (Leicester).

Replacements: T. Rodber (Northampton) for Dallaglio (29-30); P. de Glanville (Bath) for Carling (35).

Scorers: T: Sleightholme. C: Grayson. PG: Grayson (6). DG: Grayson.

Ireland: S. Mason (Orrell); S. Geoghegan (Bath), J. Bell (Northampton), M Field (Malone), N. Woods (Blackrock); D. Humphreys (London Irish), N. Hogan (Terenure, capt); N. Popplewell (Newcastle), A. Clarke (Northampton), P. Wallace (Blackrock), G. Fulcher (Cork Constitution), W. McBride (Malone), V. Costello (St Mary's College).

Replacement: C. McCall (Bangor) for Field (16).

Scorers: PG: Mason (4). DG: Humphreys.

Referee: E. Murray (Scotland).

WALES 16 FRANCE 15 (Arms Park, Cardiff, 16 March 1996)

The Welsh Dragon breathed fire for the first time in two years and destroyed France's Five Nations Championship aspirations. The margin of their victory to end a record run of eight straight Five Nations defeats was minimal, but in terms of courageous commitment and power play from their dynamic pack, they were the width of the Channel Tunnel ahead of the struggling French.

Neil Jenkins was the Welsh hero. Replacing Arwel Thomas, the Pontypridd stand-off returned to score 11 points to crown a fine display on his 39th appearance for Wales. He raised his points tally to 430 with three penalty goals and a conversion for Rob Howley's try.

The wooden spoon was never an option for the Welsh team and Jenkins' unerring accuracy with the boot left the jaded French a beaten and demoralised force, despite a second-half rally in which Emile Ntamack added a second try to Thomas Castaignede's first-half effort.

Former Welsh full-back J.P.R. Williams said afterwards: 'It was a reward for all the re-building we've done this season and, despite the fact that our win gave the Five Nations Championship to England, it doesn't take the gloss off the Welsh achievement.'

John Humphreys, the Welsh captain, apologised for giving a clenched fist salute at the end by adding: 'I've never behaved like that before but then I've never felt like that. It's the best day of my life.'

Wales: J. Thomas; I. Evans (Llanelli), L. Davies (Neath), N. Davies (Llanelli), G. Thomas (Bridgend); N. Jenkins (Pontypridd), R. Howley (Bridgend); C. Loader (Swansea), J. Humphreys (Cardiff, capt), J. Davies (Neath), G. Llewellyn (Neath), D. Jones, E. Lewis (Cardiff), G. Jones (Llanelli), H. Taylor (Cardiff).

Scorers: T: Howley. C: Jenkins. PG: Jenkins (3).

France: J-L. Sadourny (Colomiers); E. Ntamack (Toulouse), S. Glas (Bourgoin), O. Campan (Agen), P. Saint-Andre (Montferrand, capt); T. Castaignede (Toulouse), G. Accoceberry (Begles); C. Califano (Toulouse), J-M. Gonzalez (Bayonne), F. Tournaire (Narbonne), A. Benazzi (Agen), O. Roumat (Dax), R. Castel (Toulouse), L. Cabannes (Racing), S. Dispagne (Toulouse).

Replacements: O. Brouzet (Grenoble) for Dispagne (63); R. Ibanez (Dax) for Castel (76).

Scorers: T: Castaignede, Ntamack. C: Castaignede. PG: Castaignede.

Referee: B. Stirling (Ireland).

Will Carling

The England Captain's Log

1965: Born Bradford-on-Avon, Wilts, 12 December, son of Army brigadier.
1984: Leaves Sedbergh School, goes to Durham University. Captains England Schools 18 Group.
1987: Plays for England B in 22-9 win over France B.
1988: Wins first full England cap in 10-9 defeat by France in January. In November becomes, at 22, youngest England captain since 1931. Appointed by Geoff Cooke, putting him in charge of World Cup 91 campaign.
1989: Shin splints injury forces him to miss the Lions tour of Australia.
1990: Rejects £400,000 offer to turn pro with Warrington.
1991: Leads England to first Grand Slam since 1980 and runners-up to Australia in World Cup.
1992: First England captain to achieve back-to-back Grand Slams. Awarded OBE.
1993: Lions debut in first Test v New Zealand. Dropped for second Test.
1994: Wins 50th cap against Romania.
1995: Wins third Grand Slam. England reach semi-final in World Cup.
1996: Leads England to Five Nations title on his world record 59th and final appearance as captain. Announces decision to quit as captain after Championship decider against Ireland. Ends captaincy with 44 wins, one draw, 14 defeats.

Five Nations Championship

Winners, Triple Crowns and Grand Slams

CHAMPIONS		WHITEWASH
1883	England†	Ireland
1884	England†	Ireland
1885	Not completed	
1886	England and Scotland	
1887	Scotland	
1888	Ireland, Scotland, Wales	
1889	Scotland	
1890	England and Scotland	
1891	Scotland†	Ireland
1892	England†	
1893	Wales†	
1894	Ireland†	
1895	Scotland†	Ireland
1896	Ireland	
1897	Not completed	
1898	Not completed	
1899	Ireland†	England
1900	Wales†	
1901	Scotland†	England
1902	Wales†	Scotland
1903	Scotland†	England
1904	Scotland	
1905	Wales†	England
1906	Ireland and Wales	
1907	Scotland†	
1908	Wales*	
1909	Wales*	
1910	England	France
1911	Wales*	Scotland
1912	England and Ireland	France
1913	England*	France
1914	England*	France, Scotland
1915-19	World War 1	
1920	England, Scotland, Wales	Ireland
1921	England*	
1922	Wales	

1923	England*	
1924	England*	France
1925	Scotland*	France
1926	Ireland and Scotland	France
1927	Ireland and Scotland	
1928	England*	
1929	Scotland	France
1930	England	
1931	Wales	
1932	England, Ireland, Wales	
1933	Scotland†	
1934	England†	
1935	Ireland	
1936	Wales	
1937	England†	
1938	Scotland†	
1939	England, Ireland, Wales	
1940-46	World War 2	
1947	England and Wales	Scotland
1948	Ireland*	
1949	Ireland†	
1950	Wales*	
1951	Ireland	
1952	Wales*	Scotland
1953	England	Scotland
1954	England†, Wales, France	Scotland
1955	France, Wales	
1956	Wales	
1957	England*	France
1958	England	
1959	France	
1960	England†, France	Ireland
1961	France	
1962	France	
1963	England	
1964	Scotland, Wales	
1965	Wales†	
1966	Wales	
1967	France	
1968	France*	Scotland
1969	Wales†	

CHAMPIONS		WHITEWASH
1970	France, Wales	
1971	Wales*	
1972	Not completed	England
1973	Five-way tie	
1974	Ireland	
1975	Wales	
1976	Wales*	England
1977	France*	Ireland
1978	Wales*	Scotland
1979	Wales†	
1980	England*	
1981	France*	Ireland
1982	Ireland†	
1983	France, Ireland	
1984	Scotland*	Ireland
1985	Ireland†	Scotland
1986	France, Scotland	Ireland
1987	France*	
1988	France, Wales	
1989	France	
1990	Scotland*	Wales
1991	England*	
1992	England*	Ireland
1993	France	
1994	Wales	
1995	England*	Wales
1996	England†	

*Denotes Grand Slam
†Denotes Triple Crown

Notes: Whitewash is losing all Championship games in season. The tournament became Five Nations contest when France joined in 1910. Reverted to Four Nations from 1932-39 when France banned because players were paid at club level. England did not compete in 1888 and 1889, declining membership of new International Rugby Board. Disputes marred uncompleted Championships in 1885, 1897, 1898. In 1972 Scotland and Wales refused to play in Dublin because of Ulster violence. Trophy first awarded 1993. Wales won 1994 title on tie-break rule adopted in 1993. Until 1992 teams level on points shared title.

Other Test Matches

(from 1 July 1995 to 30 June 1996)

22/07/1995 New Zealand 28 Australia 16 (Auckland) (Bledisloe Cup, 1st Test)

New Zealand: G.M.Osborne (North Harbour); J.W.Wilson (Otago), F.E.Bunce (North Harbour), W.K.Little (North Harbour), J.T.Lomu (Counties); A.P.Mehrtens (Canterbury), G.T.M.Bachop (Canterbury); C.W.Dowd (Auckland), S.B.T.Fitzpatrick (Auckland) (capt), O.M.Brown (Auckland), R.M.Brooke (Auckland), I.D.Jones (North Harbour), M.R.Brewer (Canterbury), Z.V.Brooke (Auckland), J.A.Kronfeld (Otago).

Replacement: M.N.Jones (Auckland) for Z.Brooke (50).

Scorers: Lomu (T), Mehrtens (C, 2D, 5P).

Australia: M.Burke (NSW); D.P.P.Smith (Queensland), J.S.Little (Queensland), T.J.Horan (Queensland), J.W.Roff (ACT); S.Bowen (NSW), S.Merrick (NSW); D.J.Crowley (Queensland), P.N.Kearns (NSW) (capt), M.N.Hartill (NSW), W.W.Waugh (NSW), J.A.Eales (Queensland), V.Ofahengaue (NSW), B.T.Gavin (NSW), D.T.Manu (NSW).

Replacement: P.W.Howard (Queensland) for Burke (29).

Scorers: Ofahengaue (T), Roff (C, 2P), Burke (P).

Referee: R.Megson (Scotland).

29/07/1995 Australia 23 New Zealand 34 (Sydney) (Bledisloe Cup, 2nd Test)

Australia: M.Burke (NSW); D.P.P.Smith (Queensland), J.S.Little (Queensland), T.J.Horan (Queensland), J.W.Roff (ACT); S.Bowen (NSW), S.Merrick (NSW); M.N.Hartill (NSW), P.N.Kearns (NSW) (capt), E.J.A.McKenzie (NSW), W.W.Waugh (NSW), J.A.Eales (Queensland), V.Ofahengaue (NSW), B.T.Gavin (NSW), D.T.Manu (NSW).

Replacements: D.I.Campese (NSW) for Smith (40), P.W.Howard (Queensland) for Burke (56-57).

Scorers: Smith (T), Ofahengaue (T), Burke (2C, 3P).

New Zealand: G.M.Osborne (North Harbour); J.W.Wilson (Otago), F.E.Bunce (North Harbour), W.K.Little (North Harbour), J.T.Lomu (Counties); A.P.Mehrtens (Canterbury), G.T.M.Bachop (Canterbury); C.W.Dowd (Auckland), S.B.T.Fitzpatrick (Auckland) (capt), O.M.Brown (Auckland), R.M.Brooke (Auckland), I.D.Jones (North Harbour), M.R.Brewer (Canterbury), Z.V.Brooke (Auckland), M.N.Jones (Auckland).

Replacements: J.A.Kronfeld (Otago) for M.Jones (40), R.W.Loe (Canterbury) for Dowd (77-79).

Scorers: Wilson (T), Bunce (2T), Lomu (T), Mehrtens (T, 3C, P).

Referee: B.Stirling (Ireland).

02/09/1995 South Africa 40 Wales 11 (Ellis Park, Johannesburg)

South Africa: A.J.Joubert (Natal); J.T.Small (Natal), J.C.Mulder (Transvaal), H.P.Le Roux (Transvaal), J.Olivier (Northern Transvaal); J.T.Stransky (WP), J.H.Van Der Westhuizen (Northern Transvaal); S.Swart (Transvaal), J.Dalton (Transvaal), M.H.Hurter (Northern Transvaal), J.J.Wiese (Transvaal), K.S.Andrews (WP), J.F.Pienaar (Transvaal) (capt), G.H.Teichman (Natal), R.J.Kruger (Northern Transvaal).

Scorers: Small (T), Mulder (T), Wiese (T), Pienaar (T), Teichman (T), Stransky (3C, 3P).

Wales: W.J.L.Thomas (Cardiff Institute); I.C.Evans (Llanelli), G.Jones (Llanelli), G.Thomas (Bridgend), S.D.Hill (Cardiff); N.R.Jenkins (Pontypridd), A.P.Moore (Cardiff); C.D.Loader (Swansea), J.M.Humphreys (Cardiff) (capt), J.D.Davies (Neath), P.Arnold (Swansea), D.Jones (Cardiff), A.Gibbs (Newbridge), H.T.Taylor (Cardiff), A.M.Bennett (Cardiff).

Replacements: A.P.Moore (Swansea) for D.Jones (6), G.R.Jenkins (Swansea) for Gibbs (40), M.Taylor (Swansea) for G.Thomas (69).

Scorers: Bennett (T), N.Jenkins (2P).

Referee: J.Dumé (France).

14/10/1995 France 34 Italy 22 (Buenos Aires) (Latin Cup)

France: J-L.Sadourny (Colomiers); E.Ntamack (Toulouse), A.Hyardet (Castres), Y.Delaigue (Toulon), P.Saint-Andre (Montferrand) (capt); C.Deylaud (Toulouse), G.Accoceberry (Begles); F.Tournaire (Narbonne), J-M.Gonzales (Bayonne), C.Califano (Toulouse), O.Brouzet (Grenoble), O.Merle (Montferrand), P.Benetton (Agen), A.Carminati (Brive), M.Lievremont (Perpignan).

Scorers: Sadourny (2T), Ntamack (T), Carminati (T), Deylaud (4C, 2P) .

Italy: P.Vaccari (Calvisano); F.Roselli (Roma), S.Bordon (Rovigo), I.Francescato (Treviso), F.Mazzariol (Treviso); M.Bonomi (Milan), A.Troncon (Treviso); M.Dal Sie (San Dona), C.Orlandi (Milan), M.Cuttitta (Milan) (capt), M.Giacheri (Treviso), P.Pedroni (Milan), A.Sgorlon (San Dona), C.Checchinato (Rovigo), O.Arancio (Catania).

Replacements: M.Platania (Milan) for Bordon (38), M.Giovanelli (Milan) for Arancio (67).

Scorers: Troncon (T), Bonomi (C, 4P, D).

Referee: Mr Chiciu (Romania).

17/10/1995 France 52 Romania 8 (Tucuman) (Latin Cup)

France: J-L.Sadourny (Colomiers); E.Ntamack (Toulouse), P.Arlettaz (Perpignan), R.Dourthe (Dax), P.Saint-Andre (Montferrand) (capt); T.Castaignede (Toulouse), P.Carbonneau (Toulouse); S.Graou (Auch), O.Azam (Montferrand), L.Benezech (RCF), F.Pelous (Dax), O.Merle (Montferrand), A.Carminati (Brive), C.Juillet (Montferrand), M.Lievremont (Perpignan).

Replacements: P.Benetton (Agen) for Lievremont (63), A.Hyardet (Castres) for Sadourny (72), Y.Delaigue (Toulon) for Dourthe (72).

Scorers: Arlettaz (2T), Castaignede (T, 4C, D, 2P), Pelous (T), Carminati (T), Lievremont (T), Delaigue (T).

Romania: V.Maftei (Napoca); M.Olovasu (RCG Bucharest), Luca, M.Nedelcu (Steaua), G.Solomie (Timisoara); V.Prospiteanu (Steaua), Dragnea; I.Salageanu (CSM Sibiu), M.Radoi (Dinamo), L.Costea (Steaua), C.Cojocariu (Bayonne), A.Gealapu (Steaua), M.Marin (Farul), C.Draguceanu (Steaua), A.Guranescu (Dinamo).

Replacements: G.Vlad (Dinamo) for Radoi (32), A.Girbu (Farul Constanta) for Cojocariu (51), V.Flutur (Minerul) for Marin (52).

Scorers: Vlad (T), Maftei (D).

Referee: E.Sklar (Argentina).

21/10/1995 France 47 Argentina 12 (Buenos Aires) (Latin Cup)

France: J-L.Sadourny (Colomiers); E.Ntamack (Toulouse), R.Dourthe (Dax), T.Castaignede (Toulouse), P.Saint-Andre (Montferrand) (capt); C.Deylaud (Toulouse), P.Carbonneau (Toulouse); C.Califano (Toulouse), J-M.Gonzales (Bayonne), L.Benezech (RCF), F.Pelous (Dax), O.Merle (Montferrand), A.Carminati (Brive), C.Juillet (Montferrand), P.Benetton (Agen).

Replacements: O.Azam (Montferrand) for Gonzales (49), M.Lievremont (Perpignan) for Carminati (64), A.Hyardet (Castres) for Dourthe (73), O.Brouzet (Grenoble) for Pelous (73).

Scorers: Ntamack (2T), Castaignede (T), Saint-Andre (2T), Carbonneau (2T), Deylaud (3C, 2P).

Argentina: E.Jurado (Jockey Club); J-M.Luna (Cordoba), D.Cuesta Silva (San Isidoro), S.Salvat (Alumni) (capt), M.Teran (Tucuman); L.Arbizu (Belgrano), A.Pichot (San Isidoro); M.Urbano (Buenos Aires), J.Angelillo (San Isidoro), F.Mendez (Natal), G.Llanes (La Plata), R.Perez (Rosario), S.Irazoqui (Palermo), C.Viel (Newman), R.Martin (San Isidoro).

Replacement: D.Albanese (San Isidoro) for Teran (40).

Scorers: Luna (4P).

Referee: Mr Morandin (Romania).

28/10/1995 Italy 6 New Zealand 70 (Bologna)

Italy: M.Ravazzolo (Calvisano); P.Vaccari (Calvisano), S.Bordon (Rovigo), I.Francescato (Treviso), F.Mazzariol (Treviso); M.Bonomi (Milan), A.Troncon (Treviso); M.Cuttitta (Milan) (capt), C.Orlandi (Milan), F.Properzi-Curti (Milan), P.Pedroni (Milan), M.Giacheri (Treviso), M.Giovanelli (Milan), A.Sgorlon (San Dona), C.Checchinato (Rovigo).

Replacements: O.Arancio (Catania) for Giovanelli (62), M.Piovene (Padova) for Bordon (71), G.Filizzola (Calvisano) for Piovene (77).

Scorers: Bonomi (2P).

New Zealand: J.W.Wilson (Otago); E.J.Rush (North Harbour), F.E.Bunce (North Harbour), W.K.Little (North Harbour), J.T.Lomu (Counties); S.D.Culhane (Southland), S.T.Forster (Otago); C.W.Dowd (Auckland), S.B.T.Fitzpatrick (Auckland) (capt), O.M.Brown (Auckland), I.D.Jones (North Harbour), R.M.Brooke (Auckland), B.P.Larsen (North Harbour), Z.V.Brooke (Auckland), M.N.Jones (Auckland).

Scorers: Wilson (T), Rush (T), Little (2T), Lomu (2T), Fitzpatrick (T), I.Jones (T), Z.Brooke (T), M.Jones (T), Culhane (7C, 2P) .

Referee: G.Gadjovich (Canada).

11/11/1995 France 22 New Zealand 15 (Toulouse) (1st Test)

France: J-L.Sadourny (Colomiers); E.Ntamack (Toulouse), R.Dourthe (Dax), T.Castaignede (Toulouse), P.Saint-Andre (Montferrand) (capt); A.Penaud (Brive), P.Carbonneau (Toulouse); L.Benezech (RCF), M.De Rougemont (Toulon), C.Califano (Toulouse), O.Merle (Montferrand), F.Pelous (Dax), P.Benetton (Agen), A.Benazzi (Agen), A.Carminati (Brive).

Replacement: D.Berty (Toulouse) for Sadourny (46).

Scorers: Sadourny (T), Dourthe (T), Saint-Andre (T), Castaignede (2C, P).

New Zealand: J.W.Wilson (Otago); E.J.Rush (North Harbour), F.E.Bunce (North Harbour), W.K.Little (North Harbour), J.T.Lomu (Counties); S.D.Culhane (Southland), S.T.Forster (Otago); C.W.Dowd (Auckland), S.B.T.Fitzpatrick (Auckland) (capt), O.M.Brown (Auckland), I.D.Jones (North Harbour), R.M.Brooke (Auckland), B.P.Larsen (North Harbour), Z.V.Brooke (Auckland), M.N.Jones (Auckland).

Replacement: G.M.Osborne (North Harbour) for Wilson (54).

Scorers: Culhane (5P).

Referee: P.Marshall (Australia).

11/11/1995 Wales 19 Fiji 15 (Cardiff)

Wales: W.J.L.Thomas (Llanelli); I.C.Evans (Llanelli), G.Thomas (Bridgend), N.G.Davies (Llanelli), W.T.Proctor (Llanelli); N.R.Jenkins (Pontypridd), A.P.Moore (Cardiff); C.D.Loader (Swansea), J.M.Humphreys (Cardiff) (capt), L.Mustoe (Cardiff), A.P.Moore (Swansea), D.Jones (Cardiff), J.C.Quinnell (Llanelli), H.T.Taylor (Cardiff), A.M.Bennett (Cardiff).

Replacements: D.A.Williams (Swansea) for Davies (34), G.R.Jenkins (Swansea) for Humphreys (32-36).

Scorers: N.Jenkins (T, 3P), A.Moore (T).

Fiji: F.Rayasi (King Country); P.Bale (Canterbury), S.Sorovaki (Wellington), L.Little (King Country), M.Bari (Tavua); J.Waqa (Nadroga), J.Raulini (Easts); J.Veitayaki (King Country) (capt), G.Smith (Waikato), E.Natuivau (Suva), A.Nadolo (Suva), E.Katalau (Poverty Bay), I.Tawake (Nadroga), T.Tamanivalu (Brothers), D.Rouse (Nadi).

Replacement: R.Bogisa (Tavua) for Waqa (40).

Scorers: Bari (T), Rayasi (T), Waqa (C, P).

Referee: P.O'Brien (New Zealand).

12/11/1995 Italy 21 South Africa 40 (Rome)

Italy: Frederico; Williams (Milan), S.Bordon (Rovigo), I.Francescato (Treviso), Mazzucato; D.Dominguez (Milan), A.Troncon (Treviso); F.Properzi-Curti (Milan), C.Orlandi (Milan), M.Cuttitta (Milan) (capt), M.Giacheri (Treviso), P.Pedroni (Milan), O.Arancio (Catania), A.Sgorlon (San Dona), M.Giovanelli (Milan).

Scorers: Arancio (T), Orlandi (T), Dominguez (C, 3P)

South Africa: A.J.Joubert (Natal); J.T.Small (Natal), J.C.Mulder (Transvaal), H.P.Le Roux (Transvaal), C.M.Williams (WP); J.T.Stransky (WP), J.H.Van Der Westhuizen (Northern Transvaal); T.G.Laubscher (WP), J.Dalton (Transvaal), A.Van Der Linde (Natal), M.G.Andrews (Natal), J.J.Wiese (Transvaal), R.J.Kruger (Northern Transvaal), J.F.Pienaar (Transvaal) (capt), F.J.Van Heerden (WP).

Scorers: Mulder (T), Le Roux (T), Pienaar (T), Penalty Try, Stransky (4C, 4P).

Referee: S.Lander (England).

18/11/1995 England 14 South Africa 24 (Twickenham)

England: J.E.B.Callard (Bath); R.Underwood (Leicester), W.D.C.Carling (Harlequins) (capt), J.C.Guscott (Bath), D.P.Hopley (Wasps); M.J.Catt (Bath), K.P.P.Bracken (Bristol); J.Leonard (Harlequins), M.P.Regan (Bristol), V.E.Ubogu (Bath), M.O.Johnson (Leicester), M.C.Bayfield (Northampton), T.A.K.Rodber (Northampton), B.B.Clarke (Bath), R.A.Robinson (Bath).

Replacements: L.B.N.Dallaglio (Wasps) for Rodber (66), P.R.de Glanville (Bath) for Carling (79).

Scorers: De Glanville (T), Callard (3P).

South Africa: A.J.Joubert (Natal); J.Olivier (Northern Transvaal), J.C.Mulder (Transvaal), H.P.Le Roux (Transvaal), C.M.Williams (WP); J.T.Stransky (WP), J.H.Van Der Westhuizen (Northern Transvaal); T.G.Laubscher (WP), J.Dalton (Transvaal), A.Van Der Linde (Natal), M.G.Andrews (Natal), J.J.Wiese (Transvaal), R.J.Kruger (Northern Transvaal), J.F.Pienaar (Transvaal) (capt), F.J.Van Heerden (WP).

Replacements: J.T.Small (Natal) for Olivier (46), R.A.W.Straeuli (Transvaal) for Kruger (63).

Scorers: Williams (2T), Van Der Westhuizen (T), Stransky (3P).

Referee: J.Fleming (Scotland).

18/11/1995 France 12 New Zealand 37 (Parc des Princes) (2nd Test)

France: J-L.Sadourny (Colomiers); E.Ntamack (Toulouse), R.Dourthe (Dax), T.Castaignede (Toulouse), P.Saint-Andre (Montferrand) (capt); A.Penaud (Brive), P.Carbonneau (Toulouse); L.Benezech (RCF), M.De Rougemont (Toulon), C.Califano (Toulouse), O.Merle (Montferrand), F.Pelous (Dax), P.Benetton (Agen), A.Benazzi (Agen), A.Carminati (Brive).

Replacements: S.Graou (Colomiers) for Benezech (40), M.Lievremont (Perpignan) for Carminati (70).

Scorers: Saint-Andre (2T), Castaignede (C).

New Zealand: G.M.Osborne (North Harbour); E.J.Rush (North Harbour), W.K.Little (North Harbour), F.E.Bunce (North Harbour), J.T.Lomu (Counties); S.D.Culhane (Southland), J.W.Marshall (Southland); C.W.Dowd (Auckland), S.B.T.Fitzpatrick (Auckland) (capt), O.M.Brown (Auckland), I.D.Jones (North Harbour), R.M.Brooke (Auckland), M.N.Jones (Auckland), Z.V.Brooke (Auckland), L.J.Barry (North Harbour).

Replacement: R.W.Loe (Canterbury) for Dowd (75).

Scorers: Osborne (T), Rush (T), Lomu (T), I.Jones (T), Culhane (C, 5P).

Referee: P.Marshall (Australia).

18/11/1995 Ireland 44 Fiji 8 (Lansdowne Road)

Ireland: J.E.Staples (Harlequins) (capt); R.M.Wallace (Garryowen), M.J.Field (Malone), J.C.Bell (Northampton), S.P.Geoghegan (Bath); P.A.Burke (Cork Constitution), C.L.Saverimutto (Sale); N.J.Popplewell (Wasps), T.J.Kingston (Dolphin), P.S.Wallace (Blackrock), G.M.Fulcher (Cork Constitution), N.P.Francis (Old Belvedere), J.W.Davidson (Dungannon), P.S.Johns (Dungannon), S.D.Corkery (Terenure).

Replacements: A.T.H.Clarke (Northampton) for Kingston (45), S.McCahill (Sunday's Well) for Field (68-69), H.D.Hurley (Old Wesley) for Popplewell (69-70), W.D.McBride (Malone) for Davidson (75).

Scorers: Staples (T), R.Wallace (T), Geoghegan (T), P.Wallace (T), Francis (T), Johns (T), Burke (4C, 2P).

Fiji: F.Rayasi (King Country); P.Bale (Canterbury), S.Sorovaki (Wellington), L.Little (King Country), M.Bari (Tavua); J.Waqa (Nadroga), J.Raulini (Easts); J.Veitayaki (King Country) (capt), G.Smith (Waikato), E.Natuivau (Suva), E.Katalau (Poverty Bay), A.Nadolo (Suva), T.Tamanivalu (Brothers), I.Tawake (Nadroga), W.Masirewa (Counties).

Scorers: Masirewa (T), Waqa (P).

Referee: P.O'Brien (New Zealand).

18/11/1995 Scotland 15 Western Samoa 15 (Murrayfield)

Scotland: R.J.S.Shepherd (Melrose); M.Dods (Northampton), G.P.J.Townsend (Northampton), A.G.Shiel (Melrose), K.McK.Logan (Stirling County); C.M.Chalmers (Melrose), B.W.Redpath (Melrose); D.I.W.Hilton (Bath), J.A.Hay

(Hawick), A.P.Burnell (London Scottish), G.W.Weir (Melrose), D.F.Cronin (Bourgoin), R.I.Wainwright (West Hartlepool) (capt), I.R.Smith (Gloucester), S.J.Reid (Boroughmuir).

Replacement: S.J.Campbell (Dundee HSFP) for Smith (Temporary-twice).

Scorer: Dods (5P).

Western Samoa: V.Patu (Vaiala); B.Lima (Marist), T.Vaega (Te Atatu), G.Leaupepe (Te Atatu), A.Telea (Petone); D.Kellett (Marist), J.Filemu (Wellington); P.Fatialofa (Marist), T.Leiasamaiva'o (Moataa), M.Mika (Otago University), P.Leavasa (Apia), L.Falaniko (Marist), S.Kaleta (Ponsonby), P.Lam (Marist) (capt), S.Vaifale (Marist).

Scorers: Kaleta (T), Leaupepe (T), Kellett (C, P).

Referee: T.Henning (South Africa).

16/12/1995 England 27 Western Samoa 9 (Twickenham)

England: M.J.Catt (Bath); D.P.Hopley (Wasps), W.D.C.Carling (Harlequins) (capt), J.C.Guscott (Bath), R.Underwood (Leicester); P.J.Grayson (Northampton), M.J.S.Dawson (Northampton); C.G.Rowntree (Leicester), M.P.Regan (Bristol), J.Leonard (Harlequins), M.O.Johnson (Leicester), M.C.Bayfield (Northampton), T.A.K.Rodber (Northampton), B.B.Clarke (Bath), L.B.N.Dallaglio (Wasps).

Scorers: Underwood (T), Dallaglio (T), Grayson (C, 5P).

Western Samoa: V.Patu (Vaiala); B.Lima (Marist), T.Vaega (Te Atatu), G.Leaupepe (Te Atatu), A.Telea (Petone); D.Kellett (Marist), J.Filemu (Wellington); M.Mika (Otago Univ), T.Leiasamaiva'o (Moataa), P.Fatialofa (Marist), P.Leavasa (Apia), L.Falaniko (Marist), S.Kaleta (Ponsonby), S.Vaifale (Marist), P.Lam (Marist) (capt).

Replacement: S.Smith (Helensville) for Kaleta (26-27) and for Falaniko (73).

Scorer: Kellett (3P).

Referee: I.Rogers (South Africa).

06/01/1996 US Eagles 18 Ireland 25 (Atlanta)

US Eagles: M.Williams (Aspen); V.Anitoni (Yankees), R.Green (OMBAC), M.Scharrenberg (Golden Gate), M.Delai (OMBAC); M.Alexander (Denver Barbarians), A.Bachelet (Old Blues) (capt); G.McDonald (Washington), T.Billups (Old Blues), J.Rissone (Seattle), L.Gross (Cincinnati), A.Freeman (Charlotte), R.Randell (United), R.Tardits (Mystic River), D.Lyle (OMBAC).

Replacement: J.Walker (Aspen) for Randell, second half.

Scorers: Walker (T), Tardits (T), Alexander (C, P, D).

Ireland: J.E.Staples (Harlequins) (capt); R.M.Wallace (Garryowen), J.C.Bell (Northampton), K.McQuilkin (Bective Rangers), S.P.Geoghegan (Bath); E.P.Elwood (Lansdowne), C.L.Saverimutto (Sale); N.J.Popplewell (Newcastle),

T.J.Kingston (Dolphin), P.S.Wallace (Blackrock), G.M Fulcher (Cork Constitution), N.P.Francis (Old Belvedere), V.C.P.Costello (St Mary's), S.D.Corkery (Cork Constitution), P.S.Johns (Dungannon).

Replacement: P.A.Burke (Cork Constitution) for Elwood (49).

Scorers: R.Wallace (T), Elwood (C, 3P), Burke (3P).

Referee: G.Gadjovich (Canada).

16/01/1996 Wales 31 Italy 26 (Cardiff)

Wales: W.J.L.Thomas (Llanelli); I.C.Evans (Llanelli), L.B.Davies (Neath), M.E.Wintle (Llanelli), W.T.Proctor (Llanelli), A.C.Thomas (Bristol), A.P.Moore (Cardiff); A.L.P.Lewis (Cardiff), J.M.Humphreys (Cardiff) (capt), J.D.Davies (Neath), G.O.Llewellyn (Neath), D.Jones (Cardiff), E.W.Lewis (Cardiff), H.T.Taylor (Cardiff), R.G.Jones (Llanelli).

Scorers: J.Thomas (T), I.Evans (2T), A.Thomas (2C, 4P).

Italy: M.Ravazzolo (Calvisano); P.Vaccari (Calvisano), I.Francescato (Treviso), T.Visentin (Treviso), F.Roselli (Roma); D.Dominguez (Milan), A.Troncon (Treviso); M.Cuttitta (Milan) (capt), C.Orlandi (Milan), E.Properzi-Curti (Milan), O.Arancio (Catania), M.Giacheri (Treviso), P.Pedroni (Milan), J.Gardner (Treviso), A.Sgorlon (San Dona).

Replacements: M.Bonomi (Milan) for Visentin (65), M.dal Sie (San Dona) for Orlandi (74).

Scorers: Gardner (T), Properzi-Curti (T), Dominguez (2C, 4P).

Referee: G.Black (Ireland).

20/04/1996 France 64 Romania 12 (Aurillac)

France: R.Dourthe (Dax); D.Venditti (Bourgoin), O.Campan (Agen), S.Glas (Bourgignon), P.Saint-Andre (Montferrand) (capt); A.Penaud (Brive), G.Accoceberry (Begles); F.Tournaire (Narbonne), H.Guiraud (Nimes), C.Califano (Toulouse), O.Merle (Montferrand), H.Miorin (Toulouse), M.Lievremont (Perpignan), C.Moni (Nice), T.Labrousse (Brive).

Replacements: J-L.Jordana (Pau) for Tournaire (69), E.Ntamack (Toulouse) for Venditti (72), P.Carbonneau (Toulouse) for Accoceberry (75), F.Pelous (Dax) for Merle (75).

Scorers: Glas (2T), Penaud (T), Califano (3T), Moni (T), Labrousse (2T), Ntamack (T), Dourthe (7C).

Romania: V.Brici (Farul); R.Fugici (Sibiu), R.Gontineac (Cluj), Luca, G.Solomie (Timisoara); V.Propisteanu (Steaua), D.Neaga (Dinamo); I.Salageanu (CSM Sibiu), V.Tufa (Dinamo), G.Vlad (Dinamo), C.Cojocariu (Bayonne), S.Ciorescu (Auch), A.Gealapu (Steaua), T.Brinza (Cluj University), O.Slusariuc (Dinamo).

Scorer: Propisteanu (3P, D).

Referee: Mr Atorasagasti (Italy).

07/06/1996 New Zealand 51 Western Samoa 10 (Napier)

New Zealand: C.M.Cullen (Manawatu); J.W.Wilson (Otago), F.E.Bunce (North Harbour), S.McLeod (Waikato), J.T.Lomu (Counties); A.P.Mehrtens (Canterbury), J.W.Marshall (Canterbury); O.M.Brown (Auckland), S.B.T.Fitzpatrick (Auckland) (capt), C.W.Dowd (Auckland), R.M.Brooke (Auckland), I.D.Jones (North Harbour), M.N.Jones (Auckland), Z.V.Brooke (Auckland), J.A.Kronfeld (Otago).

Scorers: Cullen (3T), Wilson (T), McLeod (T), Marshall (T), Brown (T), Mehrtens (5C, D, P).

Western Samoa: T.Fa'amasino (Vaimoso); B.Lima (Marist), T.Vaega (Te Atatu), G.Leaupepe (Te Atatu), A.Telea (Petone); J.Filemu (Wellington), T.Nu'uali'itia (Te Atatu); P.Fatialofa (Manukau), T.Leiasamaiva'o (Wellington), B.Reidy (Marist St Pats), S.Smith (Helensville), L.Falaniko (Marist), P.Leavasa (Apia), P.Lam (Auckland) (capt), S.Vaifale (Marist).

Replacement: T.Samania (Muatu and King County) for Fa'amasino (55).

Scorers: Telea (T), Fa'amasino (C, P).

Referee: T.Henning (South Africa).

09/06/1996 Australia 56 Wales 25 (Ballymore, Brisbane) (1st Test)

Australia: M.Burke (NSW); D.I.Campese (NSW), J.W.Roff (ACT), T.J.Horan (Queensland), A.R.Murdoch (NSW); P.W.Howard (Queensland), G.M.Gregan (ACT); R.Harry (NSW), M.Caputo (ACT), E.J.A.McKenzie (NSW), J.A.Eales (Queensland) (capt), G.J.Morgan (ACT), O.Finegan (ACT), D.J.Wilson (Queensland), D.T.Manu (NSW).

Replacement: M.C.Brial (NSW) for Manu (60).

Scorers: Roff (T), Murdoch (T), Howard (T), Caputo (T), Morgan (T), Wilson (T), Manu (T), Burke (6C, 3P).

Wales: W.T.Proctor (Llanelli); I.C.Evans (Llanelli), L.B.Davies (Neath), N.G.Davies (Llanelli), G.Thomas (Bridgend); N.R.Jenkins (Pontypridd), R.Howley (Bridgend); C.D.Loader (Swansea), J.M.Humphreys (Cardiff) (capt), J.D.Davies (Neath), G.O.Llewellyn (Harlequins), D.Jones (Cardiff), S.M.Williams (Neath), H.T.Taylor (Cardiff), R.G.Jones (Llanelli).

Replacements: M.Voyle (Newport) for D.Jones (43-46), L.Mustoe (Cardiff) for J.Davies (69).

Scorers: Proctor (T), Llewellyn (T), Taylor (T), Jenkins (2C, 2P).

Referee: G.Wahlstrom (New Zealand).

15/06/1996 New Zealand 62 Scotland 31 (Carisbrook, Dunedin) (1st Test)

New Zealand: C.M.Cullen (Manawatu); J.W.Wilson (Otago), F.E.Bunce (North Harbour), S.McLeod (Waikato), J.T.Lomu (Counties); A.P.Mehrtens (Canterbury), J.W.Marshall (Canterbury); C.W.Dowd (Auckland), S.B.T.Fitzpatrick (Auckland) (capt), O.M.Brown (Auckland), I.D.Jones (North Harbour), R.M.Brooke (Auckland), M.N.Jones (Auckland), Z.V.Brooke (Auckland), J.A.Kronfeld (Otago).

Replacement: E.J.Rush (North Harbour) for Lomu (48).

Scorers: Cullen (4T), Lomu (T), Mehrtens (T, 7C, P), Marshall (T), M.Jones (T), Z.Brooke (T).

Scotland: R.J.S.Shepherd (Melrose); C.A.Joiner (Leicester), R.Eriksson (London Scottish), I.C.Jardine (Stirling County), K.McK.Logan (Stirling County); G.P.J.Townsend (Northampton), G.Armstrong (Newcastle); D.I.W.Hilton (Bath), K.D.McKenzie (Stirling County), P.H.Wright (Boroughmuir), D.F.Cronin (Bourgoin), G.W.Weir (Newcastle), R.I.Wainwright (Watsonians) (capt), E.W.Peters (Bath), I.R.Smith (Gloucester).

Scorers: Joiner (T), Townsend (T), Peters (T), Shepherd (2C, D, 3P).

Referee: W.Erickson (Australia).

22/06/1996 Australia 42 Wales 3 (Sydney Football Stadium) (2nd Test)

Australia: M.Burke (NSW); D.I.Campese (NSW), J.W.Roff (ACT), T.J.Horan (Queensland), B.Tune (Queensland); P.W.Howard (Queensland), S.Payne (NSW); R.Harry (NSW), M.Caputo (ACT), E.J.A.McKenzie (NSW), G.J.Morgan (ACT), J.A.Eales (Queensland) (capt), O.Finegan (ACT), M.C.Brial (NSW), D.J.Wilson (Queensland).

Replacements: S.Larkham (ACT) for Tune (1-8) and for Burke (59), D.J.Crowley (Queensland) for McKenzie (9), M.Foley (Queensland) for Caputo (43), D.T.Manu (NSW) for Foley (70).

Scorers: Burke (T, 2C, 2P), Roff (T), Horan (T), Morgan (T), Finegan (T), Foley (T), Eales (C).

Wales: W.T.Proctor (Llanelli); I.C.Evans (Llanelli), G.Thomas (Bridgend), N.G.Davies (Llanelli), S.D.Hill (Cardiff); N.R.Jenkins (Pontypridd), R.Howley (Bridgend); C.D.Loader (Swansea), J.M.Humphreys (Cardiff) (capt), L.Mustoe (Cardiff), G.O.Llewellyn (Harlequins), D.Jones (Cardiff), A.Gibbs (Newbridge), H.T.Taylor (Cardiff), S.M.Williams (Neath).

Replacements: A.L.P.Lewis (Cardiff) for Loader (18-31), D.James (Bridgend) for N.Davies (77).

Scorer: Jenkins (P).

Referee: C.Hawke (New Zealand).

22/06/1996 New Zealand 36 Scotland 12 (Eden Park, Auckland) (2nd Test)

New Zealand: C.M.Cullen (Manawatu); J.W.Wilson (Otago), F.E.Bunce (North Harbour), W.K.Little (North Harbour), E.J.Rush (North Harbour); A.P.Mehrtens (Canterbury), J.W.Marshall (Canterbury); C.W.Dowd (Auckland), S.B.T.Fitzpatrick (Auckland) (capt), O.M.Brown (Auckland), I.D.Jones (North Harbour), R.M.Brooke (Auckland), M.N.Jones (Auckland), Z.V.Brooke (Auckland), J.A.Kronfeld (Otago).

Replacements: M.R.Allen (Taranaki) for Dowd (35-36), B.P.Larsen (North Harbour) for M.Jones (60-61), A.R.Cashmore (Auckland) for Wilson (69).

Scorers: M.Jones (T), Z.Brooke (T), Kronfeld (2T), Penalty Try, Mehrtens (4C, P).

Scotland: R.J.S.Shepherd (Melrose); A.G.Stanger (Hawick), S.Hastings (Watsonians), I.C.Jardine (Stirling County), K.McK.Logan (Stirling County); G.P.J.Townsend (Northampton), G.Armstrong (Newcastle); D.I.W.Hilton (Bath), K.D.McKenzie (Stirling County), B.Stewart (Edinburgh Academicals), D.F.Cronin (Bourgoin), G.W.Weir (Newcastle), R.I.Wainwright (Watsonians) (capt), E.W.Peters (Bath), I.R.Smith (Gloucester).

Replacement: D.A.Stark (Boroughmuir) for Jardine (25).

Scorers: Shepherd (T, C), Peters (T).

Referee: W.Erickson (Australia).

22/06/1996 Argentina 27 France 34 (Buenos Aires) (1st Test)

Argentina: L.Criscuolo (Alumini); M.Pfister (Tucuman), F.Garcia (Alumni), F.del Castillo (Jockey Club), F.Soler (Cordoba); J.L.Cilley (San Isidoro), A.Pichot (San Isidoro); M.Reggiardo (Mal del Plata), C.Promanzio (Duendes), R.Grau (Mendoza), P.Sporleder (Curupayti) (capt), J.Simes (Cordoba), P.Buabse (Los Tarcos), R.Martin (San Isidoro), P.Camerlinckx (Regatas).

Replacement: J.Legora (Cordoba) for del Castillo (50).

Scorers: Garcia (T), Soler (T), Penalty Try, Cilley (2C, P).

France: J-L.Sadourny (Colomiers); E.Ntamack (Toulouse), R.Dourthe (Dax), T.Castaignede (Toulouse), P.Saint-Andre (Montferrand) (capt); A.Penaud (Brive), G.Accoceberry (Begles); M.De Rougemont (Toulon), F.Tournaire (Narbonne), C.Califano (Toulouse), O.Merle (Montferrand), O.Roumat (Dax), F.Pelous (Dax), P.Benetton (Agen), A.Benazzi (Agen).

Replacement: M.Lievremont (Perpignan) for Benetton (69).

Scorers: Ntamack (2T), Dourthe (T, 2C, P), Castaignede (T, C), Saint-Andre (T).

Referee: R.Davies (Wales).

29/06/1996 Australia 74 Canada 9 (Ballymore, Brisbane)

Australia: M.Burke (NSW); B.Tune (Queensland), D.J.Herbert (Queensland), T.J.Horan (Queensland), D.I.Campese (NSW); S.Bowen (NSW), S.J.Payne (NSW); D.J.Crowley (Queensland), M.Bell (NSW), A.Heath (NSW), G.J.Morgan (ACT), J.A.Eales (Queensland) (capt), O.Finegan (ACT), M.C.Brial (NSW), D.J.Wilson (Queensland).

Scorers: Burke (3T, 9C, 2P), Tune (T), Herbert (T), Horan (T), Campese (T), Payne (T), Wilson (2T).

Canada: (All Br Columbia unless stated) S.Stewart; D.Lougheed (Ontario), S.Gray, D.Clarke (Newfoundland), W.Stanley; B.Ross, J.Graf (capt); R.Bice, M.Cardinal, R.Snow (Newfoundland), C.Whittaker, M.James, A.Charron (Ontario), J.Hutchinson, I.Gordon.

Replacement: G.Mosgrove for Charron (temporary).

Scorer: Ross (3P).

Referee: A.Watson (South Africa).

29/06/1996 Argentina 15 France 34 (Buenos Aires) (2nd Test)

Argentina: L.Criscuolo (Alumni); D.Albanese (San Isidoro), F.Garcia (Alumni), J.Legora (Cordoba), F.Soler (Cordoba); J.Cilley (San Isidoro), A.Pichot (San Isidoro); M.Reggiardo (Mal del Plata), C.Promanzio (Deundes), R.Grau (Mendoza), P.Sporleder (Curupayti) (capt), J.Simes (Cordoba), P.Buabse (Los Tarcos), P.Camerlinckx (Regatas), R.Martin (San Isidoro).

Scorer: Cilley (5P).

France: J-L.Sadourny (Colomiers); E.Ntamack (Toulouse), R.Dourthe (Dax), T.Castaignede (Toulouse), P.Saint-Andre (Montferrand) (capt); A.Penaud (Brive), P.Carbonneau (Toulouse); J-L.Jordana (Pau), M.De Rougemont (Toulon), C.Califano (Toulouse), O.Merle (Montferrand), O.Roumat (Dax), F.Pelous (Dax), P.Benetton (Agen), A.Benazzi (Agen).

Scorers: Ntamack (T), Saint-Andre (T), Pelous (T), Benetton (T), Castaignede (C 3P), Dourthe (P).

Referee: C.Thomas (Wales).

A Internationals

21/10/95 Wales A 10 Fiji 25 (Bridgend)

Wales A: J.Thomas (Llanelli); A.Harris (Swansea), M.Taylor (Swansea), G.Thomas (Bridgend), W.Proctor (Llanelli); A.Davies (Cardiff), P.John (Pontypridd) (capt); A.Lewis (Cardiff), R.McBryde (Llanelli), S.John (Llanelli), G.Prosser (Pontypridd), A.Moore (Swansea), A.Gibbs (Newbridge), O.Lloyd (Llanelli), S.Williams (Neath).

Replacements: M.Voyle (Newport) for Prosser (51), L.Mustoe (Cardiff) for Lewis (78).

Scorers: Penalty Try, Davies (C, P).

Fiji: F.Rayasi (King Country); M.Bari (Tavua), S.Sorovaki (Wellington), L.Little (King Country), P.Bale (Canterbury); R.Bogisi, J.McClennan; T.Tamanivalu (Brothers), W.Masirewa (Counties), D.Rouse (Nadi), E.Katalau (Poverty Bay), I.Tawake (Nadroga), J.Veitayaki (King Country) (capt), E.Batimala, E.Natuivau (Suva).

Scorers: Bale (2T), Masirewa (T), Bari (T), Bogisi (C, P).

Referee: P.Thomas (France).

12/11/95 Scotland A 9 Western Samoa 26 (Hawick)

Scotland A: S.Lang (Heriot's FP); H.Gilmour (Heriot's FP), S.Nichol (Selkirk), I.Jardine (Stirling County), D.Stark (Boroughmuir); S.Welsh (Hawick), G.Armstrong (Jed-Forest) (capt); G.Wilson (Boroughmuir), G.Ellis (Currie), S.Paul (Heriot's FP), I.Elliot (Hawick), S.Campbell (Dundee HSFP), E.Peters (Bath), J.Amos (Gala), B.Renwick (Hawick).

Scorer: Welsh (3P).

Western Samoa: S.Leaega (Suburbs); V.Patu (Vaiala), T.Vaega (Te Atatu), G.Leaupepe (Te Atatu), A.Telea (Petone); D.Kellett (Marist), J.Filemu (Wellington); M.Mika (Otago University), T.Leiasamaiva'o (Moataa), P.Fatialofa (Marist), L.Falaniko (Marist), P.Leavasa (Apia), S.Kaleta (Ponsonby), S.Vaifale (Marist), P.Lam (Marist) (capt).

Scorers: Vaifale (T), Lam (T), Kellett (2C, 3P, D).

Referee: A.Spreadbury (England).

12/12/95 England A 55 Western Samoa 0 (Gateshead)

England A: T.Stimpson (West Hartlepool); J.Sleightholme (Bath), A.Blyth (West Hartlepool), W.Greenwood (Harlequins), J.Naylor (Orrell); A.King (Bristol Univ), A.Gomarsall (Wasps); K.Yates (Bath), P.Greening (Gloucester), D.Garforth (Leicester), G.Archer (Bristol), R.West (Gloucester), M.Corry (Bristol), R.Hill (Saracens), A.Diprose (Saracens) (capt).

Scorers: Gomarsall (2T), Greenwood (3T), Greening (T), Hill (T), Garforth (T), Stimpson (6C, P).

Western Samoa: A.Autagavaia (Suburbs); T.Faaiuaso (Police), S.Leaega (Suburbs), K.Tuigamala (Scopa), F.Fereti (Apia); C.Burnes (University), M.Vaea (Marist); B.Reidy (Marist St Pats), O.Matauiau, G.Latu (Vaimoso), S.Lemamea (Scopa), M.Birtwistle (Suburbs) (capt), L.Taala (Police), S.Smith (Helensville), M.Iupeli (Marist).

Referee: K.McCartney (Scotland).

6/1/96 Italy 29 Scotland A 17 (Rieti)

Italy: M.Ravazzolo (Calvisano); P.Vaccari (Calvisano), I.Francescato (Treviso), T.Visentin (Treviso), F.Roselli (Roma); D.Dominguez (Milan), A.Troncon (Treviso); M.Dal Sie (San Dona), C.Orlandi (Milan), F.Properzi-Curti (Milan), M.Giacheri (Treviso), P.Pedroni (Milan), O.Arancio (Catania), J.Gardner (Treviso), A.Sgorlon (San Dona) (capt).

Replacement: R.Favaro (Treviso) for Pedroni (56).

Scorers: Visentin (T), Arancio (T), Vaccari (T), Gardner (T), Dominguez (3C, P).

Scotland A: R.Shepherd (Edinburgh Academicals); C.Joiner (Melrose), S.Hastings (Watsonians), I.Jardine (Stirling County), K.Logan (Stirling County); G.Townsend (Northampton), B.Redpath (Melrose); D.Hilton (Bath), K.McKenzie (Stirling County), P.Wright (Boroughmuir), S.Campbell (Dundee HSFP), S.Murray (Edinburgh Academicals), S.Reid (Boroughmuir), E.Peters (Bath), R.Wainwright (West Hartlepool) (capt).

Replacement: G.Weir (Melrose) for Reid (65).

Scorers: Redpath (T), Townsend (P), Shepherd (3P).

Referee: G.Simmonds (Wales).

19/1/96 Ireland A 26 Scotland A 19 (Donnybrook, Dublin)

Ireland A: C.O'Shea (London Irish); S.Mason (Orrell), J.Gallagher (Blackheath), S.McCahill (Sunday's Well), N.Woods (Blackrock); D.Humphreys (London Irish), A.Rolland (Blackrock) (capt); P.Flavin, S.Byran, P.Wallace (Blackrock), D.Tweed (Ballymena), M.O'Kelly (St Mary's), V.Costello (St Mary's), E.Miller (Leicester), A.Foley (Shannon).

Replacement: L.Toland (Old Crescent) for Miller (51).

Scorers: Wallace (T), Mason (T, C, 3P), Penalty Try.

Scotland A: S.Lang; C.Glasgow (Heriot's FP), G.Shiel (Melrose), R.Eriksson (London Scottish), J.Kerr (Watsonians); S.Welsh (Hawick), G.Armstrong (Newcastle) (capt); M.Browne (Melrose), D.Ellis (Currie), B.Stewart (Edinburgh Academicals), M.Norval (Stirling County), D.Cronin (Bourges), P.Walton (Newcastle), J.Amos (Gala), B.Renwick (Hawick).

Scorers: Kerr (T), Walton (T), Welsh (3P).

Referee: J.Pearson (England).

19/1/96 France A 15 England A 25 (Stade Jean Bouin, Paris)

France A: O.Toulouze (Grenoble); D.Venditti, S.Glas (Bourgoin), C.Lamaison (Bayonne), L.Arbo (Perpignan); Y.Delaigue (Toulon), F.Galthie (Colomiers) (capt); J-J.Crenca (Agen), H.Guiraud (Nimes), F.Tournaire (Narbonne), Y.Le Meur (Racing), J-P.Versailles (Montferrand), L.Mallier (Grenoble), C.Juillet (Montferrand), P.Farner (Begles-Bordeaux).

Replacement: F.Bilot (Toulouse) for Le Meur (39).

Scorers: Lamaison (5P).

England A: T.Stimpson (West Hartlepool); D.Hopley (Wasps), W.Greenwood, P.Mensah (Harlequins), A.Adebayo (Bath); A.King (Bristol Univ), A.Gomarsall (Wasps); R.Hardwick (Coventry), P.Greening (Gloucester), D.Garforth (Leicester), G.Archer (Bristol), D.Sims (Gloucester), M.Corry (Bristol), R.Jenkins (Harlequins), A.Diprose (Saracens) (capt).

Scorers: Stimpson (T, C, 5P), King (D).

Referee: B.Smith (Ireland).

31/1/96 England A 24 New South Wales 22 (Leicester)

England A: T.Stimpson (West Hartlepool); P.Hull (Bristol), A.Blyth (West Hartlepool), W.Greenwood (Harlequins), A.Adebayo (Bath); A.King (Bristol Univ), A.Healey (Orrell); R.Hardwick (Coventry), R.Cockerill, D.Garforth (Leicester), G.Archer (Bristol), J.Fowler (Sale), M.Corry (Bristol), R.Hill (Saracens), A.Diprose (Saracens) (capt).

Scorers: Greenwood (T), Blyth (T), King (C, 2P), Stimpson (2P).

New South Wales: M.Burke (Eastwood); A.Murdoch (Gordon), J.Madz (West Harbour), R.Tombs (Northern Suburbs), D.Campese (Randwick); S.Bowen (Southern Districts), S.Payne (Eastern Surburbs); R.Harry (Sydney Univ), M.Bell (Northern Suburbs), M.Hartill (Gordon), W.Waugh (Randwick), S.Domoni (Northern Suburbs), W.Ofahengaue (Manly), D.Manu (Eastwood), T.Gavin (Eastern Suburbs) (capt).

Replacement: A.Blades (Gordon) for Harry (54).

Scorers: Manu (T), Burke (C, 5P).

Referee: D.Davies (Wales).

2/2/96 Scotland A 38 France A 32 (Myreside)

Scotland A: S.Lang; C.Glasgow (Heriot's FP), G.Shiel (Melrose), R.Eriksson (London Scottish), D.Stark (Boroughmuir); S.Welsh (Hawick), D.Patterson (West Hartlepool); M.Brown (Melrose), G.Ellis (Currie), S.Stewart (Edinburgh Academicals), D.Burns (Bouroughmuir), D.Cronin (Bourges) (capt), P.Walton (Newcastle), N.Broughton (Melrose), S.Renwick (Hawick).

Replacement: S.Laing (Instonians) for Welsh (72).

Scorers: Cronin (2T), Stark (T), Renwick (T), Welsh (3C, 4P).

France A: C.Lamaison (Bayonne); S.Venditti (Bourgoin), Y.Delaigue (Toulon), O.Campan (Agen), D.Berty (Toulouse); G.Merceron (Montferrand), F.Galthie (Colomiers) (capt); F.Tournaire (Narbonne), H.Giraud (Nimes), J-L.Jordana (Pau), H.Moirin (Toulouse), J-P.Versailles (Montferrand), C.Moni (Nice), S.Dispagne (Toulouse), T.Labrousse (Brive).

Scorers: Delaigue (2T), Venditti (T), Campan (T), Lamaison (T, 2C), Merceron (D).

Referee: H.Lewis (Wales).

16/2/96 Wales A 22 Scotland A 32 (Swansea)

Wales A: C.Cormack (Pontypridd); S.Hill (Cardiff), M.Wintle (Llanelli), M.Taylor (Swansea), G.Evans (Llanelli); M.Lewrie (Bridgend), P.John (Pontypridd); C.Loader (Swansea), R.McBryde (Llanelli) (capt), S.John (Llanelli), M.Voyle (Newport), J.Wakeford (Cardiff), M.Workman (Newport), O.Williams (Cardiff), M.Williams (Pontypridd).

Replacement: A.Davies (Cardiff) for Lewrie (2).

Scorers: Taylor (T), McBryde (T), Evans (T), Davies (2C, P).

Scotland A: S.Lang; C.Glasgow (Heriot's FP), G.Shiel (Melrose), R.Eriksson (London Scottish), D.Stark (Boroughmuir); S.Welsh (Hawick), D.Patterson (West Hartlepool); M.Brown (Melrose), G.Ellis (Currie), B.Stewart (Edinburgh Academicals), D.Burns (Boroughmuir), D.Cronin (Bourges) (capt), P.Walton (Newcastle), N.Broughton (Melrose), S.Renwick (Hawick).

Replacements: S.Nicol (Selkirk) for Eriksson (56-64), G.Burns (Stewart's Melville FP) for Patterson (56).

Scorers: Stark (2T), Broughton (T), Welsh (C, 5P).

Referee: S.Piercy (England).

1/3/96 Ireland A 25 Wales A 11 (Donnybrook, Dublin)

Ireland A: C.O'Shea (London Irish); R.Wallace (Garryowen), R.Henderson (London Irish), S.McCahill (Sunday's Well), J.Topping (Ballymena); E.Elwood (Lansdowne), A.Rolland (capt); P.Flavin (Blackrock Coll), P.Cunningham (Garryowen), A.McKeen (Lansdowne), M.O'Kelly (St Mary's Coll), N.Francis (Old Belvedere), A.Foley (Shannon), L.Toland (Old Crescent), B.Walsh (London Irish).

Scorers: Henderson (T), Walsh (T), Foley (T), Elwood (2C, 2P).

Wales A: R.Jones (Neath); S.Hill (Cardiff), M.Taylor (Swansea), M.Wintle, G.Evans (Llanelli); A.Davies (Cardiff), P.John (Pontypridd); C.Loader (Swansea), R.McBryde (Llanelli) (capt), S.John (Llanelli), M.Voyle (Newport), P.Jones (Llanelli), A.Gibbs (Newbridge), M.Williams (Pontypridd), S.Davies (Swansea).

Scorers: S.Davies (T), A.Davies (2P).

Referee: D.Gillet (France).

2/3/96 Italy A 19 England A 22 (L'Aquila)

Italy A: X.Pertile (Roma); M.Perziano, T.Visentin (Treviso), G.Filizzola (Calvisano), P.Donati (Treviso); A.Scanavacca (Rovigo), A.Troncon (Treviso) (capt); A.Castellani (L'Aquila), G.De Carli (Roma), D.Sie Mauro (San Dona), P.Alessandro (Rovigo), D.Scaglia (Treviso), M.Giovanelli (Milan), R.Rampazzo (Padua), J.Gardner (Treviso).

Scorers: Perziano (T), Scanavacca (C, 4P).

England A: P.Hull (Bristol); D.O'Leary, P.Mensah (Harlequins), A.Blyth (West Hartlepool), A.Adebayo (Bath); A.King (Bristol Univ), A.Gomarsall (Wasps); K.Yates (Bath), P.Greening (Gloucester), R.Hardwick (Coventry), J.Fowler (Sale), D.Sims (Gloucester), C.Sheasby, R.Jenkins (Harlequins), A.Diprose (Saracens) (capt).

Replacement: W.Greenwood (Harlequins) for Blyth (78).

Scorers: Gomarsall (T), King (C, 5P).

Referee: H.Rohr (Germany).

15/3/96 England A 56 Ireland A 26 (Richmond)

England A: T.Stimpson (West Hartlepool); P.Hull (Bristol), W.Greenwood (Harlequins), N.Greenstock (Wasps), A.Adebayo (Bath); A.King (Bristol Univ), A.Gomarsall (Wasps); R.Hardwick (Coventry), R.Cockerill (Leicester), D.Garforth (Leicester), C.Murphy (West Hartlepool), D.Sims (Gloucester), M.Corry (Bristol), R.Jenkins (Harlequins), A.Diprose (Saracens) (capt).

Scorers: Gomarsall (T), Adebayo (T), Stimpson (T), King (T, 6C, 2P, D), Diprose (T), Garforth (2T).

Ireland A: C.O'Shea (London Irish); R.Wallace (Garryowen), R.Henderson (London Irish), S.McCahill (Sunday's Well), J.Topping (Ballymena); E.Elwood (Lansdowne), A.Rolland (Blackrock Coll) (capt); P.Flavin (Blackrock Coll), J.Byrne (Blackrock Coll), A.McKeen (Lansdowne), M.O'Kelly (St Mary's Coll), N.Francis (Old Belvedere), A.Foley (Shannon), L.Toland (Old Crescent), B.Walsh (London Irish).

Scorers: O'Shea (T), Wallace (2T), Francis (T), Elwood (2P).

Referee: G.Gadjovich (Canada).

15/3/96 Wales A 13 France A 34 (Newport)

Wales A: R.Jones (Neath); S.Hill (Cardiff), M.Taylor (Swansea), J.Funnell (Neath), G.Evans (Llanelli); S.Connor (Abertillery), P.John (Pontypridd) (capt); A.Lewis (Cardiff), B.Williams (Neath), S.John (Llanelli), M.Voyle (Newport), P.Arnold (Swansea), A.Gibbs (Neath), V.Davies (Cardiff), M.Workman (Newport).

Scorers: Penalty Try, Connor (C, 2P).

France A: S.Venditti (Bourgoin); M.Marfaing (Toulouse), C.Paille, Y.Delaigue (Toulon), D.Berty (Toulouse); L.Mazas (Colomiers), P.Carbonneau (capt); C.Soulette, O.Azam (Montferrand), J-L.Jordana (Pau), H.Moirin (Toulouse), L.Bonventre, C.Moni (Nice), L.Loppy (Toulon), T.Labrousse (Brive).

Scorers: Delaigue (T), Labrousse (T), Venditti (T), Berty (T), Mazas (T, 4C, 3P).

Referee: A.Lewis (Ireland).

Under 21 and Schools Rugby

Ireland, who have always flourished at U21 level, took a well-deserved Triple Crown in their annual series of games against the Home Unions and would have welcomed an opportunity to play France's outstanding squad — the two countries, for mainly financial reasons, have never met at this level.

The Irish, coached by former Ireland and British Lions centre David Irwin, looked to play positive rugby at all times and started in the best possible fashion with a 23-10 win over England at Franklin's Gardens, Northampton. Ballymena's flying wing James Topping, who played for Ireland in the Hong Kong sevens later in the season, as well as in the Peace International, scored two tries and fly-half Fergal Campion, from St Mary's College, completed the victory by kicking 13 points. England were at full strength but had to be content with a try from Andy Gomarsall and a conversion and penalty by Simon Binns.

Next came the Scots at Blackrock in Dublin, and a convincing 21-9 win based on forward domination, before the finale against Wales at Wicklow on St David's Day. Prop Barry McConnell and wing James Cunningham scored tries, while the reliable Campion added 12 points to his 16-point haul against the Scots. One curiosity surrounding Ireland's season is that London Irish's Sussex-born centre Justin Bishop starred in all three games but decided late in the season to opt for England and subsequently donned the white shirt against Italy in May.

England, beset by availability problems and their own inconsistency, were disappointing for much of the season, following their defeat against the Irish with an unconvincing 21-18 win over Scotland at Gateshead. Their nadir came against France at the Recreation Ground, Bath, in April when they were hammered 40-3. A number of key players were, in partial mitigation, absent because of the CIS U21 County final at Twickenham the following day, but it was England's worst defeat at this level.

Much better was their 39-10 win over Italy in May, when the influence of new coach Clive Woodward was clear. Woodward boldy selected schoolboys Paul Sampson and Dave Thompson at full-back and wing respectively and England's vibrant performance bodes well for this season.

Scotland had just a victory over Italy to show for their endeavours, but were positive and entertaining throughout and only really came unstuck against France at Myreside. John Funnell, later to make the senior Wales squad to tour Australia, was outstanding for the Welsh and the emergence of Abertillery fly-half Shaun Connor was a bonus.

A debate currently rages over the relevance of Under 21 rugby. At club level, clubs are increasingly looking to nurture young players in a Development XV where more experienced players can lend a guiding hand. At international level, however, it remains a significant stepping stone en route to full international honours.

U21 International summary 1995-96

England 10 Ireland 23 (Franklin's Gardens, 15 November 1995)
England: T: Gomarsall. C: Binns. PG: Binns.
Ireland: T: Topping (2). C: Campion (2). PG: Campion (2). DG: Campion.

England 21 Scotland 18 (Gateshead, 12 December 1995)
England: T: Benton, Catling. C: Binns. PG: Binns (2). DG: Binns.
Scotland: T: Bulloch, McLeish. C: Duncan. PG: Duncan. DG: Duncan.

Italy 10 Scotland 31 (Rieti, 9 January 1996)
Italy: T: Piovan. C: Mazzariol. PG: Mazzariol.
Scotland: T: Reed (2), Murray, Pen try. C: McKee (4). PG: McKee.

Ireland 21 Scotland 9 (Stradbrook, Blackrock, 19 January 1996)
Ireland: T: McIlreavy, Egan. C: Campion. PG: Campion (2). DG: Campion.
Scotland: PG: McKee (3).

Scotland 3 France 29 (Myreside, Edinburgh, 2 February 1996)
Scotland: DG: Richards.
France: T: Nadau, Lombard, Lievremont, Gabin. C: Bruzy (3). DG: Bruzy.

Wales 25 Scotland 21 (St Helen's, Swansea, 16 February 1996)
Wales: T: Funnell, G Jones, Hawkins. C: Connor (2). PG: Connor (2).
Scotland: T: Goldie, A Bulloch. C: Richards. PG: Richards, Dalgleish. DG: Dalgleish

Ireland 20 Wales 12 (Wicklow, 1 March 1996)
Ireland: T: Cunningham, McConnell. C: Campion (2). PG: Campion. DG: Campion.
Wales: T: Manning, Connor. C: Connor.

England 3 France 40 (Recreation Ground, Bath, 19 April 1996)
England: PG: Jones
France: T: Gabin (2), Lazerges, Nadau, Bory, Sannier. C: Bruzy (3). PG: Bruzy (2)

Italy 10 England 38 (Milan, 11 May 1996)
England: T: Rees (2), Luger, Benton, Sampson. C: Sampson, Jones. PG: Jones. DG:
Jones.
Italy: T: not known. C: Mazzariol. PG: Mazzariol.

Schools

Ireland Schools repeated the Triple Crown exploits of their U21 squad, although
their last game was unbearably close, the Irish beating Wales 13-12 at Ravenhill.

Ireland started their representative season with a convincing 37-12 victory over
Scotland in Cork, wing Cormac Dowling showing exceptional pace to score two tries,
and four days later it required a huge team effort in Hull to end England's
three-season unbeaten run against Five Nations opposition. Fly-half Brian
O'Mahony landed four penalties as Ireland pinched a vital 12-9 victory. At Ravenhill
it was captain Barry Gibney who scored the decisive try against Wales and Ireland's
continued excellence at both U21 and Schools level gives great hope for the future.

England impressed in defeating Scotland and France, but generally the team did
not perform to its true potential. Lacking the size and power up front of previous
years, they were much more vulnerable and Wales forced a draw while Ireland
deservedly won. Captain and centre Joe Ewens did, however, emerge as an exceptional talent and it will be surprising if he doesn't make an immediate impact at
senior level.

Scotland struggled, using 32 players in four games including flanker Peter Phillips,
son of the Princess Royal and Mark Phillips, who played against France and Wales
and appeared as a replacement against Ireland. Lampeter full-back Daniel Jones was
the outstanding player for Wales, who played attractive rugby to defeat Scotland and
France, draw with England and nearly spoil the Irish celebrations.

Colston's Collegiate were again the premier school in England, with only Millfield
threatening their unbeaten record. Centres Joe Ewens and Paul Pritchard, scrum-half
Ricky Pellow and wing Nathan Millett were all capped by England 18 Group and
Colston's retained the *Daily Mail* U18 Cup at Twickenham by defeating QEGS
Wakefield 20-0 in a repeat of the 1995 final – Millett scoring two tries and lock Alex
Brown adding a third. The *Daily Mail* U15 tournament went to RGS High Wycombe
who defeated Wellington 17-13 in a free-flowing game, wings Nick Duncombe and
Ross Deering scoring tries for the winners.

Other outstanding schools in the 1995-96 season included Millfield, who lost only
to Colston's, Sedbergh, King's Macclesfield, Hymer's College in Hull, RGS Lancaster, John Fisher in Purley, Yarm School Cleveland and Radley.

In Northern Ireland, the Ulster Bank Schools Cup was shared for the first time since 1964 when Regent House, with fly-half John Anderson to the fore, drew 9-9 against Methodist College, Belfast, in front of a capacity crowd at Ravenhill on St Patrick's Day. In Scotland, St Aloysius College defeated Peebles HS 13-12 to win the Schools Cup for a record fifth time, while in Wales Ysgol Glantaf became the first school, as opposed to sixth form college, to win the Welsh School Cup by defeating Gowerton 10-8.

Stonyhurst were the outstanding side on the sevens circuit, emerging as convincing 29-10 winners over Glantaf in this year's Open competition at the Shell National Schools Sevens at Rosslyn Park. They arrived at Rosslyn Park having won six consecutive tournaments at the North of England Invitation Sevens, Hulme GS, Christ College Brecon, Mount St Mary's, Birkenhead and Stonyhurst itself. Their squad of ten throughout was unchanged, namely captain Paul Howard, Rupert Seldon, Mark Morris, Tony Rogerson, James Gildea, Dipo Alli, John Kehoe, Iain Balshaw, Joey Garcia and Gerard Maughan.

The Festival tournament at Rosslyn Park was won by Bryanston who survived a thrilling semi-final against Wellington (27-26). Ed Hallett, son of RFU secretary Tony, scored the vital late try. In the final, scores from captain Ben Leigh (2), Dryston Howell and David Pace accounted for Cheltenham 26-14.

RGS Guildford took the Junior Schools tournament and St Olave's the Prep School title.

Schools 18 Group Internationals 1995-96

Scotland 12 France 18 (Murrayfield, 22 December 1995); Wales 30 Scotland 3 (Brewery Field, 5 January 1996); Wales 16 France 7 (Mountain Ash, 24 February 1996); Scotland 7 England 50 (Hawick, 27 March 1996); England 7 Wales 7 (Bridgwater and Albion, 30 March 1996); France 11 England 14 (Vannes, 6 April 1996); Ireland 37 Scotland 12 (Cork, 6 April 1996); England 9 Ireland 12 (Hull Ionians, 10 April 1996); Ireland 13 Wales 12 (Ravenhill, 17 April 1996).

CIS Insurance County and Divisional Championship 1995-96

Final

Gloucestershire 17 Warwickshire 13 (Twickenham, 20 April 1996)

The advent of the professional game meant that the 1996 County Championship final between Gloucestershire and Warwickshire at Twickenham almost certainly represented the end of an era. The new rugby calendar carries what Rugby Union's new regime might term 'more meaningful' fixtures and the lucrative club contracts snapped up by players will deny many of them an opportunity to declare themselves available for less relevant competitions.

So, Gloucestershire's 17-13 County Championship final victory over Warwickshire, at Twickenham, on 20 April 1996 became something of a watershed spectacle in the game's rapidly changing world. It was seen by many as amateurism's last stand, with a paltry 7,500 spectators 'lost' in the largely deserted stands at rugby's headquarters.

The 96th final of a devalued tournament at Twickenham started brightly when Andrew Stanley, Gloucestershire's captain, peeled off the back of a lineout for a try after five minutes. Then Ian Patten made a break for Julian Davis to score a second try for Gloucestershire. Warwickshire staged a second-half revival. Mark Warr scored a try on the hour and Matt Gallagher's kicking cut the deficit to only four points as Gloucestershire full-back Tim Smith kept the final score in doubt by missing three second-half penalties.

Yet it was Smith's late penalty that had stolen a 16-13 victory over Surrey in the semi-finals at Imber Court, while Warwickshire's forward dominance had routed Lancashire 36-16 in the other semi. The three-year CIS sponsorship of the County and Divisional competitions ended with Stanley raising the trophy to mark his county's 16th title win.

Gloucestershire: T. Smith (Gloucester); J. Perrins (Gloucester), D. Edwards (Berry Hill), L. Osborne (Gloucester), D. Morgan (Cheltenham); R. Mills (Lydney), J. Davis (Lydney); R. Phillips (Cheltenham), N. Nelmes (Lydney), S. Baldwin (Gloucester OB), A. Knox (Lydney), T. Clink (Cheltenham), J. Brain (Cheltenham), A. Stanley (Gloucester, capt), I. Patten (Coventry).

Scorers: T: Stanley, Davis. C: Smith (2). PG: Smith.

Warwickshire: A. Parton (Henley); J. Minshull (Kenilworth), M. Curtis (Coventry), M. Palmer (Rugby), D. Watson (Rugby); M. Gallagher (Nottingham), M. Warr (Sale); G. Tregilgas (Coventry, capt), R. Burdett (Rugby), S. Revan (Rugby), M. Ellis (Rugby), S. Smith (Rugby), P. Bowman (Rugby), S. Carter (Rugby), M. Fountaine (Bristol).

Replacement: A. Ruddlesdin (Long Buckby) for Ellis (69).

Scorers: T: Warr. C: Gallagher. PG: Gallagher (2).

Referee: B. Campsall (Yorkshire).

CIS Insurance County Championship Results 1995-96

Staffs 55 E Mids 29; Durham 29 Cumbria 14; Northumberland 24 Cheshire 22; Leics 6 Warwicks 37; Lancs 20 Yorks 14.

Dorset 12 Wilts and Berks 13; Devon 14 Oxon 20; Herts 6 Glos 21; Sussex 15 Kent 22; Middx 33 Hants 10; Surrey 17 Cornwall 11; Somerset 19 E Counties 12; Cheshire 26 Yorks 22; Durham 30 Northumberland 16; Lancs 27 Cumbria 20; E Mids 7 N Mids 39; Warwicks 37 Notts, Lincs and Derbys 3.

Berks 22 Bucks 0; Oxon 10 Glos 34; Devon 26 Herts 28; Kent 27 Hants 31, Sussex 17 Middx 25; Cornwall 44 E Counties 6; Surrey 25 Somerset 22; Cheshire 33 Durham 31; Cumbria 14 Yorks 30; Northumberland 9 Lancs 11; Notts, Lincs and Derbys 8 Leics 34; N Mids 33 Staffs 16.

Cumbria 18 Cheshire 22; Durham 16 Lancs 19; Yorks 28 Northumberland 19; Bucks 13 Dorset and Wilts 42; Herts 37 Oxon 13; Middx 10 Kent 10; Hants 20 Sussex 3; E Counties 13 Surrey 32; Somerset 42 Cornwall 22; Glos 19 Devon 0.

Play-offs, Midlands semi-finals: N Mids 38 Leics 28; Warwicks 57 Staffs 7; North: Lancs 23 Cheshire 22; Yorks 27 Durham 22; Northumberland 32 Cumbria 10.

Play-offs, Midlands: Warwicks 39 N Mids 5; Southern: Berks 20 Glos 26; Middx 14 Surrey 18.

County Championship semi-finals: Lancs 16 Warwicks 36; Surrey 13 Glos 16.

County Championship final: Glos 17, Warwicks 13.

CIS Divisional Championship 1995-96

Midlands 36 London and SE 34; South West 15 North 38; South West 11 Midlands 16; North 18 London and SE 9; London and SE 11 South West 26; Midlands 42 North 45.

County Championship and Divisional Competitions 1996-97

The big battalions of the County Championship in the North and Midlands have been kept apart until the quarter-final stages of the 1996-97 competition, with Warwickshire, Lancashire and Yorkshire in separate sections of the 12-club draw.

Warwickshire, the 1995-96 beaten finalists, are in Pool 2 along with Northumberland, Cheshire and Notts, Lincs and Derbys, the winners of that group meeting the highest-ranked runners-up in the three pools at home in the quarter-finals.

Lancashire have one home pool game, against Leicestershire, and travel to Cumbria and East Midlands, while Yorkshire have home matches against Durham and Staffordshire before travelling to North Midlands.

Winners of that group are away in the quarter-finals, which, if traditional form is maintained, could involve a Roses clash. Quarter-final winners will go into a national draw involving the top two counties from the Southern section.

Fixtures 1996-97

North and Midlands, Nov 30: Cumbria v Lancs; Northumberland v Cheshire; Yorks v Durham; E Mids v Leics; Notts, Lincs and Derbys v Warwicks; Staffs v N Mids. Dec 7: Lancs v Leics; Cheshire v Warwicks; Durham v N Mids; Cumbria v E Mids; Northumberland v Notts, Lincs and Derbys; Yorks v Staffs. Dec 14: E Mids v Lancs; Notts, Lincs and Derbys v Cheshire; Staffs v Durham; Leics v Cumbria; Warwicks v Northumberland; N Mids v Yorks.

Southern, Nov 30: Oxon v Herts; Middx v Bucks; Dorset and Wilts v Berks; Kent v Glos; Somerset v Devon; Hants v E Counties; Cornwall v Sussex. Dec 7: Herts v Surrey; Bucks v Devon; Berks v E Counties; Glos v Sussex; Middx v Somerset; Dorset and Wilts v Hants; Kent v Cornwall. Dec 14: Somerset v Bucks; Hants v Berks; Cornwall v Glos; Surrey v Oxon; Devon v Middx; E Counties v Dorest and Wilts; Sussex v Kent.

Jan 18: Quarter-finals; March 8: Semi-finals; April 19: Final, Twickenham.

English County Champions

Year	Champion	Year	Champion
1889	Yorkshire	1949	Lancashire
1890	Yorkshire	1950	Cheshire
1891	Lancashire	1951	E Midlands
1892	Yorkshire	1952	Middlesex
1893	Yorkshire	1953	Yorkshire
1894	Yorkshire	1954	Middlesex
1895	Yorkshire	1955	Lancashire
1896	Yorkshire	1956	Middlesex
1897	Kent	1957	Devon
1898	Northumberland	1958	Warwickshire
1899	Devon	1959	Warwickshire
1900	Durham	1960	Warwickshire
1901	Devon	1961	Cheshire
1902	Durham	1962	Warwickshire
1903	Durham	1963	Warwickshire
1904	Kent	1964	Warwickshire
1905	Durham	1965	Warwickshire
1906	Devon	1966	Middlesex
1907	Devon/Durham	1967	Surrey/Durham
1908	Cornwall	1968	Middlesex
1909	Durham	1969	Lancashire
1910	Gloucestershire	1970	Staffordshire
1911	Devon	1971	Surrey
1912	Devon	1972	Gloucestershire
1913	Gloucestershire	1973	Lancashire
1914	Midlands	1974	Gloucestershire
1920	Gloucestershire	1975	Gloucestershire
1921	Gloucestershire	1976	Gloucestershire
1922	Gloucestershire	1977	Lancashire
1923	Somerset	1978	N Midlands
1924	Cumberland	1979	Middlesex
1925	Leicestershire	1980	Lancashire
1926	Yorkshire	1981	Northumberland
1927	Kent	1982	Lancashire
1928	Yorkshire	1983	Gloucestershire
1929	Middlesex	1984	Gloucestershire
1930	Gloucestershire	1985	Middlesex
1931	Gloucestershire	1986	Warwickshire
1932	Gloucestershire	1987	Yorkshire
1933	Hampshire	1988	Lancashire
1934	E Midlands	1989	Durham
1935	Lancashire	1990	Lancashire
1936	Hampshire	1991	Cornwall
1937	Gloucestershire	1992	Lancashire
1938	Lancashire	1993	Lancashire
1939	Warwickshire	1994	Yorkshire
1947	Lancashire	1995	Warwickshire
1948	Lancashire	1996	Gloucestershire

The Cross-Code Series

Wigan 82 Bath 6 (Maine Road, 8 May 1996)

Martin Offiah, who cut his rugby teeth with Rosslyn Park, predictably emerged as the star of this unique meeting at Manchester City FC, returning from a painful back injury to score six tries for Wigan en route to a crushing victory over Bath under rugby league rules.

A crowd of 20,148 saw exactly why Wigan have dominated their code to such an extent over the last decade, their bewildering running skills and superior fitness threatening at times to render the game a farce. Despite their best players on the night Henry Paul and Andrew Farrell – being withdrawn in the first half, Wigan amassed 16 tries in total.

Bath only avoided total humiliation by digging deep in the second half, as their organisation improved, and tackling for their lives. In truth, they faced an impossible task, facing the greatest RL club side in history just four days after a draining Pilkington Cup final against Leicester with precious little preparation. They were also missing their Scottish international contingent, Jeremy Guscott, who firstly refused to play and was then injured anyway, and Ben Clarke, who had signed for Richmond the previous day and was also injured.

'Wigan are a fantastic side. They're so hard to stop with their lines of running, in particular the pack. They come on at pace,' said Bath captain Phil de Glanville afterwards. 'But a couple more practice sessions and it might have been 50 instead of 80.' Perhaps.

Wigan, professional at all times, refused to gloat and accepted that the tables could be turned when the two sides reconvened at Twickenham. 'It took a lot of guts to come up here and take us on,' said Wigan captain Shaun Edwards, who once captained England Schools 16 Group at rugby union. 'We know that Bath had problems preparing and the timing wasn't ideal, but we respect them for what they have done.'

Wigan: K Radlinski; J Robinson, V Tuigamala, G Connolly, M Offiah; H Paul, S Edwards; N Cowie, M Hall, T O'Connor, S Haughton, M Cassidy, A Farrell.

Replacements: R Smyth, C Murdock, S Quinnell, A Johnson.

Scorers: T: Offiah (6), Tuigamala, Robinson (2), O'Connor, Johnson, Quinnell, Murdock, Farrell, Hall, Paul. C: 9

Bath: A Lumsden; J Sleightholme, P de Glanville, F Waters, A Adebayo; M Catt, J Callard; K Yates, I Sanders, M Haag, A Vander, S Ojomoh, A Robinson.

Replacements: R Butland, N Redman, N McCarthy, E Pearce.

Scorers: T: Callard. C: Callard.

Referee: R Smith (Castleford)

Bath 44 Wigan 19 (Twickenham, 25 May 1996)

Bath exacted a degree of revenge in another hugely entertaining encounter, much enjoyed by a crowd of 40,000, but again the abiding memory was of the speed and versatility of Wigan's backs who scored three sparkling second-half tries on limited rations.

Bath's forward power, as predicted, was much too much for Wigan and could have destroyed the game as a spectacle. It was to their credit, therefore, that Bath did not overdo the rolling mauls and attempted to play a more open style of game, which brought Wigan into play and produced a fine spectacle.

Two tries for Adedayo Adebayo, a searing effort from John Sleightholme and a penalty try saw Bath lead 25-0 at half-time, an advantage they soon increased with scores by Catt and de Glanville. Wigan replied in superb fashion with two length-of-the-field scores, both finished by Chris Murdock and a typical blockbusting effort from Va'aiga Tuigamala, returning to Twickenham where he played for the 1993 All Blacks.

Financial necessity obviously played a considerable part in the staging of the series, with both sides thought to have earned £200,000 out of the games. Wigan had been knocked out of the RL Challenge Cup competition and were looking to recoup lost income, while Bath needed to raise cash to help fund their wages bill for 1996-97.

But only a complete cynic would assess the meetings in purely financial terms. The fringe benefits were that players, supporters and administrators have forged close links and friendships where previously only suspicion existed.

'There will be a unified game in five years,' said RFL chief executive Maurice Lindsay afterwards. 'It will be difficult for the two games not to merge,' added RFU secretary Tony Hallett. After 101 years peace had finally broken out between the two codes.

Bath: J Callard; A Lumsden, P de Glanville (capt), A Adebayo, J Sleightholme; M Catt, I Sanders; K Yates, G Dawe, V Ubogu, M Haag, N Redman, E Pearce, A Robinson, S Ojomoh.

Replacements: N McCarthy for Ubogu (43), J Ewens for Sleightholme (56), R Butland for Adebayo (71), G French for Dawe (72)

Scorers: T: Pen try, Adebayo (2), Sleightholme, de Glanville, Sanders, Catt. C: Callard (3). PG: Callard.

Wigan: K Radlinski; J Robinson, H Paul, G Connolly, M Offiah; J Lydon, C Murdock; T O'Connor, M Hall, N Cowie, A Farrell (capt), G West, S Tatupu, V Tuigamala, S Quinnell.

Replacements: M Cassidy for Lydon (40), S Haughton for Quinnell (47).

Scorers: T: Murdock (2), Tuigamala. C: Farrell (2)

Referee: B Campsall (Yorkshire)

Varsity Match 1995

Cambridge University 21 Oxford University 19 (Twickenham, 12 December 1995)

A hitherto pedestrian Varsity match came alive in the final five minutes with three scores, including a controversial penalty try, awarded against Oxford by Tony Spreadbury for persistent infringement. Cambridge eventually emerged from the drama and excitement to take the Bowring Bowl and the closing moments of this 114th Varsity match will have added greatly to the fixture's folklore.

It was in the 76th minute, with Oxford leading 16-9, that Cambridge pressed hard on the Oxford line in Twickenham's south-west corner. Oxford had already been warned after a number of offside offences and as Cambridge laid siege to the line, at least three dark blue defenders were again offside and Mr Spreadbury made his fateful decision.

Robert Ashforth kicked the simple conversion to level the scores at 16-16 but resilient Oxford marched straight back upfield and a third penalty from David Humphreys seemingly ensured a 19-16 triumph. Not so. Cambridge launched one final attack in injury time through wing David Casado, whose high kick put Oxford's South African full-back Pierre du Preez in trouble. The Cambridge pack quickly robbed du Preez of possession and Ashforth threw out a long spin pass to hooker Jonathan Evans, who proved unstoppable from 20 yards. Earlier, the game had been dominated by Humphreys, Oxford's dapper young Irish fly-half, who went on to win international honours later in the season. A product of Ballymena Academy, the Ulsterman kicked a dropped goal in reply to Ashforth's early penalty and then added two penalties before threading his way through for a fine individual try which he converted himself.

Cambridge's only reply at this stage was two further penalties from Ashforth, who enjoyed mixed fortunes with his place-kicking. The light blue cause was not helped by a nasty head injury to Dan Maslen which resulted in the Gloucester scrum-half departing with concussion, while Oxford were also inconvenienced by an injury to their France A centre Jerome Riondet. For much of the second half the game spluttered disappointingly on, but the late fireworks were well worth waiting for.

Cambridge: M Singer (Wycliffe College and Homerton); D Casado (Ampleforth and St Edmund's), T Whitford (The Leys and Homerton), S Cottrell (Christ Coll Christchurch, NZ, and St Edmund's, capt); S Sexton (Dublin HS and Hughes Hall); R Ashforth (Bradford GS and Peterhouse), D Maslen (Rendcomb Coll, Cirencester, and St Edmund's); L Mooney (St Boniface Coll, Plymouth, and Hughes Hall), J Evans (Emanuel GS, Swansea, and Homerton), N Holgate (Armthorpe CS, Doncaster, and Robinson), R Bramley (QEGS Wakefield and St Edmund's), C Simpson (Hills Road Sixth Form Coll, Cambridge, and Homerton), M Hyde (St Ignatius, Sydney, and St Edmund's), R Earnshaw (Yarm School, Cleveland, and St John's), S Surridge (St Kentigern Coll, Auckland, and Wolfson). *Replacement:* B Ryan (St Benedict's, Ealing, and Homerton) for Maslen (34).

Scorers: T: Pen try, Jones. C: Ashforth. PG: Ashforth (3).

Oxford: P du Preez (Queen's Coll, Queenstown, SA, and Keble); S Rush (Harrow and Mansfield), Q de Bruyn (Diocesan Coll, Cape Town, SA, and Keble), J Riondet (Lycée La Kanal, Paris, and Mansfield), T Howe (Banbridge Acad and Keble, capt); D Humphreys (Ballymena Acad and St Cross), M Butler (King Edward VI, Lichfield, and St Edmund Hall); C Norton (St Andrew's Coll, Grahamstown, and Keble), K Svoboda (Centennial School, Belleville, Ontario, and Templeton), D Penney (Mount Pearl HS, Newfoundland, and Wolfson), N Basson (Diocesan Coll, Cape Town, SA, and St Cross), P Coveney (Clongowes Wood Coll, Kildare, and New Coll), M Riley (St Gerard's, Bray, and St Anne's), M Orsler (King's, Canterbury, and Christ Church), R Yeabsley (Haberdashers' Aske's and Keble). *Replacements:* M Mermagen (St Bartholomew's, Newbury, and Keble) for Riondet (39-43, 48).

Scorers: T: Humphreys. C: Humphreys. PG: Humphreys (3). DG: Humphreys.

Referee: A Spreadbury (Somerset).

Cambridge lead the series 53-48, with 13 matches drawn.

Peace International

Ireland XV 38 Barbarians 70 (Lansdowne Road, Dublin, 17 May 1996)

This unique Peace International was born initially out of despondency that the IRA ceasefire had again broken down and proved a spectacular success for the co-organisers, Hugo MacNeill, a southern Catholic, and Trevor Ringland, a Protestant from Northern Ireland.

The former Ireland and British Lions colleagues bumped into each other shortly after the ceasefire had broken down in London in February and wondered if a match against the Barbarians at Lansdowne Road might not be an appropriate way for Irish rugby fans, and many others, to express their disgust at the renewal of hostilities.

The answer was very definitely 'Yes' with nearly 40,000 fans braving a cold and blustery afternoon to enjoy a typically free-flowing game against a star-studded Barbarians, not to mention a day of festivities and the pre-match musical entertainment, courtesy of top Irish band, the Corrs.

'We just wanted to send the message out that whatever violence the IRA perpetrate, they don't speak for rugby people in Ireland or rugby people in general,' said MacNeill.

The occasion received vital initial support from South Africa's World Cup captain Francois Pienaar and Australian star David Campese. Ultimately, injury prevented the celebrated duo from playing, but both flew from their respective countries to support the occasion and display their solidarity for the message rugby was trying to convey.

In the game itself, the Barbarians proved much too strong for an Ireland side that was admittedly using the opportunity to experiment and blood young players. The Barbarians scored ten tries with Jonathan Callard converting the lot and victory was only marred by a leg injury to captain Phil de Glanville. Ireland, with Vic Costello and Rob Henderson to the fore, recovered to amass six tries themselves and all proceeds went to charities devoted to the furtherance of peace in Ireland.

Ireland XV: S Mason (Orrell); R Wallace (Garryowen), J Bell (Northampton), R Henderson (London Irish), J Topping (Ballymena); D Humphreys (London Irish), N Hogan (Terenure, capt); H Hurley (Old Wesley), A Clarke (Northampton), A McKeen (Lansdowne), G Fulcher (London Irish), J Davidson (Dungannon), E Halvey (Saracens), D McBride (Malone), V Costello (St Mary's)

Replacements: P Johns (Dungannon) for Halvey (3), M Field (Malone) for Bell (37), P Flavin (Blackrock) for Hurley (38); P Burke (Cork Con) for Humphreys (45), C Saverimutto (Sale) for Hogan (54), Hogan for Henderson (72).

Scorers: T: Henderson, Costello (2), Wallace, Burke, Topping. C: Mason (4)

Barbarians: J Callard (Bath); E Rush (North Harbour), P de Glanville (Bath, capt), P Sella (Agen), R Underwood (Leicester); S Bachop (Otago), J Roux (Transvaal); G Rowntree, R Cockerill, D Garforth (Leicester), O Brouzet (Grenoble), N Redman, S Ojomoh (Bath), L Cabannes (Racing), D Richards (Leicester)

Replacements: W Greenwood (Harlequins) for de Glanville (25), M Brewer (Canterbury) for Richards (50), L Jarvis (Pontypridd) for Rush (56).

Scorers: T: Underwood (2), Redman, Roux, de Glanville, Sella, Rush, Cockerill, Greenwood, Jarvis. C: Callard (10)

Referee: D Bevan (Wales)

Sanyo Cup

Leicester 31 World XV 40 (Twickenham, 21 April 1996)

The inaugural Sanyo Cup - to be played between the Courage League champions and a World Select – was greeted with a glorious warm spring afternoon and a better than expected crowd of 31,700, who enjoyed a game that happily never quite degenerated into an exhibition.

Leicester, in the middle of a gruelling fortnight that saw their squad play five vital League or Cup matches, could probably have done without the added distraction of this game, but the income generated was vital as they plan for their professional future. Sanyo have signed a three-year contract with the RFU whereby the Courage League champions, whoever they might be, will play a World XV in an annual fixture, although there is a thought that this could be changed to early season to avoid the pressure Leicester found themselves under.

Tigers were nonetheless at full strength and thoroughly enjoyed themselves as they raced into a 31-12 half-time lead, with a searing individual effort from Steve Hackney their best score. The half-time break was the signal for coaches Ian Smith and Paul Dodge to make wholesale changes as the urge to avoid unnecessary injuries became overwhelming. The World XV also brought on their replacements, and improved dramatically after the break to score 28 unanswered points.

Of those on view, nobody impressed more than Fiji's Sevens star Waisale Serevi who buried the lie that he can't play fifteens. Serevi impressed initially at full-back and then at fly-half after an injury to Thierry Lacroix forced the World XV to rejig their back division.

Leicester: J Liley; S Hackney, S Potter, R Robinson, R Underwood; N Malone, A Kardooni; G Rowntree, R Cockerill, D Garforth, M Johnson, M Poole, C Tarbuck, N Back, D Richards (capt).

Replacements: D West for Cockerill (40), J Hamilton for Kardooni (40), J Wells for Richards (60), J Harris for Liley (62), D Jelley for Garforth (72).

Scorers: T: Tarbuck (2), Hackney, Potter, Richards. C: Liley (3).

World XV: W Serevi (Fiji); T Underwood (England), P Sella (France, capt), T Lacroix (France), Y Yoshida (Japan); G Townsend (Scotland), G Bachop (New Zealand); N Popplewell (Ireland), J Humphreys (Wales), P Fatialofa (Western Samoa), Gareth Llewellyn (Wales), D Jones (Wales), I Macdonald (South Africa), L Cabannes (France), J Joseph (New Zealand).

Replacements: G Johnson (South Africa) for Lacroix (27), A Pichot (Argentina) for Bachop (40), R Martin (Argentina) for Cabannes (40), S Latu (Japan) for MacDonald (40), T Matsuda (Japan) for Yoshida (40), M Regan (England) for Humphreys (75).

Scorers: T: Serevi, Cabannes, Joseph, Sella, Pichot, Matsuda. C: Serevi (5).

Referee: E Morrison (England).

Middlesex Sevens 1996

Wigan, having dismissed Bath 82-6 just three days earlier in the first of their double-headers, breathed life into the Save & Prosper Middlesex Charity Sevens with another display of their exceptional power and pace, which thrilled a capacity 61,000 crowd at Twickenham and helped raise over £400,000 for charity.

In the absence of England's leading internationals – only Wasps' Lawrence Dallaglio was prepared to put his reputation on the line and emerged with flying colours – Wigan were the class act throughout a long day, scoring 25 tries in four games. Martin Offiah, a semi-finalist with Rosslyn Park in 1986 and a finalist with Park a year later, helped himself to six, despite missing Wigan's semi-final with Leicester with a jarred knee.

Offiah, though, was just one in a battery of astounding attacking talents, with captain Shaun Edwards, Jason Robinson, Gary Connolly, Va'aiga Tuigamala and the white-booted Henry Paul, until injured, seemingly capable of scoring at will.

'A lot of rugby union people now realise some pretty awesome athletes play rugby league,' said Edwards afterwards. 'Most people wanted us to lose but we were treated with respect and I'd like to thank the officials for inviting us here. The buzz of playing at Twickenham was fantastic. It was something I thought we would never be allowed to do.'

After dismissing Richmond 48-5 in the opening round, Wigan were fully extended by a lively Harlequins seven, who went into a 12-0 lead before losing 36-24. Next came a disappointing Leicester, who provided little threat, but Wasps scored three tries without reply before Wigan, inspired by a rather premature chorus of 'Swing low, sweet chariots' from the crowd, finally hit top gear in the final to score six unanswered tries.

'No team in union comes close to being as fit as Wigan,' said Dallaglio afterwards. 'They get up in the morning, clock on and go to the gym. The time and commitment they put in is total. They pass the ball every day. The lines they run, the quality of their support play, their wholly professional attitude is something we must look at closely.'

Dallaglio could be well pleased with his young side, in which Andy Gomarsall and Nick Greenstock underlined their potential. Elsewhere, only Wigan's friends and neighbours Orrell, who travelled down with the RL giants, caught the eye, especially the explosive Austin Healey who was making his last appearance for the club before joining Leicester.

Wigan: M Offiah (R Smyth), G Connolly, J Robinson, S Edwards (capt); S Quinnell (K Radlinski), V Tuigamala, A Farrell

Wasps: S Roiser (L Scrase), N Greenstock, A Thompson (A James), A Gomarsall; L Dallaglio, M White, P Scrivener

Middlesex Sevens: 6th round: Stirling County 29 Haywards Heath 10; Wasps 33 Bristol 12; Orrell 45 Malaysia 7; Blackheath 14 Wakefield 5; Wigan 48 Richmond 5; Harlequins 35 Gloucester 5; Sale 22 Saracens 21; Leicester 26 London Scottish 22. Quarter-finals: Wasps 24 Stirling County 12; Orrell 31 Blackheath 15; Wigan 36 Harlequins 24; Leicester 31 Sale 5. Semi-finals: Wasps 21 Orrell 12; Wigan 35 Leicester 12. Final: Wigan 38 Wasps 15.

Middlesex Sevens Past Winners

Year	Winner	Year	Winner
1926	Harlequins	1962	London Scottish
1927	Harlequins	1963	London Scottish
1928	Harlequins	1964	Loughborough College
1929	Harlequins	1965	London Scottish
1930	London Welsh	1966	Loughborough College
1931	London Welsh	1967	Harlequins
1932	Blackheath	1968	London Welsh
1933	Harlequins	1969	St Luke's College
1934	Barbarians	1970	Loughborough College
1935	Harlequins	1971	London Welsh
1936	Sale	1972	London Welsh
1937	London Scottish	1973	London Welsh
1938	Metropolitan Police	1974	Richmond
1939	Cardiff	1975	Richmond
1940	St Mary's Hospital	1976	Loughborough College
1941	Cambridge University	1977	Richmond
1942	St Mary's Hospital	1978	Harlequins
1943	St Mary's Hospital	1979	Richmond
1944	St Mary's Hospital	1980	Richmond
1945	Nottinghamshire	1981	Rosslyn Park
1946	St Mary's Hospital	1982	Stewart's Melville FP
1947	Rosslyn Park	1983	Richmond
1948	Wasps	1984	London Welsh
1949	Heriot's FP	1985	Wasps
1950	Rosslyn Park	1986	Harlequins
1951	Richmond II	1987	Harlequins
1952	Wasps	1988	Harlequins
1953	Richmond	1989	Harlequins
1954	Rosslyn Park	1990	Harlequins
1955	Richmond	1991	London Scottish
1956	London Welsh	1992	Western Samoa
1957	St Luke's College	1993	Wasps
1958	Blackheath	1994	Bath
1959	Loughborough College	1995	Leicester
1960	London Scottish	1996	Wigan RL
1961	London Scottish		

Hong Kong Sevens 1996

The Cathay Pacific Hongkong Bank Sevens celebrated their 21st birthday with another riotous carnival of action and colour at the futuristic Hong Kong Stadium, with New Zealand, inspired by the try-scoring feats of Chris Cullen, winning the title for a third consecutive year.

Cullen, like Jonah Lomu the previous year and Glen Osborne in 1994, arrived in Hong Kong as a promising but relatively unknown Kiwi and departed a household name. New Zealand have regularly chosen to test their talented youngsters in this demanding tournament and have reaped handsome benefit.

Cullen scored an incredible 18 tries in six matches, including a world record seven in their opening game against hapless Sri Lanka. He represented New Zealand Schools in 1993 and appeared for Manawatu in 1995 before being capped by New Zealand Colts and starring for Wellington in the inaugural Super 12s. Cullen opened his international account with a hat-trick on his debut against Western Samoa in June and followed that with four against Scotland.

One of the quickest players ever seen in Hong Kong, Cullen is a perfectly balanced runner and has a footballing brain to match. All these qualities were seen during New Zealand's 19-17 victory over Fiji in an absorbing final, notably in the first half when he created a sensational try for Waisake Masirewa. Finding himself under intense pressure behind his own goal line, Cullen wiggled and squirmed his way out of three tackles before straightening up under his own post, dismissing a fourth defender with a burst of pace and sending Masirewa away unchallenged.

New Zealand had taken the lead with a penalty try when Waisale Serevi tripped Cullen as he closed in on yet another try, but Fiji's sevens captain made amends soon after with a brilliant counter-attack which fashioned a score for Setareki Naivaluwaqa. New Zealand, however, clinched the title with a second try for Masirewa, although Fiji did score a consolation try from Joppe Tuikabe.

The New Zealanders had been fully stretched in an entertaining semi-final against England who, although losing 42-19, became the only team to score three tries against the Kiwis, Neil Back, Chris Sheasby and Austin Healey all crossing the line. England worked hard to contain the threat of Jonah Lomu and generally succeeded, though Dave Scully will still be feeling the effects of one tackle. Lomu did, however, provide one highlight with a superb 50-yard American football pass which made a simple opening for the ever-present Cullen.

England manager Andrew Harriman had worked hard to secure the release of his top players and was rewarded with a squad that lacked only Lawrence Dallaglio of England's acknowledged sevens experts. After comfortable group victories over Singapore, Argentina and Scotland, they hit top form in the quarter-final against Western Samoa, winning 27-7, but victory was to prove costly with captain Damian Hopley damaging cruciate knee ligaments late in the game which prevented him playing against New Zealand.

England undoubtedly rank in the world's top four, but preparation is still a problem their squad flew to Hong Kong directly from a strenuous Courage League weekend while New Zealand and Fiji had enjoyed a month's preparation including the Fiji Invitations Sevens the previous week.

Of the other British teams, a committed Welsh squad performed best, with two early tries from Robert Howley and Gareth Thomas surprising Fiji in the quarter-final before Serevi and Co recovered their poise. Ieuan Evans put his reputation on the line and emerged with much credit, so much so that Australia requested that he act as a bench replacement for their semi-final against Fiji. Much to his delight the former Wales captain got on for the final 30 seconds.

The new tournament proved a great success, with eight groups of three being replaced by six groups of four with the top two teams progressing to the knockout stages of the main competition. The opening group games were all played under floodlights on the Friday night, another successful innovation. There will be no Hong Kong Sevens in 1997 when the Hong Kong RFU will host the RWC Sevens, but the tournament is expected to return in 1998.

HONG KONG SEVENS 1996: *Quarter-finals*: New Zealand 49 Ireland 0; England 27 Western Samoa 7; Australia 19 Canada 5; Fiji 28 Wales 12. *Semi-finals*: New Zealand 42 England 19; Fiji 24 Australia 7. *Final*: New Zealand 19 Fiji 17. *Plate final*: France 45 Hong Kong 12. *Bowl*: Japan 55 Namibia 21.

Hong Kong Sevens winners:

1976	Cantabrians	Plate:	Hong Kong		
1977	Fiji	Plate:	Tonga		
1978	Fiji	Plate:	Fiji		
1979	Australia	Plate:	Papua New Guinea		
1980	Fiji	Plate:	Japan		
1981	Barbarians	Plate:	Tonga		
1982	Australia	Plate:	Korea		
1983	Australia	Plate:	Korea		
1984	Fiji	Plate:	Australia	Bowl:	Sri Lanka
1985	Australia	Plate:	Tonga	Bowl:	Hong Kong
1986	New Zealand	Plate:	USA	Bowl:	Papua New Guinea
1987	New Zealand	Plate:	Fr Barbarians	Bowl:	Hong Kong
1988	Australia	Plate:	USA	Bowl:	Taipei
1989	New Zealand	Plate:	Tonga	Bowl:	Netherlands
1990	Fiji	Plate:	Hong Kong	Bowl:	West Germany
1991	Fiji	Plate:	Argentina	Bowl:	Korea
1992	Fiji	Plate:	Hong Kong	Bowl:	Romania
1993	Western Samoa	Plate:	Tonga	Bowl:	Romania
1994	New Zealand	Plate:	Korea	Bowl:	Hong Kong
1995	New Zealand	Plate:	Canada	Bowl:	Hong Kong
1996	New Zealand	Plate:	France	Bowl:	Japan

Rugby Transfers

The following major signings were made by clubs over the last year:

BATH
Richard Webster (Salford), Henry Paul (Wigan RL, match contract), Dan Lyle (US Eagles)

BEDFORD
Mike Rayer (Cardiff), Martin Offiah (Wigan RL), Jeff Probyn (Wasps), Paul Turner (Sale), Martin Pepper (Harlequins), Stuart Anderson, Robert Scott (both L. Scottish)

BLACKHEATH
John Gallagher (Harlequins), Andre Stoop (Keighley RL), Chris Wilkins, Chris Braithwaite, Matt Griffiths, Steve Shortland (all Wasps), Thomas Billups, Raymond Lehner (both US Eagles)

BRISTOL
Robert Jones (Swansea), David Corkery (Cork), Paul Burke (Cork), Fraser Waters (Bath), Patrick Chennery (Montpellier)

CARDIFF
Gwyn Jones (Llanelli), Leigh Davies (Neath), Robert Howley (Bridgend), Justin Thomas (Llanelli), David Young (Salford RL), Lee Jarvis (Pontypridd)

COVENTRY
Andy Blackmore (Bristol), Jez Harris (Leicester), Richie Robinson (Leicester), Wayne Kilford, Andy McAdam (Leicester), Andrew Smallwood, Matt Gallagher (both Nottingham)

GLOUCESTER
Trevor Woodman, Bill Nicholas, Dave Timmington, Steve Johnson (all Bath), Chris Catling (Exeter)

HARLEQUINS
Gareth Llewellyn (Neath), Glyn Llewellyn (Neath), Keith Wood (Garryowen), Laurent Benezech, Mike Corcoran (London Irish), Laurent Cabannes (Racing Club), Dan Luger (Orrell), Matthew Evans (Cardiff Inst)

LEEDS
Phil Davies (Llanelli), Colin Stephens (Llanelli), Gerry Ainscough (Orrell), Mark Appleson (Sale), Diccon Edwards (Castleford RL), Gavin Baldin (Wakefield), Mike Shelley (West Hartlepool)

LEICESTER
Austin Healey (Orrell), Craig Joiner (Melrose), Will Greenwood (Harlequins), Neil Fletcher (Moseley), Greg Austin (Huddersfield RL), Rob Liley (Sale)

LONDON IRISH
Conor O'Shea (Lansdowne), Gabriel Fulcher (Cork), Vic Costello (St Mary's College),
Jeremy Davidson (Dungannon), Niall Woods (Blackrock)

NEWCASTLE
Rob Andrew, Steve Bates, Dean Ryan, Nick Popplewell (all Wasps), Tony Underwood
(Leicester), Gary Armstrong (Jed-Forest), Doddie Weir (Melrose), Peter Walton
(Northampton), Tim Stimpson (West Hartlepool), Garath Archer (Bristol), Andrew
Blyth (West Hartlepool)

ORRELL
Frano Botica (Castleford RL), Steve Cook (West Hartlepool), David Lyon (Leigh RL)

PONTYPRIDD
Nathan Jones (Bridgend), John Evans (Cardiff Inst), Gareth Thomas (Bridgend)

RICHMOND
Adrian Davies (Cardiff), Andy Moore (Cardiff), Ben Clarke (Bath), Scott Quinnell
(Wigan RL), Jim Fallon (Leeds RL), Richard West (Gloucester), Darren Compton
(Bath), Chris Clarke (Bath), Simon Mason (Orrell), Brian Moore (Harlequins), Craig
Quinnell (Llanelli), Steve Cottrell (ex-Cambridge Univ), Neil Martin (Moseley), Rob
Leach (West Hartlepool)

SALE
John Devereux (Widnes RL), Dewi Morris (unattached), John Mitchell (Waikato), Phil
Winstanley (Orrell), Sean Fletcher (Waterloo), Adrian Hadley (Widnes RL)

SARACENS
Michael Lynagh (Treviso), Philippe Sella (Agen), Eddie Halvey (Shannon), Tony
Copsey (Llanelli), Kyran Bracken (Bristol), Paul Wallace (Blackrock College), Michael
Walker (Garryowen), Paddy Johns (Dungannon)

SWANSEA
Stuart Evans (Grenoble), Adam Palfrey (Cardiff), Arwel Thomas (Bristol), Andy
Booth (Cardiff), Robbie Jones (Bridgend)

TREORCHY
Rowland Phillips (Workington RL), Kevin Ellis (Maesteg), Andrew Dibble (Pontypool)

WASPS
Gareth Rees (Newport), Alex King (Bristol Univ), Damian Cronin (Bourges), Simon
Mitchell (Harlequins), Chris Sheasby (Harlequins), Paul Sampson (England Colts),
Mike Griffiths (Cardiff)

WEST HARTLEPOOL
Kevin Moseley (Newport), Matt Silva (Newport), Stephan John, Mark Ring, Chris
John (all Cardiff), Jamie Connolly (Canterbury, NZ), Wayne De Jong (Sydney)

The British Lions in South Africa

The British Lions have mounted eight officially recognised tours to South Africa, when the four Home Unions have co-operated fully, but prior to the 1910 visit British Select XVs toured the country on three occasions, when the Springboks awarded caps for the internationals. A tour party in 1891 was captained by Bill MacLagan of London Scottish and won all 19 games on tour with Randolph Aston, a 15-stone centre from Cambridge University and Blackheath, scoring 30 tries. A cup, donated by shipping magnate Sir Donald Currie, was presented to the Province considered to have provided the sternest opposition – in this case Griqualand West. The trophy is now contested in South Africa's premier domestic competition, the Currie Cup.

Five years later, a British XV returned under the captaincy of Johnny Hammond, winning 19 of their 21 games but losing for the first time in a Test match, in Cape Town. Hugely popular tourists, many returned in less happy circumstances to fight in the Boer War. Indeed, Irish forwards Tom Crean and Robert Johnston both won the VC for their gallantry in battle. By 1903 the Springboks had gradually gained the ascendancy, a trend that was to continue throughout the century until 1974. In 1903, Mark Morrison's side drew the first two Tests in Johannesburg and Kimberley but lost the series in Cape Town.

The 1910 tour party was the first officially to represent the Home Unions, but also suffered defeat going down 2-1, despite winning a Test in Port Elizabeth. The 1924 Lions, led by Old Merchant Taylors' forward Ronald Cove-Smith fared no better, losing 3-0, with just a 3-3 draw in Port Elizabeth to provide consolation.

Massive interest surrounded the 1938 series, with the Lions outgunned but defiant and competitive in the extreme. South Africa won the first Test at Ellis Park, Johannesburg, 26-12, in a game notable for Welsh full-back Viv Jenkins kicking three huge penalty goals, including two from his own half. The Lions also lost the second Test but concluded the tour in memorable style with a 21-16 win in Cape Town.

After World War Two, Robin Thompson's squad continued in similar vein in 1955 with a dramatic and exciting series ending all-square at 2-2. Danie Craven considered Thompson's Lions to be the finest side to ever visit South Africa. A world record 95,000 crowd watched the Lions win the first Test 23-22 at Ellis Park, scoring five tries in the process. The two combatants shared the honours in the next two Tests and South Africa convincingly squared the series in Port Elizabeth with a 22-8 victory.

The 1962 and 1968 Lions, led by Arthur Smith and Tom Kiernan respectively, did well enough at Provincial level without ever really raising their game in the Tests. Both series were lost 3-0 and British rugby began to despair of ever matching South Africa on their own patch. That was until Willie John McBride and Syd Millar combined forces as captain and coach in 1974.

The Lions had good reason to be confident after their successful trip to New Zealand in 1971, but to go through a modern-day tour of South Africa unbeaten was a remarkable achievement. After the Lions won a muddy first Test in Cape Town, South Africa were humiliated on the hard grounds of Pretoria and Port Elizabeth and only recovered their lost pride at Ellis Park where they secured a 13-13 draw, albeit after the referee missed an obvious try by Fergus Slattery.

Bill Beaumont's 1980 tour was set against a growing world-wide abhorrence of apartheid but, as befitted England's much respected captain, his side conducted themselves with dignity and, despite being badly affected by injuries, contributed to a close-fought series. After three narrow defeats, victory in the final Test in Pretoria was sweet and well deserved.

Previous tours to South Africa

1891 (A British XV win series 3-0)

30.7.1891 South Africa 0 British XV 4 (Port Elizabeth)
29.8.1891 South Africa 0 British XV 3 (Kimberley)
5.9.1891 South Africa 0 British XV 4 (Cape Town)

1896 (A British XV win series 3-1)

30.7.1896 South Africa 0 British XV 8 (Port Elizabeth)
22.8.1896 South Africa 8 British XV 17 (Johannesburg)
29.8.1896 South Africa 3 British XV 9 (Kimberley)
5.9.1896 South Africa 5 British XV 0 (Cape Town)

1903 (South Africa win series 1-0)

26.8.1903 South Africa 10 British XV 10 (Johannesburg)
5.9.1903 South Africa 0 British XV 0 (Kimberley)
12.9.1903 South Africa 8 British XV 0 (Cape Town)

1910 (South Africa win series 2-1)

6.8.1910 South Africa 14 British Lions 10 (Kimberley)
27.8.1910 South Africa 3 British Lions 8 (Port Elizabeth)
3.9.1910 South Africa 21 British Lions 5 (Cape Town)

1924 (South Africa win series 3-0)

16.8.1924 South Africa 7 British Lions 3 (Durban)
23.8.1924 South Africa 17 British Lions 0 (Johannesburg)
13.9.1924 South Africa 3 British Lions 3 (Port Elizabeth)
20.9.1924 South Africa 16 British Lions 9 (Cape Town)

1938 (South Africa win series 2-1)

6.8.1938 South Africa 26 British Lions 12 (Johannesburg)
3.9.1938 South Africa 19 British Lions 3 (Port Elizabeth)
10.9.1938 South Africa 16 British Lions 21 (Cape Town)

1955 (Series drawn 2-2)

6.8.1955 South Africa 22 British Lions 23 (Johannesburg)
20.8.1955 South Africa 25 British Lions 9 (Cape Town)
3.9.1955 South Africa 6 British Lions 9 (Pretoria)
24.9.1955 South Africa 22 British Lions 8 (Port Elizabeth)

1962 (South Africa win series 3-0)

23.6.1962 South Africa 3 British Lions 3 (Johannesburg)
21.7.1962 South Africa 3 British Lions 0 (Durban)
4.8.1962 South Africa 8 British Lions 3 (Cape Town)
25.8.1962 South Africa 34 British Lions 14 (Bloemfontein)

1968 (South Africa win series 3-0)

8.6.1968 South Africa 25 British Lions 20 (Pretoria)
22.6.1968 South Africa 6 British Lions 6 (Port Elizabeth)
13.7.1968 South Africa 11 British Lions 6 (Cape Town)
27.7.1968 South Africa 19 British Lions 6 (Johannesburg)

1974 (British Lions win series 3-0)

8.6.1974 South Africa 3 British Lions 12 (Cape Town)
22.6.1974 South Africa 9 British Lions 28 (Pretoria)
13.7.1974 South Africa 9 British Lions 26 (Port Elizabeth)
17.7.1974 South Africa 13 British Lions 13 (Johannesburg)

1980 (South Africa win series 3-1)

31.5.1980 South Africa 26 British Lions 22 (Cape Town)
14.6.1980 South Africa 26 British Lions 19 (Bloemfontein)
28.6.1980 South Africa 12 British Lions 10 (Port Elizabeth)
12.7.1980 South Africa 13 British Lions 17 (Pretoria)

Overall record: South Africa W18, British Lions W8, D4.

The 1997 Lions, who will be managed by Fran Cotton, who toured with the triumphant 1974 party, will contest a three-Test series with internationals at Cape Town, Durban and Johannesburg. They will also play the South African Barbarians at Welkom four days before the final Test and the Emerging Springboks at Wellington prior to the first Test. Ian McGeechan, who coached the 1989 Lions in Australia and the 1993 Lions in New Zealand, makes history by being appointed coach for a third time.

1997 tour schedule

May 24 v Eastern Province Inv XV (Port Elizabeth)
May 28 v Western Province (Cape Town)
May 31 v Free State (Bloemfontein)
June 4   v Transvaal (Johannesburg)
June 7   v Northern Transvaal (Pretoria)
June 11 v South East Transvaal (Witbank)
June 14 v Natal (Durban)
June 17 v Emerging Springboks (Wellington)
June 21 v SOUTH AFRICA (Cape Town)
June 24 v Border (East London)
June 28 v SOUTH AFRICA (Durban)
July 1   v SA Barbarians (Welkom)
July 5   v SOUTH AFRICA (Johannesburg)

Top Referees

BEVAN, William Derek (Wales)
Took charge of an international match for a world record 26th time when he refereed
the Five Nations Championship match between Scotland and Ireland at Murrayfield in
February 1996. In achieving that feat, Derek moved ahead of his fellow Welshman
Clive Norling (25 Tests). A leading international referee for a decade, he has officiated
in the three World Cups. He controlled the 1991 World Cup final at Twickenham
between England and Australia. Appointed for the second Test between South Africa
and New Zealand in Pretoria on 24 August 1996, he refereed a SWALEC Cup final for
the fourth time in May 1996 when Neath played Pontypridd. An electrical training
officer, Derek's ambition is to maintain fitness and reputation to gain appointment to
the 1999 World Cup panel.

BLACK, Gordon (Ireland)
Took control of his first full international in January 1996 when he refereed the match
between Wales and Italy. Started refereeing in the 1977-78 season and has been on the
International Exchange List for nine years. Gordon played for the famous Lansdowne
Road-based Wanderers Club but was advised to retire after breaking his leg twice. He
took up coaching but turned to refereeing full-time and was appointed to the Leinster
provincial panel in 1987. A Dublin bank manager, married to Alyson with a son Gary,
Gordon established a foothold on the international scene when he controlled the match
between Scotland Schools and Wales Schools at Melrose in 1989.

CAMPSALL, Brian (England)
The 1996-97 season represents Brian's fifth season on the RFU referees panel. Brian is a
member of the RFU National Development squad. He made his debut as a full Test
referee in Scotland's victory over Ireland at Lansdowne Road in January 1996. He
officiated in the Dubai Sevens in November 1993, the Rugby World Cup qualifying
tournament in Romania in March 1994, and helped control the Hong Kong Sevens in
1994-95. A teacher, married with a daughter, Brian is celebrating his 13th season as a
leading referee.

DOYLE, Owen Edward (Ireland)
One of the game's leading referees for more than 10 years, Owen made his international
debut in 1984 when Scotland beat Wales in Cardiff. A marketing director, he took up
the whistle in 1970 when a back injury forced his retirement from the game after giving
short but distinguished playing service to Leinster Schools and for University College,
Dublin. A music lover and fluent in the French language, he made an early impact as a
referee when he took charge of a game between a French Select side and the touring
Australians. The most important challenge of his career was to control the match
between Scotland and South Africa at Murrayfield in November 1994.

DUMÉ, Joel (France)
Made his international debut when he took charge of the Five Nations Championship
match between Wales and England at Cardiff in 1993. He controlled the Scotland-
Wales game at Murrayfield that season also, and in 1994 refereed both Tests between
Australia and Ireland in Brisbane and Sydney, followed by the World Cup pool B match
between Western Samoa and Italy in East London, South Africa in 1995. He sent off
Garin Jenkins when newly crowned world champions South Africa thrashed Wales
40-11 at Ellis Park, Johannesburg, in 1995. A resident of Bordeaux, where he works as
an area sales manager for a catering company, Joel's education as a match official
involved exchange visits to Scotland and Wales after qualifying as a French Federation
referee in 1983.

ERICKSON, Wayne John (Australia)
Made his debut when he took charge of both Scotland's matches against Argentina in
Buenos Aires in 1994. Then refereed England's match against Canada at Twickenham

in December that year. Wayne, a former tight-head prop and veteran of more than 100 first-grade matches in Sydney's premier league, graduated from Australia's College of Physical Education. His refereeing exploits have taken him to New Zealand, Tonga, Uruguay and Argentina. He is employed by the Australian Rugby Union as a divisional manager in charge of team travel, kit and accommodation. He is also responsible for planning international rugby tours to his native Australia.

FLEMING, Jim (Scotland)

Jim is one of four referees to appear in all three World Cup tournaments and took charge of his 24th international when England played South Africa at Twickenham in November 1995. Scotland's most experienced referee, Jim's career with the whistle began 23 years ago when injury (concussion) forced him to quit when playing for Boroughmuir School. He took charge of his first international – Ireland v England, Dublin 1985 – in his 12th season. He claims to retain vivid memories of Michael Kiernan's late dropped goal which clinched a sixth Triple Crown for Ireland. He controlled the 1991 World Cup quarter-final match between Ireland and Australia in Dublin and broke a finger and severed tendons in his right hand during the match. But he returned to Lansdowne Road a week later to referee the semi-final between Australia and New Zealand.

HENNING, Tappa (South Africa)

Made his international debut in the match between Scotland and Western Samoa at Murrayfield in November 1995 after completing a highly successful first season in control of Currie Cup matches in South Africa. Tappa was a scrum-half for Eastern and Transvaal Under-20s before graduating to Northern Transvaal B as a centre threequarter. Knee problems forced him to stop playing for Pretoria Police in 1987 and he took up the whistle. A sports organiser at the police training centre in Pretoria, he gained experience in local minor leagues before taking charge of the Currie Cup final between Natal and Western Province in 1995.

LANDER, Steve (England)

Controlled the 1996 Pilkington Cup final between Bath and Leicester. He has officiated in three internationals, appearing in both the World Cup and Five Nations Championship. Born in Hampshire and married to Philippa, with two children, Thomas and Grace, Steve was educated at Chester College before becoming a teacher in Oxfordshire. He began refereeing in 1982 with the Oxfordshire Society and then transferred to the Liverpool Society in 1986. He was appointed to the RFU referees panel in 1989 and promoted to the international panel in 1994. He has refereed matches in England, Ireland, Scotland, Wales and France and took charge of the France v Tonga match in the 1995 World Cup. Steve is Head of Faculty for Creative Arts and Technology at Birkenhead Sixth Form College.

LASAGA, Nicolas (France)

Made his full international debut at Murrayfield when Scotland played Romania in April 1995. From the Basque coast, Nicolas was a promising back-row forward for Saint-Jean-de-Luz before work commitments for the French National Electricity Company persuaded him to retire. His uncle, Michel Dubernet, who refereed the 1971 French Club Championship final, persuaded him to take up refereeing. He has refereed in the French First Division for more than 10 years. His appointments have included the A international clash between Ireland and England in Dublin in January 1995 and he was a touch judge at the Wales v England game in February 1995.

McCARTNEY, Kenneth (Scotland)

Refereed the Five Nations Championship match between England and Wales at Twickenham in 1996. Became a prolific try-scorer for the legendary Hawick 'Green Machine' in the 1970s. He was twice Scotland's top domestic try-scorer. A firefighter with the Lothian and Borders Brigade and a Scottish Lawn Tennis Association development officer, Ken played rugby for the South of Scotland. He thought nothing of refereeing a school match in the morning before playing for Hawick after a light lunch. Encouraged by Hawick's famous television rugby commentator, Bill McLaren, he rose swiftly through the refereeing ranks. Three years after retiring as a player, he was back in the Scotland First Division as a ref. By 1990 he was good enough to join the international list and he controlled the Five Nations Championship match between France and Ireland that same season. Since then he has officiated all over the world, taking charge of South Africa's 1995 World Cup pool victory over Romania. Married to Pat, with three daughters, Jan, Lyn and Rhae, Ken represented Scotland juniors at tennis, winning the Border senior title in 1968 and was runner-up in the 1970 Scottish U-18 Championship.

McHUGH, David Thomas Michael (Ireland)
Made his international debut in Bucharest when Wales clinched a World Cup victory over Romania in 1994. David refereed the France-Scotland Five Nations Championship match in Paris in 1995 and South Africa's 1995 World Cup 'battle' against Canada when he sent-off three players. A fruit importer living with his wife and four children in Douglas, County Cork, he was given charge of the Heineken European Club Cup final between Cardiff and Toulouse in January 1996.

MEGSON, Ray (Scotland)
Survived an horrific fall from the roof of his Edinburgh home in 1994, when he damaged his shoulder and missed half a season but returned to revive his career as one of rugby's top international referees. A solicitor-advocate, he was born in Sheffield, but raised in Australia where he played all his early rugby. He returned to his childhood roots in 1991 when he took charge of a match between Australia and New Zealand. An international panel referee for more than 10 years, he has controlled three England-Wales matches (1987, 1991, 1992).

MÉNÉ, Didier (France)
At 30, became the youngest international referee in French rugby history when he was appointed to the panel in 1994. He took control of the Hong Kong Sevens final between Australia and New Zealand that year. Didier made his international debut in 1994 in the World Cup qualifying match between Argentina and USA in Buenos Aires. Refereed Wales v South Africa in the same year. Took charge of the Wales-England match at Cardiff in 1995 and was no stranger to the Principality after learning his trade as an exchange ref in the Welsh League two years earlier. A Catalan, he works as an engineer for BP Chemicals and lives near Marseille.

MORRISON, Ed (England)
Joined Steve Lander on the plane for the 1995 World Cup as one of England's two representatives and took charge of the World Cup final. He joined the Bristol Referees Society in 1981-82 when injury prevented him from continuing as a player. Steady progress was rewarded by his appointment to the RFU A-list in 1987-88. He was promoted to the RFU referees panel the following season. He made the international panel in 1989-90 and refereed his first international in 1990-91. With Steve Howard, he was one of England's two referees at the 1991 World Cup. Ed's travels have taken him to Argentina, Australia, South Africa and most parts of Europe. He lists his hobbies as 'all sports and a quiet drink'.

MURRAY, Edward (Scotland)
Took charge of his first match in 1980-81 after playing as a centre threequarter for Greenock. Made his debut as an international referee when England played Ireland at Twickenham in the Five Nations Championship decider last March. A chartered accountant, Ed was appointed to Scotland's international panel in December 1994 but was given a long wait before taking his bow at Twickenham.

O'BRIEN, Patric (New Zealand)
New Zealand's 'referee of the year' in 1995, 'Paddy' made his international debut in charge of Wales' match against Fiji at Cardiff in November 1995. He gained selection to the three-man New Zealand international panel for the first time in 1994. He played senior provincial rugby for seven years before taking up the whistle. He officiated in the

match between Hawkes Bay and the 1993 British Lions. Married to Carolyn, he has two children, Danielle and Hamish, and works as a sports administrator in Invercargill.

PEARSON, John (England)

Added to the international referees panel in 1994 as reward for distinguished record on the RFU panel since 1987. Began refereeing with Kent Society in 1977, he was promoted to the A-list in 1983. Moved to Durham in 1985. Took charge of his first international when France played Wales in January 1995. He has refereed all over the world, including Australia, Argentina, Bermuda, Fiji, France, Israel, Portugal, South Africa and Yugoslavia. Refereed the Pilkington Cup final 1995 between Bath and Wasps. Also controlled the Argentinian National final 1992. John lives in Cleveland and is responsible for physical education and health with Cleveland County Council. Sent off Sale's Paul Turner for punching Orrell captain Dewi Morris in October 1994, but later conceded he had dismissed the 'wrong man' after consulting television video.

ROGERS, Ian (South Africa)

Has refereed since the age of 17 and, with the retirement of Freek Burger, is South Africa's senior match official. Took charge of his first international when Wales played Zimbabwe in Bulawayo, May 1993, but made big headlines for sending off Philippe Sella in his 100th international appearance for France against Canada, Ottawa, 1994. 'I had warned him twice. There was no alternative.' An estate agent with a fine tenor voice, he sings in Durban's 'Pig and Whistle' pub once a week.

SPREADBURY, Tony (England)

Celebrated explosive debut as an international match official when he sent off Abdel Benazzi in the match between Australia and France in Sydney six years ago. Gave up playing for Combe Down at 17 after suffering injuries in a cycling accident. He has been a member of the international panel since 1990 and has taken charge of eight full internationals. A paramedic with the Avon Ambulance Service, he says he resembles a 'Brussels sprout' when wearing uniform. He is the first Somerset Society ref to become an international official. Born and bred in Bath, he is married to Philippa and has two sons, Christopher and Robert. Despite his cycling accident, he has never lost his love of two wheels, preferring a Honda motorbike these days. He refereed the 113th Varsity match between Cambridge and Oxford at Twickenham in December 1995, after returning from a seven-state USA tour, holding clinics and reffing territorial tournaments.

STIRLING, Brian William (Ireland)

He completed the 'set' of refereeing the major rugby playing countries when he controlled the 1996 Five Nations Championship match between Wales and France in Cardiff last March, his 10th major Test. A primary school headmaster from Greenisland, Belfast, he begins his 10th season on the Irish international panel this season. He made his debut when England played Fiji at Twickenham in 1989, and his career at the top has included two Tests between Argentina and New Zealand, 1991, the England-Scotland game in 1993 and 1995, and Australia v New Zealand in 1995. A former University of Ulster hooker and a keen golfer, Brian is married to Beatrice and has three boys. He claims rugby's decision to go 'open' has increased the pressure on referees.

THOMAS, Clayton (Wales)

A former Neath fly-half, he ran the line twice in the 1994 Five Nations Championship before making his international debut as a referee in the 1995 game between Scotland and Canada at Murrayfield. He refereed the 1995 SWALEC Cup final between Pontypridd and Swansea and his international appearances include last season's Murrayfield spectacular between Scotland and France. Born in Neath in 1950, his refereeing career began 15 years ago. Steady progress with the whistle culminated in his promotion to referee Ireland B against Argentina in 1990. He is head of physical education at Cwrt Sart Comprehensive in Briton Ferry, where he has taught for more than 20 years.

Principal Fixtures 1996-97

Saturday 31 August

RFU COURAGE LEAGUE
Division One
Orrell v Bath
Bristol v London Irish
Saracens v Leicester
Northampton v West Hartlepool
Sale v Wasps
Harlequins v Gloucester
WRU LEAGUE
Division One
Dunvant v Ebbw Vale
Neath v Pontypridd
Newport v Caerphilly
Newbridge v Treorchy
Swansea v Cardiff
Bridgend v Llanelli
SRU TENNENTS LEAGUE
Division One
Boroughmuir v Hawick
Currie v Heriot's FP
Melrose v Stirling County
Jed-Forest v Watsonians

Tuesday 3 September

WRU LEAGUE
Division One
Caerphilly v Dunvant
Ebbw Vale v Newbridge
Pontypridd v Cardiff
Llanelli v Neath
Swansea v Newport
Treorchy v Bridgend

Saturday 7 September

RFU COURAGE LEAGUE
Division One
Bristol v Orrell
Leicester v Bath
London Irish v Northampton
Wasps v Saracens
West Hartlepool v Harlequins
Gloucester v Sale
Division Two
Bedford v Nottingham
Blackheath v Rotherham
Coventry v Richmond
London Scottish v Rugby
Moseley v Wakefield
Newcastle v Waterloo

WRU LEAGUE
Division One
Newbridge v Dunvant
Bridgend v Ebbw Vale
Caerphilly v Swansea
Newport v Pontypridd
Neath v Treorchy
Cardiff v Llanelli
Division Two
UWIC v Llandovery
SW Police v Maesteg
Bonymaen v Abercynon
Aberavon v Pontypool
Cross Keys v Blackwood
Abertillery v Ystradgynlais
SRU TENNENTS LEAGUE
Division One
Heriot's FP v Boroughmuir
Watsonians v Melrose
Stirling County v Currie
Harwick v Jed-Forest

Wednesday 11 September

SRU TENNENTS LEAGUE
Division One
Hawick v Heriot's FP
Boroughmuir v Stirling County
Currie v Watsonians
Jed-Forest v Melrose

Saturday 14 September

RFU COURAGE LEAGUE
Division One
Orrell v Leicester
Northampton v Bristol
Bath v Wasps
Harlequins v London Irish
Saracens v Gloucester
Sale v West Hartlepool
Division Two
Blackheath v Bedford
Richmond v Rotherham
Rugby v Coventry
Wakefield v London Scottish
Waterloo v Moseley
Nottingham v Newcastle
WRU LEAGUE
Division One
Dunvant v Swansea
Ebbw Vale v Neath
Pontypridd v Caerphilly
Llanelli v Newport
Treorchy v Cardiff
Newbridge v Bridgend

Division Two
Maesteg v UWIC
Llandovery v Bonymaen
Aberavon v SW Police
Abercynon v Cross Keys
Ystradgynlais v Pontypool
Blackwood v Abertillery
SRU TENNENTS LEAGUE
Division One
Watsonians v Boroughmuir
Stirling County v Hawick
Melrose v Currie
Heriot's FP v Jed-Forest
RFU Pilkington Cup, first round
RFU Junior Knockout Competition, first round

Tuesday 17 September
WRU LEAGUE
Division Two
Abercynon v UWIC
Blackwood v Llandovery
Maesteg v Abertillery
Ystradgynlais v Bonymaen
Aberavon v Cross Keys
SW Police v Pontypool

Wednesday 18 September
WRU LEAGUE
Division One
Bridgend v Dunvant
Cardiff v Ebbw Vale
Caerphilly v Llanelli
Neath v Newbridge
Swansea v Pontypridd
Newport v Treorchy

Saturday 21 September
RFU COURAGE LEAGUE
Division One
Northampton v Orrell
Wasps v Leicester
Bristol v Harlequins
Gloucester v Bath
London Irish v Sale
West Hartlepool v Saracens
Division Two
Bedford v Richmond
Rotherham v Rugby
Coventry v Wakefield
London Scottish v Waterloo
Moseley v Nottingham
Newcastle v Blackheath

WRU LEAGUE
Division One
Dunvant v Pontypridd
Ebbw Vale v Newport
Treorchy v Caerphilly
Newbridge v Cardiff
Llanelli v Swansea
Bridgend v Neath
Division Two
Bonymaen v UWIC
Cross Keys v Llandovery
Maesteg v Aberavon
SW Police v Ystradgynlais
Abertillery v Abercynon
Pontypool v Blackwood
SRU TENNENTS LEAGUE
Division One
Heriot's FP v Stirling County
Hawick v Watsonians
Boroughmuir v Melrose
Jed-Forest v Currie

Saturday 28 September
RFU COURAGE LEAGUE
Division One
Orrell v Wasps
Harlequins v Northampton
Leicester v Gloucester
Sale v Bristol
Bath v West Hartlepool
Saracens v London Irish
Division Two
Rugby v Bedford
Wakefield v Rotherham
Waterloo v Coventry
Nottingham v London Scottish
Blackheath v Moseley
Richmond v Newcastle
WRU LEAGUE
Division One
Neath v Dunvant
Caerphilly v Ebbw Vale
Pontypridd v Llanelli
Newport v Newbridge
Swansea v Treorchy
Cardiff v Bridgend
Division Two
UWIC v Aberavon
Llandovery v Abertillery
Ystradgynlais v Maesteg
Bonymaen v Cross Keys
Blackwood v SW Police
Abercynon v Pontypool
SRU TENNENTS LEAGUE
Division One
Currie v Boroughmuir
Melrose v Hawick

Watsonians v Heriot's FP
Jed-Forest v Stirling County

Tuesday 1 October
WRU LEAGUE
Division Two
Blackwood v UWIC
Aberavon v Llandovery
Maesteg v Bonymaen
SW Police v Cross Keys
Ystradgynlais v Abercynon
Pontypool v Abertillery

Saturday 5 October
ITALY v WALES, Rome
RFU COURAGE LEAGUE
Division One
Harlequins v Orrell
Gloucester v Wasps
Northampton v Sale
West Hartlepool v Leicester
Bristol v Saracens
London Irish v Bath
Division Two
Bedford v Wakefield
Rotherham v Waterloo
Coventry v Nottingham
London Scottish v Blackheath
Moseley v Richmond
Newcastle v Rugby
WRU LEAGUE
Division Two
Cross Keys v UWIC
Pontypool v Llandovery
Maesteg v Blackwood
Abertillery v Bonymaen
Aberavon v Ystradgynlais
SW Police v Abercynon
SRU TENNENTS LEAGUE
Division One
Stirling County v Watsonians
Heriot's FP v Melrose
Hawick v Currie
Boroughmuir v Jed-Forest

Saturday 12 October
HEINEKEN EUROPEAN CUP
Pool A:
Pontypridd v Treviso
Bath v Edinburgh
Pool B:
Llanelli v Leinster
Pau v South of Scotland
Pool C:
North and Midlands v Ulster
Brive v Neath

Pool D:
Munster v Milan
Wasps v Cardiff
EUROPEAN CONFERENCE
Pool A:
Newbridge v Glasgow
Agen v Newport
Sale v Montferrand
Pool B:
Bristol v Treorchy
Bridgend v Castres
Pool C:
Orrell v Dunvant
Toulon v Northampton
Pool D:
Swansea v London Irish
Gloucester v Ebbw Vale
RFU COURAGE LEAGUE
Division Two
Waterloo v Bedford
Nottingham v Rotherham
Blackheath v Coventry
Richmond v London Scottish
Rugby v Moseley
Wakefield v Newcastle
WRU LEAGUE
Division Two
UWIC v Ystradgynlais
Llandovery v SW Police
Abercynon v Maesteg
Bonymaen v Pontypool
Blackwood v Aberavon
Cross Keys v Abertillery
RFU Pilkington Cup, second round
RFU Junior Knockout Competition,
second round

Tuesday 15 October
WRU LEAGUE
Division Two
UWIC v Maesteg
Bonymaen v Llandovery
SW Police v Aberavon
Cross Keys v Abercynon
Pontypool v Ystradgynlais
Abertillery v Blackwood

Wednesday 16 October
HEINEKEN EUROPEAN CUP
Pool A:
Treviso v Dax
Edinburgh v Pontypridd
Pool B:
Leinster v Leicester
South of Scotland v Llanelli

Pool C:
Ulster v Harlequins
Neath v North and Midlands
Pool D:
Cardiff v Munster
Milan v Toulouse
EUROPEAN CONFERENCE
Pool A:
Glasgow v Sale
Newport v Newbridge
Pool B:
Treorchy v Bridgend
Dinamo Bucharest v Bristol
Pool C:
Northampton v Orrell
Pool D:
London Irish v Bourgoin
Ebbw Vale v Swansea
Gloucester v Begles

Saturday 19 October
HEINEKEN EUROPEAN CUP
Pool A:
Dax v Edinburgh
Pontypridd v Bath
Pool B:
Leicester v South of Scotland
Llanelli v Pau
Pool C:
Harlequins v Neath
North and Midlands v Brive
Pool D:
Toulouse v Cardiff
Munster v Wasps
EUROPEAN CONFERENCE
Pool A:
Sale v Newport
Newbridge v Agen
Pool B:
Bridgend v Dinamo Bucharest
Bristol v Narbonne
Pool C:
Connacht v Northampton
Orrell v Toulon
Pool D:
Bourgoin v Ebbw Vale
Swansea v Gloucester
Begles v London Irish
RFU COURAGE LEAGUE
Division Two
Bedford v Rotherham
Coventry v London Scottish
Moseley v Newcastle
Nottingham v Blackheath
Richmond v Rugby
Wakefield v Waterloo

WRU LEAGUE
Division Two
Abertillery v UWIC
Maesteg v Llandovery
SW Police v Bonymaen
Aberavon v Abercynon
Pontypool v Cross Keys
Ystradgynlais v Blackwood

Saturday 26 October
HEINEKEN EUROPEAN CUP
Pool A:
Bath v Dax
Edinburgh v Treviso
Pool B:
Pau v Leicester
South of Scotland v Leinster
Pool C:
Brive v Harlequins
Neath v Ulster
Pool D:
Wasps v Toulouse
Cardiff v Milan
EUROPEAN CONFERENCE
Pool A:
Agen v Sale
Newport v Glasgow
Newbridge v Montferrand
Pool B:
Narbonne v Bridgend
Dinamo Bucharest v Treorchy
Bristol v Castres
Pool C:
Northampton v Dunvant
Orrell v Padova
Pool D:
Gloucester v Bourgoin
Ebbw Vale v London Irish
Swansea v Begles
RFU COURAGE LEAGUE
Division Two
Newcastle v Bedford
Rotherham v Coventry
London Scottish v Moseley
Waterloo v Nottingham
Blackheath v Richmond
Rugby v Wakefield
WRU LEAGUE
Division Two
UWIC v Blackwood
Llandovery v Aberavon
Bonymaen v Maesteg
Cross Keys v SW Police
Abercynon v Ystradgynlais
Abertillery v Pontypool

Tuesday 29 October

WRU LEAGUE
Division Two
Llandovery v UWIC
Maesteg v SW Police
Abercynon v Bonymaen
Pontypool v Aberavon
Blackwood v Cross Keys
Ystradgynlais v Abertillery

Thursday 31 October

RFU COURAGE LEAGUE
Division One
Orrell v Gloucester
Sale v Harlequins
Wasps v West Hartlepool
Saracens v Northampton
Leicester v London Irish
Bath v Bristol

Saturday 2 November

HEINEKEN EUROPEAN CUP
Pool A:
Dax v Pontypridd
Treviso v Bath
Pool B:
Leicester v Llanelli
Leinster v Pau
Pool C:
Harlequins v North and Midlands
Ulster v Brive
Pool D:
Toulouse v Munster
Milan v Wasps
EUROPEAN CONFERENCE
Pool A:
Sale v Newbridge
Glasgow v Agen
Montferrand v Newport
Pool B:
Bridgend v Bristol
Treorchy v Narbonne
Pool C:
Connacht v Orrell
Padova v Northampton
Pool D:
Bourgoin v Swansea
London Irish v Gloucester
Begles v Ebbw Vale
RFU COURAGE LEAGUE
Division Two
Bedford v Moseley
Coventry v Newcastle
Rotherham v London Scottish
Nottingham v Wakefield
Richmond v Waterloo

Blackheath v Rugby
WRU LEAGUE
Division Two
Pontypool v UWIC
Ystradgynlais v Llandovery
Maesteg v Cross Keys
Aberavon v Bonymaen
SW Police v Abertillery
Blackwood v Abercynon
RFU Pilkington Cup, third round
RFU Junior Knockout Competition, third round

Saturday 9 November

SCOTLAND v AUSTRALIA,
  Murrayfield
RFU COURAGE LEAGUE
Division One
Sale v Orrell
West Hartlepool v Gloucester
Harlequins v Saracens
London Irish v Wasps
Northampton v Bath
Bristol v Leicester
Division Two
London Scottish v Bedford
Newcastle v Rotherham
Moseley v Coventry
Rugby v Nottingham
Waterloo v Blackheath
Wakefield v Richmond
WRU LEAGUE
Division One
Dunvant v Llanelli
Ebbw Vale v Swansea
Newbridge v Caerphilly
Treorchy v Pontypridd
Neath v Cardiff
Bridgend v Newport
Division Two
UWIC v Abercynon
Llandovery v Blackwood
Abertillery v Maesteg
Bonymaen v Ystradgynlais
Cross Keys v Aberavon
Pontypool v SW Police

Saturday 16 November

Heineken European Cup, semi-finals
European Conference, semi-finals
RFU COURAGE LEAGUE
Division Two
Bedford v Coventry
Rotherham v Moseley
London Scottish v Newcastle
Nottingham v Richmond

Blackheath v Wakefield
Rugby v Waterloo
WRU LEAGUE
Division One
Cardiff v Dunvant
Pontypridd v Ebbw Vale
Newport v Neath
Swansea v Newbridge
Llanelli v Treorchy
Caerphilly v Bridgend
Division Two
SW Police v UWIC
Abercynon v Llandovery
Maesteg v Pontypool
Blackwood v Bonymaen
Aberavon v Abertillery
Ystradgynlais v Cross Keys
SRU TENNENTS LEAGUE
Division One
Hawick v Boroughmuir
Stirling County v Melrose
Heriot's FP v Currie
Watsonians v Jed-Forest

Saturday 23 November

ENGLAND v ITALY, Twickenham
SRU TENNENTS LEAGUE
Division One
Jed-Forest v Hawick
Boroughmuir v Heriot's FP
Currie v Stirling County
Melrose v Watsonians
RFU Pilkington Cup, fourth round
*RFU Junior Knockout Competition,
    fourth round*

Saturday 30 November

**ENGLAND v NEW ZEALAND
BARBARIANS, Twickenham**
IRELAND v AUSTRALIA, Dublin
**FRANCE v SOUTH AFRICA (first
Test), TBA**
WRU LEAGUE
Division One
Dunvant v Treorchy
Ebbw Vale v Llanelli
Neath v Caerphilly
Newbridge v Pontypridd
Cardiff v Newport
Bridgend v Swansea
SRU TENNENTS LEAGUE
Division One
Stirling County v Boroughmuir
Heriot's FP v Hawick
Watsonians v Currie
Melrose v Jed-Forest

Saturday 7 December

**BARBARIANS v AUSTRALIA,
    Twickenham**
**FRANCE v SOUTH AFRICA (second
Test), Paris**
RFU COURAGE LEAGUE
Division One
Orrell v West Hartlepool
Saracens v Sale
Gloucester v London Irish
Bath v Harlequins
Wasps v Bristol
Leicester v Northampton
WRU LEAGUE
Division One
Newport v Dunvant
Treorchy v Ebbw Vale
Caerphilly v Cardiff
Llanelli v Newbridge
Swansea v Neath
Pontypridd v Bridgend
SRU TENNENTS LEAGUE
Division One
Jed-Forest v Heriot's FP
Hawick v Stirling County
Boroughmuir v Watsonians
Currie v Melrose
**IRU INSURANCE CORPORATION
    LEAGUE**
Division One
Old Wesley v Old Belvedere
Ballymena v Terenure College
St Mary's College v Old Crescent
Garryowen v Blackrock College
Lansdowne v Dungannon
Cork Constitution v Instonians
Young Munster v Shannon

Tuesday 10 December

Varsity Match, Twickenham

Saturday 14 December

**ENGLAND v ARGENTINA,
    Twickenham**
SCOTLAND v ITALY, Murrayfield
WALES v SOUTH AFRICA, Cardiff
**IRU INSURANCE CORPORATION
    LEAGUE**
Division One
Blackrock College v Old Wesley
Terenure College v Garryowen
Old Crescent v Lansdowne
Shannon v Cork Constitution
Instonians v St Mary's College
Dungannon v Ballymena
Old Belvedere v Young Munster

Saturday 21 December

WRU LEAGUE
Division One
Ebbw Vale v Dunvant
Pontypridd v Neath
Caerphilly v Newport
Treorchy v Newbridge
Cardiff v Swansea
Llanelli v Bridgend
Division Two
UWIC v Bonymaen
Llandovery v Cross Keys
Aberavon v Maesteg
Ystradgynlais v SW Police
Blackwood v Pontypool
Abercynon v Abertillery
SRU TENNENTS LEAGUE
Division One
Melrose v Boroughmuir
Watsonians v Hawick
Stirling County v Heriot's FP
Currie v Jed-Forest
**IRU INSURANCE CORPORATION
    LEAGUE**
Division One
Old Wesley v Terenure College
Old Belvedere v Blackrock College
Ballymena v Old Crescent
St Mary's College v Shannon
Garryowen v Dungannon
Lansdowne v Instonians
Young Munster v Cork Constitution
RFU Pilkington Cup, fifth round
*RFU Junior Knockout Competition, fifth
    round*

Saturday 28 December

RFU COURAGE LEAGUE
Division One
Saracens v Orrell
London Irish v West Hartlepool
Sale v Bath
Bristol v Gloucester
Harlequins v Leicester
Northampton v Wasps
Division Two
Nottingham v Bedford
Rotherham v Blackheath
Richmond v Coventry
Rugby v London Scottish
Wakefield v Moseley
Waterloo v Newcastle
WRU LEAGUE
Division One
Dunvant v Caerphilly
Newbridge v Ebbw Vale

Cardiff v Pontypridd
Newport v Swansea
Bridgend v Treorchy
Neath v Llanelli
Division Two
Aberavon v UWIC
Abertillery v Llandovery
Maesteg v Ystradgynlais
Cross Keys v Bonymaen
SW Police v Blackwood
Pontypool v Abercynon

Saturday 4 January

IRELAND v ITALY, Dublin
Heineken European Cup, final
European Conference, final
RFU COURAGE LEAGUE
Division One
Orrell v London Irish
Bath v Saracens
West Hartlepool v Bristol
Leicester v Sale
Gloucester v Northampton
Wasps v Harlequins
Division Two
Bedford v Blackheath
Rotherham v Richmond
Coventry v Rugby
London Scottish v Wakefield
Moseley v Waterloo
Newcastle v Nottingham
WRU LEAGUE
Division One
Dunvant v Newbridge
Ebbw Vale v Bridgend
Swansea v Caerphilly
Pontypridd v Newport
Treorchy v Neath
Llanelli v Cardiff
Division Two
UWIC v Cross Keys
Llandovery v Pontypool
Blackwood v Maesteg
Bonymaen v Abertillery
Ystradgynlais v Aberavon
Abercynon v SW Police

Saturday 11 January

RFU COURAGE LEAGUE
Division One
West Hartlepool v Orrell
Sale v Saracens
London Irish v Gloucester
Harlequins v Bath
Bristol v Wasps
Northampton v Leicester

Division Two
Richmond v Bedford
Rugby v Rotherham
Wakefield v Coventry
Waterloo v London Scottish
Nottingham v Moseley
Blackheath v Newcastle
WRU LEAGUE
Division Two
Ystradgynlais v UWIC
SW Police v Llandovery
Maesteg v Abercynon
Pontypool v Bonymaen
Aberavon v Blackwood
Abertillery v Cross Keys
**IRU INSURANCE CORPORATION
    LEAGUE**
Division One
Dungannon v Old Wesley
Terenure College v Old Belvedere
Old Crescent v Garryowen
Shannon v Lansdowne
Instonians v Ballymena
Cork Constitution v St Mary's College
Blackrock College v Young Munster

Saturday 18 January
IRELAND v FRANCE, Dublin
SCOTLAND v WALES, Edinburgh
RFU COURAGE LEAGUE
Division One
Orrell v Sale
Gloucester v West Hartlepool
Saracens v Harlequins
Wasps v London Irish
Bath v Northampton
Leicester v Bristol
Division Two
Bedford v Rugby
Rotherham v Wakefield
Coventry v Waterloo
London Scottish v Nottingham
Moseley v Blackheath
Newcastle v Richmond
County Championship, quarter-finals

Saturday 25 January
**IRU INSURANCE CORPORATION
    LEAGUE**
Division One
Old Wesley v Old Crescent
Old Belvedere v Dungannon
Blackrock College v Terenure College
Ballymena v Shannon
Garryowen v Instonians
Lansdowne v Cork Constitution

Young Munster v St Mary's College
RFU Pilkington Cup, sixth round
*RFU Junior Knockout Competition, sixth
    round*

Saturday 1 February
**ENGLAND v SCOTLAND,
    Twickenham**
WALES v IRELAND, Cardiff

Saturday 8 February
RFU COURAGE LEAGUE
Division One
Gloucester v Orrell
Harlequins v Sale
West Hartlepool v Wasps
Northampton v Saracens
London Irish v Leicester
Bristol v Bath
Division Two
Wakefield v Bedford
Waterloo v Rotherham
Nottingham v Coventry
Blackheath v London Scottish
Richmond v Moseley
Rugby v Newcastle
WRU LEAGUE
Division One
Swansea v Dunvant
Neath v Ebbw Vale
Caerphilly v Pontypridd
Bridgend v Newbridge
Newport v Llanelli
Cardiff v Treorchy
Division Two
UWIC v Abertillery
Llandovery v Maesteg
Bonymaen v SW Police
Abercynon v Aberavon
Cross Keys v Pontypool
Blackwood v Ystradgynlais
SRU TENNENTS LEAGUE
Division One
Heriot's FP v Watsonians
Hawick v Melrose
Boroughmuir v Currie
Stirling County v Jed-Forest
**IRU INSURANCE CORPORATION
    LEAGUE**
Division One
Instonians v Old Wesley
Old Crescent v Old Belvedere
Shannon v Garryowen
Cork Constitution v Ballymena
St Mary's College v Lansdowne
Dungannon v Blackrock College
Terenure College v Young Munster

Saturday 15 February

IRELAND v ENGLAND, Dublin
FRANCE v WALES, Paris
SRU TENNENTS LEAGUE
Division One
Jed-Forest v Boroughmuir
Currie v Hawick
Melrose v Heriot's FP
Watsonians v Stirling County

Saturday 22 February

IRU INSURANCE CORPORATION
LEAGUE
Division One
Old Wesley v Shannon
Old Belvedere v Instonians
Terenure College v Dungannon
Blackrock College v Old Crescent
Ballymena v St Mary's College
Garryowen v Cork Constitution
Young Munster v Lansdowne
RFU Pilkington Cup, quarter-finals
*RFU Junior Knockout Competition,
   quarter-finals*

Saturday 1 March

ENGLAND v FRANCE, Twickenham
SCOTLAND v IRELAND, Edinburgh
WRU LEAGUE
Division One
Dunvant v Bridgend
Ebbw Vale v Cardiff
Llanelli v Caerphilly
Newbridge v Neath
Pontypridd v Swansea
Treorchy v Newport

Saturday 8 March

RFU COURAGE LEAGUE
Division One
Orrell v Harlequins
Wasps v Gloucester
Sale v Northampton
Leicester v West Hartlepool
Saracens v Bristol
Bath v London Irish
Division Two
Bedford v Waterloo
Rotherham v Nottingham
Coventry v Blackheath
London Scottish v Richmond
Moseley v Rugby
Newcastle v Wakefield

WRU LEAGUE
Division One
Pontypridd v Dunvant
Newport v Ebbw Vale
Caerphilly v Treorchy
Cardiff v Newbridge
Swansea v Llanelli
Neath v Bridgend
Division Two
UWIC v Pontypool
Llandovery v Ystradgynlais
Cross Keys v Maesteg
Bonymaen v Aberavon
Abertillery v SW Police
Abercynon v Blackwood
IRU INSURANCE CORPORATION
LEAGUE
Division One
Cork Constitution v Old Wesley
Shannon v Old Belvedere
Old Crescent v Terenure College
St Mary's College v Garryowen
Lansdowne v Ballymena
Instonians v Blackrock College
Dungannon v Young Munster
County Championship, semi-finals

Saturday 15 March

WALES v ENGLAND, Cardiff
FRANCE v SCOTLAND, Paris
IRU INSURANCE CORPORATION
LEAGUE
Division One
Old Wesley v St Mary's College
Old Belvedere v Cork Constitution
Terenure College v Instonians
Dungannon v Old Crescent
Blackrock College v Shannon
Garryowen v Lansdowne
Young Munster v Ballymena

Saturday 22 March

RFU COURAGE LEAGUE
Division One
Wasps v Orrell
Northampton v Harlequins
Gloucester v Leicester
Bristol v Sale
West Hartlepool v Bath
London Irish v Saracens
Division Two
Rotherham v Bedford
London Scottish v Coventry
Newcastle v Moseley
Blackheath v Nottingham
Rugby v Richmond

Waterloo v Wakefield

IRU INSURANCE CORPORATION LEAGUE

Division One

Lansdowne v Old Wesley
St Mary's College v Old Belvedere
Shannon v Terenure College
Ballymena v Garryowen
Cork Constitution v Blackrock College
Instonians v Dungannon
Old Crescent v Young Munster
RFU Junior Knockout Competition, semi-finals

Saturday 29 March

RFU COURAGE LEAGUE

Division One

Orrell v Northampton
Leicester v Wasps
Harlequins v Bristol
Bath v Gloucester
Sale v London Irish
Saracens v West Hartlepool

WRU LEAGUE

Division One

Dunvant v Neath
Ebbw Vale v Caerphilly
Llanelli v Pontypridd
Newbridge v Newport
Treorchy v Swansea
Bridgend v Cardiff

IRU INSURANCE CORPORATION LEAGUE

Division One

Old Wesley v Ballymena
Old Belvedere v Lansdowne
Terenure College v Cork Constitution
Old Crescent v Instonians
Dungannon v Shannon
Blackrock College v St Mary's College
Young Munster v Garryowen
RFU Pilkington Cup, semi-finals

Saturday 5 April

RFU COURAGE LEAGUE

Division One

Leicester v Orrell
Bristol v Northampton
Wasps v Bath
London Irish v Harlequins
Gloucester v Saracens
West Hartlepool v Sale

Division Two

Bedford v Newcastle
Coventry v Rotherham
Moseley v London Scottish

Nottingham v Waterloo
Richmond v Blackheath
Wakefield v Rugby

WRU LEAGUE

Division One

Llanelli v Dunvant
Swansea v Ebbw Vale
Caerphilly v Newbridge
Pontypridd v Treorchy
Cardiff v Neath
Newport v Bridgend

IRU INSURANCE CORPORATION LEAGUE

Division One

Garryowen v Old Wesley
Ballymena v Old Belvedere
St Mary's College v Terenure College
Shannon v Old Crescent
Lansdowne v Blackrock College
Cork Constitution v Dungannon
Instonians v Young Munster

Saturday 12 April

RFU COURAGE LEAGUE

Division One

Orrell v Bristol
Bath v Leicester
Northampton v London Irish
Saracens v Wasps
Harlequins v West Hartlepool
Sale v Gloucester

Division Two

Moseley v Bedford
Newcastle v Coventry
London Scottish v Rotherham
Wakefield v Nottingham
Waterloo v Richmond
Rugby v Blackheath

IRU INSURANCE CORPORATION LEAGUE

Division One

Old Belvedere v Garryowen
Terenure College v Lansdowne
Cork Constitution v Old Crescent
Instonians v Shannon
Dungannon v St Mary's College
Blackrock College v Ballymena
Young Munster v Old Wesley

Saturday 19 April

RFU COURAGE LEAGUE

Division One

Bath v Orrell
London Irish v Bristol
Leicester v Saracens
West Hartlepool v Northampton

Wasps v Sale
Gloucester v Harlequins
Division Two
Bedford v London Scottish
Rotherham v Newcastle
Coventry v Moseley
Nottingham v Rugby
Blackheath v Waterloo
Richmond v Wakefield
WRU LEAGUE
Division One
Dunvant v Cardiff
Ebbw Vale v Pontypridd
Bridgend v Caerphilly
Newbridge v Swansea
Neath v Newport
Treorchy v Llanelli
Division Two
UWIC v SW Police
Llandovery v Abercynon
Pontypool v Maesteg
Bonymaen v Blackwood
Abertillery v Aberavon
Cross Keys v Ystradgynlais
County Championship final, Twickenham

Saturday 26 April
RFU COURAGE LEAGUE
Division One
Orrell v Saracens
West Hartlepool v London Irish
Bath v Sale
Gloucester v Bristol
Leicester v Harlequins
Wasps v Northampton
Division Two
Coventry v Bedford
Moseley v Rotherham

Newcastle v London Scottish
Richmond v Nottingham
Wakefield v Blackheath
Waterloo v Rugby
WRU LEAGUE
Division One
Treorchy v Dunvant
Llanelli v Ebbw Vale
Caerphilly v Neath
Pontypridd v Newbridge
Swansea v Bridgend
Newport v Cardiff

Saturday 3 May
RFU COURAGE LEAGUE
Division One
London Irish v Orrell
Saracens v Bath
Bristol v West Hartlepool
Sale v Leicester
Northampton v Gloucester
Harlequins v Wasps
WRU LEAGUE
Division One
Dunvant v Newport
Ebbw Vale v Treorchy
Cardiff v Caerphilly
Newbridge v Llanelli
Neath v Swansea
Bridgend v Pontypridd
*RFU Junior Knockout Competition final,
   Twickenham*

Saturday 10 May
RFU Pilkington Cup final, Twickenham

Saturday 17 May
Middlesex Sevens finals, Twickenham